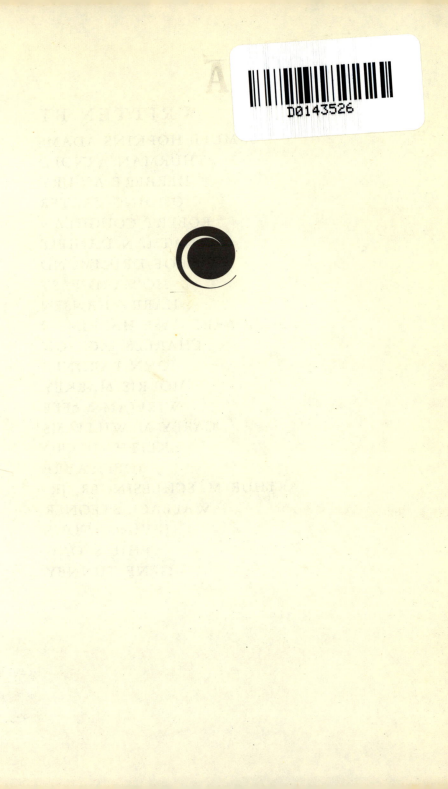

WRITTEN BY
SAMUEL HOPKINS ADAMS
THURMAN ARNOLD
HERBERT ASBURY
HODDING CARTER
ROBERT COUGHLAN
JONATHAN DANIELS
ROSCOE DRUMMOND
HOWARD FAST
HARRY HANSEN
MARGARET CASE HARRIMAN
CHARLES JACKSON
JOHN LARDNER
MORRIS MARKEY
WILLIAM McFEE
CAREY McWILLIAMS
KEITH MUNRO
JOEL SAYRE
ARTHUR M. SCHLESINGER, JR.
WALLACE STEGNER
IRVING STONE
PHIL STONG
GENE TUNNEY

THE
ASPIRIN
AGE

1919 ✻ 1941

EDITED BY
ISABEL LEIGHTON

A Clarion Book
Published by Simon and Schuster

A CLARION BOOK
PUBLISHED BY SIMON AND SCHUSTER
ROCKEFELLER CENTER, 630 FIFTH AVENUE
NEW YORK, NEW YORK 10020
ALL RIGHTS RESERVED
INCLUDING THE RIGHT OF REPRODUCTION
IN WHOLE OR IN PART IN ANY FORM
COPYRIGHT 1949 BY SIMON & SCHUSTER, INC.

EIGHTH PAPERBACK PRINTING
SBN-671-20062-3
LIBRARY OF CONGRESS CATALOG CARD NUMBER: 49-9336
MANUFACTURED IN THE UNITED STATES OF AMERICA
PRINTED BY MURRAY PRINTING CO., FORGE VILLAGE, MASS.
BOUND BY ELECTRONIC PERFECT BINDERS, INC.

"Izzy and Moe" by Herbert Asbury was originally published in *The American Mercury* under the title of "When Prohibition Was in Flower": Copyright, 1946, The American Mercury, Inc.

"Huey Long" by Hodding Carter was originally published in *The American Mercury:* Copyright, 1949, The American Mercury, Inc.

"The Man on the Ledge" by Joel Sayre was originally published in *The New Yorker* in a slightly different form: Copyright, 1949, The New Yorker Magazine, Inc.

"My Fights with Jack Dempsey" by Gene Tunney originally appeared in *Sport* Magazine.

FOR A.
"As it was in the beginning, is now, and ever shall
be, world without end."

Book of Common Prayer: Matins
I. L. B.

☼ Table of Contents

✸ Editor's Preface

THIS IS *a story of America between two wars, told in terms of the most significant, or typical, or utterly fantastic news events of the gaudy and chaotic years that separated Versailles and Pearl Harbor. From the troubled vantage point of 1949, the United States of the twenties and thirties appears, in retrospect, as a strange, uncharted, and enchanted land; so many of the personalities and events that challenged our imaginations during that time now seem almost to have been part of a spell . . . hectic, frenzied, not always beneficent . . . cast over the entire country. We seem to have fluctuated between headaches: sometimes induced by prohibition, more frequently by the fevered pace of the times. During these throbbing years we searched in vain for a cure-all, coming no closer to it than the aspirin bottle. Hence:* The Aspirin Age.

Twenty-two prominent authors, all closely connected with the period, have written expressly for this book the chapters that follow. Some of the events are described by active participants; others are retold by reporters who were on the scene or by specially qualified observers. Who was more integral a part of the struggle against the Kingfish, Huey Long, than Hodding Carter? Who could have been closer to the Dempsey-Tunney fight than Gene Tunney himself?

This is, I hope, no mere chronicling of arresting events, but rather a re-creation of a strange and almost somnambulistic time when America was much younger in spirit than it ever can be again. A time too close, still, for historical appraisal, yet too distant to be accurately assessed by most of us. They were years of high tragedy and low comedy, of truth and delusion, of complacency and hysteria. Sacco and Vanzetti died in this period, and so did prohibition. Much else came to life. Some of it, I hope, is here.

ISABEL LEIGHTON

THE ASPIRIN AGE

1919 ✳ 1941

The Forgotten Men of Versailles

BY HARRY HANSEN

When Harry Hansen attended the Paris Peace Conference in 1919 he was a seasoned, but not too hard-boiled, war correspondent. He began his newspaper career carrying papers in Davenport, Iowa, and held all the editorial positions on his home-town newspaper before he entered college. He edited the university graduates' magazine, promoted books for the University of Chicago Press, and did his first war reporting for the Chicago *Daily News* from the German front lines in Belgium in 1914. His Peace Conference reports were syndicated throughout the country by the North American Newspaper Alliance and appeared in the New York *Globe*. Mr. Hansen has written *The Adventures of the Fourteen Points* (1919), about the making of the Treaty of Versailles; *Midwest Portraits* (1923), the first book to contain studies of Sherwood Anderson and Carl Sandburg; several other books of nonfiction and a novel. He became literary editor of the New York *World* and later of the New York *World-Telegram,* and is now editor of the *World Almanac.*

✷ 1

EXACTLY THIRTY years have passed since that gray day in Paris when President Poincaré of France formally opened the Peace Conference that was to result in the Treaty of Versailles. Gray skies above; a gray stone building on the Quai d'Orsay; black motorcars, flying little flags, carrying men in top hats and military coats to the doors; and fewer than five hundred spectators idling around the wrought-iron gates—this is my memory of January 18, 1919.

Few of us who presented press cards at the entrance and stretched out necks to get a glimpse of the formalities in the Salle d'Horloge could have forecast the far-flung consequences of this meeting. No doubt there were statesmen, especially such veterans as Georges Clemenceau, who looked on this as one of the periodic adjustments of power and a division of spoils and advantages. We Americans, on the other hand, spoke of it as the final act in crushing military aggression, in outlawing war and guaranteeing the protection of minorities by international agreement. Had we not forced on the European Allies a set of principles that contradicted some of their established practices, threatened agreements to divide the spoils made between them in secret treaties, and gained their assent to a world union to keep the peace? Had we not, by incorporating these conditions in the terms of the armistice, practically guaranteed the rehabilitation of Germany and its future co-operation?

The limousine flying a white eagle on a blue ground and carrying the President of the United States to the opening session had implications of latent power, but already Woodrow Wilson was being measured by his equals as a man with human limitations. "We are going to have difficulties with this Presbyterian," Clemenceau had said, as he read Wilson's speech at Manchester declaring that the balance of power was responsible for Europe's woes and must go. Retorting before the Chamber of Deputies, Clemenceau had declared that he remained faithful to the balance of power; "this system of alliances, which I do not renounce, shall be my guiding thought at the Conference . . . so that there can be no separation in peace of the four powers that have fought side by side."

Now they sat near each other at the big U-shaped table in the Salle, an overdressed hall dating from the boastful era of the Second Empire. At their backs rose a white marble mantelpiece, surmounted by a gold clock and a marble statue of Liberty holding aloft a torch. The French, who did not believe that "open covenants, openly arrived at" applied to the press, had barred the way of correspondents by placing tables as barriers under the three arches that led to a gallery overlooking the grounds of the building, which was the Ministry of Foreign Affairs. Through these openings we were permitted to gaze at the men who had seats at the green table. They were not men of equal status, despite the professed democratic procedure. Top place belonged to representatives of the principal belligerents, with full powers; then came subordinate delegations from the British Dominions and India, whose exact position was still to be determined; also men from states with special or limited interests, and finally those from states that had broken off relations with the Germans, without fighting in the field.

It was not easy to see or hear in this comparatively small chamber, but we could observe Woodrow Wilson, serious, lantern-jawed, listening gravely as the President of France declared that "America, the daughter of Europe, crossed the ocean to wrest her mother from the humiliation of thralldom and to save civilization." Such phrases were familiar to American ears; they were the common coin of our idealistic appraisal of a tough job, and the President who sat there had electrified American public opinion with similar, though better expressed, sentiments. Beside him sat the plenipotentiaries he had named and whose choice had been ridiculed by the opposition in the United States as a multiplication of mouthpieces. While General Tasker H. Bliss, military representative on the Supreme War Council, was not included in this criticism, Robert Lansing, Secretary of State, Henry White, one-time Ambassador in Paris, and Colonel E. M. House were specifically indicated, and the reservation that Mr. White was a Republican did not mollify Republicans in the Senate, who felt that the President's disregard of the Senate, though legal, was arbitrary and partisan.

It was Woodrow Wilson who proposed that Clemenceau, "the grand young man of France," be made permanent chairman of the conference, and that spirited leader, wearing gray silk gloves, a black tie, and round white cuffs, and looking more like a bulldog than a tiger, took charge. Beside him sat Stephen Pichon, Louis-Lucien Klotz, André Tardieu, and Jules Cambon; on the other side of Woodrow Wilson sat David Lloyd George, animated and eager, Andrew Bonar Law, Lord Milner, Arthur J. Balfour, still without a title, and George N. Barnes. Marshal Foch, dignified and handsome in his powder-blue uniform, sat near the French delegation, as a privileged guest; then, as our eyes roved over the assembly, we identified Vittorio Orlando, firmly determined to realize the aspirations of Italy as a great power; the Marquis Saionzi, Baron Makino, and Viscount Chinda of Japan; Paul Hymans of Belgium, Sir Robert Borden of Canada, W. M. Hughes of Australia, Eleftherios Veniselos of Greece, Lou Tseng-Tsiang and Chengting Wang of China, the Maharaja Ganga Singh Bahadur, the turbaned representatives of the Arab kingdom of Hedjaz, and many others whose names were associated with causes and demands.

This was the first formal session in public and as much of an open meeting as the Peace Conference ever achieved. There were to be others like it—the reading of the Covenant of the League of Nations, for instance, in this same room, and the flamboyant signing of the treaty of peace by two insignificant Germans in the Hall of Mirrors of the Bourbon kings at Versailles. But open negotiations proved impractical from the first; decisions had to be reached by the five great powers, which organized the Supreme Council, or Council of Ten; this shrank to the Council of Four, in which Woodrow Wilson, David Lloyd George, Georges Clemenceau, and Vittorio Orlando tackled major issues, occasionally expanding to the Council of Five when Japan's interests were involved.

Thus, at the very outset, President Wilson's principle of "open covenants, openly arrived at" was set aside. Ray Stannard Baker was named by the President to head a bureau through which news of American activities was to be filtered to the American press. This was no surprise to such seasoned men as Frank Simonds, Mark Sullivan, Richard V. Oulahan, Laurence Hills, Clinton Gilbert, and David Lawrence, who had found their way through the Wilsonian labyrinth in Washington, but it startled some of the rest of us, and led to formal protests by Herbert Bayard Swope, Arthur D. Krock, Paul Scott Mowrer, and other energetic men. Indeed, at the first session, David Lawrence showed his disregard of official barriers by vaulting over the tables and buttonholing Lloyd George, an incident that sticks in my memory because the next day the American Secretary of State, Robert Lansing, made a point of reproving Lawrence for what he termed a breach of good conduct.

There were other men in the American delegation who had no illusions about the hard, preparatory work necessary to negotiations. Several years before Colonel E. M. House, at the President's request, had begun a systematic effort to compile political, economic, and geographic information on all subjects likely to come up at the final settlement. The work of Walter Lippmann and David Hunter Miller had clarified principles for Woodrow Wilson and shaped some of his most important declarations. James T. Shotwell, Charles Seymour, James Brown Scott, George Louis Beer, Archibald Coolidge, Isaiah Bowman, Charles H. Haskins, and others of like stature had worked without stint to provide essential data; a whole library had been accumulated and moved to Paris aboard the *George Washington,* the ship that carried the President and the American delegation to Europe.

Through these agencies, which occupied offices in the Hôtel Crillon and adjoining buildings, President Wilson was furnished not only with information but with summaries of interviews with representatives of many nations who wanted help from the Peace Conference. Thus Colonel E. M. House became an important source of information; his rooms adjoined those in which Robert Lansing, Henry White, and General Bliss daily exchanged views on the weather with the press, and I have a vivid memory of Herbert Bayard Swope striding firmly toward Colonel House's apartment, with Arthur D. Krock always two steps behind him, ignoring the blandishments of the Secretary of State.

For although Woodrow Wilson had instituted a "censorship" of conference news, it was quite impossible to keep matters secret; other nations had too much at stake not to invite the co-operation of world opinion. We did not have to ferret out information in odd corners of Paris; we were overwhelmed by requests for interviews, invitations to social affairs where politics would be served with tea and cakes, and tons of printed propaganda. But communication with the United States was still chiefly by cable, and there were no radio commentators to give a blow-by-blow version of the conference.

The conflicting issues were apparent long before the conference met, and every day were debated in the newspapers. Political leaders especially were eager to influence public opinion, because this was the principal support of Woodrow Wilson. His prestige with the people of Europe was enormous, because of his stand for democratic principles and the rights of minorities. His formal entry into Paris resembled that of a conquering hero; it was estimated that one hundred thousand Frenchmen were packed into the Place de la Concorde to cheer his arrival at the Crillon. This popularity the French leaders tried to counteract.

Before the conference met Europeans had suggested to Colonel

House that the President, as head of a state, could not confer with men who did not possess equal authority. The President replied that prime ministers and premiers were executives of their own countries, holding powers similar to his own. Opposition also arose in the United States, where it was felt that his position as arbitrator would be compromised if he went to Europe; this was brought to his attention by Herbert Hoover, American member of the Supreme Economic Council, battle-scarred by his altercations with Europeans. But the President gave no heed to these well-meant warnings; his subsequent experiences proved them right.

It was not yet customary to take a poll of the opinions of the man on the street in 1919; had he been consulted he would have insisted, with a prideful swagger, that the President go to Europe and give orders right and left. For the war had been a great American enterprise; the public had believed the President when he said, "The world must be made safe for democracy," and was convinced that American troops had won the war for the Allies. Yet there was a strong counterpoint in the demand that the boys be brought back from Europe, now that the job was done. The Army, too, clamored for leave in Paris and a quick trip home. Moreover, its letters were filled with gripes about prohibition, which, the men declared, "was put over on us when we couldn't object." Their attitude was expressed by the cartoonist Wallgren in the *Stars and Stripes,* when he portrayed the lady of the Statue of Liberty welcoming the veterans back by holding aloft a beer mug, upside down.

When the conference was organized the five big powers took over all the important work, giving such meager representation on committees to the nineteen junior nations, or "powers with special interests," that one after another of their delegates protested. Many of these men were important in their own countries—Paul Hymans was Minister of Foreign Affairs for Belgium, Joao Calogeras had been Minister of Finance for Brazil, Eleftherios Veniselos was Prime Minister of Greece, Lou Tseng-Tsiang was Minister of Foreign Affairs for China, and young Eduard Beneš was Minister of Foreign Affairs of the newly constituted Czechoslovak republic

These and others were put in their place by Clemenceau. He said flatly that the five great powers had twelve million men under arms at the time of the armistice, and their dead could be counted by millions. If they had not intended to create a society of nations, the five great powers need have consulted only themselves in the settlement. The smaller nations might state their case, at any time. But the great questions should come before the five. "And to give you my reason frankly," he said, "it is because I could not, we would not, agree that any committee should have the right to dictate to the five great powers."

So actually Wilson, Lloyd George, Clemenceau, and Orlando made the peace amid bitter arguments and recriminations. Once the debate became so personal that Clemenceau threatened to assault Lloyd George. Threats to leave the conference were made by several delegations; the Japanese were prepared to withdraw over Shantung; President Wilson once ordered the *George Washington* to be ready to take him home; and the Italian delegation actually withdrew when all its claims were not granted.

It was easy to subscribe to the principle that only a just peace would restore Europe to political and economic health, but every nation interpreted this to mean the rectification of its own grievances. France was determined to get guarantees against further aggression by the Germans; it asked the return of Alsace-Lorraine; the cession of the Saar, in which the population was more German than French; the permanent occupation of the Rhineland; full payment for all damages inflicted by the Germans and, to supplement the League of Nations, a defensive alliance with Great Britain and the United States. Japan was so determined to succeed the Germans in Shantung that the President opposed this as a violation of the territory of China.

Italy asked fulfillment of the Treaty of London, whereby Britain and France had agreed to vast concessions to draw Italy into the war. Italy had been promised the Trentino to the Brenner, Trieste, a large slice of the Dalmatian coast with strategic islands, and spheres of influence in Asia Minor. The Italian demands conflicted with several of the Fourteen Points; moreover, the needs of the new states of Czechoslovakia and Yugoslavia had to be satisfied. Italy now also demanded the port of Fiume, which had an Italian majority, but had been specifically reserved for the Croats in the Treaty of London.

2.

MANY EVENTS of the Peace Conference were dramatic and spectacular, and some gave evidence of emotional tension behind calm fronts, but none exceeded in general interest the appearance of a delegation of royal Arabs from the hot sands of the desert, escorted by a man who was to become a strange, unsettling figure in Near East diplomacy— Lawrence of Arabia. Their arrival brought before the unsuspecting members of the Council of Four the conflicting problems of Asia Minor, which bedevil the nations to this day.

Here two British factions confronted each other, one supporting the Balfour effort to create a Jewish homeland in Palestine, the other backing the claims of the Sherif of Mecca, Hussein, to all the lands of Asia Minor liberated from the Turks. A complicating factor was the insistence of the French that the council honor the letter of the Sykes-Picot secret agreement, which divided Asia Minor into French and British zones and left the Arabs in a subordinate position. The British who opposed this argued that the greatest contribution to victory had been made by General Edmund Allenby's expedition, which, with the help of the Arabs, threw the Turks out of the country.

In this connection the British and French had a job for the United States: keeping order in Armenia. This was the toughest spot in the Near East at the time. They thought the plight of the Armenians, who had been cut down by both Turks and Greeks, would appeal to the humanitarian instincts of the Americans. However, our representatives considered the idea too dangerous for consideration.

The struggle of the Arabs was dramatized for me the day the Emir Feisal pitched his tent amid the red velvet carpets, the damask hangings, and the white and gold walls of the Hôtel Continental in the Rue de Rivoli. That house held memories of the Second Empire, and for a short time during this conference an aged woman in black, once known as the Empress Eugénie, received diplomats here and warned them never again to permit Germany to have an armed force.

The Emir Feisal was a tall Arab with sensitive features, a fringe of beard, long well-groomed fingers, and the refined bearing of the educated man who listens attentively to the trite mumblings of others. He

had come as the representative of his father, Hussein, who had proclaimed himself King of the Hedjaz with British support. His apartments were guarded by turbaned Negroes, and inside were other Negroes who spoke in deep voices as they performed the offices of
hospitality.

The men of the prince's entourage favored European dress, but
over it they wore long robes of black wool, while picturesque turbans
were held fast by a number of gold cords across the forehead. On the
day I first saw him, the Emir was also wearing a black robe with a gold
cloth turban. In his belt stuck a pistol with a jeweled handle. Before the
Council of Four, I have been told, he also wore a scimitar. His manner
was free of all formality. He was there to get recognition for the King of
the Hedjaz as head of the new Arabian federation, and he spoke politely
but firmly in French of the vital help the Arabs had given the Allies and
the recognition by Britain of their independent sovereignty.

But the Emir Feisal was not to be the sole spokesman for Hedjaz. He
had hardly completed his remarks when an English officer in uniform,
wearing a turban like the others, came unobtrusively into the room. He
was a man of medium height, with strong features, of which his firm
chin was most prominent. Without any explanation he introduced himself as Colonel Lawrence. The prince at once yielded the floor to him.
The story of his dashing campaigns as officer of liaison between General
Allenby and the Arabs was just becoming current.

Colonel Lawrence talked freely and with the evident determination
to impress the company with the validity of the Arabian claims. He
described their war exploits, but omitted his part in the fighting, calling
himself an archaeologist who had been pressed into service in an
emergency. He said there was no possible doubt about the rightness of
the Arab position. He was so completely at ease and so persuasive that
soon he had most of the company sitting on the carpet with him, as in
an Arab tent. After he had described the holy city of Mecca, which
was closed to unbelievers, someone asked him: "Were you ever in
Mecca?"

"If anyone said I was, I should deny it," replied Colonel Lawrence.

From Colonel Lawrence I received a circumstantial statement of the
Arab attitude toward the Zionist movement for a Jewish homeland in

Palestine. The Arabs were willing to make concessions to the Jews without, however, yielding sovereignty to any of the territory. "We have a kinship with the Jews," the Emir Feisal had said. "Both Jews and Arabs are Semitic. We are cousins." But Colonel Lawrence made specific the proposed political relationship. "The King of the Hedjaz has no objection to giving autonomy to the Zionists in the land they ask, from Dan to Beersheba," he said. But sovereignty would have to rest with the Arabs.

And here the abiding hope for a homeland where harassed Jews could flourish, where Hebrew would be the official tongue, was confronted by the Arab determination to rule what had been Turkey in Asia, both having British political groups behind them. While the delegation from Hedjaz pressed this point of view on the Council of Four, the spokesmen for the Zionists, Chaim Weizmann, Nahum Sokolow, M. Ussischkin, and several other leaders, asked the conference to guarantee Palestine as an autonomous state under British protection, as foreshadowed in the Balfour Declaration.

Zionism gained many adherents in Britain just before the first World War, when Dr. Weizmann urged the formation of a haven in Palestine for Jews persecuted in Czarist Russia, Poland, Rumania, and other lands of Eastern Europe. The proposal was supported in the United States by many influential Jews, including Dr. Stephen S. Wise, Louis Marshall, Louis D. Brandeis, and Felix Frankfurter. Not all were agreed on the form of government, but they recognized the need.

Strange to record, the Germans were the first to make amelioration of restrictions on Jews an issue in the first World War, because it served their purpose to get help from them in Poland and Russia. In the same year the British recognized the Jewish interest in Palestine briefly in the Sykes-Picot agreement with France, but David Lloyd George later called the plan for French and British zones "a crude hacking of the Holy Land." The German General Staff made the gesture of asking Turkey, its ally, to remove some of the Jewish burdens, and the British prevailed on the Russians to grant some concessions. The Russian Revolution gave the Jews freedom of worship and full citizenship, but when the Bolshevists came into power the confiscation of private business and the suppression of religious organizations hurt the Jews.

Many elements combined to make Britain the champion of Zionism
—political opportunity no less than moral duty. But there is no doubt
of the sincerity of Arthur J. Balfour, Foreign Secretary, who led the
cause in the British Cabinet. There he won the support of Sir Mark
Sykes, David Lloyd George, Lord Robert Cecil, General Jan Christian
Smuts, Lord Alfred Milner, and other leaders. It is on record, however,
that among those opposed were influential British Jews who feared a
rise in anti-Semitic feeling if the Jews gained political importance as
a national group.

In 1917 Balfour came to the United States with the British War
Commission, and discussed the project of the Jewish homeland with
American Zionists. Among them was Louis D. Brandeis, associate
justice of the Supreme Court, who urged a British protectorate for
Palestine, but opposed its partition between France and Britain. During
this visit Balfour gave President Wilson, on May 17, 1917, a report
on the Sykes-Picot treaty, the Treaty of London, and other so-called
"secret" agreements entered into between Britain and her European
allies, the existence of which had become known when Leon Trotsky
rifled the Czar's diplomatic archives. While the treaties were referred to
frequently by Colonel E. M. House and American diplomats abroad
in reports home, the President adopted the attitude that, since the
United States was not a party to them, final decisions would have to be
reached at the Peace Conference.

The opinions gathered on this journey affected the famous Balfour
Declaration, which was issued November 2, 1917, and expressed both
the high hopes and the political doubts that have affected British
foreign policy. Dr. Weizmann, Lord Rothschild, and other Zionists
drew it up in consultation with Balfour. It pledged British support for
the national home, but made the reservation that "nothing shall be
done which may prejudice the civil and religious rights of the existing
non-Jewish communities of Palestine," a phrase continuously invoked
by the Arab opposition ever since.

Even while the Emir Feisal and Colonel Lawrence were pleading
the cause of the Arabs in Paris, reports of violent attacks on Jews and
other minorities came to the Council of Four from Asia Minor. Moreover, delegations pressed their demands for liberation from restrictions

and persecutions in Poland, Rumania, Hungary, Bulgaria, Lithuania, Latvia, Estonia, Czechoslovakia, and Yugoslavia. An especially urgent request for an investigation of the excesses in Syria came from Dr. Howard Bliss, an American with great prestige in the Near East. As a result an American commission went to Asia Minor and eventually recommended that the United States accept a mandate for Armenia. This, however, was contrary to the wish of the Americans, who invoked the technical excuse that they had not been at war with Turkey, to cover their determination not to get embroiled in Near East animosities. It was the British who wanted to shoulder that responsibility in 1919, and who found it an intolerable burden in 1948.

The day after the Jewish representatives made their plea for Palestine, a remarkable letter, filled with the spirit of good will, was sent by the Emir Feisal to Felix Frankfurter. In it he spoke of the deep sympathy with which the Arabs, "especially the educated among us," looked upon the Zionist movement, and said the Arab deputation considered the Zionist proposals both "modern and proper." "We will do our best," he continued, "in so far as we are concerned, to help them through; we will wish the Jews a most hearty welcome home. . . . The Jewish movement is national and not imperialist; our movement is national and not imperialist; there is room in Syria for us both."

3.

FOUR DAYS after the formal opening of the Peace Conference, the Council of Five surprised Paris by boldly tackling the problem of Russia. Acting on a suggestion from David Lloyd George, President Wilson proposed a meeting of all warring Russian factions, with representatives of the conference, in the hope of establishing peace among them, leading to a fair election. The proposal was met with general skepticism by the French, whose stake was in a conservative government that would recognize the Czar's obligations to France, and who were outraged by the excesses of the extremists, whom we then called the Bolsheviki.

The day of the announcement I met William Allen White in the Palais Dufayel, the sumptuous residence on the Avenue des Champs

Élysées that had been set aside for the press. He was grinning at the announcement that he and George D. Herron, a socialist writer living in Switzerland, had been named to represent the United States at a conference of all the Russians on the main island of Principo, in the Sea of Marmora. "I hear they call it the isle of dogs," he said. "So they pick on me to go there and knock the Russians' heads together. How does that strike you?"

Throughout the conference the Emporia editor took the high seriousness with a grain of salt and observed events in the light of his plain, Kansas point of view. His reports from Paris never lost the human touch. One day, on a visit to Strasbourg, I came upon him standing in front of a statue of Gutenberg. "There's the fellow who started all our troubles," he remarked.

But Russia was a serious matter, a dread specter that hung over the meditations in Paris. Among the delegations were men who wanted the troops to "restore order" and fight a preventive war, but who realized public opinion in Great Britain and the United States would never support it. The first reaction to the fall of the Romanovs had been favorable. The new state of the people was welcomed by the workers and plain citizens of the world. But presently the moderate party, which was organizing the state on representative lines, lost control. The extreme Bolshevist elements under Lenin suppressed the Constituent Assembly and established the dictatorship of the Communist party. Repudiating the Czar's agreements with the Allies, they accepted the Draconian peace terms of the Germans at Brest Litovsk.

This debacle had immediate repercussions in Western Europe. It abrogated the secret treaties Russia had made with Great Britain and France, opened Asia Minor to controversy, and robbed France of its expected support for controlling the Rhineland. It repudiated the huge loans France had made to Russia, and thus made France the center of conservative reaction. It started remnants of the Czar's armies and independent groups campaigning for help from the Allies and associated powers in a general fight on the Bolshevists. Yet in Washington, far from the upheaval, Woodrow Wilson calmly set down, as the sixth of his Fourteen Points, recognition of the integrity of Russia, asking "an unhampered and unembarrassed opportunity for the independent determination of her own political development and national policy," with a welcome "into the society of nations under institutions of her own choosing, and more than a welcome, assistance."

Despite this calm declaration, the President was subjected to continued pressure to intervene in Russia. David R. Francis, the American Ambassador on the ground, demanded immediate intervention against the terror on the grounds of humanity. When Bolshevist troops killed an English army captain who was guarding the British embassy in Petrograd (later called Leningrad), the British arrested the Soviet representative in London, Maxim Litvinov, and his staff. There were agitations for supporting the White Russian leaders, Kolchak and Denikin, with arms, but President Wilson resolutely refused to become involved in the civil war.

Britain had sent some support to Kolchak and the United States had sent small detachments to protect our interests and stores in Archangel and Murmansk and to help cover the retreating Czech army of fifty thousand men, which had been promised a safe journey to the Pacific and ships home. General William S. Graves was in charge of a Siberian contingent, which helped protect Vladivostok as much against the land-hungry Japanese as against the Bolshevists. While Senator Hiram Johnson was attacking the administration and demanding the immediate withdrawal of American troops from Russia, the President was warding off arguments from Britain and France to get him to send more.

The French were openly skeptical toward the Principo meeting. When Paris was first suggested as the site, Clemenceau opposed it forthwith. "No country would be found willing to receive their envoys," he declared, referring to the Soviets. The Central Russian Committee in Paris, which included representatives of the Kerensky, Omsk, Archangel, and Ekaterinodar factions, refused to have anything to do with the meeting. The only acceptance, to the great surprise of the conference, came from the Soviets, but was accompanied by conditions that practically canceled it.

Thus the Principo conference never became a reality, and William Allen White and Dr. Herron pursued their journalistic tasks in Paris without interruption. In the meantime word leaked out that a secret attempt was being made by the Americans to get an agreement with the Soviet regime. William C. Bullitt and Lincoln Steffens had made a trip into Russia and returned with proposals for an armistice and a basis of settlement, agreed to by Lenin and Chicherin in terms far more lenient than anyone expected. But this, too, failed of acceptance. The chief contribution of this remarkable pilgrimage was Lincoln Steffens' electrifying but slightly inaccurate statement: "I have seen the future and it works!"

4.

THE GREAT achievement of the Peace Conference was the League of Nations. Even though the American Congress rejected this work of an American President, it is a milestone in the history of man's slow progress toward the control and outlawry of war. For twenty years afterward the American people deluded themselves by thinking that, because the League sat in far-off Geneva and we had no official association with it, it did not concern us.

Yet the United States could not cut itself off from world affairs. Both the Republican and Democratic administrations compromised by sending observers and supporting organizations and commissions that got around the technicality of nonmembership. But without our political support, the League was preponderately a British bulwark, and it could not make its sanctions against Italy effective in the Ethiopian crisis. It took a second World War, with its terrible cost, to bring the United States into the United Nations. If a nation can sit in sackcloth and ashes, the United States should do so for its selfish rejection of the League.

The League grew out of the conviction, especially strong in Britain, that if the nations had possessed an agreement to discuss their disputes before shooting—now called a cooling-off period—the war of 1914, with its incalculable consequences, would have been averted. Baron Phillimore was one of the leading supporters of the plan, and General J. Christian Smuts brought forward the idea of trusteeships—mandates—for the German colonies and backward peoples. President Wilson made the League one of the objectives of the war and, by incorporating it in the Fourteen Points, obtained agreement to other proposals by the implied promise that the United States would help guarantee the peace of Europe.

The American public, always strongly responsive to a humanitarian appeal, favored the general project of an international organization to keep the peace. But when reports came from Paris that Great Britain would probably gain most of the German colonies, that France demanded the Rhineland, that Japan was slicing Shantung off China's territory, and that the American Army and Navy would have to take orders from the League and protect whatever boundaries the conference agreed on, a reversal of opinion set in.

This was not wholly a matter of political opposition to a Democratic administration. A people descended from immigrants, many of whom had left Europe to avoid military service, clung to Washington's counsel of independent action and Jefferson's advice against entangling alliances. Suspicions of British land-grabbing, fanned by memories of the unpopular Boer War, had not entirely died out. The Irish in America, sympathizing with a strong Sinn Fein element, argued against permanent association with the British Empire. The German element was still eager to see Germany reconstituted as a strong power. The disillusion that always sets in when practical measures have to supplement ideal projects worked against American participation in European affairs.

There is still an erroneous impression that Woodrow Wilson brought home a completed Covenant of the League of Nations and gave it to the Senate with a "take it or leave it" flourish. Actually, proposals by such Republicans as Elihu Root and William H. Taft had been acted on, and individual Senators had been consulted through various agencies. The Senate was directly responsible for the statement in Article XXI that nothing in the Covenant should affect the validity of international agreements such as treaties of arbitration, regional understandings, and the Monroe Doctrine. President Wilson explained that "regional understandings" comprised tariff agreements and measures affecting immigration. The right to withdraw from the League was also included in deference to American wishes.

The chief Senate criticism was directed against Article X, which had been drawn up by President Wilson. This declared that members of the League would respect and preserve against external aggression the territorial integrity and existing political independence of its members, and that the council would "advise upon the means by which this obligation shall be fulfilled." The Republican opposition contended that this affected the constitutional right of Congress to declare war and would make it necessary for the United States to guarantee all the boundaries determined by the conference, many of which the Senate considered violations of national rights. There was also criticism of the seats accorded the British Dominions, by which, it was argued, Britain could outvote the United States.

In reply the President pointed out that making war was the prerogative of Congress, as also was the appropriation of money for that purpose; the League could advise action, but could not enforce it. Moreover, the following articles of the Covenant dealt in detail with means of subjecting disputes to investigation and arbitration, and the Permanent Court of International Justice would still further advance the cause of peace. The President made much of the argument that the League had machinery to rectify mistakes and abuses and to deal with matters not specifically named in the treaty. On the subject of representation of the Dominions of the British Empire, he explained that these had sent armies under their own leaders and had many of the prerogatives of nations in the British Commonwealth; that they were truly entitled to seats above the claims of minor nations.

Unfortunately, the League became the subject of bitter controversy, during which Henry Cabot Lodge, Hiram W. Johnson, William E. Borah, Medill McCormick, and other Republican leaders toured the country denouncing our departure from traditional American independence from Europe. They spoke to huge, enthusiastic crowds; in the Midwestern breadbasket they were greeted with emotional frenzy. An eagerness to be free of Europe's troubles could not be diverted by Woodrow Wilson's plea of necessity. The President in turn appealed to the country, but he found it difficult to discuss the treaty on an oratorical level. His tragic breakdown while on tour and his subsequent defeat give him the aspect of a martyr to principle, but it was evident that he no longer spoke for the majority of his countrymen.

That he was not willing to compromise further has been held against him. Colonel E. M. House is responsible for the statement that before the final vote on ratification he visited Senator Lodge and asked him to name the minimum changes that were necessary to make the treaty acceptable to the Senate. Senator Lodge took a printed copy of the treaty and wrote the changes in the margin, none of them drastic enough to affect the usefulness of the instrument. Colonel House sent this document to the White House, where the President was seriously ill. It was not acknowledged. Later Mrs. Wilson said that Colonel House's negotiations with Senator Lodge broke Woodrow Wilson's heart. Colonel House declared that twenty Democratic Senators would have voted for the treaty on a compromise; even with their votes counted against ratification, the treaty was defeated by the narrow margin of six votes short of the necessary two-thirds.

In the year of acrimonious debate that followed, President Wilson, ailing and completely out of the public eye, made no effort to mend matters. Repeated attempts to ratify the treaty met with firm opposition in the Senate. A simple resolution of nine words, saying "that peace exists between the United States and Germany," was shelved when reservations were proposed. The Senate took the occasion to request the President to invite foreign governments to plan disarmament and an international court. These and other proposals failed. When the Senate and the House finally agreed on a joint resolution, declaring peace with Germany and Austria-Hungary, it was vetoed by President Wilson. The House failed to pass the measure over his veto.

The Wilson administration went out of office with its great effort for international peace frustrated by the conservative, nationalist opposition. President Warren G. Harding on April 12, 1921, asked the Congress to "declare a state of peace, which all America craves." He took the opportunity to criticize his predecessor, but admitted that the United States still faced certain duties in Europe, not only in enforcing just reparations but in aiding the restoration of world economy. "It would be unwise to undertake to make a statement of future policy with respect to European affairs in such a declaration of a state of peace," he warned. "In correcting the failure of the executive, in negotiating the most important treaty in the history of the nation, to recognize the constitutional powers of the Senate, we would go to the other extreme, equally objectionable, if Congress or the Senate should assume the function of the executive." Mr. Harding recommended "the existing treaty," if reservations safeguarding American interests and securing freedom from inadvisable commitments could be added.

Once more the matter of making peace went into the mill, this time with both a Republican President and a Republican Congress trying to find an acceptable way. It was accomplished by a joint resolution dated July 2, 1921, and took effect by an exchange of ratifications, but it was November 14, 1921, before the President proclaimed that war had ended in July. Yet this rejection of Europe was a delusion. The United States could no longer dwell in isolation, no matter how intensely it wished to do so.

There is little doubt that the Senators who steadfastly refused to commit the country to membership in the League of Nations had the welfare of the nation at heart, even though accused of acting out of hatred for Woodrow Wilson. They continued their attempts to safeguard American interests in foreign engagements long after Wilson had passed from the scene. They, too, could not reject Europe entirely. Indeed, the initiative for co-operation often came from the Republican party.

Harding, Coolidge, and Hoover, all Republicans, formally called conferences for the limitation of armaments or joined other nations in them. President Harding attempted to get the United States into the Permanent Court of International Justice, the World Court, even though it was associated with the League of Nations. President Coolidge pressed the matter in 1926 and membership was actually voted by both the Senate and the House, but one of the American reservations was found inacceptable by the Court. President Hoover made a new attempt in 1930, which failed. In 1935, when Franklin D. Roosevelt was President, another effort was made to join the Court, but the opposition succeeded once more, amid unparalleled misrepresentation of the true issues.

5.

THE PEACE CONFERENCE of Paris was the largest and most momentous of international conferences held since the Congress of Vienna had attempted to restore the Europe that Napoleon had splintered. Like Vienna, it had its full-dress events, but instead of balls where royalty danced, and High Mass in the field, attended by military staffs in full regalia, its most important events were plenary sessions. At one of these the League of Nations Covenant was formally presented; at another, in the Hôtel Grand Trianon at Versailles, the German envoys received the terms to which they were to subscribe. The most dramatic of all events was the signing of the treaty in the Hall of Mirrors at Versailles. In this long, narrow gallery, where Louis XIV had paraded, where Benjamin Franklin had attended levees, and where Bismarck had proclaimed the German Reich in 1871, diplomats of all ranks gaped to see two scapegoats affix their obscure names to the document in the name of Germany.

The rest of Paris was filled with the rattle of typewriters and the showers of pamphlets, multigraphed documents, and leaflets; members of investigating bodies, boards of inquiry and research, dashed about the boulevards in taxicabs collecting views and statistics. Sometimes an official delegation from one small state would occupy a hotel next door to that occupied by the unofficial, but highly vocal, opposition. In the meantime restaurants and cafés were filled with men in uniform, on leave, while at night the streets were densely packed with restless Yanks, each with three days and a pocketful of pay at his disposal.

In the midst of this hurly-burly Georges Clemenceau was shot by an assassin one morning, just after leaving his house to go to his office, in the Ministry of War, an old formal eighteenth-century palace. Clemenceau was hit in a shoulder-blade and in the flesh near a lung; the rest of the bullets went into the body of the motorcar. The assassin, a twenty-three-year-old lad, member of a Communist federation, told the police: "I am a Frenchman and an anarchist." Clemenceau never lost his calm and ironic detachment; he joked with the doctors about the assassin's marksmanship. " 'He shoots too well,' I said when I found myself hit," he explained to President Poincaré, but later he wondered why a man who had been trained for army duty should have missed dispatching him and wasted so many bullets. Two weeks after the incident the indestructible Clemenceau was able to attend a meeting of the council.

If the Council of Four meant to keep silent about its deliberations, those who appeared before it did not; nor could the council suppress the identities of those who came and went. Since each nation had special claims to press, its delegates were always ready to talk, or to let secretaries drop hints to the press. What was talked about in secret in the morning was passing around Paris, with suitable emendations, by afternoon. While there were few interviews "at the highest level," I recall that Italy's Prime Minister, Vittorio Orlando, argued Italy's case with all the persuasive powers of a trained lawyer; he had an impressive personality and is, at this writing, the only surviving member of the Big Four.

At one end of the Avenue des Champs Élysées stood the Hôtel Crillon; here the American Commission and numerous subsidiary groups had their headquarters. At the other end, near the Etoile, was the Astoria; here the British transacted business. One large room had been equipped with long tables covered with green cloth to serve the journalists of all nations; here Sir Robert Cecil explained the rights of minorities and the policy of the League, and J. Christian Smuts described the new colonial system, henceforth called mandates and allocated by the League.

Miles away, on the Boulevard Raspail, was the Hôtel Lutétia, where the Chinese Government presented arguments for recognizing the territorial integrity of China. The Chinese appealed first to the inner man; their hospitality was the most lavish of all at the conference. After huge quantities of food had been served, Lou Tseng-Tsiang, Minister of Foreign Affairs, and Chenting Thomas Wang, former Minister of Agriculture and Commerce, would quietly recite the misdeeds of the Germans in seizing Kiaochow (Shantung) and then remind us that the Germans had been forced out by the Japanese, who were now in possession of an Ally's goods.

Nearly everybody lost face in the Shantung controversy. The Japanese had demanded all German rights from Germany "with a view of eventual restoration of the same to China." In this Great Britain, then bound to Japan by a treaty, acquiesced. Now China demanded immediate restitution. Baron Makino contended this would be a slur on Japan's good name. Only Japan could restore the properties to China. China did not believe Japanese promises. Britain would not interfere. President Wilson, trying hard to keep the open-door principle in view, finally agreed to let the Japanese remain in possession on their promise to restore the property to China. For this he was severely criticized. But in 1922, with British and American pressure in operation, Japan restored the territory. China did not get it back free, however. She had to pay well for her property, especially for the railroad that she had built.

The aspirations of Italy, and the effort of the French and British governments to fulfill the promises they had made to get Italy's help in the war, brought about the hottest controversy of the conference. Here President Wilson faced the acid test of his ideas on national integrity and self-determination. It was the Italian problem, likewise, that caused the first rift between Wilson and Colonel E. M. House, who had tried to establish a basis for compromise, and apparently had promised too much.

Since Britain and France had made lavish promises of other people's territory to Italy, Italy expected the bargain to be kept. But the Americans considered the terms too costly. When the disagreement became acute President Wilson appealed to the Italian people, over the heads of their representatives, to revise their extreme demands in the interest of friendly relations with their neighbors. It was a noble document, intended to reach not only the Italian public but the people of Britain and France, where the newspapers were accusing the President of unrealistic meddling.

The *Morning Post* of London called his statement "Wild West diplomacy," and the *Daily Express* spoke of it as the "rabies of democracy." Yet the President merely explained that the United States had not been a party to the Treaty of London; that it, too, had made sacrifices of blood and treasure for the good of all, to establish a just peace; that this peace was in jeopardy if national groups were not given the freedom to live. He had already violated his principles by agreeing to place a huge population of Austrians under Italian rule.

But the Italians would not scale down their demands, and Vittorio Orlando, Baron Sonnino, and the rest of the delegation left for Rome. At first they were given noisy ovations by large crowds, but in the next few weeks they were blamed for not forcing their views on the Big Four. The Cabinet of Orlando fell.

The agitation to possess Fiume, which had been blocked in Paris, even though the city contained more Italians than Croats, took the form of an irresponsible military campaign by irregulars under Gabriele d'Annunzio, the poet. He "occupied" the city, gave out flamboyant proclamations, and reviewed troops. The subsequent history of Fiume is fantastic, for an Italian Prime Minister, Giolitti, had to send a warship to dislodge D'Annunzio. Through a long series of negotiations with the Yugoslavs by Mussolini, concessions of territory were made, though Italy retained the port. The diversion of shipping to other ports had reduced the importance and value of Fiume by the time the second World War broke out.

Thus all the principles that had won such general approval when proclaimed by President Wilson plagued him at every turn. The rights of minorities were the most difficult to apply. The compromise on the Saar provided for a plebiscite under the League in fifteen years. The attempt to reconstitute Poland and give it a proper outlet to the sea opened new wounds and laid the basis for the next World War. Poland was formed without the consent of Russia. The Polish Corridor, from Silesia to Danzig, had nearly three million Germans in it and cut across German territory. The Free City of Danzig was strongly resented by the Germans, who dominated it, and in the 1930's the National Socialists organized a strong party there and introduced a *Gauleiter*. Attempts to make a bargain with Poland, ousting the League of Nations and returning Danzig to Germany in exchange for concessions elsewhere, were made by Hitler, but rejected by Poland.

The Treaty of Versailles was also responsible for the situation that led to the dispute over the Sudeten Germans and the compromise of Munich. When the new nation of Czechoslovakia was formed, it was given the boundaries that Bohemia had as a member of the Austro-

Hungarian monarchy. This included the Sudeten Germans, who had felt at home under Austrian rule. When Hitler began to agitate for the inclusion of all Germans in his Reich, the Sudetens became the object of his propaganda.

6.

ONE OF THE SIGNIFICANT ACCOMPLISHMENTS of the treaty was to set in motion the International Labor Organization. This attempt to better working conditions everywhere had the strong support of the English-speaking nations, but their attitudes differed radically. The British wanted an international parliament of labor with power to make laws effective in all member nations. The Americans, led by Samuel Gompers, with William Green among his advisers, were strongly opposed to a superstate and adhered to the position, so long supported by the American Federation of Labor, of working through the established national agencies.

The Constitution of the International Labor Organization was an achievement. Even before it was adopted generally a labor conference met in Washington at the invitation of the President and took up such important matters as the eight-hour day, the forty-eight-hour week, and protection for women and children in industry. The United States did not immediately become a member because it did not ratify the treaty, but in 1934 Congress accepted an invitation to the United States to join, and this nation became one of the chief industrial states in the organization. This was another instance of American participation in a body founded by the Treaty.

James T. Shotwell considered the I.L.O. and the League as the two constructive accomplishments of the conference and pointed out that they provided for the future: "The only institutions which last are living institutions," said he; "and the very condition of living is change." He also stressed the view of the treaty makers that it was better to use governments already established in a community of effort rather than to weaken them in their sovereignty.

7.

THE SERIOUS FACE and reserved bearing of Woodrow Wilson became a familiar sight to those who attended the formal sessions of the Peace Conference, but the public, which had greeted him tumultuously, saw him only as he entered or left his limousine. He attended several exercises prepared by the French, but sat through no state dinners. Once the National Opera invited him to be its guest and to name his preference in opera, and he chose Rameau's classic ballet of *Castor and Pollux,* and sat with great dignity in a box with Mrs. Wilson and Admiral Grayson. Maurice Chevalier and Mistinguett were appearing nightly at the Casino de Paris; I believe he would have enjoyed them more, had he been at liberty to slip quietly into the theater.

Sometimes I saw him walk into the Hôtel Crillon to call on Colonel E. M. House; he would exchange a word with men he knew and step quickly into the little elevator, a slim figure in a single-breasted topcoat and felt hat, with the businesslike air of an accountant. After the cooling of his relations with Colonel House, it was said that Wilson had been affronted because he had met members of the Council of Four emerging from Colonel House's rooms. I doubted this inference, for the Colonel had been authorized to have numerous contacts with these men in the line of duty. Actually he was an indefatigable consultant and interviewer, though his personality suggested secret doings of deep import.

President Wilson was cordial to men who worked with him, such as David Hunter Miller and Ray Stannard Baker. Mr. Baker, as press relations officer, assisted by Arthur Sweetser, who adopted the League of Nations as a career, prepared the "communiqués" of the day's work and had them mimeographed. His position as a journalist, eager to put the Americans in a good light, and as the confidant of the President, who had no feeling for publicity, was difficult. The President had refused to grant interviews on the progress of the negotiations, and cards sent in at the Villa Murat and the Hôtel Bischoffsheim (a private *palais,* not a hotel) were returned by attendants. Mr. Baker endeavored to salvage information, but could not go beyond his instructions; however, if cornered he could always suggest an authority who ought to be consulted.

It was Woodrow Wilson's great concern for the success of the Covenant of the League of Nations that overcame his reluctance to recognize the usefulness of the press. One morning he appeared unexpectedly at Robert Lansing's press conference in the Hôtel Crillon. There he spoke freely for fifty-five minutes on the League, but warned: "I am not to be quoted. Not even as the highest authority.' Everyone knows who is meant by the 'highest authority.' " It was on this occasion that he made his first comment on the freedom of the seas, answering a query about the fate of his second point by declaring, "The joke's on me," and explaining that under the League the issue would not be raised, for there would be no neutrals and no neutral rights to violate.

Woodrow Wilson had immense dignity and reserve, but he also was self-sufficient. He made no attempts to mollify the public. It always seemed to me that his smile did not reach his eyes. Yet an intelligent Englishman, who observed him during his great welcome in London, said to me: "He has such a winning smile!" It was surprising to find that surface impressions meant much to the stolid British. Actually, Wilson was unlike the majority of Americans, to whom "passing the time of day" is an essential preliminary to more serious intercourse. The ability to put visitors at ease, possessed in a superlative degree by Franklin D. Roosevelt, was lacking in Wilson. But it should be added that Wilson's Assistant Secretary of the Navy did not possess it, in 1919, to the degree acquired later by careful application.

It was interesting to watch the French bring all sorts of influences to bear on President Wilson, in order to impress him with their views. From the day of his arrival they agitated for a journey through the devastated regions, hoping this would soften his stand against extensive reparations and territorial security. Wilson, who knew what they were about, was reluctant to go; he wanted to get down to business. His delay was impolitic, for eventually he did have to make a trip to Rheims and other ruined cities. Eventually, too, he had to give in to reparation claims, which had been severely contested, and which some authorities predicted, rightly, would contain the germs of a new war.

Mrs. Wilson has told how, in first passing through Soissons, the President found few to greet him. On his return from Rheims he was supposed to take another route, but actually returned through Soissons. Now the streets were filled with French troops, who cheered him noisily and demanded that he address them. When he realized that the troops had been purposely kept in barracks before, so that he might not be affected by their enthusiasm, he became sad and thoughtful.

President Wilson is the great tragic figure of the Peace Conference. He expressed, better than any leader of his generation, the high aspirations of the common man for equality of opportunity in individual and public life. No one rose higher above the limitations of sectionalism, nationalism, and commercial imperialism. No one fought more tenaciously for principles rather than expedience. He was, even in failure, a tremendous influence for world solidarity rather than national interest, for the good of the human race rather than the advantages Americans might gain by being powerful.

But he demonstrated anew that the fortunes of people in the mass are affected by the limitations of the individuals who lead them. Whatever the social forces that determine the direction taken by a nation, the final decision is often a personal one, in which the temperament of the leader plays a vital part. Woodrow Wilson had tenacity, but also stubbornness; vision, but also myopia; a sense of personal responsibility for the general welfare and a defiant conviction that his judgment was accurate. This made him the architect of the League of Nations; this in turn lost him his American support, and the peace.

For the principal leaders of the opposition, such as Henry Cabot Lodge and Hiram W. Johnson, Wilson had not only hatred but contempt. He saw in their actions no desire to serve their country, but only to gain partisan advantage. To his dying day Colonel E. M. House was not certain whether Senator Lodge acted from patriotic motives or the determination to sabotage the work of a Democratic President, but Woodrow Wilson, there is reason to believe, never doubted that Lodge was ready to wreck anything to gain a Republican advantage.

8.

THE TREATY WAS NOT NEGOTIATED with the vanquished; it was forced upon them. The negotiations were between the victors, over the spoils. This enabled Hitler later to denounce the treaty as dictated—*"Das Diktat von Versailles."* When the Germans had received the treaty at the Hôtel Grand Trianon, their first reply was about sixty-five thousand words long: "It took Lloyd George all day to read it," said Lord Riddell. The fundamental objection by the chief of the delegation, Count von Brockdorff-Rantzau, that it did not conform to the conditions of the armistice, based on the Fourteen Points and two subsequent declarations by President Wilson, was sound.

He raised another objection that was to reverberate down the years—his rejection of war guilt. It is characteristic of hurt German pride that the Germans translated "responsibility" as *Schuld,* or guilt. The Austrian and Hungarian versions did not mention guilt. The victors needed to establish responsibility so that they could exact reparations. The German delegate demanded that an impartial commission search the archives of all belligerents and establish the culpability of nations and individuals. To this the victors did not respond.

The major influence for strong repressive measures was France, which demanded political control over all German land west of the Rhine. This was scaled down to demilitarization of the left bank and an area extending fifty kilometers east of the river. A commission was named to supervise enforcement. The treaty was explicit about penalties: "In case Germany violates in any manner whatever the provisions . . . she shall be regarded as committing a hostile act against the powers signatory of the present treaty and as calculating to disturb the peace of the world." The Treaty of Locarno of 1925, signed by Britain, France, Italy, and Germany, was intended to define rights and discourage still further violation of the treaty, but on March 7, 1936, Hitler poured thirty thousand troops into the restricted Rhenish territory and declared the terms of Locarno violated by treaties signed by France with Poland and the Soviet Union. Germany, which had joined the League in 1926, in the days of the Weimar Republic, was taken out of the League by Hitler in 1935.

The treaty tackled the old difficulty of the race in armament by recommending a reduction in armament. The defeated nations were stripped of their military power and strongly restricted in future building operations, but when the League proved powerless to enforce these provisions Hitler defied them and rearmed. The other powers made repeated attempts to lift the burden of military and naval armament. The United States initiated several important conferences and supported others.

The first conference on naval armament at Washington established a ratio for building capital ships by Great Britain, the United States, Japan, France, and Italy, which was observed from 1922 to 1936. In 1927 President Coolidge called a conference on naval armament at Geneva, but with France and Italy absent, it failed to reach an agreement. In 1930 Great Britain, the United States, and Japan signed a new treaty at London; it was in effect until 1936, when Japan withdrew from all engagements. Japan had left the League in 1935 because of the opposition to its long series of aggressive acts against China, beginning with the occupation of Mukden in 1931. In 1932 President Hoover initiated a conference on armament at Geneva, suggesting that every nation reduce its strength by one-third. When Japan finally withdrew the other powers agreed to raise the tonnage of capital ships to forty-five thousand and the caliber of the largest guns to sixteen inches, so that the naval race was on once more.

The Treaty of Versailles is an important milestone in human progress. It established an international union of states to adjudicate disputes in a legal manner without immediate resort to war. It recognized the right of minorities and backward peoples to unhampered development, instead of colonial exploitation. These were steps in advance, but they were not as idealistic as would appear. Actually they responded to the need of the times.

An alliance of several states, the balance of power that Woodrow Wilson had denounced, was no longer sufficient to halt the terrible destructiveness of modern warfare; what was needed was general backing for continuing mediation and redress of grievances. Colonies were becoming more costly and difficult to defend; Great Britain, challenged in Ireland and India, was in no position to absorb the bulk of the German colonies; by pooling them under the mandate system of the League Britain gained supervision without complete responsibility. Obviously both measures were infringements of that idea of absolute sovereignty that went back to the days of absolute monarchs; in actual practice every nation makes concessions to others that may be construed as abridgment of sovereign rights, just as individuals recognize the claims of communal living.

The big failures of the treaty were inherent in the national systems that it represented. In reshuffling boundaries to the advantage of the victors, the treaty shifted authority from one group to another, without solving nationalist aspirations and antagonisms. No ideal arrangement could have been devised, short of the complete submergence of national identities in a European confederation.

Another mistake came in exacting reparations that became too heavy to bear, and thus proved as detrimental to the creditor as to the defeated. The French led in this demand, but it must be remembered that in subsequent negotiations the United States also presented its bill for the costs of the occupation of Germany. The failure of Germany to live up to its agreements led to two military occupations of the Ruhr, the later one encountering a show of passive resistance in the reviving German state. The collapse of German currency and other financial difficulties led to the adjustments by experts known as the Dawes plan and the Young plan, both attempts to balance the budget and provide for a steady flow of reparations payments; these became complicated with the demand of the United States for payments on debts incurred here by the Allies, and with the external loans of Germany, which helped to finance German recovery.

These difficulties proved the economic interdependence of the modern world. Subsequent experiences showed that a central authority, such as the League, cannot enforce its decisions without general support, and that victors cannot force new boundaries and political conditions on losers permanently without providing power for continued supervision. The latter truth was recognized primarily by France and to some extent by Britain; it was completely disregarded by the United States.

Even the terrible experiences of the second World War taught us nothing; we again disbanded the greater part of our military machine and shut down our vital war factories, yet continued to give orders to nations under arms. The stupidity of this practice is once more apparent; our right to speak has been challenged on the primitive basis of street-corner strategy: "If you want to know who's boss, start something." Once more yielding to the strong anti-military, pacifist, and isolationist feelings of the American people, we stand in danger of further disasters, in a world jealous of our wealth and resentful of our interference.

The Treaty of Versailles may have been set aside by Hitler, but it was considered binding by the other signatories. When the powers that defeated Nazi Germany named their International Military Tribunal to bring the Nazi aggressors before a court, they remembered the violations of the treaty. That instrument had made an attempt to provide for the trial of individuals "accused of having committed acts in violation of the laws and customs of war," to which the Germans assented. However, the Germans protested bringing William II to trial, or labeling their leaders as aggressors.

When the Dutch assumed full responsibility for interning the Kaiser, the Allied governments dropped the hot issue of "hang the Kaiser." Eventually the Germans agreed to trials of war criminals at Leipzig, but the results were so disappointing that the prosecutions were not continued. Germany was not then an occupied country, and the desire to re-establish a prosperous Europe as soon as possible had great weight in the attitude taken toward Germany.

A quarter of a century later the powers set up their tribunal at Nuremberg and confronted the Nazi leaders with specific violations of the Treaty of Versailles. They specified that the Nazi leaders, in addition to committing crimes against peace and violating many other treaties and conventions, were responsible for these specific acts in contravention of the treaty: occupying and fortifying the Rhineland; annexing Austria, Memel, Danzig, Bohemia, and Moravia; creating an air force; establishing compulsory military service; and increasing the Army and the Navy beyond treaty limitations.

9.

WHEN THE TREATY-MAKING had been concluded, the victorious powers staged their great historic scene, the signing of the treaty in the
Hall of Mirrors of the palace of Versailles on June 28, 1919. That the
French public would look upon this as the culminating event in the
defeat of Germany was to be expected; what happened was that officials
and diplomats, who had been arguing with one another until now, likewise esteemed this their mighty hour. The spirit of the day was one of
rejoicing in the final victory rather than in the beginning of peace, and
everywhere, along the wide avenues leading to the Place d'Armes, before the headquarters of various delegations and inside the cobbled
courtyard of the palace itself, French troops, foot and cavalry, in their
finest uniforms, reminded visitors of how important this day was to
France.

Yet none of the high-ranking Germans who had conducted the war
was present at this final act. The German Kaiser was a fugitive in
Holland, protected by the Dutch; General von Hindenburg had retired
to his country home and General Ludendorff was fuming in private,
stripped of authority; the Imperial Ministry had yielded to a pro-
visional government, and even the original plenipotentiaries, led by
Count von Brockdorff-Rantzau, had refused to accept the terms, declaring, "We will sign neither our own death sentence nor a deprivation
of our rights or our honor." Faced with the threat of military occupation, the German Government agreed to sign and sent two cabinet
members, hitherto unknown to diplomacy, to affix their names to the
document. They were Hermann Müller and Johann Bell, and at the direction of Clemenceau they signed the treaty on approximately the
spot where King William I of Prussia had been proclaimed German
Emperor on January 18, 1871.

Whatever misgivings the leading statesmen had, they must have felt,
at that hour, that they had completed the first steps toward a lasting
peace. The element of gaiety was uppermost, and even Clemenceau,
Lloyd George, and Wilson locked arms and hurried merrily down the
paths to watch the fountains disgorge the water that had been labori-
ously pumped up for days from the Seine. Even though China, at the

last moment, refused to sign, in protest at the Japanese occupation of Shantung, Italy did, in the persons of Sonnino, Imperiali, and Crespi. France had obtained the major part of her demands, including the promise of reparations from Germany and the coal of the Saar, and Clemenceau had in his pocket a supplementary treaty with Great Britain and the United States in which both promised to come to the aid of France in any future attack.

Whether Woodrow Wilson really believed that the Senate of the United States would ratify such a treaty we have no way of knowing; it was France's price for supporting in full the terms of the League. The President, who was the first to sign the Treaty of Versailles after the Germans, left Paris that evening with a "thank you" note to his hosts, the French nation; with him traveled Mrs. Wilson, Margaret Wilson, Admiral Grayson, and his secretaries. His train did not reach Brest until nearly noon the following day, when, amid the booming of cannon and the playing of the "Star-Spangled Banner," he boarded a gunboat and was taken to the *George Washington* in the roadstead. As the band struck up "La Marseillaise," President Wilson remarked to one of the French officials: "I hope there will be no more wars; in any case, no great war."

General Smuts was right when he summed up the conference: "Not Wilson, but humanity, failed in Paris."

The Noble Experiment of Izzie and Moe

BY HERBERT ASBURY

Herbert Asbury has been an eager student of American morals and mores for a good many years. One of sixteen children in a strictly churchgoing family, he worked in his younger days as a printer's devil, a freight loader on Mississippi River boats, a handy man in a lumber yard, a professional baseball player, and a newspaper reporter and re-write man. His magazine article "Hatrack," about a skinny prostitute in his home town of Farmington, Missouri, was perhaps the most famous piece of writing ever published in the old *American Mercury* (April 1926), and was promptly banned in Boston. Mr. Asbury has written books about the gaudier aspects of life in old New York, Chicago, New Orleans, and San Francisco, and it is natural he should take a special interest in those two delightful figures of the prohibition era, Izzie Einstein and Moe Smith. For several years during the war he was on the staff of *Collier's Weekly*. He has since resigned.

✵ 1.

PROHIBITION WENT into effect throughout the United States on January 16, 1920, and the country settled back with an air of "Well, *that's* settled." There had been a liquor problem. But a Law had been passed. Naturally, there was no longer a liquor problem. No prophet arose to foretell the awful things that were coming—the rum ships prowling off the coasts, the illicit breweries and distilleries, the boot-leggers and the speakeasies, the corruption of police and judiciary, the hijackers and their machine guns, the gang wars, the multimillionaire booze barons, the murders and assassinations, the national breakdown of morals and manners, and all the rest of the long train of evils that sprang from the Eighteenth Amendment.

Nor did anyone imagine that the Amendment and its enabling legislation, the Volstead Act, would be difficult to enforce. It was THE LAW, and by and large the American people were law-abiding. The common attitude was expressed, somewhat flamboyantly, by John F. Kramer, the first Prohibition Commissioner. "This law," he said, "will be obeyed in cities large and small, and in villages, and where it is not obeyed it will be enforced. The law says that liquor to be used as a beverage must not be manufactured. We shall see that it is not manufactured. Nor sold, nor given away, nor hauled in anything on the surface of the earth or under the earth or in the air." The Anti-Saloon League estimated that prohibition could be enforced for less than $5,000,000 a year, so eager were the people to enter the shining gates of the dry Utopia. Congress appropriated a little more than that amount enough to set up an enforcement organization and to provide about 1,500 prohibition agents. These noble snoopers, paid an average of about $2,000 a year and hence immune to temptation, were supposed to keep 125,000,000 people from manufacturing or drinking anything stronger than near-beer. They didn't, but two of them made a spectacular try.

2.

IN A $14-A-MONTH flat on Ridge Street, in New York's lower East Side, lived a bulbous little man named Isadore Einstein, whom everyone called Izzy. He had been a salesman, both inside and on the road, but was now a minor clerk at Station K of the New York Post Office. It required very shrewd management to feed, house, and clothe his family—his wife and four children and his father—on the meager salary of a postal employee. He was looking for something better, and decided that he had found it when he read in his newspaper about the government's plans to pay enforcement agents up to $2,500 a year.

But James Shevlin, Chief Enforcement Agent for the Southern District of New York, was not enthusiastic about Izzy. "I must say, Mr. Einstein," he said, "you don't look much like a detective." And that was the truth. Probably no one ever looked less like a detective than Izzy Einstein. He was forty years old, almost bald, five feet and five inches tall, and weighed 225 pounds. Most of this poundage was around his middle, so that when he walked his noble paunch, gently wobbling, moved majestically ahead like the breast of an overfed pouter pigeon.

But Izzy was accomplished. Besides English and Yiddish, he spoke German, Polish, and Hungarian fluently, and could make headway, though haltingly, in French, Italian, and Russian. He had even picked up a few words and phrases of Chinese. Moreover, Izzy had a knack of getting along with people and inspiring confidence. No one, looking at his round, jolly face and twinkling black eyes, could believe that he was a government snooper. Down on the lower East Side in New York he was the neighborhood cutup; whenever he dropped into the corner cigar stores and the coffeehouses his witticisms and high spirits never failed to draw an appreciative crowd.

"I guess Mr. Shevlin never saw a type like me," Izzy said afterward. "Maybe I fascinated him or something. Anyhow, I sold him on the idea that this prohibition business needed a new type of people that couldn't be spotted so easy."

Whatever the reason, Izzy got the job.

"But I must warn you," said Shevlin, "that hunting down liquor sellers isn't exactly a safe line of work. Some law violator might get mad and try to crack a bottle over your head."

"Bottles," said Izzy, "I can dodge."

Izzy's first assignment was to clean up a place in Brooklyn which the enforcement authorities shrewdly suspected housed a speakeasy, since drunken men had been seen staggering from the building, and the air for half a block around was redolent with the fumes of beer and whiskey. Several agents had snooped and slunk around the house; one had watched all one afternoon from a roof across the street, and another had hidden for hours in an adjoining doorway, obtaining an accurate count of the number of men who entered and left. But none had been able to get inside. Izzy knew nothing of sleuthing procedures; he simply walked up to the joint and knocked on the door. A peephole was opened, and a hoarse voice demanded to know who was there.

"Izzy Einstein," said Izzy. "I want a drink."

"Oh, yeah? Who sent you here, bud? What's your business?"

"My boss sent me," Izzy explained. "I'm a prohibition agent. I just got appointed."

The door swung open and the doorman slapped Izzy jovially on the back.

"Ho! ho!" he cried. "Come right in, bud. That's the best gag I've heard yet."

Izzy stepped into a room where half a dozen men were drinking at a small, makeshift bar.

"Hey, boss!" the doorman yelled. "Here's a prohibition agent wants a drink! You got a badge, too, bud?"

"Sure I have," said Izzy, and produced it.

"Well, I'll be damned," said the man behind the bar. "Looks just like the real thing."

He poured a slug of whiskey, and Izzy downed it. That was a mistake, for when the time came to make the pinch Izzy had no evidence. He tried to grab the bottle but the bartender ran out the back door with it.

"I learned right there," said Izzy, "that a slug of hooch in an agent's belly might feel good, but it ain't evidence."

So when he went home that night he rigged up an evidence-collector. He put a small funnel in the upper left-hand pocket of his vest, and connected it, by means of a rubber tube, with a flat bottle concealed in the lining of the garment. Thereafter, when a drink was served to him, Izzy took a small sip, then poured the remainder into the funnel while the bartender was making change. The bottle wouldn't hold much, but there was always enough for analysis and to offer in evidence. "I'd have died if it hadn't been for that little funnel and the bottle," said Izzy. "And most of the stuff I got in those places was terrible."

Izzy used his original device of giving his real name, with some variation, more than twenty times during the next five years. It was successful even after he became so well known, and so greatly feared, that his picture hung behind the bar in many speakeasies, that all might see and be warned. Occasionally Izzy would prance into a gin-mill with his badge pinned to his lapel, in plain sight, and shout jovially, "How about a drink for a hard-working prohibition agent?" Seeing the round little man trying so hard to be funny, everyone in the place would rush forward to hand him something alcoholic, and Izzy would arrest them and close the joint.

3.

ONCE HE WENT into a gin-mill where three huge portraits of himself, framed in what he described as "black, creepy crape," ornamented the back bar. He asked for a drink, and the bartender refused to serve it.

"I don't know you," he said.

"Why," said Izzy, laughing. "I'm Izzy Epstein, the famous prohibition detective."

"Get the name right, bud," growled the bartender. "The bum's name is Einstein."

"Epstein," said Izzy. "Don't I know my own name?"

"Maybe you do, but the low-life you're trying to act like is named Einstein. E-i-n-s-t-e-i-n."

"Brother," said Izzy, "I ain't never wrong about a name. It's Epstein."

"Einstein!" roared the bartender.

"Epstein!" shouted Izzy.

"You're nuts!" yelled the bartender, furiously. "I'll bet you anything you want it's Einstein!"

"Okay," said Izzy. "I'll bet you the drinks."

The bartender called his other customers, and after much argument and pointing to Izzy's pictures, they agreed that the name was Einstein. So Izzy—or rather the government—had to buy nine drinks, and the bartender served them, and shortly after went to jail.

After Izzy had been an enforcement agent for a few weeks, he began to miss his old friend Moe Smith, with whom he had spent many pleasant evenings in the East Side coffeehouses. Like Izzy, Moe was a natural comedian, and, also like Izzy, he was corpulent. He tipped the scales at about 235 pounds, but he was a couple of inches taller than Izzy and didn't look quite so roly-poly. Moe had been a cigar salesman, and manager of a small fight club at Orchard and Grand Streets, New York City, and had invested his savings in a little cigar store, where he was doing well. Izzy persuaded him to put a relative in charge of the store, and to apply for a job as enforcement agent.

Moe could probably have got on the enforcement staff by his own efforts, for his background and experience were at least as good as those of nine-tenths of the agents who were hired, but he obtained the post a little quicker through Izzy's recommendation. As soon as he was sworn in as an agent, he and Izzy teamed up together, and most of the time thereafter worked as a pair. Their first assignment took them to Rockaway Beach, near New York, where they confiscated a still and arrested the operator. This man apparently took a great liking to Izzy, for after he got out of jail he made several trips to New York especially to urge Izzy to go on a fishing trip with him.

"I'll take you three miles out to sea," he said. "You'll have quite a time."

But Izzy firmly declined the invitation. "Sure he'll take me out to sea," he said, "but will he bring me back? He could leave me with the fishes."

In those early days of the noble experiment everything that happened in connection with prohibition was news, and some of New York's best reporters covered enforcement headquarters. Casting about for a way to enliven their stories and provide exercise for their imaginations, they seized upon the exploits of Izzy and Moe. The two fat and indefatigable agents supplied human-interest material by the yard; moreover, they were extraordinarily co-operative. They frequently scheduled their raids to suit the convenience of the reporters and the newspaper photographers, and soon learned that there was more room in the papers on Monday morning than on any other day of the week.

One Sunday, accompanied by a swarm of eager reporters, they established a record by making seventy-one raids in a little more than twelve hours. On another they staged a spectacular raid for the benefit of Dr. John Roach Straton, a famous hell-buster of the period, and the congregation of the Calvary Baptist Church in West Fifty-seventh Street, of which Dr. Straton was pastor. Izzy and Moe timed their raid, on a small café near the church, to coincide with the dismissal of Dr. Straton's flock after morning services, and the members of the congregation reached the street in time to see the agents rolling barrels of whiskey

out of the café and smashing them with hatchets. This raid made everybody happy, except, of course, the man who owned the whiskey.

Hundreds of stories, a great many of them truthful, were written
about Izzy and Moe and their grotesque adventures, and they probably
made the front pages oftener than any other personages of their time
except the President and the Prince of Wales.

Izzy especially gained great renown, for he was the acknowledged
leader of the team. The New York *Tribune* called him "the master
mind of the Federal rum ferrets." O. O. McIntyre, in his syndicated
column, informed his readers that Izzy had "become as famous in
New York as the Woolworth Building," and that "no morning paper
is complete without some account of his exploits." Wayne B. Wheeler,
General Superintendent of the Anti-Saloon League and the man who
lobbied the prohibition law through Congress, graciously expressed
his approval of Izzy's feats in a personal letter. "The bootlegger who
gets away from you," he wrote, "has to get up early in the morning."
In fact, it didn't matter how early a bootlegger got up, Izzy was usually
ahead of him.

"Izzy does not sleep," reported the Brooklyn *Eagle*. "He's on the
job day and night, and accomplishes more for the drys than half a dozen
anti-saloon leagues. It's getting so now that a saloonkeeper hesitates in
serving the wants of his oldest and best-known customer, for fear that
he may suddenly develop into Izzy. A few more Izzies scattered over
the country and the U. S. would be bone dry, parched, and withered."

4.

What the newspapers enjoyed most about Izzy and Moe was their
ingenuity. Once they went after a speakeasy where half a dozen dry
agents had tried without success to buy a drink. The bartender positively wouldn't sell to anyone he didn't know. So on a cold winter night
Izzy stood in front of the gin-mill, in his shirt sleeves, until he was red
and shivering and his teeth were chattering. Then Moe half-carried
him into the speakeasy, shouting excitedly:

"Give this man a drink! He's just been bitten by a frost!"

The kindhearted bartender, startled by Moe's excitement and upset by Izzy's miserable appearance, rushed forward with a bottle of whiskey. Moe promptly snatched the bottle and put him under arrest.

One of Izzy's most brilliant ideas was always to carry something on his raids, the nature of the burden depending upon the character of the neighborhood and of a particular speakeasy's clientele. When he wanted to get into a place frequented by musicians, for example, he carried a violin or a trombone, and if, as sometimes happened, he was asked to play the instrument, he could do it. He usually played "How Dry I Am." On the East Side and in the poorer sections of the Bronx, if the weather permitted, Izzy went around in his shirt sleeves carrying a pitcher of milk, the very pattern of an honest man on his way home from the grocery. Once in Brooklyn he was admitted to half a dozen gin-mills because he was lugging a big pail of dill pickles. "A fat man with pickles!" said Izzy. "Who'd ever think a fat man with pickles was an agent?"

When Izzy operated on the beaches around New York he always carried a fishing rod or a bathing suit; he had great success one day at Sheepshead Bay with a string of fish slung over his shoulder. The doorman of the Assembly, a café in Brooklyn which catered to judges and lawyers, let him in without question because he wore a frock coat and carried a huge tome bound in sheepskin. Once inside, Izzy opened his book and adjusted a pair of horn-rimmed spectacles and, with lips moving and brow furrowed, marched with stately tread across the room and barged into the bar. Without lifting his eyes from the book, he called sonorously for "a beverage, please," and the fascinated bartender poured a slug of whiskey before he realized what he was doing. When Izzy and Moe visited Reisenweber's, a famous and expensive resort on Broadway, they carried two lovely blondes and wore "full-dress tuxedos," with rings on their fingers, sweet-smelling pomade on their hair, and huge imitation-pearl studs in their shirt fronts. The headwaiter asked them for references when they ordered liquor, and Izzy searched his pockets and pulled out the first card he found. It happened to be the card of a rabbi, with which Izzy planned to ensnare a sacramental-wine store. But the headwaiter, a man of scant perception, bowed deferentially and sold them a bottle of whiskey. "He deserved to be arrested," said Izzy, indignantly. "Imagine! A rabbi with a blonde and no beard!"

Up in Van Cortlandt Park, in New York City, near the public play-ing fields, was a soft-drink establishment which was suspected of being one of the retail outlets of a big rum ring. Many complaints were made to enforcement headquarters that customers had become tipsy after a few shots of the soda water sold in the place; one woman wrote that by mistake her milk shake had been filled with gin. Bad gin, too, she added. The job of getting the evidence was given to Izzy. It proved a difficult task, for the owner of the joint would sell liquor to no one he didn't know personally. So on a Saturday afternoon in November Izzy assembled a group of half a dozen dry agents, clad them in foot-ball uniforms, and smeared their arms and faces with fresh dirt. Then Izzy tucked a football under his arm, hung a helmet over his ears, and led them whooping and rah-rahing into the suspected speakeasy, where they shouted that they had just won the last game of the season and wanted to break training in a big way. The speakeasy owner, pleased at such a rush of business, sold each agent a pint of whiskey. "Have fun, boys," he said. "The same to you," said Izzy, handing him a summons.

Flushed with this striking success, which showed that at heart he was a college boy, Izzy went to Ithaca, N. Y., to investigate a complaint by officials of Cornell University that some soda fountains near the campus were not confining their sales to pop. Izzy disguised himself as an undergraduate by putting on a little cap and a pair of white linen knickers, not so little, and for several days strolled about the campus. He hummed snatches of Cornell songs which he had learned, and played safe by addressing everyone with a mustache as "Professor," and everyone with a beard as "Dean." Having located the soda foun-tains which sold liquor, he dashed into them one by one, establishing himself as a student by shouting, "Sizzle Boom! Sizzle Boom! Rah! Rah! Rah!" The speakeasy boys thought he was a comedian, which indeed he was, and they gladly sold him all the booze he wanted, after which he went from place to place distributing "diplomas," or sum-monses.

From Cornell, and without the blessing of the student body, Izzy rushed into Harlem to investigate a complaint about a grocery store. "The man charged me two dollars for a can of tomatoes," a woman wrote to enforcement headquarters, "and when I got it home I found there was nothing in it but a lot of nasty-smelling water. My husband he grabbed it and ran out of the house and I ain't seen him since. I want you to arrest that man." Izzy disguised himself as a Negro, with his face blackened by burnt cork and a rich Southern accent rolling off his tongue. He visited the store and awaited his turn in a long line of impatient customers. He found that to buy a half-pint of whiskey (four dollars) a customer asked for a can of beans. If he wanted gin (two dollars) he asked for tomatoes. Izzy bought both beans and tomatoes and came back next day with a warrant and a truck. Besides the groceryman, he hauled away four hundred bottles of gin, some empty cans, a canning machine, three barrels of whiskey, and a barrel of pickles which contained one hundred small bottles of gin. "Pickles was a kind of hobby of mine," he said, "and I could always tell if anything was wrong with a barrel."

The trail of illegal liquor led Izzy and Moe into some mighty queer places, but they followed wherever it led, and were always ready with the appropriate disguise. Dressed as a longshoreman, Izzy captured an Italian who used his cash register as a cellarette; its drawers were filled with little bottles of booze. In the guise of a mendicant, Izzy pawned an old pair of pants for two dollars in Brooklyn, and snooping about the pawnshops a bit found ten thousand dollars' worth of good liquor wrapped in clothing that had been left as pledges. He got into the Half Past Nine Club, on Eighth Avenue, as a prosperous poultry salesman, playing tipsy and carrying a sample, and found a large stock of liquor in a stuffed grizzly bear.

When he made an investigation of a snooty delicatessen on Madison Avenue, which catered exclusively to the carriage trade, Izzy got himself up as a Park Avenue dude, with evening clothes, a huge imitation diamond stud, and a gold-headed cane. He snooped around, acting hard to please, until he found that many of the beribboned baskets of fruit had bottles tucked away in them. Next morning he returned with a warrant, and was just about to enter the store to serve it when a young man drove up in a truck. "Hey, mister," he said, "do me a favor, will you? I gotta deliver some stuff here and they told me to be careful. Take a look inside and see if everything looks okay." Izzy glanced into the delicatessen and reported that everything looked wonderful. Then he arrested the young man and confiscated his truck and stuff, which was fifty cases of liquor. In the delicatessen Izzy found five hundred more cases.

One of Izzy's largest and most important hauls came as the result of a visit to a graveyard on the outskirts of New York. He had gone to the cemetery to attend the burial services of a friend, and, as usual, kept his eyes open. Just as the car in which he was riding turned into the cemetery gates, he saw two men come out of the back door of a house across the street, look furtively about, and then carry a large galvanized can across the yard into a shed. This looked suspicious, so when the services were over, instead of returning to New York, Izzy hid in some shrubbery. At sundown, when the cemetery gates had been closed, he moved to a tombstone directly across from the house, and crouched behind it. For three hours he watched and listened. Several times he thought he caught a whiff of mash, but nothing happened.

Izzy returned to New York about midnight, but without evidence to justify making a raid or asking for a warrant. So he evolved a scheme, for he was convinced that dirty business was afoot in the house. Next day he and Moe appeared at the cemetery office, two very seedy-looking characters, clad in rags and obviously down on their luck. They asked for work as gravediggers. The superintendent said there were no jobs open but changed his mind when they offered to dig graves for half price. They worked in an obscure corner of the cemetery until the time came to close the gates, then they told the superintendent that they needed money badly and would like to work overtime. He agreed, and left them there with their picks and shovels. After he had gone they moved to an unused area near the fence, across from the house, and began to dig. About an hour later a man came out of the house, stood on the porch watching them for a few minutes, then crossed the road and leaned idly against the fence.

"Hard work, ain't it, boys?" he asked.

"Yeah," said Moe. "Thirsty work, too. I'd give ten dollars for a pint right now."

"Five, anyway," said Izzy.

The man said nothing, and after a few minutes went back into the house. Then Izzy had another idea. He and Moe quickly dug three or four shallow holes, and were working on a fifth when the man returned. When he got within hearing distance Moe called to Izzy:

"How many more we got to dig tonight?"

"Ten," said Izzy.

"My God!" exclaimed the man. "What happened? Somebody blow up a hotel?"

"Well, that's the way it goes," said Izzy. "Sometimes nobody dies for a long time, then all of a sudden a lot of people make up their minds at the same time."

"It wouldn't be so bad," said Moe, "if we could get a drink."

"You boys come over to the house after a while," the man said. "Maybe I can fix you up."

Half an hour later Izzy and Moe put away their tools, climbed the fence, and strolled across the road. The man greeted them cordially, and introduced them to two others as hard-working gravediggers. The party adjourned to the kitchen, where Izzy bought a pint of whiskey for six dollars, having beat the price down from ten. Then while Moe covered the three prisoners with his gun, Izzy kicked in the door of an adjoining room, from which came the heavy odor of fermenting mash. There he found three big stills running full blast, fifty-one barrels containing alcohol, and a dozen bottles of essences and chemical coloring, used to give the new hooch the appearance, and something of the flavor, of the real stuff. In another room Izzy discovered a large quantity of counterfeit labels and government revenue stamps. The hosts had the job of carrying all this stuff out and loading it on a truck.

5.

FOR MORE than five years the whole country laughed at the antics of Izzy and Moe, with the exception of the ardent drys, who thought the boys were wonderful, and the bootleggers and speakeasy proprietors, who thought they were crazy and feared them mightily. And their fear was justified, for in their comparatively brief career Izzy and Moe confiscated 5,000,000 bottles of booze, worth $15,000,000, besides thousands of gallons in kegs and barrels and hundreds of stills and breweries. They smashed an enormous quantity of saloon fixtures and equipment, and made 4,392 arrests, of which more than 95 per cent resulted in convictions. No other two agents even approached this record.

Nearly all of their victims were small-fry bootleggers and speakeasy operators, although they raided and confiscated a considerable number of large stills and breweries. Their largest single haul was 2,000 cases of bottled whiskey and 365 barrels of whiskey and brandy, which they found in a Bronx garage. And they made one terrifying swoop up and down Broadway which put the finishing touches to such celebrated night-life resorts as Jack's, the Ted Lewis Club, Shanley's, the Beaux Arts, and Reisenweber's.

Neither Izzy nor Moe molested hip-flask toters; nor, unlike other agents who made themselves obnoxious to the general public, did they go barging into restaurants sniffing at glasses and snatching bottles off tables. "Personally," wrote Izzy, "I never saw any call for such tactics. I did my work quietly, and extended courtesy to any law violator I had to deal with. If it was a high-class place I was pinching, I'd sometimes even let the manager collect his dinner checks so he wouldn't be stuck for the food he'd served. Even in tough places I never abused my power. I used the name of the law and not blackjacks."

Izzy and Moe made many spectacular raids in Chicago, Detroit, and other cities ruled by the gangsters and the beer barons, but they never encountered Al Capone, Johnny Torrio, Frankie Yale, or any of the other great hoodlums who were the real beneficiaries of the Eighteenth Amendment. If they had, there is little doubt that they would have taken the triggermen in their stride, for neither Izzy nor Moe lacked courage. Izzy didn't approve of guns, and never carried one. Moe lugged a revolver around occasionally, but in five years fired it only twice. Once he shot out a lock that had resisted his efforts, and another time he shot a hole in a keg of whiskey. Izzy said later that guns were pulled on him only twice. The first time was on Dock Street, in Yonkers, N. Y., where he had spent a pleasant and profitable evening with raids on five speakeasies. To make it an even half dozen, he stepped into a sixth place that looked suspicious, bought a slug of whiskey for sixty cents, and poured it into the funnel in his vest pocket. While he was arresting the bartender, the owner of the joint came into the bar from another part of the house.

"He pulled an automatic from behind the bar," wrote Izzy. "She clicked but the trigger jammed. It was aimed right at my heart. I didn't like that. I grabbed his arm and he and I had a fierce fight all over the bar, till finally I got the pistol. I don't mind telling you I was afraid, particularly when I found the gun was loaded."

On another occasion an angry bartender shoved a revolver against Izzy's stomach. But Izzy didn't bat an eye; he calmly shoved the gun aside.

"Put that up, son," he said, soothingly. "Murdering me won't help your family."

Fortunately, the bartender had a family, and Izzy's warning brought to his mind a vision of his fatherless children weeping at the knee of their widowed mother, who was also weeping. He stopped to think. While he was thinking, Moe knocked him cold.

On one of his swings around the so-called enforcement circuit, Izzy made up a sort of schedule showing the length of time it took him to get a drink in various cities. New Orleans won first prize, a four-star hiss from the Anti-Saloon League. When Izzy arrived in the Crescent City he climbed into an ancient taxicab, and as the machine got under way he asked the driver where he could get a drink.

"Right here, suh," said the driver, and pulled out a bottle. "Fo' bits."

Time—thirty-five seconds.

In Pittsburgh, disguised as a Polish mill worker, Izzy bought a drink of terrible whiskey in eleven minutes. Just seventeen minutes after he got off the train in Atlanta, he walked into a confectionery shop on Peachtree Street, bought a drink, and arrested the proprietor. In Chicago he bought a drink in twenty-one minutes without leaving the railroad station, and duplicated this feat in St. Louis. In Cleveland it took twenty-nine minutes, but that was because an usher in a vaudeville theater, who had offered to take him to a speakeasy, couldn't leave his job right away. In Baltimore, Izzy got on a trolley car and asked the conductor where he could find a speakeasy. "In the next block," the conductor replied. Time, fifteen minutes. It took longer in Washington than anywhere else; Izzy roamed the city for a whole hour before he could locate a gin-mill. He finally had to ask a policeman, who provided him with the necessary directions.

6.

DURING THE SUMMER of 1925 the almost continual stories about Izzy and Moe in the newspapers got on the nerves of high prohibition enforcement officials in Washington, few of whom ever got mentioned in the papers at all. National headquarters announced that any agent whose name appeared in print in connection with his work would be suspended, and perhaps otherwise punished, on the ground that publicity brought discredit to the service. At the same time a high official called Izzy to Washington and spoke to him rather severely. "You get your name in the newspaper all the time, and in the headlines, too," he complained, "whereas mine is hardly ever mentioned. I must ask you to remember that you are merely a subordinate, not the whole show." For a while Izzy really tried to keep away from the reporters and out of the papers, but both he and Moe had become public personages, and it was impossible to keep the newspapermen from writing about them. When they refused to tell what they had done, the reporters invented stories about them, so a stream of angry denials and protests continued to come from Washington.

Finally, on November 13, 1925, it was announced that Izzy and Moe had turned in their gold badges and were no longer prohibition agents. Izzy's story was that he had been told he was to be transferred to Chicago. He had lived in New York since he was fifteen years old, and had no intention of ever living anywhere else, so he refused to go, and "thereby fired myself." Government officials, however, said that Izzy and Moe had been dismissed "for the good of the service." Off the record they added, "The service must be dignified. Izzy and Moe belong on the vaudeville stage." Most of the newspapers took the position that the whole problem of enforcement belonged on the vaudeville stage. The New York *Herald Tribune* said, "They [Izzy and Moe] never made prohibition much more of a joke than it has been made by some of the serious-minded prohibition officers."

Both Izzy and Moe went into the insurance business, and did well. They dropped out of the public eye, and remained out except for an occasional Sunday feature story, and a brief flurry of publicity in 1928, when Izzy went to Europe and returned with some entertaining accounts of his adventures. Izzy died in New York on February 17, 1938, by which time his four sons had all become successful lawyers.

Aimee Semple McPherson: "Sunlight in My Soul"

BY CAREY MCWILLIAMS

Carey McWilliams was Sister Aimee McPherson's neighbor during most of her gaudy career in Los Angeles. His verdict that Sister was a genuine force for tolerance and brotherhood—as well as a tempestuous, oversexed, and desperately frustrated woman—may cause surprise, but it carries special authority. Mr. McWilliams was Commissioner of Housing and Immigration in California during four depression years. He has written several books about social problems and minority groups, the most recent of which is *A Mask for Privilege* (1947), a study of anti-Semitism, as well as a study of Southern California and a biography of Ambrose Bierce.

✸ 1.

THIS IS THE STORY of a sad lady. Aimee Semple McPherson was most frequently characterized in her lifetime as a gay and dynamic person. At different times and by a variety of observers, she was pictured as a misplaced queen of musical comedy; a woman who "might have been a great actress" (of course she *was* a great actress); a siren of "a magnetism such as few women since Cleopatra have possessed." But such notions are essentially false. She was lonely and sad, as only a person suddenly catapulted into the floodlight of unbearable fame can be lonely; indeed, as only a woman who has lost the talisman of personal happiness, lost it far away and long ago, and tracks it endlessly through troubled dreams and cruel fantasies, can be sad.

She was not particularly attractive. Her features had "a certain heaviness"; the framework of her body was, by a slight but fatal margin, too broad and angular; and her legs were of the stovepipe variety, a detail that distressed her keenly—she always wore long skirts to hide her ankles. She had a finely shaped head, abundant tawny hair, fine eyes, and a good skin, and these items, as one biographer wrote during her lifetime, "complete the list of her natural assets."

But not quite, for she possessed two additional "assets" of great potency. One was her voice. It was a voice that the ordeal of thousands of sermons, preached on street corners, in outdoor pavilions, in camp meeting tents, and in large city auditoriums in the days before microphones, had strained and coarsened. It was the husky, vibrant "contralto of the midway," a voice of range and power, which she had learned to use with rare dramatic skill. Above all, I remember the deep huskiness of that voice, the occasional throaty richness, the suggestion of stifled laughter.

The other "asset" was an astonishing physical vitality, a little overpowering, to be sure, but charged with zest and bounce and brilliant tone. In a really beautiful woman, the vibrant voice, scaled not to the boudoir but the auditorium, and the insistent hyperthyroid vitality, would have been conspicuous incongruities. But she was just sufficiently attractive, in an angular, robust way, to carry off the voice and the high personal magnetism.

Here a paradox must be noted. She suggested sex without being sexually attractive. The suggestion was to be found, perhaps, in some quality of the voice; some radiation of that astonishing physical vitality. While constantly emanating sex, she lacked the graceful presence, the subtlety of manner, the mysterious reticence of a real siren. There was about her a trifle too much masculine vigor: the hips were too wide; the shoulders too broad; the neck too thick; the wrists and ankles too large. But wherever she moved or stirred, sex was present, at least in its public aspects, its gross implications; sex in headlines, sex emblazoned in marquee lights.

Perhaps it was this overly dramatic manifestation of sex that, in some curious manner, accounts for the fact that men apparently became disenchanted at close range. Being in love with her must have been rather like living in a one-room apartment with a radio going full blast night and day. Hence the sadness. For when she advanced on love with all the klieg lights blazing, Eros shrank away into the mist and darkness, and she was left alone, with all that hard brilliant lighting; with all those numberless watts of energy still cruelly ablaze.

2.

SHE WAS BORN Aimee Elizabeth Kennedy—most probably in an actual manger. The time, October 9, 1890; the place, a small farm near Ingersoll, Ontario, Canada. Her mother, Minnie Kennedy, later known to millions as "Ma" Kennedy, had once been a stalwart Salvation Army lass but had abandoned the trombones, the demure bonnets, and the vigorous marching, to marry a devout farmer many years her senior. Frustration was the penalty which a cheated life had demanded of the mother, frustration and an aggressive will-to-power. The mother-daughter relationship was always a tense one, with much bitterness and recrimination; many feuds and reconciliations; repeated estrangements followed by the constantly reasserted dominance of the mother. Always the mother considered it her special mandate, as she once said, "to keep Sister Aimee in the harness—to rein her in when she was inclined to scamper." Desperate as were her struggles, Aimee could never quite succeed in extricating herself from this pattern of earlier childhood domination.

The first major rebellion occurred in 1907, when Aimee, "a little country girl of seventeen with tawny hair braided into a bun at the back of her neck and bedecked with a crisp, vivid bow that reached from ear to ear," to use her own words, fell in love with Robert Semple, an itinerant Pentecostal minister. Ma, of course, protested vigorously: "Just wait, my lady," she said, "I will attend to you." But Aimee, young in years, was strong in purpose. Although reared in a devout household, it seems that "the churning sands of the quagmire of disbelief" eddied about her at this time. In the local library, she had discovered Darwin, Voltaire, Tom Paine, and Robert G. Ingersoll, and these men "had done their work well." She loved to dance and sing and had a highly prized collection of ragtime music, including such favorites as "Mandy Lee," "Under the Old Apple Tree," and "Rufus Rastus Johnson Brown."

But this early girlish frivolity vanished the instant that big, six-foot, heavily sweating, clarion-voiced Robert Semple appeared in the town of Ingersoll to summon the wayward to account. His words, as Aimee later wrote, "sank into my heart like a swift-flung arrow." Following Semple from meeting to meeting, she finally said to him: "Oh, Mr. Semple, what a blessed privilege it would be to bear the light into the darkest corners of heathendom." After reporting this remark to her autobiography, she quickly adds: "Now, I wasn't hinting. Nothing was farther from my mind. But suddenly one of my hands was imprisoned in his and I heard him softly saying: 'Aimee, dear, will you become my wife?' At this point, I closed my eyes and we knelt together. The room seemed suddenly filled with angels. As we prayed . . . my girlish heart suddenly began to pound against my ribs—like a caged, tropical bird beating its wings against the bars that kept it from the golden, mellow sunlight of a South Sea Island paradise. Love, triumphant, powerful and elemental, was surging and taking possession of me like a giant set free."

Ma Kennedy had suffered her first, perhaps her last, serious defeat: "the tropical bird" had momentarily escaped from its cage. Not the slightest premonition of disaster haunted Aimee on the eve of her wedding. In a dream of bliss eternal, the wedding presents (she later wrote) "became mixed with wedding cakes and pieces, a cut-glass-and-silver cruet chased salt and pepper holders around in endless circles. The horn-handled carving set chased the roast chickens around the festive board, wedding dress and veil floated up, up, up, on a mountain of presents to reach the orange wreath which rested on top, then with the slip of foot on a jelly-roll, a harmless dream fell, down, down, down into marshmallow whipped-cream cake with icing three feet deep."

After their marriage, the Semples did a stint of preaching in Chicago; visited Semple's parents in England; and then sailed for China as missionaries. Not long after their arrival in China, Semple was stricken with "the dread Eastern fever" and died in the English hospital on "the peak" at Hong Kong. One month after his death, Aimee gave birth to her first child, a girl. "I called her Roberta Star," she wrote, "because she was my star of hope." And hope she needed: a penniless nineteen-year-old widow, alone in Hong Kong, with a child to support. A gift of sixty dollars provided the burial and funeral expenses, and the China missions chipped in to buy her passage back to the States. Coming home on the *Empress of China*, she conducted religious services for the passengers, who in turn collected a purse to buy her ticket home. It was apparently at this point in her career that Aimee began to cultivate Elijah's ravens, forever on the wing, bringing her gifts and supplies, presents and purses, with that mysterious and timely efficiency that the Lord reserves for his favorites.

Joining her parents, who, in the China interval, had moved to New York, Aimee sought to recapture, as she put it, "the elusive bluebird of happiness." In an effort to find it, she returned for a time to the farm in Canada with her baby; came back to New York; left shortly for a period of free-lance missionary work in Chicago; and returned to New York "simply besieged with a restless loneliness." When a gentleman would escort her across a street intersection or when, in a restaurant, she would see "a man draw out a chair for his companion," in these and a thousand ways she was reminded that she "yearned for a nest of her own." Since such loneliness was obviously unendurable, she married again, this time Harold McPherson, a grocery clerk, by whom she had another child, Rolf McPherson. That this marriage was far from happy is indicated by the complete omission from her autobiography of any dreams about "marshmallow whipped-cream cakes" or South Sea Island paradises. Only this one cryptic reference: "It was at this time that I married again."

A year and a half after her marriage, experiencing "the clarion-call that brooks no denial," she set forth on the sawdust revival trail that was to terminate in fame and fortune at the rainbow's end in Southern California. In 1921 a divorce action was filed by McPherson; the charge, desertion. An embittered man, McPherson complained of Aimee's "dual personality." She had love for all the world under the big tent of the revival meetings, he said, but "wildcat habits" in the home. A witness at the divorce hearing testified that Aimee was "a great actress who could throw herself into a fit at any time." There was obviously nothing in this marriage for either party but frustration and bitterness. "I do not wish to come in contact with her in any way, shape, or form," McPherson said in 1926. "I would much rather give up the pleasure of seeing my own son than put up with even the slightest connection with my former wife."

The incident that started Aimee on her way to achieving the unique distinction of being "the world's most pulchritudinous evangelist" occurred in Canada, when she received a "call" to conduct a series of revival meetings in a neighboring town. Sensing the necessity of using novel tactics to attract crowds, she did not, as her biographer reports, "call to the public to come to her revival meetings." On the contrary, she "stood on a chair at the street corner, motionless, silent, rigidly erect, with closed eyes and lifted arms—praying." Soon a crowd gathered about this strange figure of a woman entranced, whispering, murmuring, speculating. Once the crowd had reached the right proportion, Aimee's eyes suddenly snapped open and she shouted: "Quick! Follow me!" and away she raced to the revival hall with the crowd in hot pursuit. When the last straggler was in the hall, the vibrant contralto voice commanded: "Shut the doors. Don't let anyone out!"

Following this successful venture in soul-saving, Aimee set forth on her own, lugging the children along, with Ma Kennedy in charge of collections. Their worldly possessions, at this time, consisted of the usual paraphernalia of traveling evangelists: a car and a tent. In addition to preaching, Aimee drove the car, looked after the children, and staked out the tent, becoming, as she later said, an expert on tents, familiar with every detail of center poles, ridge poles, push poles, block and tackle, guy ropes, wooden stakes, iron stakes, nails, and sledge hammers. "For the next two years, in summer and in winter, north or south, I worked by day and dreamed by night in the shadow of a tent." Thousands of miles they traveled, from Maine to Florida, up and down the Eastern seaboard. These were the years in which Aimee developed her special evangelical techniques, became a practiced and skillful showman, and acquired her deep understanding of "the folks." It was in these years that she formulated her Foursquare Gospel creed: the literal infallibility of the Bible; conversion; physical healings by religious means; and the personal return of Jesus Christ to this earth. Publishing a little magazine, *The Foursquare Monthly,* she began to acquire a small but loyal following. As the crowds became larger, and the take greater, the tent was supplanted by the lecture hall and the city auditorium.

After following this glory road for several years, Aimee decided to go to California, preaching through Kansas, Oklahoma, and Arizona to pay expenses. Messiahs, like the pioneers, have always moved westward in America. Long before Aimee started for Los Angeles, an evangelical circuit had been carefully worked out by her numerous rivals and predecessors: summer in the East, spring and fall in the Middle West, winter in Florida or Southern California. Thus in 1917, when she was twenty-six years old, with two children and a mother to support, she packed her belongings in a car and, herself at the wheel, set forth for the land of dreams, the land of the Sun-Down Sea, Southern California.

3.

IT WAS TWILIGHT when they arrived in Los Angeles—"a delight in the antechamber of Heaven, an eternity of beauty packed into the space of half an hour." Two days later they held a revival meeting; within a week they had rented the Philharmonic Auditorium, seating thirty-five hundred people. "Heart-hungry multitudes," she wrote, "came and filled it to overflowing." Between the date of this first visit to California in 1918 and her return in 1921, Aimee made four transcontinental and trans-Pacific tours, with the Foursquare Gospel ménage, holding revival meetings in Canada, New Zealand, and Australia. But all the while she was thinking and dreaming of the Zion that was Southern California and of the temple she would one day build in that land of milk and honey.

She returned in 1921, to hold a series of meetings in San Diego, home of the sick and aged, city of suicides, California's famous jumping-off place. Between 1911 and 1927, five hundred people committed suicide in San Diego. Seventy per cent of the suicides were put down to "despondency and depression over ill health." A haven for invalids, the rate of sickness in San Diego has ranged as high as twenty-four per cent of the population, as compared with a national average of six per cent. Whether by accident or design, Aimee had selected the pre-destined setting for her emergence as a "miracle woman."

Before discovering the untapped well of sickness and despondency in San Diego, she had first sought to attract attention to her meetings by novel publicity stunts—scattering evangelical tracts from an airplane and holding revival meetings in Jack Kearns's boxing arena. But it was a great outdoor meeting in the Organ Pavilion at Balboa Park in San Diego that really lifted Aimee out of the mill-run of small-time evangelists into the big money. Attended by thirty thousand people, this meeting was sponsored by the San Diego churches, with two rows of ministers seated on the platform with Sister.

It was at this meeting that her first sensational "miracles" were performed. When a middle-aged paralytic rose from her wheel chair and took a few stumbling steps, San Diego's legion of incurables, its sick and ailing, started for the platform. "On they came," wrote Aimee, "hobbling up the steps with their crutches," as a surge of hysteria gripped the vast audience. "Those healings," she later wrote, "were the one topic of conversation on the streets, in hotel lobbies, even in the theaters." Seemingly quite by accident, she had discovered that healing sessions "were immensely valuable as attractions."

It should be noted, however, that Sister never contended that she was a miracle woman or that she could actually heal the sick. "I am not a healer," she once said; "Jesus is the healer. I am only the little office girl who opens the door and says, 'Come in.' "

After this sensational meeting in San Diego, her fame spread quickly throughout the Pacific Coast, the West, and the Middle West, a fame which she immediately exploited by a series of overflowing revival meetings. At the end of this tour Aimee decided to return to Los Angeles and found a church—nay, a temple! Why travel senselessly about the country, she reasoned, when a co-operating providence had gathered in one city a rich sample of "the folks" who were everywhere eager to receive her message? That the Lord wanted her to build a temple in Los Angeles was at least circumstantially revealed by the manner in which thousands and tens of thousands of these same "folks" continued to migrate to the city every year. Here revival meetings could be conducted not on a seasonal but on a year-round basis. "An enormous village" rather than a city, Los Angeles yearned for an urban evangelism designed to appeal to former rural residents.

On January 1, 1923, Angelus Temple, by the rushes of Echo Park Lake, was officially opened in Los Angeles. While trumpeters blared, Aimee pulled the strings that unveiled an electrically illuminated, rotating cross atop the Temple that could be seen at night for a distance of fifty miles. An incredibly ugly structure, the Temple, and Sister's rococo residence, adjoining it, were supposed to have cost $1,500,000. The Temple itself eventually came to include an auditorium with a seating capacity of 5,000, a $75,000 broadcasting station, a great commissary, a theological seminary with hundreds of "students," a vast organ, a collection of costumes for Aimee and her choir which would do credit to a motion-picture studio, a "Cradle Roll Chapel" for babies, and a "Miracle Room" filled with hundreds of discarded crutches, wheel chairs, trusses, and artificial aids of all kinds. From the opening of the Temple to the present time, groups of Templites, in relay teams, have been praying continuously, day and night, in response to the ten thousand "requests for prayer" which are said to reach the Temple every month. At one time, the payroll of the Temple averaged $7,000 a week.

Here Aimee proceeded to entertain "the folks": with pageants, picture slides of the Holy Land, music, dramatized sermons, shows, circuses, and, of course, the healing sessions. Before her death, she had baptized forty thousand people in the Temple, established four hundred branch churches or "lighthouses," and located 178 missionary stations throughout the world. The basic elements of her formula were: a simple, easily remembered, four-point gospel; lively and unconventional preaching methods; an extraordinary flair for publicity; the familiar technique of self-dramatization in the role of a messiah; and an inexhaustible skill in improvising things for people to do. But the most important factor in her success was the way in which she "substituted the cheerfulness of the playroom for the gloom of the morgue." She completely abjured the hell-fire techniques of old-style evangelism. At one of her early meetings in Florida, an assistant had shouted to an indifferent bystander: "Brother, do you know that you are on the way to perdition?" Annoyed by this remark, Aimee later told him: "Even if it were true, that is not the way to win souls to Christ." She reveled in love and happiness. She invited the folks to feel at home, to relax, to have a good time. She released their minds from frightful visions of eternal damnation. Instead, she gave them "flowers, music, golden trumpets, red robes, angels, incense, nonsense, and sex appeal."

She had come, of course, to the right place to launch an evangel of joyousness. In the decade 1920-1930, 1,270,000 new residents swept into the County of Los Angeles, with the peak of this movement being reached in 1923, the year the Temple was founded. In most instances, newcomers could not find the church of their childhood; or, if they did, there was something about the impishly impious sunlight of the region that undermined their interest in "the old-style religion." Migration severs allegiances and weakens old loyalties. It creates the social fluidity out of which new cults grow and flourish. Nine out of ten of Aimee's followers were converts from the orthodox Protestant creeds, migrants from small-town and farming areas in the Middle West. Full of nostalgia for the corn belt but mightily intrigued by sunny California, aching with loneliness and the feeling of "wanting to know someone," they found their heart's desire in Angelus Temple, Sister Aimee, and the Shared Happiness of Kindred Souls.

With rare ingenuity, Aimee kept the Ferris wheels and merry-go-rounds of religion going night and day. Her showmanship was superb; her timing matchless; her dramatic instinct uncanny. When, at the close of her sermon, she asked the sinners to come forward and be saved, her voice was low, compassionate, and tender; the lights were dimmed; the music mournful and pleading. Then, as the slow, sad, solemn procession started down the aisles, she would suddenly shout, "Ushers, jump to it! Turn on the lights and clear the one-way street for Jesus!" As the lights blazed on and the organ boomed, the meeting would suddenly start to bounce and jump.

Once I saw her stage a memorable dramatization of the triumph of Good over Evil. On the stage was an illuminated scoreboard. As the lights dimmed in the auditorium, one could see the forces of Good advancing on the citadels of Evil, stalking up ravines, scaling mountains, jumping precipices. To the flash of godly gunfire and the blaze of holy artillery, the forces of General Evil began to retreat. Then a miniature blimp came floating over the scoreboard terrain. A soldier of Good fired a single shot, exploded the blimp, and an ugly grimacing Devil landed on the stage with a thud as the spotlight centered on an unfurled American flag.

On another occasion she staged a fourteen-hour Holy Ghost rally of continuous preaching, with a team of preachers spelling each other. When one minister collapsed with fatigue, Aimee leaped up to take his place. "What makes people jump out of their seats?" she demanded. "If there's a fire under you, you just can't stand still. Did you ever try sitting on a hot stove?" In a second, the crowd was shouting and clapping, dancing and stomping, collapsing in the aisles.

Not only had Aimee picked the right place in which to found a new cult, but she had opened the Temple at precisely the right time. In the early 1920's, Los Angeles, like the rest of the country, was beginning to experience a major boom. The postwar period, so full of restlessness, with its craze for entertainment and passion for frivolity, had already given birth to the Jazz Age. The flapper had arrived, a little tipsy, with short skirts and bobbed hair. It was a time for petting and necking; for flasks and roadside taverns; for movie "palaces" and automobiles. Los Angeles itself was just emerging from a long period of glacial fundamentalism, its ice age of Protestant orthodoxy. In near-by Hollywood, the movie colony was in its "purple period," full of scandal and commotion. All America was stepping out on an emotional binge, and Aimee was determined to lead the parade on a grand detour to Heaven.

Allowing for the fortunate location and the excellent timing, her phenomenal success still represents a great personal triumph. In the space of a few years, from 1921 to 1926, this obscure grass widow skyrocketed to fame and fortune. When she first arrived in Los Angeles her worldly possessions, according to her own statement, consisted of one hundred dollars in cash and a broken-down automobile. By 1926 she owned a temple and residence worth more than a million dollars and was collecting money as few ministers have ever been able to collect it. In Los Angeles she was more than just a household word: she was a folk hero and a civic institution; an honorary member of the fire and police departments; a patron saint of the service clubs; an official spokesman for the community on problems grave and frivolous. Without quite realizing what she had done, Aimee had breathed new life and meaning into an ancient and powerful myth. The myth was that of the miracle-worker, the faith-healer, the one who comes to lift the ancient bondage. That the messiah in this new revelation was an attractive woman only gave the myth a new piquancy and a certain fitness for the times.

But in the midst of all this ever-mounting ease, security, and prestige, Aimee began to feel a return of the old sadness. "It isn't all a bed of roses," she said, "this thing of being in a high place as a leader. Sometimes I wish I didn't have to carry on the Lord's work in such a conspicuous capacity." Long years of one-night stands had bred in her something of the chronic restlessness of the circus performer, but now she was caught up by fortune, caged by fame. In the midst of multitudes, her loneliness was more acute than ever. She was the dynamo that kept the Temple lights burning, and there was no way by which she could escape from her work or elude the spotlight that focused on her every move and action.

While her physical stamina was great, the endless round of her public activities was not only tiresome but had begun to be boring. In 1926 she was thirty-six years old; Robert Semple was a memory; and she had been divorced from McPherson for five long years. The great drama was about to unfold. Throughout her life she had fought off "the blues," as she said, by whistling or singing the hymn with the refrain that goes "sunlight, sunlight in my soul today." Now a new sunlight, the sunlight of a new love, was to flood her soul.

4.

IT WAS in 1925 that Sister Aimee first heard the voice from the radio control room in the tower of the Temple, a cultivated, soothing, sympathetic voice that said: "You sound as though you were tired tonight, Mrs. McPherson," or "You have done splendidly tonight." The voice was that of Kenneth G. Ormiston, the Temple's radio operator. Not a member of the Foursquare cult, Ormiston was a man of some sophistication and intelligence. Unfortunately, he was married. But marriage for Sister was out of the question anyway since she was publicly and irrevocably committed to the doctrine that divorced persons should not remarry as long as the other spouse lived. After some weeks of chatting intermittently over the radio phones, wth growing interest and intimacy, they met one night on the steps of the Temple, and Mrs. McPherson drove him to his home.

In a matter of weeks the Temple buzzed with gossip that Sister was engaging in indiscreet conversations on the radio with the man in the tower and spending an inordinate amount of time in his office. What the Temple minions did not know, but probably suspected, was that night after night a car drove up to the Temple residence, blinked its light to a waiting figure on the balcony, paused for a moment, and drove on. A year later they were to hear Agnes Callahan, a maid at the Ambassador Hotel, testify that, in the latter part of 1925, Sister McPherson had occupied a room at the Ambassador on six occasions and that "every day Mrs. McPherson came in" Ormiston was seen entering her room. They were also to hear a house detective of the Ambassador testify that he, too, had seen the radio operator entering Mrs. McPherson's room at the Ambassador during Christmas week in 1925. Not that this testimony shook their belief in the purity of Sister's intentions, which, in their eyes, remained angelic.

In January of 1926, largely at Ma Kennedy's insistence, Aimee left for Europe and a tour of the Holy Land, the trip being financed, of course, by a special "love offering" of the faithful. Although Mrs. Kennedy insisted that she, too, needed a vacation, she was not invited to accompany her daughter. In London, Sister had a large meeting in Albert Memorial Hall on Easter Sunday (she was the first woman ever to hold religious services in Albert Memorial Hall) and became a great favorite of the London press. It was at this period that Aimee began to respond to the compulsions and vogues of the Jazz Age. Her dowdy evangelical dress of yesteryear was suddenly replaced by new and scandalous splendor. She appeared in London with "a coiffeur that might have been done in Bond Street, pale yellow silk jumper, black silk gown, short skirts, and flesh-colored silk stockings"—the raiment of a bride. Startling reports began to drift back to California of visits to night clubs and regal shopping expeditions in Paris. Whether Ormiston met Aimee in Europe and accompanied her to the Holy Land is uncertain, but it is known that he was absent from California for a period that would have made it possible for him to have gotten at least a glimpse of fair Jerusalem and its ancient walls.

Shortly after her return to Los Angeles in May, 1926, Sister began to lay the foundation, psychological and metaphysical, for her subsequent disappearance. Affecting an air of sadness and foreboding, she would occasionally preface her sermons with such remarks as "When I am gone," "If I should die soon," and "I may not be with you always." On May 6 she cabled a minister in England asking him to substitute for her at Angelus Temple. On three subsequent days, Ormiston was registered at the Virginia Hotel in Long Beach, where a car registered in the name of Aimee Semple McPherson was parked in the garage for three hours. The garage attendant later testified that he had seen a woman, carrying a briefcase stamped with Mrs. McPherson's name, leave the car and enter the hotel. On May 9 Ormiston registered at the Alexandria Hotel, in Los Angeles, under the name of "Frank Gibson," and there Mrs. McPherson was also registered on the ninth and tenth. Using the name "George McIntyre," Ormiston appeared in Carmel on May 14, paid three months' rent on a cottage, and told the landlord that he was leaving for San Diego but would return in a day or so with his invalid wife. The stage was now set, the curtain about to ascend.

5.

IT IS DIFFICULT now to recapture the emotional climate and the pattern of events of the month of May in the year 1926, a period that seems utterly lost in the mists of time. A few items from the Los Angeles newspapers on the morning of May 18, 1926, collected by Sister Aimee's faithful chronicler, Miss Mavity, may serve to bring back a slight nostalgic remembrance: "DRY BATTLE FLARES UP IN SENATE. Roald Amundsen announces from Nome, Alaska, that he will abandon polar expeditions, following successful flight across the pole in the dirigible *Norge*. Two men sail from New York in an attempt to break the world's record for speedy encirclement of the globe by boat and plane. AMERICAN EMBASSY BOMBED IN BUENOS AIRES. President Coolidge returns to Washington after a cruise in the

Mayflower." It was a period of stunts, escapades, and broken records. The "long week end" was far advanced. The sun of the Coolidge prosperity was ablaze on the land, and rum-runners with flashlights and machine guns were busy off the Malibu coast.

In the early afternoon of this day Aimee drove not to Carmel but to the beach at Venice near Los Angeles, accompanied by her faithful secretary, Emma Schaeffer. A strong and sturdy swimmer, Aimee donned a green bathing suit in a room at the Ocean View Hotel and sauntered out to a beach tent near the shore. For a time she sat in the tent, working on notes for a sermon to be delivered the following Sunday on the perennial subject of "Lightness and Darkness." After working for a while on the sermon, Sister dispatched Miss Schaeffer on an inconsequential errand. But when Miss Schaeffer returned she found the tent deserted. By late afternoon the extras were out: Sister McPherson had disappeared! Thousands of people gathered about the Temple to hear Mother Kennedy sorrowfully proclaim: "She is with Jesus— pray for her!" while additional thousands milled around the Ocean View Hotel in Venice and scanned the ocean for signs and portents.

During the succeeding thirty-two days armies of the faithful kept a night and day vigil at the Temple and at the beach, where they built bonfires, wept, prayed, moaned, and sang hymns. Patrols were sent up and down the beach; airplanes swept low over the waters; and deep-sea divers prowled the ocean floor, looking for the body of a marathon swimmer in a green bathing suit. A girl committed suicide. One of the deep-sea prowlers died of exposure. On May 20 an ecstatic follower, glimpsing an image of Aimee on the bright, shimmering waters of the Pacific, was forcefully restrained from plunging into the waves. On May 23 one Robert Browning, twenty-six, leaped into the sea crying, "I'm going after her," and was drowned. Mother Kennedy chartered an airplane to scatter flowers on the watery grave. A reward of $25,000 was offered and, at a great meeting in the Temple, a collection estimated at $36,000 was taken for a memorial to Aimee. (Mrs. Kennedy later admitted under oath the receipt of $4,690 in cash and a much larger sum in pledges; no part of this collection was ever returned.)

On May 27 the name of Ormiston was, for the first time, mentioned in the front-page stories devoted to Sister's disappearance. The city gasped when it learned that Ormiston had left his position at the Temple two weeks after Aimee had departed for the Holy Land and the Paris millinery shops; that he had been in New York in February, 1926; and that he had not returned to the West Coast until March. It gasped again, and began to whisper, when it learned that Ormiston's wife had reported him as "missing" to the Sheriff's office after he had left the Temple. And it scented real scandal when it learned that Ormiston had stayed at a hotel in Venice late in March and again in April. The day after his name was first mentioned in the news, Ormiston nonchalantly reappeared in Los Angeles, visited the "search" headquarters which Mother Kennedy had established at the beach, and answered a few meaningless questions put to him by a detective. When taken to police headquarters for further questioning, however, he excused himself on the usual pretext and promptly vanished.

It is quite apparent that up to this point Aimee thoroughly intended to disappear, not momentarily but permanently. Permanent disappearance was, in truth, the only solution to an otherwise insoluble dilemma. To have continued her intrigue with Ormiston would have been to run the risk of certain exposure. Marriage, even if peace might have been made with the suspicious Mrs. Ormiston, was unthinkable so long as Harold McPherson survived. To have abandoned the ministry for romance would have been to shatter the illusions of her thousands of trusting followers. Merely to have run away would have solved nothing. One of the most famous women of her day, she would certainly have been identified sooner or later, wherever she went.

It was only natural, therefore, that she should have thought of the parable of Christ walking on the waves. To disappear at the beach, to leave the illusion of having vanished into the cool blue waters of the Pacific, seemed a practical solution and it undoubtedly appealed to her sense of Biblical history. But once her name was publicly linked with that of Ormiston, the illusory nature of this childish, love-blind fancy was quickly demonstrated. Now, to preserve the myth in which thirty thousand people believed, a reappearance became as essential as the original disappearance.

6.

AT HALF-PAST one o'clock on the morning of June 23, Sister Aimee stumbled out of the dark to knock at the door of a cottage in Agua Prieta, across the U. S.-Mexican border from Douglas, Arizona. The days and nights between the first mention of Ormiston's name in the newspapers and her dramatic reappearance at Agua Prieta must have been filled with an almost unsustainable tension and excitement, of excursions and alarums, quick entrances and exits, numberless sharp turns and desperate improvisations. For after May 27 the press of the entire State of California and its law-enforcement officials were watching every highway, searching every train, pursuing every lead. And at times they were hot on the trail.

On the morning of May 29, Ormiston, accompanied by a woman, called for his car, which had been stored in Salinas, a town near Carmel. Later that day the same couple registered as "Mr. and Mrs. Frank Gibson" at the Andrews Hotel in San Luis Obispo, farther down the coast. The original plan seems to have called for Aimee's reappearance nearer Los Angeles, with a lurid tale of kidnaping and detention in Topanga Canyon. But, en route at night from San Luis Obispo south, the car driven by Ormiston, accompanied by the lady, was stopped on the highway near Santa Barbara by a newspaper reporter. Although the reporter was suspicious, he had no warrant to detain the couple. Realizing the danger, Ormiston had promptly doubled back toward San Francisco. Just how "Mr. and Mrs. Gibson" ever managed to elude their pursuers and get from San Francisco to Agua Prieta, Mexico, must remain one of the most celebrated California mysteries. Circumstantial evidence reveals a trail that probably led from San Francisco to Nevada, from Nevada to a ranch in Arizona, and from there across the border— no mean feat in itself. In any case, two men and a woman, acting most furtively, were seen ducking into the Foreign Club at Agua Prieta on June 20.

Sister Aimee's reappearance in Douglas, with her fanciful account of the kidnapers "Rose" and "Steve" and "Jake," was one of the most sensational news stories of the 1920's. It hit the front page in almost every newspaper in the world. Over a hundred thousand words of copy were filed by reporters from Douglas in a single day. Submitting to a mass interview in her hospital room in Douglas, she said: "Why should I disappear? To rest? I was not tired. Amnesia? I never suffered that. Publicity? That is absurd. Love—" and here Sister Aimee broke into gales of laughter.

Returning to Los Angeles in a private car, she was accorded a thunderous, a historic welcome. Not even the visits of Woodrow Wilson, William Howard Taft, and the King of Belgium had occasioned such a reception. Thirty thousand people thronged the station when she arrived. Seated in a wicker chair decked with flowers, she was carried from the train through the lane of flowers to a rose-draped automobile. A white-robed Temple band led the procession through streets on which a hundred thousand Angelenos had gathered "to welcome Aimee home." As she stepped on the platform at Angelus Temple, the thousands assembled there were chanting:

> *"Coming back, back, back,*
> *Coming back, back, back,*
> *Our sister in the Lord is coming back.*
> *There is shouting all around*
> *For our sister has been found;*
> *There is nothing now of joy or peace we lack."*

That Aimee's disappearance and return should have been one of the great news stories of the decade is not surprising. It contained, as has been said, all the right ingredients: sex, mystery, underworld characters, spooks, kidnapers, the ocean, hot desert sands, an escape, and a thrilling finale. It was a story made for the period, a period that invested the trivial with a special halo, that magnified the insipid, that pursued cheap sensationalism with avidity and passion. While admittedly quite a story, the "kidnaping" of Sister Aimee became invested with the proportions of a myth and the dimensions of a saga in the great vacuum of the age. It was a kind of compendium of all the pervading nonsense, cynicism, credulity, speakeasy wit, passion for debunkery, sex-craziness, and music-hall pornography of the times. Ribald Aimee stories circulated with a velocity rivaled only by those of a later period about Mae West—whom, in a sense, Aimee preceded. Burlesque comics parodied

Sister's antics and mannerisms. The owner of a hamburger joint in Los Angeles named his place "Aimee's Shack," in honor of the building in which she was supposed to have been held captive in Mexico.

In this slapstick version of the Great Myth, the sequence was re-versed: the Resurrection preceded the Crucifixion. Indeed, the cruci-fixion might never have occurred had not Aimee fatefully taken the initiative and sought complete civic vindication. There was a moment, after her return, when the community was willing to let bygones be bygones. As the Los Angeles *Record* editorialized: "Let's forget it. At the worst, Mrs. McPherson is accused by rumor of a moral lapse, and of lying about it afterwards like a gentleman." But she could not, she would not, let well enough alone. Goaded by the cynical stories that continued to circulate about her disappearance and fortified by an inordi-nate faith in her ability to make the kidnaping story stick, she pressed for official vindication. Over the radio and in statements to the press, she kept badgering the authorities to quit stalling and produce the "kidnapers." An investigation might easily have been avoided had she elected, on her return, to remain loftily indifferent, nobly silent. But once begun, the investigation became her spiritual scaffold. When the grand jury reported on July 20 that evidence was lacking upon which anyone could be indicted, the folly of her boldness was exposed, and the crucifixion swiftly ensued.

Two days after the grand jury filed its report, the newspapers began to tell of the "love nest" in Carmel. Four credible witnesses positively identified Sister Aimee as the "Mrs. McIntyre" who had occupied the cottage with Ormiston in May. Books left in the cottage when the "McIntyres" made their hasty exit contained passages quoted in some of Aimee's sermons, and a grocery slip was discovered with a signature identified as being in her handwriting. At this point, Ormiston, still playing hide-and-seek with the police, responded to a public appeal from Aimee by forwarding an affidavit in which he admitted having rented the cottage in Carmel, but stated that Mrs. McPherson was "entirely innocent" and referred to the lady of the cottage as "Miss X." When this document was published, a highly neurotic character sud-denly appeared on the scene and contended that her sister had been the mysterious Miss X.

Grasping blindly at these seeming corroborations of her story, Aimee once again insisted upon vindication. But, alas! the strange character turned out to be a lady wanted by the police on numerous bad-check charges and her story was exposed as a crazy hoax. The District Attorney was now compelled, by pressure of opinion, to place the whole matter once again before the grand jury. During this second investigation one of the jurors, a woman, took the highly important grocery-slip exhibit with her to the toilet and proceeded to flush it down the drain. When the other members refused to take action against this erring sister, the grand jury was summarily dismissed. But the public, its passion for scandal inflamed, its appetite for sensational detail whetted by months of furious speculation, now clamored for action. The pitch of excitement being what it was, there could be no turning back, no charitable drawing of the veil. To appease the lust for revelation, a criminal complaint was filed on September 17 charging Aimee, and others, with a conspiracy to obstruct justice. The preliminary hearing on this complaint, which consumed two months, was a feast of scandal for the public and the press. Special seats had to be built to accommodate the tongue-wagging hordes that lined the corridors, bringing their breakfasts and lunches in paper bags. Scalpers' prices of twenty-five dollars were offered reporters for the use of their passes for a single day.

That this preliminary hearing was, in effect, a protracted lynching hardly admits of doubt. For Mrs. McPherson had not committed a crime, however reprehensible her conduct may have been. But Sister had a host of enemies in Los Angeles in 1926. The fundamentalist Protestant clergy of the town were particularly indignant and bitterly envious. Six of these chivalrous gentlemen of the cloth signed a public statement, after her reappearance, demanding that she publicly answer a long list of intimate questions (the theory then current in Los Angeles was that she had disappeared for the purpose of having an abortion, a theory later conclusively refuted). Among her most implacable enemies was the Reverend Robert P. Shuler, born in a log cabin in the Blue Ridge Mountains, a graduate of Elm Creek Academy, and a primordial theologian of the hell-fire and brimstone variety. Shuler like Aimee had a radio station, and the two had long been bitter rivals.

Then, too, the business community had come to the conclusion that

Aimee's antics were "embarrassing the town." With thirty thousand devoted followers, she had of course been courted by the politicians; but, in the process of bestowing favors, she had inevitably annoyed some elements while pleasing others. The "regular" church people of the community were solidly ranged against her. Not only was the press hostile, but, in an effort to keep up the hectic sale of extras, it constantly incited her to new flights of fancy, maliciously pointed out contradictions in her story, and endlessly baited her. From the murky depths of the underworld, all sorts of curious characters emerged, some seeking to blackmail Sister, others trying to cut in on the $250,000 "Fight-the-Devil" fund that had been raised for her defense. A legion of neurotics, of the type that only Los Angeles produces in such quantity and variety, was drawn into the glare of publicity surrounding the case; while packs of salacious hounds bayed about poor Aimee, eager for the kill. If only Sister could be forced to confess her sins, to make public the intimacies of her love life, to provide a panting, sex-crazed public with the little spicy details of time and place and circumstance!

To understand the curious behavior of the law-enforcement officials toward the case—their on-again, off-again attitude—it should be recalled that Asa Keyes, the District Attorney, was shortly afterward sentenced to San Quentin Prison for corrupt conduct in office. Already trembling with apprehension, he naturally feared that Sister, with thirty thousand followers and a radio station, might, in her desperation, ignite the fuse that would blow him from office. And Sister was in a dangerous mood, fighting for her freedom, fighting valiantly to preserve the faith which she had aroused in the hearts and minds of thousands of good people. While she made mistakes, in this relentless and unevenly matched fight, her courage was indomitable, her spirit superb, and her cunning amusing and marvelous.

The nature of the fight compelled her to dramatize the trial as a crucifixion, and, in doing so, she tapped unsuspected wells of credulity and belief. For the role of devils, she conjured forth first one group and then another. Since two of the officials assigned to her case happened to be Catholics, she terrified the District Attorney by charging him with having purposefully ignited the fires of religious warfare. Then she charged that the Reverend Shuler, and his weird cohorts, were after her scalp for their own selfish purposes. To vary the theme, she would occasionally point to the existence of corruption in Los Angeles officialdom and suggest that the "vice lords" were behind her persecution. On the night of July 26 she staged a wonderful Devil's Convention at Angelus Temple, in which dozens of hideous devils, armed with pitchforks, emerged from the vapors, fumes, and fires of hell to grimace and dance on the stage. As they emerged from the dungeons of iniquity, she introduced them to the audience as the ministers of Los Angeles, members of the grand jury, law-enforcement officials, vice lords, and the "kidnapers," "Jake," "Rose," and "Steve." On the day she was first summoned before the grand jury, she advanced to the hearing room "along a hundred-foot pathway formed by a double line of her Temple staff, garbed in uniforms of white with gray-lined blue capes, holding Bibles and singing." Dressed in a stunning white-and-blue evangelical costume, Sister turned, at the door to the hearing room, Bible clasped to her breast, and said: "I am like a lamb led to the slaughter."

During the course of her trial, she adroitly diverted attention from the case, from time to time, by casual remarks, such as that she had overheard her kidnapers plotting the kidnaping of Mary Pickford. The more the evidence mounted against her, the more stoutly she maintained her innocence. After all, she said, if Daniel, St. Stephen, Shadrach, Meshach, and Abednego were kidnaped, why not Aimee? Continuing to rely on what one writer called "vehement assertion as a substitute for explanation," she was successful in what was, perhaps, her primary aim: to maintain the faith of her Temple following at all costs. The more the case went against her, the louder they prayed and the more generous were their contributions.

And, toward the finale, the prosecution had begun to make a damning case. A parade of witnesses identified her as the Mrs. McIntyre of the Carmel "love nest"; chambermaids and house detectives placed Ormiston in her hotel rooms at specific dates and times; and the telltale hotel registers were received in evidence. The fake lady who had come forward to corroborate Ormiston's affidavit confessed that Sister had given her money and "gone over" her story with her. On October 28 the Los Angeles *Examiner,* hot on the trail of the elusive Ormiston, discovered and published some extravagantly silly love letters that Aimee had written "Ralph Stringer," one of the numerous aliases used by Ormiston. And then, on December 17, Ormiston himself was finally run down in Harrisburg, Pennsylvania. It now seemed as though the long and eagerly awaited confessions would soon be made. But on January 4, 1927, District Attorney Keyes suddenly moved to dismiss the case of the People v. Aimee Semple McPherson. That he was later convicted of corruption in office may throw some light on his action (the rumor still persists in Los Angeles that a thirty-thousand-dollar payoff was involved). In any case, Aimee was "vindicated," rescued by the Lord at the zero hour. With a jubilant "Hallelujah!" she turned at once to the writing of her autobiography, *In the Service of the King,* in which she recounted once more the story of her "kidnaping" and her triumph over the forces of Evil. The ghost writer who assisted her in this enterprise was a Los Angeles reporter who had turned up most of the damning evidence against her.

7.

AS SOON as the case against her was dismissed, Sister departed on a national "rehabilitation tour." Visiting twenty-two cities, she gave a lecture (not a sermon) on "The Story of My Life," with paid admissions only. Much to her surprise, the tour seriously misfired. Somehow Sister McPherson was now just "Aimee"; the onetime miracle worker had been replaced by a woman of some notoriety. In cities where she had scored some of her greatest evangelical triumphs, she was greeted with relative indifference. Radio stations summarily revoked invitations to speak; the public balked at the idea of paid admissions; and, in some places, she spoke to half-empty halls. Nor did she fare better on her return to Los Angeles. For she promptly became involved in the first of a series of bitter public quarrels with Ma Kennedy and had to contend with numerous schisms in the ranks of her followers. Several "lighthouses" sought to secede from the Foursquare organization, and a handful of dissidents in Los Angeles questioned such expenditures as $40.50 "for beauty treatments" in Detroit. From this time on a telltale repetitive pattern can be discerned in her life, a pattern that must have reflected a mounting sense of insecurity, exhaustion, and despair. The new sequence of events had a rhythm of its own: flight, new beginnings, fiascoes, quarrels, new efforts, defeat—regularly interspersed with periods of "breakdown" and "nervous exhaustion." After the depression of 1929 the pattern became more pronounced and the tempo quickened as anxieties spiraled upward in ever-darkening clouds.

The source of her new difficulties was partly social in origin. The long week end was running out. With the repeal of prohibition, "the aspirin age" came to an end. The stock market crash demolished the crazy structure of Coolidge prosperity and the expatriates began to scurry homeward. New messiahs made their appearance in Southern California: Upton Sinclair, who promised to end poverty; Dr. Francis Townsend, the Long Beach ex-physician and realtor, who promised pensions for the aged; the Utopians who staged great pageants enacting, not the triumph of Good over Evil, but of Abundance over Scarcity; and the brothers Willis and Lawrence Allen, who switched over from the promotion of Grey-Gone, a hair tonic, to Ham N' Eggs or $30-Every-Thursday. In these new and troubled times, Aimee could survive; she could still hold the remnant of her following, now reduced to eight or ten thousand; but she could not break into the larger competitive field of public interest. She was somehow dated, old-hat, a bit of a bore.

In 1928 she went on another European tour, but no more in Europe than in America could she rekindle the old sparks of interest. While the London newspapers noticed her arrival, and still gave her space, it was space with a difference. She was no longer a world-famous evangelist but just another whacky American. Once again she was induced, without too much persuading, to visit the night spots in Piccadilly, Soho, and Limehouse; but somehow the expedition just didn't come off. When she spoke in Glasgow, malicious students adorned the platform with empty bottles and beer glasses and decorated the walls with flamboyant whiskey posters. Taking a new tack, she proceeded to launch, on the eve of the stock market crash, a series of fantastic business ventures: the Blessed Home Memorial Park, with the prices of the cemetery lots graduated in relation to their nearness to the lot which she had reserved for herself; a summer camp at Lake Tahoe ballyhooed under the slogan "Vacation with Aimee"; and a skyscraper apartment-hotel near Angelus Temple in which the faithful were to be housed until the time came to cart their remains to the Blessed Home Memorial Park. For some months she was busy with plans for a motion picture, based on her life, to be called *Clay in the Potter's Hand,* a project that, unhappily, was never consummated. In fact, all these projects were stillborn. Then she decided to promote a crusade to the Holy Land in a specially chartered liner; but only a hundred followers assembled in New York for the voyage. Interviewing Aimee on the bridge of the ship, reporters noted, for the first time, that her once beautiful chestnut-colored hair was now "bright gold" and bobbed.

On returning from this junket, there was another bitter quarrel with her mother in which Ma contended that she had been knocked down and her nose injured. To even scores, Mrs. Kennedy tipped off the reporters that Sister had had her face lifted prior to leaving for the Holy Land. A detail in itself, this face-lifting scandal momentarily threatened to do what the newspaper notoriety, the disappearance, and the trial had never done—to alienate her following. During this quarrel, the egregious Ma called in the newspaper reporters, gave a few choice details about the "kidnaping episode," and guardedly hinted that she would eventually tell all. For weeks Aimee was reported ill, suffering from nervous exhaustion, confined to a beach cottage at Malibu. Recovering from this illness, she left for the Orient and was gone nearly a year. Once again she was accorded an official "welcome home": twenty-five thousand Angelenos assembled to greet her; the usual dignitaries were on hand; and the familiar profusion of roses, red and white, showered down upon her. Now forty years of age, it seemed as though she were on the verge of a real comeback, after numerous false starts and deflated ambitions. At this turning point in her career, Aimee again fell in love.

When she first met Dave Hutton, as she later said, "my heart wanted companionship. I wanted a man—a husband. Every normal woman wants a mate." Roberta, the daughter, had married in 1930; Rolf, the son, in 1931. "At the end of each day," wrote Aimee, "after each wonderful service, our dear people, and my children, would go to their homes arm in arm, with tender words and little caresses; while I would sit in silence watching the last light extinguished in the big auditorium, and the last smiling, happy couple disappear in the darkness." Hutton, like Ormiston, was a radio man: a huge, roly-poly fellow with the features of a big fat boy. "When he first came to the Temple," Aimee later confessed, "I thought he was the answer to my prayer. I thought, poor little fool, that the roads to destiny again brought romance and religion together to walk with me in sunshine and joy."

While Hutton doubtless appeared to be the answer to her prayers, still he did not meet the specifications for the "ideal mate" which she had given the press a year or so previously. Then she had said: "He must be good-looking. He must be six feet tall or more. He must be a preacher. And he must play the trombone." But when she fell in love with Hutton, "it was not the girlish, elemental emotion of youth but rather the reawakening of a mature, tired heart." The reawakening was so powerful that she ignored her own rule that divorced persons should not remarry. After their wedding, the Huttons left for a honeymoon at Aimee's sumptuous Moorishesque castle at Lake Elsinore, a fourteen-room monstrosity decorated in gold and silver leaf. But, alas! two days after the marriage, Hutton was sued by another woman for two hundred thousand dollars' "heart balm."

On the day this case was tried, Aimee wrote, "I did not know what had happened until David arrived in the Temple limousine. 'Five thousand dollars,' he shouted at me with a wave of his hand." So shocking was the news of the verdict that she fainted dead away, and, in falling, fractured her skull on the flagstones in the courtyard. In Europe, where she went to escape the derisive howls of the Los Angeles press, she received a wire from Dave: "Take your time, honey. Don't hurry home until you are well. I miss you and nearly die of loneliness, but you come first and Daddy wants a well woman." But Daddy was to be disappointed, for the separation was permanent. A year or so later, Hutton was granted a decree of divorce.

That Aimee's career was now hopelessly disorganized is best indicated by the interminable lawsuits in which she became involved. In the twenty years prior to her death, she was sued in the courts of Los Angeles fifty-five times, with most of these suits being filed after her separation from Hutton. Included in the actions were suits for unpaid bills, broken contracts, overdue promissory notes, false arrest, malicious prosecution, asserted responsibility for the death of an aged woman, slander, and other charges. Several lawsuits were filed by relatives of Temple followers who sought to set aside various gifts and bequests. Thus Edward McNead claimed that a relative of his, under the impression that Aimee had worked a miracle, died leaving most of her property to Sister. McNead won a judgment reclaiming title to the properties in question. The same year the courts set aside a handsome bequest made to Aimee by Catherine McAdams, who, according to the court's decision, "made her will under the morbid delusion that she was required to give all or nearly all her property to the Temple," in order to be cured of cancer.

For years Aimee had been "great copy" for the Los Angeles press, but even the newspapers began to weary of her endlss lawsuits, family quarrels, and publicity stunts. Two editorials in the Los Angeles *Times* indicate the changed attitude of the community during the 1930's. In the first of these, the *Times,* not often given to Biblical allusions, proceeded to quote Scripture:

"A forward man soweth strife; and a whisperer separateth chief friends (Prov. XVI, 28);

"Death and life are in the power of the tongue; and they that love it shall eat the fruit thereof (Prov. XVIII, 21);

"Whoso keepeth his mouth and his tongue, keepeth his soul from troubles (Prov. XXI, 23);

"As a jewel of gold in a swine's snout, so is a fair woman which is without discretion (Prov. XI, 22);

"Where no wood is, the fire goeth out; so where there is no talebearer, the strife ceaseth (Prov. XXVI, 20)."

If there is any application of these reputed sayings of the wise King Solomon to the affairs of Angelus Temple, where the third (or is it the thirty-third?) slander suit that has been filed in recent months by and against Temple principals has just been announced, let it be made by those in charge of its affairs. It does seem as though the business of saving souls and setting good examples to the nonreligious could be conducted without quite so much back-biting and mud-slinging.

When this warning went unheeded, the *Times* again moralized, this time more pointedly:

It may be news. It has at least passed for such for a long time. Yet it grows repetitious. Each time now there is the quality about it of something that has happened over and over again. "She was clad modishly in a boyish outfit." "This time she wore orchids instead of gardenias." The first time it was a sensation. The second it was still good. But now it is like the ninth life of a cat; it is about worn out. . . . Many families have quarrels. Few of them with tne intense ardor of three generations succeed in becoming what might be listed as court perennials; regular customers. Family fights are not pleasant things. Sometimes they amuse the public. But even a bullfight audience grows callous and uninterested by late afternoon if the same tricks are done over and over again. . . . A news moratorium on the McPhersons *et al.* is the crying need of the day.

There seemed to be general concurrence in this verdict, for, after 1937, a partial news blackout engulfed the Temple and its denizens.

Not that Aimee's last years were lived in gloomy obscurity. On occasion she continued to dazzle the community, as when she appeared at a woman's club luncheon "gowned in black with flowing chartreuse chiffon frills at the elbows, chartreuse corsage at her throat, white fur, and a small black hat set jauntily on her head." She seemed to have discovered, with almost childish delight, some of the lighter pleasures and sillier vanities of life after she was a grandmother. Calling at the parsonage for an interview in 1936, a reporter found her dressed "in the latest sports attire, with golf clubs and tennis racquets filling the room and the phonograph playing 'Blue Skies,' the latest snappy fox-trot." Something of the old hellishness, too, was occasionally apparent, as when she celebrated her forty-eighth birthday in 1938. On this memorable occasion she appeared on the platform of Angelus Temple dressed in a red gingham frock and a sunbonnet such as she had worn on the farm in Canada. Carrying a brimming milk pail, with a collar of real foam, to the stage, she poured milk cocktails for a group of self-conscious officials and then used the empty pail to take up the collection. Leaving the stage momentarily, she reappeared in stunning white satin to preach a sermon on "My Dear Diary." During the course of this sermon, she asked the audience how many had ever lived on a farm. The entire audience stood up.

One of the last official "welcome homes" occurred in 1939, when she was greeted by bands, pom-poms, and thousands of followers who, under the direction of a cheer-leader, shouted: "S-I-S-T-E-R! Rah! Rah! S-I-S-T-E-R!" Stepping from a train and carrying a bouquet of six dozen American Beauty roses in one hand and a bird in a gilded cage in the other, she was modestly attired in a form-fitting white silk suit, fuchsia Chinese coolie hat, fuchsia veil of heavy net, fuchsia gloves and scarf, and she wore a single large gardenia.

8.

ON THE EVENING of September 26, 1944, Sister Aimee left the Hotel Leamington in Oakland, California, in a horse-drawn buggy to speak to an audience of ten thousand people in the municipal auditorium, the first meeting of a projected "magic carpet crusade." According to her son Rolf, she was later very "keyed up" and excited, perhaps because of the warm reception she had received. The topic of her sermon that night was "The Story of My Life," a favorite subject, one that she had used hundreds of times in the years from 1923 to 1944. The following morning, Sister was found unconscious in her hotel room, and she died later in the day. There were circumstances that indicated that she might have taken her own life. An autopsy was ordered after a bottle containing twenty sleeping capsules was found in her handbag. The bottle was about half full, and several capsules were scattered about the floor beside her bed. A coroner's jury returned a verdict that her death had been caused "by shock and respiratory failure due to an overdose of barbital compound and a kidney ailment." The verdict might well serve as an epitaph for the hectic years between the wars—"shock . . . respiratory failure . . . an overdose of barbital compound."

Assembled in Angelus Temple to bid Sister farewell on her "magic carpet" ascent to eternal glory, the faithful remnant sang "In the Sweet Bye and Bye," marveled at the title of her sermon for the following Sunday ("Going My Way"), and stoutly maintained that Sister would soon be resurrected. Throughout the day of September 29 ten thousand of them filed into the Temple and sorrowfully made their way to the platform to gaze at Sister in a bronze casket quilted with white silk and satin and splashed with roses and gardenias. For her last appearance on the platform of Angelus Temple, Sister was attired in the white robe and blue cape—the famous Admiral's costume—of the Foursquare faith. Her hands were folded over a Bible, which was opened, and a corsage of gardenias and red roses draped her shoulder.

She was buried, not in the ill-fated Blessed Home Memorial Park, but in a plot which she had long ago selected in Forest Lawn Memorial Park, located on "Sunrise Slope," where the statues of two large angels stand glittering in the sunlight. Forest Lawn officials reported that "the floral tributes constituted the greatest batch of flowers telegraphed since the funeral of Will Rogers." One floral piece, a huge cross, had required two carloads of flowers. The shrewdly appraising eyes of the officials estimated that fifty thousand dollars had been spent on flowers, ten thousand dollars on orchids alone. "Today," said Dr. Howard P. Courtney of Angelus Temple, "we are here to commemorate the stepping up of a country girl into God's Hall of Fame. Along with Zwingli, Huss, Wycliffe, Savonarola, Luther, Wesley, Whitfield, Knox, and Moody, Aimee Semple McPherson takes her place with the greatest of spiritual leaders."

Sister's stepping up to glory was, indeed, the culmination of an extraordinary career. A woman who could arouse such love and devotion and blind loyalty in the hearts of thousands of little people possessed qualities that perhaps justified certification to God's Hall of Fame. She believed, with all her heart, in goodness and kindness, and before this fact all else was meaningless. In a moment of desperation she had indulged in some unfortunate baiting of Catholics, but, aside from this isolated instance, the record is free of even a suggestion of bigotry, hatred, or intolerance. There was not a trace of snobbery in this woman. She conducted no "vice crusades," engaged in no snooping, and baited no radicals. She was, as a Los Angeles newspaperman once said, "neither a political hellcat nor a scandalmonger." It is not surprising, therefore, that Los Angeles has already begun to miss Sister Aimee and to wish that she were back at the Temple, chasing the Devil around with a pitchfork, calling the lonely to love in her unforgettable voice.

Nowadays her son Rolf McPherson presides, rather sedately, at Angelus Temple. The loyal remnant, reduced in number, are concentrated more densely than ever in the Echo Park neighborhood, as though they wanted to draw closer to the Temple. But Angelus Temple is no longer the great showplace by the lake. The prayer marathons continue (one relay team has been praying, now, for 118,260 hours); the lights still burn; but the old liveliness and sprightly vigor have gone. The principal project at the Temple right now is the raising of a million-dollar fund to build a memorial to Sister. I have often thought that this memorial might well take the form of a huge statue in bronze, by the waters of Echo Park Lake, with the flowing robes and the Admiral's cape, a Bible clasped in an uplifted hand, and a broad smile of mischievous triumph on Sister's face. For she was really the Queen of the Angels, this sad lady, and, if she could see that statue by the lake, I am sure that, somewhere in paradise, she would start to sing, to the brassy accompaniment of trombones, "Sunlight, sunlight in my soul today."

The Timely Death of President Harding

BY SAMUEL HOPKINS ADAMS

Samuel Hopkins Adams began his writing career on the New York *Sun* in 1891, and has published nearly thirty novels, numerous movie scripts, and half a dozen biographies, including definitive studies of Alexander Woollcott, the Gibson Girls, and Warren G. Harding himself (*Incredible Era*, 1939). His novel *Revelry* (1926), about the Harding scandals, sold more than one hundred thousand copies and was banned in Washington, D. C., and by several state legislatures. It persuaded many readers that President Harding might have been murdered—a supposition which Mr. Adams does not subscribe to, and which he rather completely demolishes in his article for this book. In preparing this new study of Harding and his times, Mr. Adams has uncovered an abundance of new and important facts, especially about Harding's dramatic final journey across the United States to Alaska, and his death soon after. Mr. Adams' latest novel, *Plunder*, is about corruption in Washington in the year 1952.

✵ 1.

A SIGH OF RELIEF breathed from the nation on August 1, 1923. That beloved President, Warren Gamaliel Harding, the idol of the man in the street, the apotheosis of the Average American, the exemplar of the triumphant commonplace who lay, stricken, in a San Francisco hotel, was on the mend. The crisis was past, the prospects were favorable.

Thus officially spoke medical incompetence, through the sick man's personal doctor. Other physicians in attendance knew better. So did those close to the President. The public was fooled.

It may be doubted whether Harding wished to live. What was planned as a carefree junket had turned to a haunted pilgrimage. Private

scandal and political disaster impended. Men do not die of broken
hearts in the poetical sense. But unrelieved apprehension, the nerve
strain of dread and disillusion and helpless wrath, can impair the
central mechanism of life. Harding's heart had collapsed. The robust
athlete who had entered the White House two years before was a
wreck; he had nothing to look forward to but months of seclusion followed by semi-invalidism which would have disqualified him from ful-
filling more than the simplest external demands of his great and rigorous office.

The threat to the President's good name was as little known to the
people at large as the state of his health. So far as they knew, Harding's
personal life was untainted; his Presidential incumbency, if undis-
tinguished, free from scandal. To an extent matched by none since
Lincoln, he was their President, simple, warm-hearted, human; the
man whom they had chosen by a record majority, who had said that
while he could not expect to be the best Chief Executive in history, he
would like to be the best-loved. If hopes and prayers could preserve life,
Harding would not have died.

Two days after the heartening and deceptive message was given out,
a blood clot reached the President's brain. He died instantly and pain-
lessly. So ended the distorted and misplaced career of an unambitious
man, ruined by being dragooned into the nation's highest office against
his better judgment.

His fellow countrymen mourned him with a sense of personal be-
reavement.

2.

HIS IS A LUCK STORY; success achieved with little effort and less ambition under the impulsion of characters stronger than his own. Born to
lowly circumstances, he came up the easy way. To draw a copybook
moral from his career, one must reverse the formula. Inertia wins the
prize.

An idle boy, son of a veterinary turned doctor through a term in a
medical diploma-mill and of an industrious midwife, young Warren
shirked the casual jobs of childhood in an Ohio hamlet, scamped an

education in a local academy, and quit schoolteaching in midyear because it was too hard work. Drifting to the small city of Marion, he,
with two associates, acquired a depreciated evening newspaper, "wholly
destitute of either circulation or reputation" by contemporary report.
The motivating idea seems to have been politics rather than journalism.
At twenty-one he was playing first base on the ball team, alto horn in
the Citizens' Cornet Band, and casual swain to the roller-skating girls.
It may well have been at the rink that he met Florence Kling DeWolfe,
daughter of the town mogul. So far apart were their social strata that
she would have been unlikely to make his acquaintance in any less
public place. She was five years older than he, a divorcée through no
fault of her own, self-willed, hot-blooded, able, and unalluring.

Amos Kling did not approve of the association. Holding up young
Harding in the courthouse, he addressed him as "you God-damned
nigger" and promised to blow his head off if he ever intruded upon the
Kling premises. It discouraged the youth. Not so Florence. She married
him anyway, and for fifteen years her father passed her on the streets
of the city without speaking. For Harding it continued to the end an
advantageous and unhappy marriage.

Dissatisfied with the haphazard conduct of her husband's newspaper,
Mrs. Harding went to the office "intending to help out for a few days
and remained fourteen years." "It was she," testifies Norman Thomas,
one of the newsboys, "who was the real driving power in the success of
the *Star*." Harding circulated in the town, making connections and
picking up news. His editorials were negligible. William Allen White
believed that Harding never wrote "a line that has been quoted beyond
the confines of his state." He pottered unsuccessfully with small politics.

Presumably he would have lived and died an unknown editor and
small-town politician had a campaign speech of his not been heard by
Harry M. Daugherty. Daugherty was a political fixer at the state capital,
quietly useful to corporations. He could not promote himself; he was
so repeatedly defeated for office that the New York *Times* likened him
to a disillusioned boxer, punch-drunk from many knockouts, who
wisely decides that his future lies in management. He picked Warren
Harding for his champion on the strength of the young orator's flam-

boyant rhetoric and statesmanlike aspect. ("He looked like a President ought to look.") Daugherty became the second potent lever in Harding's rise. He and Florence Kling Harding ran the younger man's life for him thenceforth.

Harding slipped into the State Senate on a fluke. With his talent for ingratiation, he quickly became the most popular man there. He was re-elected, and sent back for a third term, this time as Lieutenant Governor. But when he ran for Governor with Harry Daugherty managing his campaign, he was badly beaten. Easily discouraged, he was ready to quit politics. Being editor of the *Star* and Marion's most popular citizen was good enough for him.

The Daugherty-Florence Kling Harding combination had other and more ambitious ideas. The United States Senatorship was open. Would Harding make the fight? He would not. To his natural inertia was now added the reluctance born of defeat. He ran away to Florida, whither Daugherty, that inexorable promoter, "found him sunning himself like a turtle on a log and pushed him off into the water."

It was a happy push for him. Elected by a sounding majority, he joined "the most exclusive club in the world." That is precisely what it was to him. One of his secretaries made a shrewd distinction when he said that Harding "didn't like being a Senator; he liked being in the Senate." Harding himself put it this way to his fellow members:

"Mr. President: I like the fraternity of this body. I like to know that when the waters are muddy, I will be considered. I like to participate in the 'booster' proposition."

As a Senator he was negligent and neglible; almost null. Roll call found him present less than half the time. When he did appear, he refrained from voting on 35 per cent of the motions. Not one item of important legislation was presented by him. But he was having the time of his life! There was the jovial companionship of the more sportive Senators. There were golf and prize fights and baseball games; poker and drinking parties in his pleasant house and elsewhere. Thanks to his wife's vigorous management the *Star* was making money enough to support them in style.

Harding had also taken a mistress, a Marion girl who, robust and physically precocious at twelve years of age, had fallen in love with the

handsome editor and at twenty had come East to capture him, a feat of
no great difficulty. Nan Britton and the child she bore him were to com-
plicate his life and tarnish his memory. His friend, Judge Gary, President of the United Steel Corporation, obligingly found a job for her in
a handy office in New York City. She was pretty, vivacious, and intelligent. Harding's fellow sports in Washington knew of the liaison; the
girl sometimes traveled with him as his niece. Whether Mrs. Harding
also knew about her at this time is doubtful.

As preparation for the Presidency of the United States, Harding's
record while Senator is something less than impressive. His one consistent policy was to get himself re-elected.

Yet Harry Daugherty was patiently scheming with the White House
in view. To this end he must keep his man in the national arena. He had
successfully maneuvered to have Harding present Taft's name as Presidential nominee in 1912. In 1916 he secured for him the temporary
chairmanship of the Republican National Convention, where his key-
note speech met with a chilly reception in the morguelike atmosphere
of a dispirited gathering. Nevertheless it served to keep the politicos
from forgetting Warren G. Harding. At least, so believed that determined optimist, Harry Daugherty.

Too shrewd to consider his entry as anything but an outside chance,
Daugherty believed that 1920 would be the year for a long shot. Theodore Roosevelt was dead. Wilson's idealism had soured on the public
stomach. The Republicans were ready to profit by the revulsion. Almost
anyone could win on an anti-Wilson platform. The stage was set for a
possible background third-rater.

Not that the party lacked for first-rate candidates. Leonard Wood,
Frank O. Lowden, and Senator Hiram Johnson, in the first line, were
all men of stature. For less prominent possibilities there were Senators
Borah, Knox, and La Follette; Sproul of Pennsylvania, Herbert Hoover,
and Charles Evans Hughes. Modestly, Harding shrank from measur-
ing himself in such competition. His loftiest ambition was to go back
to the Senate, "a position far more to my liking than the Presidency
possibly could be." Mrs. Harding, too, was fearful. It may be that she
dreaded scandal. Or she may have been affected by the dark prevision
of a Washington crystal-gazer who had seen disaster hovering over

the Presidency of "a man born on November 2, 1865, at 2 P.M." It took all Harry Daugherty's glib blandishments to overpersuade her. He had already been to the Republican leaders, Penrose, Knox, Lodge, and others, pointing out that the party wanted "a man who would listen." His argument to his prospective candidate was that a good showing in the Presidential balloting would strengthen the Senatorial chances. It prevailed.

The nomination of 1920 with its final act of "fifteen men in a smoke-filled room at two o'clock in the morning" has become a classic set piece of American politics. Wood and Lowden, swaying in long deadlock, had exhausted each other and the delegates. Compromise was the logical solution. The leaders compromised on a man who himself had risen by the arts of compromise. Oil, which was to besmirch the Harding record, had a hand. Through Jake Hamon, a millionaire Oklahoman who expected a government oil lease or a Cabinet position or both as his *quid pro quo,* it contributed twenty-five thousand dollars to Harding's headquarters expenses, and ten times that amount (according to Hamon) to background action.

To combat the rising threat of the dark horse, the opposition went to extreme lengths. Rumors of Harding's involvement with the Britton girl swelled from a whispering campaign to written "testimony." What purported to be signed statements about the illegitimate child were circulated. Nan Britton was in Chicago, employed at Republican headquarters, to the alarm and distress of the candidate's adherents. An older scandal connecting Harding with the wife of a department store owner in Marion was raked up. All this was known to the newspapermen; none of it could be printed.

Coincidentally there appeared in rival headquarters a flood of printed leaflets purporting to prove that there was Negro blood in the Harding lineage. It was the work of Professor William Estabrook Chancellor of the College of Wooster (Ohio). There were anthropometrical data by the author, who professed to be and perhaps was an expert, affidavits from acquaintances of the Harding family in the early days, references to a full-page newspaper account in a Marion daily which had been bought up and suppressed. Chicago buzzed with the rumors. For obvious reasons, this, like the Nan Britton story, was ignored by the newspapers.

It was not to be ignored by the master minds who had all but determined to nominate Harding. One of them, Colonel George B. M. Harvey, summoned the candidate to a private conclave and thus addressed him:

"We think you may be nominated tomorrow. Before acting finally we think you should tell us, on your conscience and before God, whether there is anything that might be brought against you that would embarrass the party, any impediment that might disqualify you or make you inexpedient, either as candidate or as President."

Since Harding's official career was an open book, largely blank and certainly without any disqualifying entries, this could have alluded only to his private affairs: presumably Nan Britton and the racial smears which were an old story to him (*vide* his father-in-law's denunciation as well as sundry more or less veiled implications in the days of the *Star's* violent newspaper controversies).

Stunned and wavering, Harding asked for time to think it over, and withdrew. Had he told the full truth on either count, his hopes would have been blasted on the eve of fulfillment. After a ten-minute self-consultation which might have altered the course of American history, he emerged and said that there was no obstacle.

He was uproariously nominated on the tenth ballot.

"Harding is no world-beater," said Senator Brandegee, voicing the opinion of the inner circle, "but he's the best of the second-raters."

"I can see but one word written above his head if they make him President," cried Mrs. Harding, again in a slump of distrust, "and that word is Tragedy."

Harding's own gleeful comment was luminously in character. "I feel like a man who goes in on a pair of eights and comes out with aces full."

3.

HARDING swept the nation by a record vote. War-weary, impatient of problems too weighty for the mind in the street, cynically intolerant of a half-wrecked world's troubles, avid to get back to the nation's business of making money, people accepted that spurious coinage, "normalcy," as the goal of existence. They chose as its spokesman a man of district-leader caliber whose spiritual and moral values were those of the drugstore corner; kindly, companionable, genuinely democratic, personally (and inexplicably when one considers his associations) free of graft, adroit in the minor manipulations of politics, handsome, and with a singularly winning personality. Of statesmanship he had not an iota, nor did he profess to have. He knew nothing of history, economics, or sociology. He was neither educated nor informed. His oratory, of which he was proud, had a certain gusto but lacked originality, logic, and sometimes grammar. Intellectually undervitalized, he shrank pathetically from problems which he knew to be beyond his powers.

Modestly acknowledging his limitations, he announced his intention of surrounding himself with the Best Minds. His Cabinet was far above the average, with men of the character and caliber of Hughes, Hoover, Mellon, Wallace, Hays, and Weeks. But it was Daugherty and Fall, not these greater men, who swayed and guided him. As for the Best Minds, they spoke a language incomprehensible to him. He wanted to understand; he wished ardently to live up to the expectations of the country which had given him so impressive an endorsement. But it was too much for him. He proved the most bewildered President in our history.

"We're in the Big League now," he told his subordinates, expecting them to accept the expanded responsibilities.

Grave issues impended: unemployment, national financing, taxation, tariff readjustments, the lawlessness attending prohibition, the peace treaties, and the League of Nations. Owing to the inertia of Congress, the machinery of government was all but stalled. "Never has any President come to the tremendous office with so much unfinished business and so many fresh problems of moment," warned one of Harding's influential newspaper supporters.

The President played poker.

No rumor could have exceeded the reality [wrote Alice Roosevelt Long-worth]; the study was filled with cronies . . . the air heavy with tobacco smoke, trays with bottles containing every imaginable brand of whiskey stood about, cards and poker chips ready at hand—a general atmosphere of waistcoat unbuttoned, feet on desk, and spittoons alongside.*

Just such a gathering could be found in innumerable second-floor law offices, overlooking Courthouse Square, the nation over. Here, to be sure, the stakes were higher, the entertainment more lavish, the company more distinguished—or notorious would perhaps be the better term. But the atmosphere was identical. The small-town sport, translated to the White House, was still the life of the party.

It would be unjust to say that Harding deliberately shirked his work. He was not lazy; he was not indifferent. It would not be far from the truth to say that he was daunted. Between nomination and election he had told friends that the office was too big for him and later had touch-ingly begged Bishop Anderson to "talk to God about me every day by name and ask him somehow to give me strength for my great task."

Had the strength been there, the equipment was lacking. Harding's dreary appreciation of this was part of his tragedy. He lamented that he was "a man of limited talents from a small town. . . . I don't seem to grasp that I am President."

To any interviewer he said with disarming humility, "I don't know anything about this European stuff. You and Jud [Judson C. Welliver, one of his secretaries] get together and he can tell me later; he handles these matters for me."

As for finances: "I can't make a damn thing out of this tax prob-lem," he complained. ". . . I know somewhere there is a book that will give me the truth; but hell! I couldn't read the book."

So he went back to the genial companionship of the Poker Cabinet, where everybody was so comfortable and no questions arose to put a strain on one's mind. He was on first-name terms with the whole bunch, though they maintained the external proprieties by addressing him as "Mr. President." There was that prince of good fellows, Charley

* *Crowded Hours,* by Alice Roosevelt Longworth. Charles Scribner's Sons.

Forbes—he loved Charley—and Ned McLean, maybe not very strong in the upper story but a millionaire and a society man and not a bit stuck up about it. There was "Doc" Sawyer, who might not be the most scientific guy in the world, having had only a couple of terms in a dubious medical school, but came from the Old Home Town, played a stiff hand of poker, and was good enough for Harding. And how Doc loved the trappings of a Brigadier General which went with his job as the President's personal physician! There was "Mort" Mortimer, a personal friend as well as a reliable bootlegger who knew where the best liquor was to be found and kept his pals well supplied—and to hell with the bluenoses who beefed about the evil example of illegal drinks in the White House! There were those prime Senatorial sports, Joe Frelinghuysen and Frank Brandegee. Harry Daugherty often dropped in for the semiweekly dinner followed by poker, with his henchman Jess Smith; so did Bert Lasker of the Shipping Board, Harry Sinclair, the big oil man, and Bill Wrigley of the chewing gum family, and Albert Fall was not too busy at his job as Secretary of the Interior to contribute his dry wit and frontier stories to the occasion. They were a grand bunch. The President was in his element.

So was the President's wife. Her fears and misgivings had been appeased. She had found a new seeress who descried a Star of Destiny burning upon her forehead. The star was to guide her and, through her, her illustrious husband to glory. She did not sit in at the poker but acted as amateur Ganymede, circulating with the liquor. Harry Daugherty called her "Ma." To Ned McLean she was "Boss."

This was play. Farther downtown business was going on, the undercover business of the Harding administration on a strictly cash basis. The Ohio Gang, a loose association of minor but favored politicians, had their headquarters in a little green house at 1625 K Street. There they dealt in liquor withdrawal permits, appointments to office, illegal concessions, immunity from prosecution, pardons and paroles for criminals, and various minor grafts. It was in its way a *maison de joie* as well as a commercial center. Senators, Congressmen, Cabinet members, and other officeholders—and the place was patronized by all these classes—could find drinks at any hour and be accommodated with feminine companions from a choice list of ladies-at-call. Gaston B. Means, the most notorious confidence man of his day, and an operative of the Department of Justice, made his headquarters in the Little Green House. Thomas W. Miller, Alien Property Custodian, and E. Mont Reilly, Governor of Puerto Rico, were regulars, as was Charley Forbes. Elias H. ("Mort") Mortimer conducted his bootlegging operations from there; trucks laden with cases delivered their goods in broad daylight.

Assurance of immunity was vested in Jesse W. Smith. He was the liaison between the Department of Justice and the Little Green House on K Street. A pulpy, spluttering, timorous, loose-lipped, dressy country sport, he loved to loll on the corners, greeting his hundreds of acquaintances with stale jokes and the stock query, "Whaddaya know?" His more cautious acquaintances were perturbed by his penchant for the contemporary song whose refrain he delivered in an untuneful and leathery voice: "Good God! how the money rolls in!"

One of the potent figures on the Washington scene, Jess operated in two worlds, the minor graft of the K Street house and the large-scale operations of his sponsor, Attorney General Harry M. Daugherty. He and Daugherty lived, rent-free, in a house of Ned McLean's on a fifty-thousand-dollar-a-year scale which appeared to later investigators as incommensurate with Daugherty's twelve-thousand-dollar-a-year salary. Although he held no official position, Jess had his office in the Department of Justice, franked his mail on the Attorney General's letterhead, traveled on a departmental pass, issued authoritative orders both in person and in writing, and was, in short, "the man to see" when one had ready cash to pay for an office or a favor. Washington called it the Department of Easy Virtue.

Daugherty had been appointed by Harding on purely personal grounds, over the protests of the Best Minds. He made the job pay from the first. When he took office he had less than ten thousand dollars, with liabilities of twenty-seven thousand dollars. Two years later he had deposited in his brother's bank more than seventy-five thousand dollars. Bonds to the value of forty thousand dollars, identified by a court decision as part of a graft deal, were found at the bank, listed as the property of Harry M. Daugherty. Two hundred shares of an aircraft company which had profited by three and a half million dollars' overpayment by the government found their way into Daugherty's possession. By a singular coincidence there vanished from the Department of Justice files the dossier upon which an action for recovery was to have been based. Pardons, inexplicable except on the assumption of value received, were engineered by the Department of Easy Virtue. When criminal charges impended, the Daugherty brothers burned the bank records.

Independently Charles R. Forbes was carrying on a highly profitable line of graft. He was another personal appointment, Harding having met him while on a Senatorial junket and been charmed with his bonhomie. Chiefly because he wanted his jovial playmate at hand, the President offered him several appointments, which he declined. There was nothing in them but the salary. Salaries did not interest the ambitious applicant; he was out for bigger money. He tried for the Shipping Board and settled for the Veterans Bureau. Nearly half a billion dollars a year was allotted to this agency. He got to work upon it. He chose as counsel for the Bureau Charles F. Cramer, a California lawyer.

Soon Charley Forbes became a notable figure in the capital's night life. Lavish entertainment was the order of the day; but the Forbes parties outdid anything else in that line. He did it all on a salary of ten thousand dollars a year. Nobody seems to have questioned it. Asking questions was not good form in the Harding regime.

Hospital sites were to be selected. Forbes went on a transcontinental tour, taking along White House Bootlegger Mortimer. It was an itinerant orgy, in which the main interest, money, was not forgotten. Forbes officially approved locations, upon which the price forthwith shot up to unprecedented heights. Building contracts were let on a percentage basis for the Director of the Veterans Bureau. His report so pleased the President that he narrowly escaped being made Assistant Secretary of War, where pickings would have been scanty and precarious.

Government storehouses near Washington were heavily stocked with supplies and equipment which hospitals all over the country desperately needed. Some of the goods were old or damaged; these could properly be sold on order from the Director. But there was little in the secondhand market for Forbes. So, at a time when disabled veterans were suffering from lack of bedding, bandages, drugs, pajamas, and other prime necessities, Charley Forbes was blithely chalking the x-mark of condemnation on freight-car loads of these very articles and selling them at absurd prices to chosen firms who paid him the agreed rake-off. Sheets in the original packages, bought at $1.37, were passed along by Forbes at 27 cents the pair. Oiled paper, at 60 cents a pound, went for 5. Brand-new gauze at $1.33 per roll suffered an 80 per cent discount. And so on, all to the profit of the Director and the crooked firms with which he dealt.*

General Sawyer—who, whatever his deficiencies, was an honest man—heard rumors, made a quiet investigation, and went to the President. So did Harding's sister, Mrs. Votaw, and Harry Daugherty, the one inspired by jealousy (she had been left out of the Forbes-Mortimer junket), the other by personal dislike. Blinded as always by his personal loyalty, the President termed the accusations "an abominable libel." Against testimony strong enough to convince any but a tight-closed mind, he clung to his faith in his friend Charley.

Looting on a grander scale was in progress in the Department of the Interior. Albert B. Fall, Senator from New Mexico, had long been a Harding crony. Harding would have liked to appoint him Secretary of State (Hughes was a second or third choice), which would hardly have fallen in with the New Mexican's calculations. He was "broke," and taxes on his run-down ranch were nine years overdue. He needed money badly and quickly. Oil meant money, and the Department of the Interior meant oil. But not oil enough to satisfy Fall's scheme. Some of the most valuable (and negotiable) properties in the country had been turned over to the Navy. As soon as Fall became Secretary of the Interior, he persuaded his friend, Secretary of the Navy Denby, to turn control of the rich Teapot Dome and Elk Hills Fields over to him. Denby was not corrupt. He was simply and hopelessly stupid. High naval officers objected. But the President stood by his crony.

"I guess there will be hell to pay," he confided to a friend, "but those fellows seem to know what they're doing."

There was hell to pay—later. Fall was paid first.

Back taxes on his ranch were satisfied. The depleted property was put in prime condition and stocked with blooded cattle. Adjoining land

---

* Will Irwin in a series of articles on the Veterans Bureau estimated the government's loss on Forbes' operations at $200,000,000.

was acquired at a cost of $125,000. The Falls were living high. All this on the $12,000 salary of a Cabinet officer.

Two generous friends, both oil magnates, were responsible. Edwin L. Doheny of the Pan-American Petroleum Company wanted Elk Hills, which, he estimated, should be worth $100,000,000 to him. So he sent $100,000, surely a modest percentage, to Secretary Fall in a black satchel.

Teapot Dome ought to be worth as much, by the calculations of Harry F. Sinclair. He and some associated oil men formed the Continental Trading Company, whose funds were partly invested in Liberty bonds. These bonds to the amount of about $233,000 found their way by devious routes into Fall's possession, shortly after the Teapot Dome lease delivering the oil over to Sinclair was signed. However devious the route, Liberty bonds are always traceable by numbered coupons. These particular coupons were cashed by Albert B. Fall. Their transfer, however, had been successfully concealed. When, after two years' incumbency, Fall resigned from the Cabinet to take open employment with Sinclair, his reputation was still untainted. Harding, of course, had full confidence in him.

4.

THE YEAR 1923 opened inauspiciously for the harassed President. Congressional investigations threatened in several directions: oil, the Veterans Bureau, the Alien Property Custodian, the conduct of the Attorney General's office, the no-longer secret power of Jess Smith and the Ohio Gang, and abuses in minor departments of the administration. Unfair newspaper criticism (to the Harding type of mind any criticism is unfair) was getting under his skin.

Personal and family complications added to his distress. Mrs. Harding, if she did not know positively, suspected Nan Britton's side-door entry to the White House. There was an animated scene between husband and wife, and the mistress was packed off to Europe at Harding's expense. The Votaws were in trouble; Harding's sister Carolyn had married the Reverend Heber Votaw, who benefited by a nepotic and unfit appointment as Superintendent of Federal Prisons. Now the Department of Justice charged that the ex-missionary was protecting the dope-peddling ring which operated in the Atlanta Penitentiary. Forbes and Daugherty got into a row over that. There was jealousy and back-biting, tale-bearing and recriminations among the White House favorites.

The Harding genealogy popped up again. Professor Chancellor, he of the Chicago convention leaflets, issued a book purporting to prove the President's Afro-American lineage. Without a shadow of legality the Department of Justice sent out a gang of operatives to confiscate the volume. They bullied and browbeat the purchasers into surrendering the book with such thoroughness that less than half a dozen specimens are known to survive.

The President's health was not good. He slept ill and rose unre-freshed. Finances worried him; he was $180,000 in debt to his brokers. How could a man do his job, beset by such vexations? He planned to get away, to take a long and restful trip somewhere. Alaska. That was it! He would see new countries, take a vacation from official troubles and problems. Of course he would have to make some speeches. He didn't mind that. In fact, he rather enjoyed it. "Bloviating" (his own term for his brand of oratory) came natural to him. All the rest would be jollity and junket in the company of such carefully selected friends as Ned McLean, Charley Forbes, Mort Mortimer, Frank Brandegee, and perhaps Harry Daugherty and Jess Smith if they could get away; good pals, all, who could be relied upon to divert his mind from the burdens insistently and irritantly imposed upon it by such solemn-minded associates as Hughes and Hoover, Weeks, Work, Wallace, and Mellon.

Le roi s'amuse. The President was going to have some fun. Invita-tions were sent out.

The first intimation of a break in the program came by letter from Europe. Colonel Charles R. Forbes, traveling for his health, resigned. It was an ominous note. Harding failed to recognize its import. He urged his old crony to reconsider; but Forbes knew now that he could never stand up to the threatened Senatorial investigation. He was through.

Resignations may be interpreted one way or another. A bullet is definitive. At dead of night in the house which he had bought from the President, Forbes' right-hand man, Cramer, shot himself. A Department of Justice agent was early on the spot. He hurried to the White House and got Harding out of bed.

"Mr. President: I have a letter for you."

"Who's it from?"

"Charles F. Cramer. Mr. Cramer is dead."

"Yes, I know." (How he knew is a matter for surmise. Cramer was alone in the house when he killed himself. Had he perhaps called up the President and given notice of his intention?)

"Here is the letter, sir. It was found in his room."

"Take it away. I don't want it."

The message was destroyed, unread, by Harry Daugherty, to whom the F.B.I. man delivered it.

Shortly after the tragedy Forbes returned from Europe. A chance visitor, misdirected in the White House, was horrified at breaking in upon a scene of violence. The President of the United States had a man by the throat, shaking him and gasping out:

"You yellow rat! You double-crossing bastard!"

The victim was Charley Forbes.

It was the President's first positive disillusionment. Always a self-persuasive optimist, Harding might have been able to convince himself that Forbes' disloyalty was a sporadic instance, not symptomatic of a general condition of rottenness. But now disturbing reports that struck nearer home reached his ears, matters about which informed circles had been gossiping for months. Like the proverbial injured husband, the President of the United States is always the last to hear news affecting the honor of his house. Too many people are interested in keeping information from him.

Harding sent for Jess Smith.

Poor Jess was in eclipse. He had been evicted from his sanctum of power in the Department of Justice and banished to his native Ohio by Harry Daugherty, presumably because his loose-tongued bragging of easy money had become dangerous. Wretched in exile, he crept back to Washington. Possibly the first inkling of his error was when he was summoned to the White House.

The President had chosen his subject shrewdly. Under inquisition the pulpy grafter broke down and, in his slobbering, sputtery speech, told Harding what Washington's political underworld had successfully concealed from him for nearly two years. There is reason to believe that his revelations did not include his boss, Harry Daugherty, who was spending that very night under the White House roof.

"Go home," the President bade his visitor. "Tomorrow you will be arrested."

Jess returned to the hotel apartment that he shared with Daugherty and blew his brains out. Either before or, more probably, after the act, all his papers were conveniently burned.

The Smith disclosures shocked Harding not into political house-cleaning but into personal reform. The White House poker parties were abandoned. He told his intimates that he was "off" liquor. Nan Britton had already been banished to Europe. His nerve was shaken. He lost his taste for revelry. The plans for the Alaska trip were radically revised. Instead of an itinerant whoopee, it was now to be a serious political mission.

For the Poker Cabinet there was substituted a group of very different significance. The new Secretary of the Interior, Dr. Hubert Work, Speaker of the House Gillett, and Secretary of Agriculture Wallace were invited to go along, and Secretary of Commerce Hoover was requested by wire to join the tour at Tacoma. General Sawyer was included as guardian of the President's health, while Dr. (now Admiral) Joel T. Boone was to look after the other members of the party. There was to be a sprinkling of army and navy men, secretaries, and a number of wives. Mrs. Harding arranged to accompany the President. "Never let your husband travel without you" was one of her maxims for marital stability.

During the interval between Jess Smith's enforced exposures and the start of the journey, the President's mood was one of nerve-racked indecision. He sent for Nicholas Murray Butler to come from New York and, upon his arrival, chatted vaguely of such trivialities that the visitor never did discover why he had been summoned.

Early in the itinerary there was a touch of melodrama. A heavily veiled woman made her way into the President's suite at Kansas City and was closeted with him for nearly an hour. If the newspapers were aware of this, they practiced a discreet silence. The visitor was the wife of ex-Secretary Albert B. Fall, who was already threatened with exposure. Whatever Mrs. Fall's errand, whether to impart information, give warning, consult upon measures of defense and concealment, or demand help, it left the President moody and fearful.

At Tacoma he had an important message to deliver. The surrender of the steel industry on the twelve-hour day and the eighty-four-hour week, and the reduction of this punishing schedule to an eight-hour day and forty-eight-hour week, had been brought about by Secretary Hoover after long negotiations. Mr. Hoover wrote the announcement into the President's address. But the Hoover style, which tends to a rather classical simplicity and directness, was an incongruous insertion in the midst of the Hardingesque sonorities, which once reminded H. L. Mencken of "a string of wet sponges." When he reached the interpolated passage the President paused, stumbled, and addressed his collaborator in an aside, half jocular, half annoyed.

"Why can't you write English like I do?"

For the remainder of the speech he acquitted himself well enough.

From Tacoma on, the President was in a state of chronic jitters. He could not be quiet for five minutes on end. His one thought was to escape from thinking. To this end he organized a bridge game, with Secretaries Wallace, Work, and Hoover, Speaker Gillett and Admiral Rodman. The President played to exhaustion, twelve, fourteen, fifteen hours a day, with brief time out for luncheon and dinner. The game started immediately after breakfast and went on well into the next morning. Unlike the White House poker standards, the stakes were small; it was the escape from worries that Harding wanted. For the other players it was an endurance test. Being two more than the required number, they met it by cutting in and out for a respite of two or three hours each. The President played through every session.

By the time the West Coast was reached, his nervous demoralization was painfully apparent. It reached a pressure point at which he felt the need of relief. He sought out Secretary Hoover.

"Mr. Secretary," said he, "there's a bad scandal brewing in the administration."

The Secretary waited, but no details were forthcoming.

"What do you think I ought to do?" pursued the President. "Keep it under cover or open it up?"

It was not wholly news to Mr. Hoover. He had long distrusted and disliked Attorney General Daugherty; news of the Jess Smith suicide had reached him through the newspapers. He had not spent two years in Washington without hearing rumors of Charley Forbes' profligate expenditures on a small official salary.

"There is only one course for you, Mr. President," he replied. "Open it up completely and without delay."

Harding stared at him uncertainly, unhappily, and turned away. It was not what he had hoped to hear, though he could hardly have expected anything else from the Quaker conscience of Hoover. He never again brought up the matter. Though still slack with indecision, he did wire Harry Daugherty to come West and meet him when the tour should have returned from Alaska to Seattle.

On the Navy Transport *Henderson,* coming and going, on Alaska soil when he was not making speeches or receiving delegations, the President was indefatigably, interminably playing bridge. An airplane brought him a code message from Washington. After reading it he appeared melancholy; he shut himself away for a while. He was heard asking himself in an absent mutter what a fellow was to do when his own friends double-crossed him. Liquor being officially banned on the tour, a quart of choice bourbon was obtained from one of the correspondents for Harding's use. Doubtless he needed it. He went back to the solace of his bridge game. But his attention wavered at times; he was not up to his standard of play.

5.

THE BEGINNING of the end was at Vancouver. It was a stifling day, the hottest in years. Harding spent the day going about in an open car, making speeches. He was listless, his delivery flat and dull. At Seattle he was in worse condition. Halfway through a long address he dropped his manuscript. Hoover, who sat behind him, gathered and arranged the scattered sheets, observing with concern as he handed them back the glassy eyes and vague expression of a man who was, in fighting parlance, out on his feet. The orator rallied and finished gamely.

It was here that Harry Daugherty rejoined him by command. They were closeted long together. When the President emerged from the colloquy his face was drawn and livid. Daugherty hurried away. He did not join the private train party, nor did he see the President again, though Mrs. Harding was urgent that he should go to the bedside in San Francisco.

The Daugherty interview broke Harding's waning resistance. Forbes, his old cronies of the Ohio Gang, Albert Fall, and now his mentor and intimate, Harry Daugherty—all had betrayed him. Whom could he trust? Where could he look for advice? He was supported to the train, quivering with nervousness. It was announced that he had suffered an attack of "acute indigestion" (General Sawyer's diagnosis) from crab meat (the same authority) which he had not eaten, though other members of the party had without any ill effects.

All engagements were canceled. The Presidential train set out for San Francisco. The next morning Dr. Boone, a physician of wide experience and high standing, declared himself dissatisfied with the Sawyer diagnosis.

"There's something far more serious," he told the inner circle. "I ought to have a look at him."

Officially he had no status. The President was Dr. Sawyer's patient. But there are occasions when the public interest transcends medical ethics. Another able physician was aboard, Dr. Hubert Work, then Secretary of the Interior. The two conferred and decided to visit Harding on their own authority. Their examination convinced them of the gravity of the case. The President was suffering from a coronary thrombosis, a major impairment of the heart, the symptoms of which, by their superficial resemblance to a sharp stomach upset, had led Dr. Sawyer into error.

Specialists in San Francisco were summoned to meet the train. Arrangements were made with a sanitarium in Santa Barbara to take the patient, should he be able to go there. Even if he survived—a matter of grave doubt—he must be sequestrated for at least six months.

Should the sick man be told of the seriousness of his condition? In view of his known physical courage, an affirmative decision was made. It was assumed that he would face the issue without alarm or weakening.

He did. But his first reaction was strange and, to those in the know, rather pathetic. He directed that the rooming arrangement at the Palace Hotel be altered so that he would be between Secretaries Hoover and Work. It was as if, after the repeated treacheries which had broken him down, he craved the proximity of men whom he could trust. And he demanded fretfully to be allowed to return to Washington at the earliest possible moment. There were pressing matters there to which only he could attend. Mercifully, he had not been told of his impending invalidism.

Through the few succeeding days he was worse—he was better—pneumonia set in, the weakened heart being incompetent to pump enough blood to clear the lungs—it abated—the optimistic bulletin went forth while the specialists were profoundly concerned over their patient's increasing nervousness—the wandering blood clot struck into the brain like a bullet and the President died while his wife was soothing him with a eulogistic magazine article. The cortege across the country to Washington and thence to Ohio was everywhere held up by unparalleled throngs, mourning, weeping, praying, singing the dead man's favorite hymn. For that brief time Warren Gamaliel Harding was the well-loved President he had hoped to be.

6.

It took years to clean up the "debris of decency" which was the Harding administration's legacy to the nation. The public which had held its breath over the dying President now held its nose over the rising stench of scandal. The unfolding history of the aftermath reads like a combination of Greek tragedy and criminal court dossier. Few, indeed, of the dead man's intimate circle escaped unsullied.

Charles R. Forbes went to jail. Albert B. Fall went to jail. Alien Property Custodian Thomas W. Miller went to jail. Gaston B. Means went to jail after neatly swindling Edward B. McLean's wife out of one hundred thousand dollars. McLean, himself, went into a madhouse. Harry F. Sinclair went to jail first for refusing to answer questions on the stand and second for contempt of court in connection with jury-shadowing. Harry M. Daugherty escaped jail, thanks to two hung juries and his refusal to take the stand lest he incriminate himself. The Daugherty bank where his boodle was secreted—though insufficiently —crashed, bringing ruin to an Ohio countryside. His brother, Mally, convicted and sentenced, wriggled out on a technicality. The Attorney General was forced from office with not a shred of reputation left, but still able to boast that no charge against him was ever proven in court.

Two other members of the Harding Cabinet suffered in public esteem. Secretary of the Navy Denby resigned after revelations which proved no moral obloquy but almost unbelievable incompetence and ignorance of his job. Postmaster General Will H. Hays was shown to have acted as receiver of the Sinclair slush fund on behalf of the Republican National Committee, though his personal integrity was not impugned; none of the money stuck to his fingers.

The Ohio Gang, bereft of the advantages and privileges of Ohiohood, scattered and vanished into obscurity.

Rather than inflict the further scandal of a stock-gambling President upon the already overburdened record, Harding's personal brokers took a loss of $150,000 on the unsatisfied Presidential indebtedness and never said anything about it.

To the three previous tragedies of violence close to Harding— Hamon, Cramer, and Jess Smith—were now added two more. Elias H. Mortimer, charging that his wife was unfaithful to him with Charles Forbes, blew out his brains.

Frank Brandegee, involved in a discreditable bankruptcy, committed suicide in his Washington apartment.

Oil smeared the record. Because of participation in the Sinclair deals, a Standard Oil president (Indiana) was stripped of office by the higher authorities of the corporation. Two other oil company presidents fled beyond the reach of extradition and died in lugubrious exile. By a contradiction, not to say corruption, of the law's process, Fall was convicted of accepting a bribe from E. L. Doheny and Doheny was acquitted of giving that same bribe to Fall! But the hovering Harding tragedy descended upon him just the same. His son, who was bearer of the "little black satchel" containing Fall's hundred-thousand-dollar "loan," killed or was killed in a peculiar murder-and-suicide mystery involving him and his private secretary.

The dead President's personal record did not escape the afterwave of scandal. Nan Britton published her book, *The President's Daughter*, in 1927. In its main theme it is a convincing documentation of sordid intrigue, beginning with thirty dollars tucked into a stocking-top and ending with the White House as a place of assignation. It shamed and nauseated a nation which now asked nothing better than to forget Harding and all his works.

Though it enjoyed an equal *succès de scandale,* Gaston B. Means's volume, *The Strange Death of President Harding* (1930), bears every imprint of being a thoroughgoing fake as regards its basic thesis. Without making the charge in so many words, it advances the theory that Mrs. Harding poisoned her husband in a sort of "mercy killing," to save him from the impeachment which she foresaw. The absurdity of the allegation is sufficiently indicated by the fact that it presupposes criminal collusion after the fact by medical men of the character of Drs. Boone, Ray Lyman Wilbur, Charles Minor Cooper, and Surgeon General Sawyer (who, whatever his deficiencies, was an upright and honorable man), together with presumptive collaboration by Messrs. Hoover, Work, and others.

Unhappily, there were concomitant circumstances which could be twisted into a semblance of support for this theory. Mrs. Harding peremptorily refused to permit an autopsy. As soon as she reached Washington she collected all accessible letters and papers of the dead President, took them to Marion, and burned most of them. When Dr. Sawyer died in circumstances somewhat similar to those of Harding's death, the whisperers pointed out that Mrs. Harding was in his sanitarium at the time. The murder rumor spread widely and was accepted by a considerable part of the gossip-loving public and by a few serious (but in this case negligent) historians. Another report, equally baseless, attributed the President's death to suicide.

The anomaly of Warren Gamaliel Harding's career is that without wanting, knowing, or trying to do anything at all unusual, he became the figurehead for the most flagrantly corrupt regime in our history. It was less his fault than that of the country at large. Maneuvered by the politicians, the American people selected to represent them one whom they considered an average man. But the job they assigned to him is not an average job. When he proved incapable of meeting its requirements, they blamed him and not themselves.

That is the tragedy of Harding.

Konklave in Kokomo

BY ROBERT COUGHLAN

Robert Coughlan is a Kokomo, Indiana, boy who has special reason to remember the Ku Klux Klan. His family was Roman Catholic and lived in a neighborhood which was almost a hundred per cent Protestant and strongly pro-Klan. Mr. Coughlan's account of the Klan's great day in Kokomo and its swift rise to power in Indiana and elsewhere would seem unbelievable if we did not know it was all a part of actual history. Mr. Coughlan was born in Kokomo and attended the public schools there. Thereafter came Northwestern University, where he was graduated in 1936, a short turn with Harcourt, Brace & Co., the New York publishers, and a writing job with *Fortune*. He is now a member of the board of editors of *Life*, in charge of its text department.

☼ 1.

ON A HOT July day in central Indiana—the kind of day when the heat shimmers off the tall green corn and even the bobwhites seek shade in the brush—a great crowd of oddly dressed people clustered around an open meadow. They were waiting for something; their faces, framed in white hoods, were expectant, and their eyes searched the bright blue sky. Suddenly they began to cheer. They had seen it: a speck that came from the south and grew into an airplane. As it came closer it glistened in the sunlight, and they could see that it was gilded all over. It circled the field slowly and seesawed in for a bumpy landing. A bulky man in a robe and hood of purple silk hoisted himself up from the rear cockpit. As he climbed to the ground, a new surge of applause filled the country air. White-robed figures bobbed up and down; parents hoisted their children up for a view. A small delegation of dignitaries filed out toward the airplane, stopping at a respectful distance.

The man in purple stepped forward.

"Kigy," he said.

"Itsub," they replied solemnly.

With the newcomer in the lead the column recrossed the field, proceeded along a lane carved through the multitude, and reached a platform decked out with flags and bunting. The man in purple mounted the steps, walked forward to the rostrum, and held up his right hand to hush the excited crowd.

"My worthy subjects, citizens of the Invisible Empire, Klansmen all, greetings!

"It grieves me to be late. The President of the United States kept me unduly long counseling upon vital matters of state. Only my plea that this is the time and place of my coronation obtained for me surcease from his prayers for guidance." The crowd buzzed.

"Here in this uplifted hand, where all can see, I bear an official document addressed to the Grand Dragon, Hydras, Great Titans, Furies, Giants, Kleagles, King Kleagles, Exalted Cyclops, Terrors, and All Citizens of the Invisible Empire of the Realm of Indiana. . . .

"It is signed by His Lordship, Hiram Wesley Evans, Imperial Wizard, and duly attested.

"It continues me officially in my exalted capacity as Grand Dragon of the Invisible Empire for the Realm of Indiana. It so proclaims me by Virtue of God's Unchanging Grace. So be it."

The Grand Dragon paused, inviting the cheers that thundered around him. Then he launched into a speech. He urged his audience to fight for "one hundred per cent Americanism" and to thwart "foreign elements" that he said were trying to control the country. As he finished and stepped back, a coin came spinning through the air. Someone threw another. Soon people were throwing rings, money, watch charms, anything bright and valuable. At last, when the tribute slackened, he motioned to his retainers to sweep up the treasure. Then he strode off to a near-by pavilion to consult with his attendant Kleagles, Cyclopses, and Titans.

2.

THAT DAY, July 4, 1923, was a high-water mark in the extraordinary career of David C. Stephenson, the object of these hysterics; and it was certainly one of the greatest days in the history of that extraordinary organization the Knights of the Ku Klux Klan. The occasion was a tri-state Konklave of Klan members from Illinois, Ohio, and Indiana. The place was Melfalfa Park, the meeting place, or Klavern, of the Klan chapter of Kokomo, Indiana, the host city. Actually, although planned as a tri-state convention, it turned out to be the nearest thing to a rank-and-file national convention the Klan ever had. Cars showed up from almost every part of the country. The Klan's official estimate, which probably was not far wrong in this case, was that two hundred thousand members were there. Kokomo then had a population of about thirty thousand, and naturally every facility of the town was swamped.

The Konklave was an important day in my life. I was nine years old, with a small boy's interest in masquerades and brass bands. But I was also a Catholic, the son of a Catholic who taught in the public schools and who consequently was the object of a good deal of Klan agitation. If anything worse was to come, the Konklave probably would bring it. Every week or so the papers had been reporting Klan atrocities in other parts of the country—whippings, lynchings, tar-and-feather parties— and my father and his family were logical game in our locality.

Nevertheless, in a spirit of curiosity and bravado, my father suggested after our holiday lunch that we drive out to Melfalfa Park, which lies west of the town, to see what was happening. My mother's nervous objections were overcome, and we all got into the family Chevrolet and set out for West Sycamore Road. We saw white-sheeted Klansmen everywhere. They were driving along the streets, walking about with their hoods thrown back, eating in restaurants—they had taken the town over. But it was not until we were well out toward Melfalfa Park that we could realize the size of the demonstration. The road was a creeping mass of cars. They were draped with flags and bunting, and some carried homemade signs with Klan slogans such as "America for the Americans," or "The Pope will sit in the White House when Hell freezes over." There were Klan traffic officials every few yards, on foot, on motorcycles, or on horseback, but they were having a hard time keeping the two lanes of cars untangled and moving, and the air was full of the noise of their police whistles and shouts. The traffic would congeal, grind ahead, stop again, while the Klan families sat steaming and fanning themselves in their cars. Most of them seemed to have made it a real family expedition: the cars were loaded with luggage, camping equipment, and children. Quite a few of the latter— even those too young to belong to the junior order of the Klan—were dressed in little Klan outfits, which did not save them from being smacked when their restiveness annoyed their hot and harassed parents. The less ardent or more philosophical Klansmen had given up and had established themselves, with their picnic baskets and souvenir pillows, in shady spots all along the road and far into the adjoining fields and woods. From his gilded airplane, D. C. Stephenson must have seen a landscape dappled for miles around with little knots of white.

Since there was no way of turning back we stayed with the procession, feeling increasingly conspicuous. Finally we came to the cross road whose left branch led past the entrance to Melfalfa. We turned right and started home.

So we missed seeing the Konklave close up. But the newspapers were full of it, and people who were there have been able to fill in the details for me. The program gave a good indication of what the Klan was all about, or thought it was about. The Konklave started in midmorning with an address by a minister, the Reverend Mr. Kern of Covington, Indiana. The Reverend Kern spent most of his time warning against the machinations of Catholics and foreigners in the United States. When he finished, a fifty-piece boys' band from Alliance, Ohio, played "America" and the crowd sang. Then a band from New Castle, Indiana, played the "Star-Spangled Banner" and the Reverend Everett Nixon of Kokomo gave the invocation. These preliminaries led up to a speech by Dr. Hiram Wesley Evans, the national leader of the Klan, who had come all the way from headquarters at Atlanta, Georgia. Dr. Evans commented gracefully on the fact that the center of Klan activities seemed to have shifted from Atlanta to Kokomo, and then talked on "Back to the Constitution." In his view, the Constitution was in peril from foreigners and "foreign influences," and he urged his audience to vote for Congressmen who would legislate "to the end that the nation may be rehabilitated by letting Americans be born into the American heritage." By the time Dr. Evans finished it was lunch time, and the Klan families spread their picnic cloths through the leafy acres of Melfalfa Park. Block-long cafeteria tables lined the banks of Wildcat Creek. From these, the women's auxiliary of the Klan dispensed five thousand cases of pop and near-beer, fifty-five thousand buns, twenty-five hundred pies, six tons of beef, and supplementary refreshments on the same scale.

It was after lunch, at about 2 P.M., when the crowd was full of food and patriotic ecstasy, that D. C. Stephenson made his dramatic descent from the sky.

The rest of the day, after Stephenson's speech, was given over to sports, band concerts, and general holiday frolic. That night there was a parade down Main Street in Kokomo. And while an outside observer might have found a good deal to be amused at in the antics of the Klan during the day, no one could have seen the parade that night without feelings of solemnity. There were thirty bands; but as usual in Klan parades there was no music, only the sound of drums. They rolled the slow, heavy tempo of the march from the far north end of town to Foster Park, a low meadow bordering Wildcat Creek where the Klan had put up a twenty-five-foot "fiery cross." There were three hundred mounted Klansmen interspersed in companies among the fifty thousand hooded men, women, and children on foot. The marchers moved in good order, and the measured tread of their feet, timed to the rumbling of the drums and accented by the off-beat clatter of the horses' hoofs, filled the night with an overpowering sound. Many of the marchers carried flaming torches, whose light threw grotesque shadows up and down Main Street. Flag bearers preceded every Den, or local Klan chapter. Usually they carried two Klan flags flanking an American flag, and the word would ripple down the rows of spectators lining the curbs, "Here comes the flag! Hats off for the flag!" Near the place where I was standing with my parents one man was slow with his hat and had it knocked off his head. He started to protest, thought better of it, and held his hat in his hand during the rest of the parade.

Finally the biggest flag I have ever seen came by. It must have been at least thirty feet long, since it took a dozen or more men on each side to support it, and it stretched almost from curb to curb. It sagged in the center under a great weight of coins and bills. As it passed us the bearers called out, "Throw in! Give to the hospital!" and most of the spectators did. This was a collection for the new "Klan hospital" that was to relieve white Protestant Kokomoans of the indignity of being born, being sick, and dying under the care of nuns, a necessity then since the Catholics supported the only hospital in town. It was announced afterward that the huge flag had collected fifty thousand dollars.

When the last of the marchers had filed into Foster Park the "fiery cross" was touched off. The Klansmen sang "The Old Rugged Cross," the Klan anthem, heard a few more speeches, and then dispersed, the hardier ones to drive back to Melfalfa Park to see a fireworks exhibition. Many of them were too spent, however, emotionally and physically, to make the trip. As we sat on our front porch after watching the parade, we could see the Klansmen of our neighborhood trickling home. Some still wore their regalia, too tired to bother with taking it off before they came into sight. Others carried little bundles of white: they were the ones who still made some pretense of secrecy about being members. One of the last to come down the street was old Mrs. Crousore, who lived a few doors away. Her white robe clung damply, and her hood was pushed back. As she climbed her steps and sank solidly into a rocking chair on her porch, we could hear her groan, "Oh, my God, my feet hurt!"

Mrs. Crousore spoke with such feeling that her words seemed to summarize the whole day. My parents adopted her comment as a family joke. July 4, 1923, became for us the day when Mrs. Crousore's feet hurt. But it was clear to me when I grew a little older that my parents needed the joke as much as Mrs. Crousore needed her rocking chair. There were wild rumors in the town in the months that followed: Father Pratt, the pastor at St. Patrick's Church, was on the list for tar-and-feathering; the church was going to be burned; the Klan was going to "call" on the Jewish merchants; it was going to "get" my father and Miss Kinney, another Catholic who taught in the public schools. Considering all the violent acts committed by the Klan elsewhere in the country, it seemed quite possible that any or all of these notions might mature into action.

As it turned out, none of them did. Six years later, in 1929, when the Klan was almost dead, vandals broke into St. Patrick's and defaced some of the statuary. Perhaps they were remnants of the Klan; perhaps they were only ordinary cranks. As for my family, nothing worse happened than that a few days after the Konklave I found a small cross painted in tar on one of our front steps—an ominous sign with no aftermath. I know of no explanation for the lack of violence, for Kokomo was one of the most "Klannish" towns in the United States. Perhaps the answer lay in the dead level typicalness of the town: a population overwhelmingly white Protestant, with small, well-assimilated numbers of Catholics, Jews, foreigners, and Negroes, and an economy nicely balanced between farming and industry. There were few genuine tensions in Kokomo in 1923, and hence little occasion for misdirected hate to flame into personal violence.

It may be asked why, then, did the town take so whole-heartedly to the Klan, which made a program of misdirected hate? And the answer to that may be, paradoxically enough, that the Klan supplied artificial tensions. Though artificial, and perhaps never quite really believed in, they were satisfying. They filled a need—a need for Kokomo and all the big and little towns that resembled it during the early 1920's.

3.

IN 1923, Kokomo, like the rest of the United States, was in a state of arrested emotion. It had gone whole-hog for war in 1917-18. My own earliest memories are mostly of parading soldiers, brass bands, peach pits thrown into collection stations on Main Street to be used "for gas masks," Liberty Bonds, jam-packed troop trains, the Kaiser hung in effigy, grotesque drawings of Huns in the old *Life*. But it was mostly a make-believe war, as it turned out, and by the time it was well started it was all over.

The emotions it had whipped up, however, were not over. As Charles W. Furgeson says in *Confusion of Tongues*: "We had indulged in wild and lascivious dreams. We had imagined ourselves in the act of intercourse with the Whore of the World. Then suddenly the war was over and the Whore vanished for a time and we were in a condition of *coitus interruptus.*" To pursue the imagery, consummation was necessary. With the real enemy gone, a fresh one had to be found. Find an enemy: Catholics, Jews, Negroes, foreigners—but especially Catholics.

This seemingly strange transmutation was not really strange, considering the heritage of the times. Anti-foreignism has been a lively issue in American history since before the Republic. It became a major issue from the 1830's on, as mass migrations took place from Ireland, Germany, Scandinavia, Italy, Poland, Russia, and the Far East. Before immigration was finally curbed by the quota laws, many old-stock Americans in the South and Central West had been roused to an alarmed conviction that they were in danger of being overrun. The "foreigners" with their different ways and ideas were "ruining the country"; and hence anything "foreign" was "un-American" and a menace.

Another main stream in American history was anti-Catholicism, for the good and sufficient reason that a great many of the founding fathers had come to this continent to escape Catholic persecutions. This stream ran deep; and periodically it would emerge at the surface, as in the Know Nothing Party of the 1850's and the American Protective Association of the 1890's. It was submerged but still strong as this century began, and it came to a violent confluence in the 1920's with the parallel stream of anti-foreignism. The conscious or unconscious syllogism was: (1) foreigners are a menace, as demonstrated by the war, (2) the Catholic Church is run by a foreign Pope in a foreign city, (3) therefore the Catholic Church is a menace. Here was a suitable enemy—powerful, mysterious, international, aggressive.

To some extent, of course, the violence with which the jaws of this syllogism snapped shut was a result of parallel thinking in Washington. Wilson had been repudiated, and with him the League and the World Court, and internationalism had become a bad word. The great debates accompanying these events had stirred the country as it had not been stirred since the days preceding the Civil War, and things said then by the isolationists had been enough to frighten even normally sensible people. The exact sequence is a conundrum like that of the chicken and egg: whether the isolationist politicians led the people or whether the people drove the isolationist politicians. The postwar disillusionment that swept all ranks, including the new generation of authors, would seem to indicate the latter. Great men might have controlled the tide, but they were not to be found in the administrations of Harding and Coolidge.

There were other factors too: the deadly tedium of small-town life, where any change was a relief; the nature of current Protestant theology, rooted in Fundamentalism and hot with bigotry; and, not least, a native American moralistic blood lust that is half historical determism, and half Freud. The Puritan morality that inspired *The Scarlet Letter* and the hanging of witches spread across the country not far behind the moving frontier; it gained new strength, in fact, in the revulsion against the excesses of frontier life. But Puritanism defies human nature, and human nature, repressed, emerges in disguise. The fleshly appetites of the small townsman, when confronted by the rigid moral standards of his social environment, may be transformed into a fanatic persecution of those very appetites. The Klan, which sanctified chastity and "clean living" and brought violent punishment to sinners, was a perfect outlet for these repressions. It is significant that the favored Klan method of dealing with sexual transgressors was to strip them naked and whip them, an act of sadism.

This sexual symbolism could, with not too much effort, be made to dovetail with anti-foreignism and anti-Catholicism. Foreigners were notoriously immoral, as proven by the stories the soldiers brought back from wicked Paris. The Catholic Church, the "foreign church," must condone such things; and besides, who knew *what* went on among the priests and nuns! A staple in pornographic literature for at least one hundred years had been the "revelations" of alleged ex-priests. The Klan made use of these and other fables, such as the old and ever popular one about the mummified bodies of newborn infants found under the floor when a nunnery was torn down. Unhappily, Klan propagandists could also find real ammunition by looking back far enough in history. The Borgias were an endless mine of material, and their exploits came to be as familiar to readers of the Klan press as the lives of soap-opera characters are to modern housewives. Constant readers must, after a time, have begun to think of them as The Typical Catholic Family of the Renaissance.

Thus the Catholic Church very easily assumed, in the minds of the ignorant majority, the proportions of a vast, immoral, foreign conspiracy against Protestant America, with no less a design than to put the Pope in the White House. The Knights of Columbus were in reality a secret army pledged to this aim. They kept their guns in the basements of Catholic churches—which usually had high steeples and often were located on the highest ground in town, so that guns fired from the belfries could dominate the streets. Not all Catholics were in on the plot: for example, the Catholics you knew. These were well-meaning dupes whom one might hope to save from their blindness. My parents were generally considered to be among them. My mother's friend, Mrs. Wilson, would come often and, in a high-strung and urgent manner, try to argue the thing out. Against my mother's gentle insistences to the contrary, she would usually end up by declaring, "Now I want to tell *you*, honey! As sure as you're born, the Pope is coming over here with his shirttail aflyin'!"

Mrs. Wilson was not a completely reliable witness, since she had also once had a vision of Jesus standing on the steps of the Baptist church. But the mass acceptance of this idea was shown one day at the little town of North Manchester, Indiana, when the rumor spread that the Pope was finally pulling into town on the south-bound from Chicago to take over. A mob formed and stormed the train. To their mixed disappointment and relief, all they found on the lone day coach was a traveling salesman who was able to give satisfactory evidence that he was not the Pope in disguise.

Kokomo first began to hear about the Klan in 1920. In 1921 the local Nathan Hale Den was established, and within two years the town had become so Klannish as to be given the honor of being host city for the tri-state Konklave. (Of course its name helped: the Klan loved alliterative K's.) Literally half the town belonged to the Klan when I was a boy. At its peak, which was from 1923 through 1925, the Nathan Hale Den had about five thousand members, out of an able-bodied adult population of ten thousand. With this strength, the Klan was able to dominate local politics. In 1924 it elected the mayor, a dapper character named Silcott E. "Silk" Spurgeon, a former clothing salesman, and swept the lists for city councilmen. It packed the police and fire departments with its own people, with the result that on parade nights the traffic patrolmen disappeared, and traffic control was taken over by sheeted figures whose size and shape resembled those of the vanished patrolmen. It ran the town openly and insolently.

As in most of the thousands of other towns where the Klan thrived, there was a strong undercurrent of opposition. But as in most towns, few men were brave enough to state their disapproval openly. The Klan first appealed to the ignorant, the slightly unbalanced, and the venal; but by the time the enlightened elements realized the danger, it was already on top of them. Once organized in strength, the Klan had an irresistible weapon in economic boycott. The anti-Klan merchant saw his trade fade away to the Klan store across the street, where the store window carried a "TWK" (Trade with Klansmen) sign. The non-Klan insurance salesman hadn't a chance against the fraternal advantage of one who doubled in the evenings as a Kladd, Night-hawk, or Fury. It takes great courage to sacrifice a life's work for a principle.

It also takes moral conviction—and it is difficult to arrive at such conviction when the pastor of one's own church openly or tacitly takes an opposite stand. Kokomo's ministers, like her merchants and in-surance men, swung with the tide. Most of them, in fact, took little or no swinging, since they saw in the Klan what it professed to be: the militant arm of evangelical Protestantism. There were a few holdouts, but they remained silent; and their silence was filled by the loud ex-hortations of others such as the Reverend Everett Nixon, Klan chaplain and Klan-sponsored city councilman, and the Reverend P. E. Green-walt, of the South Main Street Methodist Church, who whipped a homemade Klan flag from his pocket as he reached the climax of his baccalaureate sermon at the high-school graduation exercises. Other ministers, while less fanatic, were perhaps no less sure that the Klan was doing God's work. They found that it stimulated church attend-ance, with a consequent and agreeable rise in collections. They found their churches visited in rotation by a Klan "team" which would appear at the door unexpectedly, stride up the aisle with Klan and

American flags flying, deposit a money offering at the foot of the pulpit, and silently depart. Generally, while this was going on, the ministers would find it in their consciences to ask the choir to sing "Onward, Christian Soldiers."

And so it went in Kokomo and in its equivalents all over the Middle West and South. The Klan made less headway in the big cities, with their strong foreign, Catholic, Negro, and Jewish populations, but from the middle-sized cities down to the country villages it soon had partial or full control of politics and commerce. Indianapolis, with a population of some two hundred thousand, was dominated almost as completely as Kokomo. D. C. Stephenson, the Grand Dragon, had his headquarters there, in a suite of offices in a downtown business building, and from there he ran the state government. "I am the law in Indiana," he said, and there was no doubt about it. He owned the legislature; he owned the Governor, a political hack named Ed Jackson; he owned most of the Representatives and both United States Senators. The Junior Senator was Arthur Robinson, a dark, thin-faced man with the eyes of a zealot and the instincts of a Torquemada. The Senior Senator was genial Jim Watson, who had his own powerful machine within the Republican party. Watson was the arch type of the cartoon politician: big, paunchy, profane, and opportunistic. He thought that he could control the Klan for his own ends, joined up, and shortly found himself swallowed by the new machine.

4.

STEPHENSON in turn took his orders, after a fashion, from Atlanta, Georgia, where Dr. Evans presided over the Invisible Empire from a sumptuous Imperial Palace on fashionable Peachtree Road. Dr. Evans was a dentist by trade and an Imperial Wizard by usurpation. He had unhorsed the previous Wizard and founder, "Colonel" William Joseph Simmons, several months before the Kokomo Konklave. It was in Kokomo, incidentally, that Evans made his first Imperial appearance before a really large Klan audience, thus giving that event an extra significance for history, since it was during his Reign that the Klan was to have its greatest triumphs and sink finally almost to its nadir.

However, in understanding the place of the Klan in American life, Dr. Evans' significance is less than "Colonel" Simmons'. Evans was shrewd, aggressive, and a good administrator, but he stepped into a going concern. The concern existed because of Simmons. And it was going not through the efforts of either Evans or Simmons but those of an obscure couple named Edward Young Clark and Mrs. Elizabeth Tyler.

The tangled story of the Klan's twentieth-century rebirth opens officially in 1915, but stems back to a day in 1901 when Simmons was sitting on a bench outside his home. The future Emperor at that time was a preacher, but wasn't doing very well at it. As he sat gazing into the sky, watching the wind drive masses of cumulus clouds along, he noticed an interesting formation. As he watched, it split into two billowy lengths, and these in turn broke up into smaller clouds that followed one another in a procession across the sky. Simmons took the phenomenon as a sign from God, and fell to his knees with a prayer.

A devotee of Southern history, Simmons was even more familiar than most Southerners with the legends of the old Ku Klux Klan. Founded in 1866 in Pulaski, Tennessee, by a group of young Confederate troopers home from the war and with time heavy on their hands, it had started out simply as a social club—a device, significantly enough, to recapture some of the lost wartime excitement and comradeship. The young ex-soldiers picked their name from *Kuklos,* the Greek word for "circle," which they transformed to Ku Klux, and framed a fantastic ritual and nomenclature for their own amusement. The idea spread, and as it spread it found a serious purpose in restoring the South to home rule. Eventually the best manhood (and much of the worst) of the South took part, with General Nathan Bedford Forrest as Imperial Wizard. Finally it degenerated into mere terrorism, and General Forrest disbanded it in 1869, but not until the Carpetbaggers had been dispersed and the Klan had become immortalized in Southern memory. It was the old Klan that the convulsed mind of Reverend Simmons saw in the clouds.

Since he had been a boy, he later recalled, he had been dreaming of organizing real Americans into an army of salvation. His cloudy vision told him what form it should take. But it was not until 1915 that he felt prepared for the great task. Meantime he carried on as a preacher, as an instructor in history at Lanier University, a dubious little enterprise that later became the official Klan university, and latterly as an itinerant organizer for the Modern Woodmen of the World. Then, on Thanksgiving night, 1915, he led a troupe of sixteen followers up Stone Mountain near Atlanta and there, "on the top of a mountain at the midnight hour while men braved the surging blasts of wild wintry mountain winds and endured temperatures far below freezing [The temperature was forty-five degrees.—R. C.], bathed in the sacred glow of the fiery cross, the Invisible Empire was called from its slumber of half a century."

What Simmons called forth was not the old Klan, however, but a greatly distorted image of it. For all its excesses, the original Klan had some constructive purposes. Its prescript shows that it was devoted to restoring Constitutional rights to white Southerners, to the protection of Southern womanhood, and to the re-establishment of home rule. It operated in secrecy for the good reason that its members would have been shot or imprisoned by federal troops had they been found out.

The new Klan adopted the costume, the secrecy, and much of the ritual of the old, but very little of the substance. Its purposes are indicated in the Kloran, or book of rules and rituals:

1. Is the motive prompting your ambition to be a Klansman serious and unselfish?

2. Are you a native born, white, gentile American?

3. Are you absolutely opposed to and free of any allegiance of any nature to any cause, government, people, sect, or ruler that is foreign to the United States of America?

4. Do you believe in the tenets of the Christian religion?

5. Do you esteem the United States of America and its institutions above all other government, civil, political, or ecclesiastical, in the whole world?

6. Will you, without mental reservation, take a solemn oath to defend, preserve, and enforce same?

7. Do you believe in clannishness, and will you faithfully practice same toward Klansmen?

8. Do you believe in and will you faithfully strive for the eternal maintenance of white supremacy?

9. Will you faithfully obey our constitution and laws, and conform willingly to all our usages, requirements, and regulations?

10. Can you always be depended on?

Only in "white supremacy" did the aims of the old and new Klans coincide, aside from the banalities about unselfishness, patriotism, and dependability. By questions 2 and 3 Simmons excluded foreigners, Jews, and Catholics, all of whom had been accepted into the original Klan, and thereby set his course in an altogether new direction.

While appropriating much of the ritual of the original, Simmons also added some mumbo-jumbo of his own. The old plus the new enveloped his converts in a weird and unintelligible system of cere-monies, signs, signals, and words. The Klan had its own calendar, so that July 4, 1923, for example, became "The Dismal Day of the Weeping Week of the Hideous Month of the year of the Klan LVII." The local "dens" were governed by an "Exalted Cyclops," a "Klaliff," "Klokard," "Kludd," "Kligrapp," "Klabee," "Kladd," "Klagaro," "Klexter," "Klokann," and "Nighthawk," corresponding respectively to president, vice-president, lecturer, chaplain, secretary, treasurer, conductor, inner guard, outer guard, investigating committee, and proctor in charge of candidates. The Klansmen sang "klodes," held "klonvocations," swore blood oaths, burned crosses, muttered pass-words ("Kotop," to which the reply was "Potok," both meaning nothing), and carried on "klonversations." The latter were an exchange of code words formed from the first letters of sentences.

Ayak	Are you a Klansman?
Akia	A Klansman I am.
Capowe	Countersign and password or written evidence.
Cygnar	Can you give number and realm?
No. 1 Atga	Number one Klan of Atlanta, Georgia.
Kigy	Klansman, I greet you.
Itsub	In the sacred, unfailing bond.

They would then *Klasp* left hands (Klan loyalty a Sacred Principle). If a known non-member approached at this fraternal moment, the one who spied him first would break off the klonversation with a warning, *"Sanbog."* (Strangers are near. Be on guard!)

Non-members were "aliens," and remained so until they were "baptized" as "citizens of the Invisible Empire," whereupon they received the "Mioak," or Mystical Insignia of a Klansman, a little red celluloid button bearing the inscrutable words "Kotop" and "Potok." Having taken the sacred oath, the new member was reminded by the Exalted Cyclops that "Mortal man cannot assume a more binding oath; character and courage alone will enable you to keep it. Always remember that to keep this oath means to you honor, happiness, and life; but to violate it means disgrace, dishonor, and *death*. May happiness, honor, and life be yours." The member's subsequent duties included absolute obedience to the Imperial Wizard, who was described in the Kloran as "The Emperor of the Invisible Empire, a wise man, a wonder worker, having power to charm and control."

Thus equipped, the Reverend Simmons set about creating his Empire. It was uphill work, however. Five years later he had enrolled only a few thousand subjects. The times, perhaps, were not quite right, but in addition the Emperor himself lacked two mundane qualities—executive ability and calculating greed. Both of these lacks were supplied in the spring of 1920, when he met Mr. Clark and Mrs. Tyler.

This couple were professional fund raisers and publicity agents whose accounts had included the Anti-Saloon League, Near East Relief, the Roosevelt Memorial Fund, and others of similar scope. Simmons' Ku Klux Klan was almost too small to be worth their attention, but they decided that it had possibilities. As Southerners, they saw in the anti-foreign, Catholic, Jewish, Negro provisions the raw material with which to appeal to four deep prejudices among other Southerners. After they took the project on Clark became King Kleagle, or second in command, and head of the promotion department, and Mrs. Tyler became his chief assistant. Simmons was left in the misty heights as Imperial Wizard and Emperor, where he was happy. Thereafter, between them, Clark and Mrs. Tyler systematized the appeals to racial and religious hatred and organized the sale of Klan memberships on a businesslike basis.

They divided the country into eight "domains," each headed by a Grand Goblin, and subdivided it into "realms," or states, each in charge of a Grand Dragon, such as Stephenson. The initiation fee was $10 of which $4 went to the Kleagle, or local solicitor, when he signed up a recruit, $1 to the King Kleagle, the state sales manager, 50 cents to the Grand Goblin, and $4.50 to Atlanta. Robes, which were made by the affiliated Gate City Manufacturing Company at a cost of $3.28, were sold for $6.50. Newspapers, magazines, Klorans, and other Klan printed matter was turned out at a substantial profit by the Searchlight Publishing Company, another Klan enterprise, and miscellaneous real estate was handled by the Clark Realty Company. The local Klaverns were supported by dues of a dollar a month, part of which was sent to the state organization. It was somewhat like a chain letter; almost everyone seemed guaranteed to make money.

Within a year and a half, this system had netted more than a hundred thousand members. It had also, according to the New York *World,* caused four killings, one mutilation, one branding with acid, forty-one floggings, twenty-seven tar-and-feather parties, five kidnapings, and forty-three threats and warnings to leave town. The *World's* exposé pricked Congress into an investigation in October, 1921. Emperor Simmons was called, but proved to be a slippery witness. The atrocities ascribed to the Klan were, he said, the work of imposters. The Klan did not permit violence, he assured the Congressmen, and cited instances wherein he had rebuked dens which disobeyed this rule by withdrawing their charters. The Klan was "purely a fraternal organization," dedicated to patriotism, brotherhood, and maintenance of law and order. Although circumstantial evidence was strong, the investigators could find no legal evidence that the Klan's national organization had caused the outrages or even approved of them, and the inquiry petered out.

However, the *World's* detective work did have one notable result. Shortly before the Congressional investigation got under way, the paper printed an account of how, two years before, Clark and Mrs. Tyler had been "arrested at midnight in their sleeping garments, in a notorious underworld resort at 185 South Pryor Street, Atlanta, run by Mrs. Tyler," and hauled off to jail, to be charged with "disorderly conduct" and possession of liquor. In the resultant furor Clark submitted his resignation to Simmons, which inspired Mrs. Tyler to issue a statement calling him "a weak-kneed quitter" and repudiating him. Simmons, who was well aware of what the couple had accomplished for the Klan, refused to take action against them. Instead, the propaganda department began to grind out denials, the *World* was branded as a "cowardly and infamous instrument of murder . . . against fair woman!" and the scandal was smoothed over.

But it left a scar. As the moral custodians of their communities, the rank-and-file Klansmen were deeply shocked by the story. Some of them were not convinced by the denials. Along with the evidence presented during the Congressional hearing, it gradually fermented into a basis for an insurgent movement within the ranks. This faction grew under the loving eye of Dr. Evans, who had deserted dentistry to become Grand Dragon of the Realm of Texas, and who had ambitions to the throne. In May, 1922, he became Kligrapp, or secretary, of the national organization, and from that vantage point accomplished a *coup d'état* the following Thanksgiving. With twelve of the fourteen members of the board of directors joining the cabal, he detached the Wizardship and all the real power from Simmons and took them himself, leaving Simmons only the cold comfort of a thousand dollars a month salary and a simple Emperorship. Simmons fought back energetically, and as a consequence, the following year, lost even this sop. "He Who Traversed the Realm of the Unknown, Wrested the Solemn Secret from the Grasp of Night, and Became the Sovereign Imperial Master of the Great Lost Mystery"—was out.

"I was in Gethsemane," Simmons wrote later, "and the gloom of its dense darkness entombed me; the cup which I drank surpassed bitterest gall, and my sweat was the sweat of blood; the hour of my crucifixion was at hand." He beckoned after his seduced flock: "Come unto ME all you who yearn and labor after Klankraft and I will give you rest. Take my program upon you and learn of me, for I am unselfish and true at heart. . . . I am the one custodian and sole Master of the sublime Mystery." But it was no use. Foxy Dr. Evans had stolen the show, and the ex-Emperor had to be content with a final cash settlement of ninety thousand dollars. He set about organizing a rival enterprise called the "Knights of the Flaming Sword," but was unsuccessful. In the mid-thirties he tried again with "The White Band," also a revival of a post-Civil War vigilante group, but had no better luck. He died in May, 1945, poor and disillusioned.

In spite of the shock of the Clark-Tyler case, the *World's* disclosures, and the Congressional investigation, the Klan continued to grow. It filled urgent needs in the contemporary psyche, and it was manifestly a good thing commercially. By the time Dr. Evans took over, it was adding thirty-five hundred members a day, and the national treasury was taking in forty-five thousand dollars a day. Within a year Evans could boast, probably with fair accuracy, of a membership of five million. Being in possession of that many adult voters, he and his henchmen naturally turned their thoughts to politics. Principles, they announced, were important to the Klan, not party labels; and accordingly the state and local organizations adopted whichever of the two major parties was stronger in its region. In the South, the Klan was Democratic, in the North, Republican. But since the Republicans were dominant nationally, both the arithmetic of membership and the ends of expediency dictated a stronger drive within that party. But 1924 was a poor year to interfere in Republican affairs. Calvin Coolidge was not only an extremely popular President, but represented in his person many of the parochial virtues that the Klan endorsed, and there was no point in contesting or even trying to bargain over his nomination. The Democratic convention was much more promising. The strongest candidate was Alfred E. Smith, Catholic, Tammany, wet, and a big-city product—in short, a symbol of everything the Klan was against. The Klan came out fighting for William Gibbs McAdoo and managed to split and stalemate the whole proceedings. It finally lost, but it also prevented Smith's nomination; and after many angry hours and smoke-filled meetings John W. Davis, a J. P. Morgan lawyer, was served up as a compromise. The Harding scandals were fresh in the minds of everyone, and 1924 logically should have been a Democratic year, but Davis lost. Considering later events, it is easy to speculate that the Klan's battle in the 1924 Democratic convention was a decisive event in United States and world history.

For Dr. Evans and his Goblins and Dragons it was an encouraging show of strength, despite their failure to nominate their man. They looked forward to 1928. Then, suddenly, there was a disaster. D. C. Stephenson, the Grandest Dragon of the Empire, made a mistake.

5.

"STEVE"—as he was usually known—kept a bust of Napoleon on his desk. And like Napoleon, he knew what he wanted. He wanted money and women and power, and later on he wanted to be President of the United States. He got plenty of the first three, and he might have got the fourth. He was a prodigy; he was at the height of his career when he was thirty-three years old. But he looked ten years older, and he encouraged his followers to refer to him as "the old man." He had a fleshy, handsome face, with blond hair, thin eyebrows, a small mouth, and small, shrewd eyes. He could be as hearty as a country drummer, and as cold as a hangman. He preached righteousness, but he was over-sexed and he drank too much. He was vain, but beyond vanity he had certainty. He could command; his orders were obeyed; he exuded power. He understood the average man.

Not much is known about his early life. He was born in 1891, evidently in Texas, and spent part of his youth in Oklahoma. He was a second lieutenant in World War I but saw no service overseas. He was married twice, but had divorced or abandoned both women by the time he moved to Evansville, Indiana, shortly after the war. There he began organizing veterans, and this took him into politics. In 1920 he entered the Democratic Congressional primary as a wet. Defeated by the Anti-Saloon League, he promptly became a dry Republican and at the same time joined the newly rising Ku Klux Klan. He became an organizer for the Klan. By 1922 he had succeeded so well that he was made organizer for the State of Indiana, and shortly afterward for twenty other states, mostly Midwestern. After a short period in Columbus, Ohio, he moved his offices to Indianapolis, and on July 4, 1923, at Kokomo he officially added the Grand Dragonship of Indiana to his portfolio. By that time he was well on his way to his first million dollars.

Within a year or so he had passed far beyond that goal. He branched out into the coal and gravel business, the tailoring business, and various other sidelines. He imported Florida real-estate salesmen and other high-pressure operators to carry Klankraft into the towns and up and down the country roads, and arranged a split with these sub-salesmen. In one eighteen-month period his personal income is estimated to have been between two and five millions. He owned one of the showplace homes of suburban Irvington, maintained a suite of rooms at a big hotel, kept a fleet of automobiles, a covey of bodyguards, and a yacht in Lake Michigan. He knew many women, and had a way with most of them.

One of the women he knew, but not very well, was Madge Oberholzer. She had a small job at the State House in the office of the State Superintendent of Public Instruction. She was not particularly attractive. Unmarried at twenty-eight, which in Indiana means ripe spinsterhood, she was a buxom 145 pounds, had a rather long nose, and wore her hair in an exaggerated upsweep that hung over her forehead. But for some reason Steve, whose taste usually ran to ripe beauties, was interested in Madge. He took her to several parties, and once, when the legislature was considering a bill that would have abolished her state job, he gallantly killed it for her.

On the night of March 15, 1925, Madge came home about ten o'clock from a date with another man. Steve had been telephoning, and when she called him back he told her he was going to Chicago and wanted her to come and see him on an important matter before he left. He would send Earl Gentry, one of his bodyguards, to escort her.

She found Steve drinking when she arrived at his home, and according to her later testimony he "forced" her to drink with him. Three drinks later he asked her to go along to Chicago. When she refused, Steve motioned to Gentry and Earl Klenck, another bodyguard, who produced guns; the three men then led her outside and into Steve's waiting car. They drove to the railroad station and boarded the midnight train to Chicago. Steve, Gentry, and Madge went into a drawing room. Gentry climbed into an upper berth and Steve shoved Madge into the lower. "After the train started," her testimony says, "Stephenson got in with me and attacked me. He held me so I could not move.

I . . . do not remember all that happened. . . . He . . . mutilated
me. . . ."

The next day in Hammond, Indiana, where Steve had the presence
of mind to get off the train to avoid the Mann Act, Madge managed
on a pretext to get hold of some bichloride-of-mercury tablets. She
swallowed six of them. By the time Steve discovered what she had done
she was deathly ill. Steve tried to get her to a hospital, then offered to
marry her, and finally drove her back to Indianapolis. He kept her in
a loft above his garage with the threat that she would stay there until
she agreed to marriage. She still refused and finally he had her taken
to her home, where she died several weeks later. Before her death she
dictated the full story to the prosecuting attorney, William H. Remy,
who was one of the few officials of Marion County that Steve did not
control.

The case caused an unimaginable uproar. Steve, who had said, "I am
the law," was calm and confident, but he took the precaution of having
the trial venued to the little town of Noblesville. A quarrel with Evans
had created factionalism in his Indianapolis stronghold, and he was
afraid of being double-crossed there. But to his shock and dismay, the
Noblesville jury found him guilty of murder in the second degree, and
the judge sentenced him to life imprisonment.

To his further shock, Governor Ed Jackson refused to pardon him.
The case had created such a bad smell that not only Jackson but nearly
all of Steve's other political allies abandoned him. Steve threatened
to bring out the "little black box" containing his records; when finally
produced, the box's contents sent a Congressman, the Mayor of Indianapolis, the Sheriff of Marion County, and various other officials to jail.
Jackson was indicted for bribery but was saved by the statute of limitations. But although Steve got his revenge, he did not get his liberty. He
tried every kind of threat and legal dodge, but every one failed. Years
later, when he had served enough time with good behavior to come
up for parole, public feeling against him was still so strong that no
governor would take the responsibility of releasing him. He stayed in
prison, in effect a political prisoner.

Steve's crude mistake was a disaster for the Klan not only in Indiana
but everywhere. His trial was a national sensation, and his conviction

was a national indictment of the organization. It became too absurd and ironic for any Goblin or Dragon to proselytize in the name of morality. The Bible Belt might dismiss the Clark-Tyler episode as malicious gossip, but it could hardly dismiss the legal conviction of one who was probably the Klan's most powerful local leader. The Klan began to break up rapidly, leaving political chaos in its wake. In Indiana, the Democratic boss, Frank P. Baker, said, "We don't want the poisonous animal to crawl into our yard and die." The Republicans earnestly disclaimed any relationship with the Klan.

The Klan tried just as eagerly to disassociate itself from Stephenson. It had nominal grounds for doing so, since Steve's differences with Evans had caused him to be read out of the organization some months before. In reply, however, Steve had merely declared his independence of Atlanta and had carried on in his own Realm with no diminution of power. The general public knew and cared little about this internal squabble. The label of "Stephensonism" was applied to the Klan as a whole, and it stuck.

The Klan died hard, however. It took a new grip on life in 1927-28, with the nomination of Al Smith again in prospect, and the old cries of "Keep the Pope out of the White House!" were heard again. Although it could not prevent Smith's nomination this time, the new wave of religious prejudice it stirred up, and the backwash of intolerance it had created in the years before, were important factors in defeating Smith for the Presidency. Thereafter it subsided again, and by the end of the decade it had only a tiny fraction of its former strength. Here and there, during the next years, one heard of it: a whipping, a castration, a cross burning. The propaganda line changed with the times. During the thirties, emphasis switched from Catholics, Negroes, Jews, and foreigners to Communism and "labor agitators." It was an unrewarding strategy, for although it may have gained contributions for employers, especially in the South, it won back few members.

The crowning irony came in 1935 when the Imperial Palace, after passing through the hands of ten owners, was finally bought for $32,500 by the Savannah-Atlanta diocese of the Catholic Church as the site for a new cathedral. Two years later at the cathedral's consecration Dr.

Evans, as a token of the spirit of tolerance of the "new Klan," posed in a friendly attitude with the Bishop G. P. A. O'Hara. This was too much for the remaining brothers. In 1939 there was another revolution from below, and Evans was disposed of in favor of Dr. James A. Colescott, a former veterinarian of Terre Haute, Indiana, and latterly Grand Dragon of the Realm of Ohio. In 1944, Dr. Colescott voluntarily returned to doctoring animals, which give him a better living, and the Klan was disbanded as a national organization. It survives under a system of state autonomy, but has no appreciable strength in any state with the possible exceptions of Georgia and Florida. There may be a few thousand members in the entire country.

6.

AND TODAY, in Kokomo, the Klan is only an old memory. The Reverend Everett Nixon carried on for years as Secretary of the Melfalfa Park Association, trying to hold together the property and few believers. But he failed, and now the park is overgrown with brush, deserted and decayed, its sagging pavilion a meeting place for bats and owls. Steve, who had his greatest moment there, is still in the state penitentiary at Michigan City, still hoping. Not long ago he made his fortieth unsuccessful petition for freedom. The accounts of his triumphs and his trial are embalmed in the brittle files of the Kokomo *Tribune* and *Dispatch*, along with the Nell Brinkley Girl and ads for the Apperson Jackrabbit. It all seems a long time ago.

Yet it was only a generation ago—time for the children who marched in the big parade, and who were held on their fathers' shoulders to see Steve's dramatic landing near Melfalfa Park, to grow up and have small children of their own. Like its population, the town seems substantially changed, with its new store fronts, its better paving, and its night-time neon glow. But in many, deeper ways, both the people and the town are much the same. And 1949 is not unlike 1920.

In his book, *The Ku Klux Klan,* James Moffatt Mecklin observes:

What impresses the student of the Klan movement at every stage is the lack, on the part of the average American, of any real insight into its significance.

Not man's innate depravity, not overt criminal acts, nor yet wicked attempts to subvert American institutions, but rather plain old-fashioned ignorance is the real enemy of the huge giant, the public, who is still the fumbling physician of our social ills.

When a new bogey appears on Main Street to take the place of the Pope, and a new organization arises to take the place of the Klan, one can only hope that the new generation will turn out to be less ignorant than the old.

Calvin Coolidge:
A Study in Inertia

BY IRVING STONE

Irving Stone was born in California in 1903 and had a varied experience as fruit picker, saxophone player, and boxer before he became a teacher of economics at the University of California. In 1934 he published *Lust for Life,* a vivid and sensationally successful biographical novel about the Dutch painter Vincent van Gogh. Since then he has made a great deal of history come to life in his books on Jack London (*Sailor on Horseback*), *Clarence Darrow for the Defense,* Jessie Fremont (*Immortal Wife*), and Eugene V. Debs (*Adversary in the House*). He lives in Beverly Hills with his wife and two children. In 1943 he published *They Also Ran,* an interesting study of the men who ran for President and were defeated. He concluded that many of the also-rans should have won, and that many of the winners should have been beaten. The 1924 presidential race between Calvin Coolidge and John W. Davis was one of the most exciting and ironic in the book.

☼ 1.

CALVIN COOLIDGE believed that the least government was the best government; he aspired to become the least President the country had ever had; he attained his desire.

By forcing government to lie supine he paved the way for a world depression which led blocks of nations to demand a form of government which would control everything. His lust for nihilism in administration made *laissez faire* seem a plan for dynamic action; he was as responsible as any individual of his age for the socialist revolution now sweeping over Europe and Asia.

In the White House he napped each afternoon through one of the most danger-fraught periods in modern history. By the very act of sleeping with his feet up on the desk he sincerely believed he was making his most valuable contribution to the American way of life: keeping the federal agencies from doing anything which he might have been obliged to permit them to do had he remained awake.

The Washington Monument pierces five hundred and fifty-five feet into the sky to symbolize the greatness of George Washington's contribution to his country; Calvin Coolidge's monument could be a hole dug straight down into the ground to commemorate all the things he failed to do for his country; a railing should be built around this monument to protect the beholder from vertigo.

He was an incorruptible man; all of his sins were sins of omission. He was a living symbol of Yankee frugality, known and trusted in the remotest corner of America. At the height of the pre-1929 stock market hysteria, when the Federal Reserve Board and nearly every economist in Washington implored the President to tighten the money market and avert the imminent crash, Coolidge issued instead a statement that the four billion dollars in brokers' loans was not too much, and that "the increase represented a natural expansion of business in the security market."

Down from his native hills of Vermont, up from the cattle ranges of Texas, out of the green fields of Kansas and the white cotton fields of Alabama, out of the factories of Detroit and the markets of Seattle poured the last of the hard-earned savings of a lifetime, of generations past, to be thrown into the bottomless pit of the stock market, leading the peoples of America directly to the loss of their homes, their farms, their shops, their jobs, their food, their physical and mental health, their confidence in their country and its democratic form of government.

Coolidge represented the residual mind of America, everything it had been and so little of what it was becoming; the fragmentary man who cared nothing for music, poetry, painting or sculpture, the drama, architecture or the ballet, for the amiabilities of social intercourse. Under his influence the ticker tapes exulted at an ever-accelerating pace while the fruits of the intellect withered. To Europe, to South America, and to the Orient we exported not our art but the products of our juvenilia and materialism.

On the afternoon of the day that Treasury Department officials laid on Calvin Coolidge's desk the documented case for immediate and drastic control of the investment market, and he turned them away, defeated by his icy silence, he went down into the basement of the White House to count the number of apples in a barrel sent him by a friend in Vermont.

While Rome burned, Nero at least made music. But President Coolidge counted apples.

In his native Vermont, politics had been an adjunct of business. His forebears had been farmers and shopkeepers at the same time that they held political office. Calvin maintained the family tradition by transferring the seat of power from the White House across Pennsylvania Avenue to the United States Chamber of Commerce. The President's initials and those of the Chamber of Commerce were the same: the two bodies became identical.

After the raucous depredations of the Harding freebooters, Coolidge restored to the people their faith in the personal honesty of their government. Yet Harding's Ohio Gang, operating from the Little Green House on K Street, took in only hundreds of thousands of dollars from "bootleggers, illegal concessions, pardons, paroles, privileges, and general graft." Coolidge's Secretary of the Treasury, Andrew Mellon, realized a profit on the stock market estimated at *three billions!* Coolidge was the most rigorously economical head the Federal Government had known for decades; this thrifty concept of government saved the taxpayers thousands of dollars; his categorical refusal to govern cost them their shirts.

Words with Calvin Coolidge were not a free medium of exchange. They were a rare and precious commodity to be spent only for the world's goods. Very early he cut the umbilical cord between thought and speech. Yet at the end of his life he was lured into loquacity, writing for seventy-five thousand dollars one of the dreariest concoctions of Sunday-school banalities ever put out by a professional publisher. Mr. Coolidge should have protected his life-long investment in silence.

He was the epitome of the joyless soul, with so little need for human warmth or communication that he couldn't envisage this need in others. When reproached for not giving any part of himself to old and trusted friends, he would cry, "But what do they want of me?" When he was five years old he underwent hours of torture before he could force himself to go through the kitchen in which his mother was entertaining friends; fifty-one years later, when he was leaving the White House, he slipped ignominiously out the back way rather than go through the ordeal of saying good-by to the staff that had served him for five years.

He was the easiest President in American history to lampoon, satirize, caricature; yet this external approach missed the inner truth of the man: both for himself and for the nation he was a tragic figure, born with an organic personality dyspepsia. There was tragedy written across his twisted face, and shortly after he left office there was tragedy written across the twisted, starving face of the nation.

The twentieth century in which he did his work was never quite as astonished at having this atavar in its midst as he was at being there. His earliest biographer comments that whenever Coolidge opened his mouth to speak, a moth flew out. But the real reason that Coolidge spoke so rarely is that he was too astounded for words: the only thing he could have said which would have adequately expressed his feelings was, "What are all you people doing here a couple of hundred years before your time?"

By what twist of fate did Calvin Coolidge, vestigial remnant of the eighteenth century, help plunge the world into a revolution apparently not scheduled in history's notebook until the twenty-first century?

2.

CALVIN was born on a Vermont farm which had been cut out of the wilderness by his forebears and worked by five generations of Coolidges. Throughout his life ran his love for the green hills and the stony earth of Vermont. He disliked cities, distrusted cosmopolitan people, and spoke contemptuously of "the affectations of the drawing room," by which he meant even the mildest form of social intercourse.

The Coolidges always had been among the most important men in their community: hard-working, resourceful farmers, mayors, aldermen, and sheriffs. Both Calvin's father and grandfather were fiercely silent and economical by nature, yet Calvin so outdid them that they were moved to oratorical lengths to comment, "He ain't gabby." Nor would Calvin do any of the other things that normal children did: play games, laugh, chat, spend a penny now and then for candy or ice cream. So economical was he that he would go down in history as the only President to save a small fortune while in the White House.

There were two soft but brief influences in Calvin's childhood: his mother and his sister. His mother became bedridden after his birth, and died when he was twelve; his warm-hearted and spontaneous sister, whom he adored, died from a burst appendix five years later. He never recovered from the loss of these two gentle women; fear of death lay permanently behind his small, chill eyes. Coolidge said admiringly of his mother, "There was a touch of mysticism and poetry in her nature." Yet all his life he fought a grim battle to put down in himself and discourage in others the slightest suspicion of mysticism or poetry. His grandmother forbade him to dance, and all his life Calvin thought that fun, joy, and sin were three-letter synonyms.

The one great passion of Coolidge's life was politics. During his childhood he drove about the countryside in his father's buggy while the elder Coolidge collected the county's taxes; he attended meetings of the citizenry at which those taxes were set and political officers were elected; he listened to his grandfather and father hear cases as justices of the peace. He was raised in the magnificent tradition of New England's town-hall government, probably the most successful form of democracy ever practiced; thus he grew up with a belief in politics as an honorable and valuable form of service.

Calvin went to the one-room stone schoolhouse in Plymouth, and after school hours and on week ends he did chores around the farm: splitting wood, milking cows, feeding the chickens and pigs, plowing behind a team of oxen. His father was a stern disciplinarian; Calvin was known to get out of his bed on a wintry night to take care of some duty he had neglected, rather than face his father's wrath the next morning. Yet the father's undemonstrative love was even greater than his sense of rigidly Puritan discipline. When Calvin had exhausted the facilities of the Plymouth school, his father sent him to the Academy at Ludlow, where he lived and studied for the next six years. The fact that John Coolidge was willing to spend what must have seemed a formidable sum of money was indicative of his desire that his boy rise in the world; and we have a picture of the father driving the twelve miles down the rough mountainside in a farm wagon to bring his son home for week ends.

In the Academy at Ludlow, Calvin was quiet, mildly studious, enjoyed books on politics, history, and forensics. Occasionally he worked of a Saturday in a toy factory in Plymouth; these few hours constituted the only intimate contact of his lifetime with industrial workers.

The pattern of his following years at Amherst College was prophetic of his next three decades. He entered as a callow, graceless youth and emerged four years later with the respect of his class and the friendship of such discerning students of human nature as Dwight Morrow. From the first class meeting he sat for hours in tombstone silence, sat through its political organization and committee meetings, doing nothing, contributing nothing except the support of his bodily presence; yet at the end of four years he was considered the class political organizer. The feat of young Calvin, who made other New Englanders appear talkative, emerging as the class orator only seemed a contradiction: he did not believe in spending words in idle pleasantries, but he cannily endorsed the use of words in political speeches because those speeches might serve a valuable purpose. In this lies the explanation of the most silent man of his age making the Fourth of July speech in his home town of Plymouth at the age of eighteen, and spending considerable time on a theme which showed the relation between oratory and history.

Calvin left Amherst with a diploma and three segments of pragmatic wisdom: first, that if he sat clear through every last political meeting he would eventually find his place in the organization; second, that he didn't have to mix socially with the men around him for his contemporaries eventually to grow to like him; and third, that if one did not try to interfere with the moral laws of the universe, which were good and enduring, everything would work out extremely well.

He had already decided that he would become a lawyer. When Dwight Morrow asked him where he was going to practice, Coolidge drawled, "Northampton is the nearest courthouse." This was his approach to life; it was not merely his speech which was laconic.

He was twenty-two when he reached Northampton, with the medium

height and wiry figure of an Indian—and Calvin was very proud of
the touch of Indian blood in the Coolidge family. His hair was a carroty
red, his features sharp, his skin pale with big freckles, his mouth thin,
and his blue eyes uncommunicative though not unkindly. In all ways
he was the essence of the prudent man, walking with "short quick
steps, his slightly rigid body giving him a rather prissy gait." His face
was expressionless, and no man ever boasted that he knew whether
Calvin Coolidge was happy or miserable. His friends of this period
said of him that "his expression remained as blithe as a mourning
card"; that he was a "sharp-nosed repository of an infinite and chilling
silence, but dependable"; and that "he was as expansive as a letter box:
anything said to him was received with a click but practically nothing
came out." His voice was a high, twangy, unmusical New England
drawl.

He secured his opportunity to read law in the Northampton firm of
Hammond and Field through a sardonic misapprehension: Judge Field
had heard Calvin give his class oration a few months before, and had
laughed at Coolidge's satiric quips at his classmates. He agreed to let
Coolidge come into his office because, as he said, "I liked to laugh and
Calvin Coolidge was very funny." A few months later someone in
Field's firm described him as "a cold and errant draft about the office."

His father was still supporting him, and so Calvin lived under the
most rigorous regime. Later, when he went up to Boston for the
legislature, he occupied a dollar-a-day inner room at a dingy hotel; nor
would he take his wife to live with him during the endless months he
served as Representative, Senator, Lieutenant Governor, and Governor.
When he got to Washington he converted the White House into a hall
bedroom: the cook quit because of his parsimony, the staff had the
jitters because of his daily inspection of the kitchens and storerooms;
the only time there was the sound of a strange voice or a bit of laughter
was when Grace Coolidge insisted that guests be invited to supper.
Not since the regime of Franklin Pierce, before the Civil War, had
the White House been so dreary.

Calvin read the law for twenty months, watched Hammond and
Field practice their profession, and listened to cases at the courthouse.
He remembered every decision he read, and where to find it. One day

when he was alone in the office, and the town coroner rushed in to ask if he could remove a corpse found in the woods, Calvin chewed his acrid cud for a moment, then put forth the dictum, "Can move body." Shortly afterward he was given an oral examination by a judge and admitted to the Bar.

He knew precisely what the law was; he did not concern himself with what the law ought to be. For him what existed was synonymous with what ought to be: for if it wasn't what it should have been, then how could it have come into existence in the first place? The word "change" never gained admission to his vocabulary.

Calvin Coolidge never intended to practice the law unless he had to; for the next quarter of a century he was actually out of politics only twenty months. He ran for office twenty times and was elected nineteen. He started at the bottom of the ladder as a precinct vote-getter and member of the Northampton City Council, working his way up to City Solicitor, State Legislator, Mayor, State Senator, President of the Senate, Lieutenant Governor, and Governor. He began his political career by going from house to house, saying to strangers: "I am running for office. I need your vote. I would appreciate it," never bothering to mention his qualifications. He ended his Massachusetts tenure by being elected by an enormous majority as Governor.

He was a civil servant of the type more native to the British than the American: his faculties were sharp, and he would do with persistent efficiency and economy every detailed task put before him. He could never be bribed; he would never be slothful; he would not deteriorate in a routine job; he would take pride and pleasure in the performance of his simple duties. Up to the door of the White House itself he served as a faithful executive clerk, dispatching the necessary minimum of governmental business with cold economy. As he had on his father's farm, he transacted the imperative residuum of chores; for the rest he sat in silence. At no time and in no office did he display the qualities of leadership; he was utterly without imagination, without ideas, without the daring of innovation; he would not have permitted himself to be caught dead making policy. Policy was something made by God, by nature, never by the chief executive of a city, a state, a nation.

He was twenty-five when he was admitted to the Massachusetts Bar, but he was not the traditional young man facing with flushed cheeks and palpitant heart a romantic future. He was already an old man, as old as he was at twelve, and as old as he would be at sixty. He had few friends, only one or two nodding acquaintances; and if he had any enthusiasms, he kept them artfully concealed. On those rare occasions when he felt the need for diversion, he would go to a beer garden after office hours, order a seidel of beer, eat two pretzels, and cogitate in lonely grandeur. The beer drunk, he would return to his hall bedroom. During his student days he had read Scott, Shakespeare, Milton, Kipling, Field, and Riley; once he had passed the Bar he seems to have put such dilatory pursuits behind him.

The year following his admission to the Bar he campaigned and got himself elected to the City Council. This was in 1898. From this day until his election to the Governorship twenty years later he held public office almost continuously. Coolidge made no promises, no bargains, and no deals; he lived this entire time under an almost fanatical economy, never acquiring a debt in order that he might never betray his office or his own character because of his need for cash. No matter how microscopic his wage, he forced himself to save a dollar or two a year. In an age when politicians were hiding tens of thousands of corporation greenbacks in locked boxes, Coolidge did no man's bidding, maintaining his self-respect so impregnably that he won the admiration of everyone who came in contact with him. His was the valuable contribution of proving that some Americans will serve in political offices with religious honesty.

His mechanism of politics was superb, but the mountain brought forth a mouse: for the content of his twenty years of service is incredibly meager. The only consistent contribution running through his career was a slimming down of the functions of the particular office he held. In his autobiography he states with pride that when he was President of the Massachusetts Senate he cut the number of bills passed by 30 per cent. As City Councilman, as City Solicitor, and later as Mayor of Northampton, the record shows him attempting to get an armory built for the local military company, and increasing teachers' salaries; as a member of the Massachusetts House of Representatives his voting record shows him supporting woman suffrage and direct election of

United States Senators, and as the co-drafter of a bill outlawing price cutting, none of which succeeded in getting passed. As a member of the Massachusetts Senate and later as its President, he supported measures for a mothers' aid bill, a bill regulating the work week of women and children, and a bill providing pensions for families of firemen.

As a member of various legislative committees, such as railroads, judiciary, banking, he simplified the mechanism of governmental control. As Governor of Massachusetts he reorganized the governing apparatus, making it more efficient and economical; he also signed the bill for which he had been working many years, establishing a forty-eight-hour week for women and children in industry.

Coolidge said about his legislative years, "I made progress because I studied some subjects sufficiently to know a little more about them than anyone else on the floor. I did not speak often but talked much with Senate personnel and came into contact with many of the businessmen of the state." William Allen White, in his superb biography of Coolidge, *Puritan in Babylon,* comments, "No one can draw so perfect a picture of the mousy, competent little country-man edging his way onward and upward on the path of glory as that he drew of himself. He won his way by diligence in Amherst. He won his way to the top in Massachusetts politics by tempering his diligence with kindly patience and a lively sense of gratitude."

He accumulated sizable debts of favors, which he advanced to everyone providing he could do so in an honest manner; he asked for no small repayments on his debt; he would go down the line for the Republican party and its members. He had a mild touch of Theodore Roosevelt progressivism. However, the higher Calvin rose in the political hierarchy the fainter became his progressivism until at last, when he crossed the threshold of the White House, there was not a symptom left of his youthful infection. In high place he began to feel that the humanitarianism he had backed in his early years was turning to radicalism. He accused liberalism of being "the claim in general that in some way government was to be blamed because everybody was not prosperous, and because it was necessary to work for a living." On being sworn in to the Presidency of the State Senate, Coolidge delivered an address called "Have Faith in Massachusetts." In what is probably his single most delightful remark, he said about this article, "The effect was beyond my expectations. Confusion of thought began to disappear and unsound legislative proposals diminish."

The four existing biographies of Calvin Coolidge do not contain a sum total of four pages of writing about his concrete services or contributions during his twenty-three years of local and State office. Coolidge was what might have been called an efficiency expert in government, except that efficiency experts consider it their job to increase production. He was an efficiency expert to decrease production. If he could have eliminated the very last duty of a councilor or legislator he would have gone with joy to the funeral.

3.

OUT OF HIS BATHROOM window each morning in Northampton, while he shaved, Calvin watched a young lady walking up the hill toward the deaf-and-dumb school, where she was a teacher. To another young man going through his ablutions he drawled, "Likely-looking young woman." When the other young man asked if he knew who she was, he replied, "No, but I'm going to marry her."

It was apparent to everyone but Calvin that he could not win the lovely Grace Goodhue, a warm-hearted, spontaneous girl, with a fine intuitive intelligence which had been sharpened by extensive reading and four years of study at the University of Vermont. One of the observers of this budding romance said that Calvin's many competitors for the hand of Miss Goodhue laughed at him, for "his conversation upon any subject bloomed, like the edelweiss, rarely and in a cold, forbidding atmosphere." Calvin had not the slightest chance—no more chance than he had to become Governor of Massachusetts or President of the United States. He won Grace Goodhue by the same method that he won political office: he outsat everybody else. Grace fell in love with him, understanding his taciturn New England nature, loving him so much that she married him against her mother's bitter protests.

Having married a young lady of outstanding qualities, Calvin Coolidge now proceeded to put her in her place. He rented half of a duplex for twenty-seven dollars and fifty cents a month, and furnished it completely. Only then did he take his wife home so that she might see where she was to live. With the courage of feminine resignation, she settled down in the flat for the next fifteen years, never stirring from it until the Coolidges moved to the Hotel Willard in Washington, following his election as Vice-President of the United States.

Calvin's one defeat in twenty political campaigns came in his marriage year of 1905, when he lost his race for the Northampton School Board because he had devoted part of the campaign period to a honeymoon in Montreal. This defeat further convinced him that it did not pay to waste one's time on frivolity. His marriage too became a grim business: guests were never brought into the home, friends never sat down to the supper table. He revealed to Grace not the slightest shred of what he was doing. "He did not trust my education," wrote Grace Coolidge in a popular magazine many years later. All she knew of her husband's activities she read in the papers. She bore him two sons, did the family wash, remained alone in her duplex during the countless months that he was in Boston, and walked away from him when, as Heywood Broun reported, he became insufferably ill-natured. Under all her burdens she never ceased loving Calvin Coolidge; women are wondrously strange.

In 1913 Frank W. Stearns, millionaire owner of a large Boston department store, had gone to Senator Coolidge's office to ask him to support a bill for new sewers for their alma mater, Amherst. Coolidge growled, "I'm sorry, it's too late," and dismissed Stearns. A short time later the Amherst Board of Trustees met to discuss the possibilities of promoting an Amherst graduate into the White House. Several of the trustees felt that Calvin Coolidge was a good man to be backed. Stearns said, "Well, if you say it's Coolidge, it's Coolidge. But the only time I ever met him he insulted me."

Without knowing that Stearns was in process of backing him, Coolidge helped pass the Amherst sewer bill the following session, thus proving to Stearns that Calvin was a sound and faithful man if one would only let him work things out in his own peculiar way. Stearns came to admire, then to love, and finally to worship Calvin Coolidge. He covered the state with the pamphlet "Have Faith in Massachusetts," and put not only his vast fortune but the full facilities of his advertising department and his power among Massachusetts corporations at Cool-idge's service. Next to Calvin himself, it was Stearns who secured him the Vice-Presidential nomination in 1920 and thus made possible his entry into the White House. Stearns' total reward was the privilege of sitting in the White House with Calvin in utter silence while the two men smoked their cigars. Coolidge was fond of Stearns and grateful for all the older man had done for him; his feeling was similar to that of the old New England farmer sitting in a rocker on the front porch of his house and saying to his wife, "When I think of what you have meant to me all these years, it's almost more than I can bear not to tell you about it."

Stearns had said, "Well, if you say it's Coolidge, it's Coolidge." The backing was now solid and the road into the Lieutenant Governorship in 1916 and the Governorship in 1918 was a matter of well-regulated and well-oiled politics.

Governor Coolidge entered the national scene in 1919 during Bos-ton's police strike, making himself a national press hero by refusing to act for the public good and the public safety until a dangerous crisis had been permitted to develop. The Boston police strike need never have broken into violence—in fact, might never have reached the boil-ing point of conflict—had Governor Coolidge been willing to exercise the normal functions of his office. His refusal to act brought on the ultimate consequence of a city without police, yet thousands of gallons of ink were spilled in his praise when he said, "There is no right to strike against the public safety by anyone, anytime, anywhere." The statement led directly to the Vice-Presidency in 1920 and the Presi-dency in 1923. It became the single greatest recommendation for the do-nothing political philosophy to be found in our history books.

In the spring of 1919 the Boston police force threatened to strike on the grounds that they were drastically underpaid, and that the living conditions at the station houses were execrable. Few people in Boston denied the justice of the policemen's claims, but Commissioner Curtis refused to admit the policemen's grievances or to negotiate with them. The police then attempted to join the American Federation of Labor so that they might have the right of collective bargaining. Commissioner Curtis promptly suspended the leaders of the union movement. The rest of the force threatened to go out on strike if their leaders were dismissed; Commissioner Curtis refused to reinstate them.

The Mayor's Citizens' Committee heartily recommended arbitration. Commissioner Curtis refused to arbitrate. During the critical week end Governor Coolidge left Boston and kept himself unavailable. When he returned to the city on Monday, Boston's Mayor Peters and the chairman of the Citizens' Committee pleaded with him to come out for arbitration. Coolidge refused to do anything. On Tuesday afternoon the policemen went on strike. Shortly after midnight mobs began raging through the city, looting and destroying. Coolidge refused to see or talk to anyone. It was not until Thursday, after still another night of rioting, that he went to a meeting of his political advisers at the Union Club, and accepted their decision that the time had come for the Governor to act. He then issued his famous fourteen-word statement, "There is no right to strike . . . etc.," called out the state militia, and broke the strike which he could have averted in its entirety six days before.

This philosophy of *laissez faire* got him into the White House in the 1920's; it proved to be the identical philosophy which brought the nation to its economic catastrophe in the 1930's. In Washington President Coolidge refused to act; the hysteria of the stock market spiral was not unlike the upward spiral of violence in Boston which Governor Coolidge condoned by his refusal to do everything in his power to avoid serious dislocation.

4.

PROBABLY the lowest point in American history between the two World Wars was that moment at 1:20 in the morning of June, 1920, when a Senatorial cabal, the most venal since the days of President Grant, nominated Warren G. Harding for the Presidency. Harding was Calvin Coolidge's alter ego: a hard-drinking, gambling man who spent many nights in the Little Green House on K Street, or in a third-rate New York hotel room with his inamorata—leaving the government in the hands of as depredatory a gang of swindlers as had been assembled in Washington since the Reconstruction.

Calvin Coolidge was nominated for Vice-President by the Republican convention as a reaction against the type of man that had been forced upon them to head the ticket. After election he served as an astute parliamentarian over the Senate. Invited by Harding to sit in at the Cabinet meetings, he became aware of the corruption and malfeasance inside the government. He said and did absolutely nothing about them.

Since he was determined not only to live within his salary as Vice-President but also to continue his savings, he and Mrs. Coolidge, whom he now took with him for the first time, moved into two rooms at the Hotel Willard. Here he was utterly ignored by official Washington, which was roistering in bootleg liquor, poker, and wads of greenbacks. When the Coolidges were invited out to dinner, Calvin accepted the invitations, though he sat through the dinners and the evenings in curdled silence. A sympathetic woman, who saw what he was suffering, asked him why he continued to dine out. He replied churlishly, "Got to eat somewhere." Another pleasant young woman who had the misfortune to be placed next to him said, "Mr. Coolidge, I've made a rather sizable bet with my friends that I can get you to speak three words this evening." Coolidge snapped nastily, "You lose." These two anecdotes, which are reported by Coolidge's biographers as being fine examples of his wit, form his complete contribution to Americana from March of 1921 up to the death of Harding in August, 1923.

The ceremony of Calvin's father swearing him into the Presidency in the Vermont farmhouse in which he had been born, reading from the Bible by kerosene lamp, was eaten up by the American people not only as colorful and characterful, but as the best possible guarantee that Coolidge would be an antidote to the rapacity of the Harding ring. In point of fact the accession of Coolidge to the Presidency at this time, when respect for our Federal Government had fallen to an estate rarely before known in American history, was good and valuable; Coolidge's demonstrable honesty restored the people's faith in their high-placed servants. What they could not realize was that the Coolidge swearing-in ceremony would be symptomatic of his regime: that he would take to Washington with him a political kerosene lamp with which to light his way in an age of vast electrodynamics.

By an actual time count, Calvin Coolidge averaged a shade under four hours of work a day while President of the United States! In his *Forty-Two Years in the White House,* Irwin Hoover, head usher who had known and observed a great many Presidents, commented acidly that Calvin Coolidge worked fewer hours and assumed fewer tasks than had any other President he had known. No man of his day could so completely have turned the Presidency into a civil service sinecure. When Will Rogers asked him how he kept fit in a job that had broken the health of Woodrow Wilson, Coolidge replied in all seriousness, "By avoiding the big problems."

He had done no sleeping in the afternoons when he was State Senator, Lieutenant Governor, or Governor of Massachusetts. Once he became President he waged an unrelenting campaign to keep his desk so clear of papers and business that he could sleep away the afternoons and be in bed again at ten o'clock at night. As President of the Massachusetts Senate he had cut the legislation by 30 per cent; as President of the United States he cut the duties of the Chief Executive by at least 70 per cent. Wherever possible he mercilessly slashed appropriations for the various federal departments and agencies, forcing them to let out men and reduce their work to a minor fraction. He used every weapon of discouragement, silence, and negation to keep the Congress from passing laws. The brunt of his day's work was pure listening: examination of a daily program shows that he received a large number of people; he listened to what they had to say, and ninety-nine times out of a hundred made no answer whatever.

Whatever self-originated work he did was party politics, quietly bringing Republican officials into line so that his renomination in 1924 was dried and boxed before the party's convention met. In like manner he had called in his debts when he wanted to become Lieutenant Governor.

His election that year was a triumph for the double negative: don't do nothing, don't say nothing. It was also a best-seller success for the newspaper reporters, from whose ranks have risen some of our most prolific fiction writers: through desire to create readable copy out of a dull original, they fabricated the image of a shrewd, droll, colorful, highly efficient and economical executive, zealously guarding the interests of the nation from his vantage point at the brain center of America. Coolidge co-operated in the gentle fraud: strangulatingly shy by temperament, he posed in outlandish costume for the news cameramen, peering out from the front pages of the papers as an Indian chief in an effort to show the people that he was a reg'lar fellow.

The stratagem worked, as every device in his political tactic had worked: for rarely has there been a public career so uniformly successful in its parts, yet such a tragic failure in its whole. The country was prosperous; relatively few had been hurt in their personal pockets by the Harding gang; people were still surfeited by what they called "Wilsonian idealism" (i.e., the attempt to achieve world peace, and to establish a liberal economy at home which would preserve the best of modern capitalism); but most important, the public scented and scurried after the bitch-in-heat inflation of the fabulous days ahead.

Coolidge won by an overwhelming margin, almost sixteen million votes to something more than eight million, over one of the most likely candidates ever nominated for the Presidency: John W. Davis, Attorney General under Woodrow Wilson, as international-minded as Coolidge was parochial, as creatively progressive as Coolidge was decayingly static, as warm-hearted as Coolidge was frigid, as capable of controlling the financial brigands as Coolidge was incapable of subjecting them even to the mildest criticism. In so far as one can second-guess history, John W. Davis would have used every legitimate agency of the Federal Government to control the stock markets and money markets; by every token of his talents, record, and character he would have sharply reduced, if not largely eliminated, the credit zoom of 1925-1929 and its attendant material collapse of 1929-1939.

5.

COOLIDGE's two lifetime virtues as a public servant manifested themselves as soon as he became President. First, his appointments were honest; he resisted the considerable politico-pressure that had made Garfield cry out under similar circumstances, "What is there in this office that makes anyone think they would want it?" Second, he gave close detailed study to those subjects on which he was going to have to make a decision. But he studied with almost the sole purpose of being able to refute and confound his visitors, and thus resist their demands for some kind of positive action. White says of him, "He was an economic fatalist with a God-given inertia. He knew nothing and refused to learn."

After Calvin Coolidge had been in the White House five months he announced in a speech that "the business of America is business." This perfect flowering of the Philistine mind became the core of his five-year regime. It was his unshakable conviction that "brains are wealth and wealth is the chief end of man."

He loaded the Tariff Commission with men representing special industries and products. These men made their tariff decisions in the best interests of their particular companies, and Coolidge thought it was right that they should do so: if the sugar men protected their own sugar industry, and the oil men protected the oil industry, and the leather men protected the leather industry, then wasn't it obvious that the best interests of the entire nation also would be served? For him it was inexorable logic that the men who ran industry and made the most money should be the exactly right and inevitable people to run the whole economy—from their great and demonstrated talents would flow prosperity for all. Any accusation that in the 1920's the apex of the American industrial world ran the show solely for its own profit, considering not at all the broad base of humanity, he would have called radicalism, of the kind he had so providentially dispelled in 1918.

This was President Coolidge's conviction. It was based on temperament. Neither fact nor condition could alter it.

There was one more step he had to take before he could assume that he was doing his full job as President: he had to give his urgent approval to the bankers and brokers. He believed in speculative credit because speculative credit created business, and from this business came the funds with which to pay the debts accumulated out of speculative credit. He therefore informed his friends in Wall Street that no federal agency would hinder them.

Family savings were being poured into local banks. Local banks poured their funds into Wall Street. Organizations of high-powered salesmen having been set up for the sale of securities, they sold bad securities when there were no good ones; bankers and investment brokers deliberately sold millions of dollars of dubious stock, for they made just as large a commission on the sale of shaky stock as they did on the sound. The savings of the nation having been absorbed by Wall Street, the people were persuaded to borrow money on their farms, factories, homes, machinery, and every other tangible asset, that they might earn high interest rates and take big profits out of the rise in the market. When Wall Street's huge foreign loans and dubious domestic loans were not repaid, America lost not only the cash of its savings but its collateral as well.

In the spring of 1927 the Federal Reserve Board, sensing the danger ahead, attempted to cut the volume of speculative trade; when Coolidge learned about this he slapped his own Board in the face with a public statement that the year would continue to be active and prosperous. When conservative businessmen became alarmed at the orgy of pyramiding stock prices, and tried to warn the country, Secretary of the Treasury Mellon came out with a statement that the saturation point had not yet been reached, or announced a new Treasury plan to approve and buttress the flow of figures and debts. The ill-assorted prosperity twins, Coolidge and Mellon, alternated in boosting the market: when in the summer of 1927 the rise in stock prices began to slow up, Coolidge publicly predicted that the future of business looked to him to be completely sound—whereupon stocks jumped twenty-six points in one day! Coolidge was enormously pleased with himself, thinking that he had increased the wealth of America by the exact ratio of this advance.

Occasionaly, with Stearns or some other trusted intimate, Coolidge would become gabby for a half hour, not asking council or seeking information, but merely spilling his thoughts on some decision or other. Then, his little orgasm of human communication spent, he would return for weeks, even months, to his continence. He also became a practical joker. His humor always had had a sadistic turn, consisting mostly of sarcasms like the one thrown at his long-winded associate on the Massachusetts Railroad Commission: "Sand your tracks, you're slipping." Now for amusement he would ring all the bells on his desk at once so that he could watch the large staff come running from distant parts of the grounds; he would ring the bell at the front gate, and then disappear before the sentry, running on the double, could reach the gate; he would walk up the long, white brocaded train of Mrs. Coolidge's new dress while she was trying it on.

How could he indulge in this moronic puerility when the world was in upheaval? How could he find time to supervise the menu of every meal served in the White House, and check his wife's bills to make sure she was not spending too much money, or being cheated? How could he spend a half hour creating a scene because a Secret Service man, to whom he had given a dime to buy a five-cent magazine, had forgotten to return the other nickel?

The answer is simple. He had nothing else to do. To fill in the dragging hours he would carry his rocker out to the White House porch and rock in full view of Pennsylvania Avenue, or wander through the hallways in his nightshirt, his spindly calves showing, or send a servant to tell Justice Hughes of the venerable beard that the barber was ready to give him a haircut and shave.

He never had been a youth. He was now spending his adolescence in the White House. But millions of Americans would grow gray-haired as a consequence of their President's second childhood.

In the summer of 1927 the Coolidges went to the Black Hills of South Dakota for a vacation, while Frank Stearns and the Republican chairmen of every state and county began setting up the machinery for Calvin's re-election the following year. There was no doubt in anyone's mind but that he would triumph as handsomely in 1928 as he had in 1924. However, one day in his office at Rapid City he dictated a ten-word message:

"I do not choose to run for President in 1928."

He then ordered twenty-five copies of the message typed and summoned the newspapermen, to whom he handed the little pieces of paper without facial or vocal expression. The reporters were stunned; one of them managed to gasp, "Mr. President, can't you give us something more on this?" Coolidge silenced them with, "There will be nothing more from this office today!"

He had taken no one into his confidence, asked counsel from neither his wife nor Frank Stearns. Mrs. Coolidge learned the news from Senator Arthur Capper, who had witnessed the scene; Stearns learned it, brutally, from the newspapers. The chairmen succumbed to shock; but

Calvin Coolidge achieved the result he had wanted: paralyzing mystification, which made him, not by deed or accomplishment, but by the simple expedient of abstruseness, the center of the world's stage and the hero of millions of spilled words.

He concealed his motives as rigorously as he had concealed his intent. The only sentence he uttered on the subject was said to Senator Capper a few moments after his coup: "Ten years in Washington is longer than any other man has had it—too long!" Rumor, gossip, and scandal washed back and across the nation: he was playing possum; he was fatally ill; his wife had threatened to divorce him if he ran again.

There was evidence to indicate that he hoped the party would overwhelm his wishes, for on the day that the convention nominated Hoover, whom Coolidge sneeringly called "The Wonder Boy," Coolidge threw himself on his bed disconsolately, lying there face down for many hours. However, by this time a number of suspicious cracks were beginning to appear in the American economy, and a sufficient number of persons had warned the President that grave, perhaps calamitous, times lay ahead. It is quite possible that Calvin Coolidge saw the hurricane coming, and that that was why he did not choose to run.

After Hoover's inauguration, the Coolidges returned to Northampton. Calvin bought a big house and grounds called "The Beeches," and wrote his memoirs for *Cosmopolitan* in his now old and shabby law offices. Northampton was wondrously proud of him; everyone wanted to stop him to shake hands and say hello.

Then came the crash of the stock market, and with it, Calvin Coolidge's world: for other men only lost their money, while Coolidge lost his faith and philosophy in life. He became discouraged, then hopeless, then ill, commenting to a friend that in other depressions it had been possible to see something solid on which to base hope, but that he could now see nothing to give ground for hope.

As a crowning symbol, the Northampton Savings Bank failed, along with thousands of others all over the country. The people of Northampton lost their homes, their factories and stores, their jobs. Destitution, illness, misery walked the streets in the eyes of Calvin Coolidge's old friends. Dimly they understood that he had not been their friend, but their mortal enemy. And dimly, Calvin Coolidge saw this understanding in their eyes.

He lived for four years after leaving the White House, lived to see his old associates and advisers discredited, his Wall Street intimates put in the dock of public opinion and branded as malefactors of American life. He lived to see Franklin D. Roosevelt move into the White House and begin to build the plain-board edifice of the common man's life on the ashes of Calvin Coolidge's collapsed and burned-out world.

In the last year or two of his life he began to understand the fullness of the tragedy that had seized the United States. Now, at last, he knew how gravely he had sinned against the little people who had trusted him, how much he had willfully added to their woes. He saw no reprieve for mankind, except in the solace of religion.

6.

COULD THE ORDINARY American citizen have known that in voting for Silent Cal he was helping usher in the deluge? Or is such wisdom available only to after-the-fact historians? The answer is as difficult to reach as it is simple to postulate: unless the human race learns wisdom before the fact it will vanish from the earth in the spiraling smoke of the atom bomb, or its twenty-first-century equivalent. The world can no longer afford its do-nothing Calvin Coolidges: the price of error has risen beyond the ability of mankind to pay and survive.

My Fights
with Jack Dempsey

BY GENE TUNNEY

James Joseph ("Gene") Tunney is a New York City boy who became one of the great celebrities of the years between the wars. In the article which follows he gives an amusing account of how he acquired the reputation of being a literary prizefighter, and a convincing explanation of what happened during the famous "long count" in Chicago. But he does not mention the fact that he retired undefeated from his heavyweight championship in 1928, with all of his huge earnings almost intact, to become a businessman of wide affairs and a prominent resident of Stamford, Connecticut. He is at present the president of a building company, board chairman of a tire and rubber concern, director of a bank, a chemical company, and Eversharp, Inc. He is the author of *A Man Must Fight* (1932) and *Arms for Living* (1941), and was once invited to lecture on Shakespeare at Yale University. During the recent war he was director of the Navy's fitness program, with the rank of Commander.

✳ 1.

THE LAUGH OF THE TWENTIES was my confident insistence that I would defeat Jack Dempsey for the heavyweight championship of the world. To the boxing public, this optimistic belief was the funniest of jokes. To me, it was a reasonable statement of calculated probability, an opinion based on prize-ring logic.

The logic went back to a day in 1919, to a boat trip down the Rhine River. The first World War having ended in victory, the Army was sending a group of A.E.F. athletes to give exhibitions for doughboys in the occupation of the German Rhineland. I was light heavyweight champion of the A.E.F. Sailing past castles on the Rhine, I was talking with the Corporal in charge of the party. Corporal McReynolds was a peacetime sports writer at Joplin, Missouri, one of those Midwestern newspapermen who combined talent with a copious assortment of knowledge. He had a consummate understanding of boxing, and I was asking him a question of wide interest in the A.E.F. of those days.

We had been hearing about a new prizefight phenomenon in the United States, a battler burning up the ring back home. He was to meet Jess Willard for the heavyweight championship. His name was Jack Dempsey. None of us knew anything about him, his rise to the challenging position for the title had been so swift. What about him? What was he like? American soldiers were interested in prizefighting. I was more than most—an A.E.F. boxer with some idea of continuing with a ring career in civilian life.

The Corporal said yes, he knew Jack Dempsey. He had seen Dempsey box a number of times, had covered the bouts for his Midwestern newspaper. Dempsey's career had been largely in the West.

"Is he good?" I inquired.

"He's tops," responded Corporal McReynolds. "He'll murder Willard."

"What's he like?" I asked.

The Corporal's reply was vividly descriptive. It won't mean anything to most people nowadays, but at that time it was completely revealing to anyone who read the sports pages. McReynolds said: "He's a big Jack Dillon."

I knew about Jack Dillon, as who didn't thirty years ago? He was a middleweight whose tactics in the ring were destructive assault —fast, shifty, hard-hitting, weaving in with short, savage punches, a knocker-out, a killer. Dillon even looked like Dempsey, swarthy, beetle-browed, and grim—a formidable pair of Jacks.

I thought the revelation over for a moment, and recalled: "Jack Dillon was beaten by Mike Gibbons, wasn't he?"

"Yes," replied the Corporal. "I saw that bout. Gibbons was too good a boxer. He was too fast. His defense was too good. Dillon couldn't lay a glove on him."

Mike Gibbons was the master boxer of his time, the height of defensive skill, a perfectionist in the art of sparring.

I said to the Corporal: "Well, maybe Jack Dempsey can be beaten by clever boxing."

His reply was reflective, thought out. "Yes," he said, "when Dempsey is beaten, a fast boxer with a good defense will do it."

This, coming from a brainy sports writer, who knew so much about the technique of the ring and who had studied the style of the new champion, aroused a breathless idea in me. My own ambition in the ring had always been skillful boxing, speed and defense—on the order of Mike Gibbons.

As a West Side kid fooling around with boxing gloves, I had been, for some reason of temperament, more interested in dodging a blow than in striking one. Fighting in preliminary bouts around New York, I had learned the value of skill in sparring. In A.E.F. boxing I had emphasized skill and defense—the more so as during this time I had hurt my hands. Previously I had been a hard hitter. Now, with damaged fists, I had more reason than ever to cultivate defensive sparring.

Sailing down the Rhine, I thought maybe I might be a big Mike Gibbons for the big Jack Dillon. It was my first inkling that someday I might defeat Jack Dempsey for the Heavyweight Championship of the World, which all assumed Jack was about to acquire.

This stuck in mind, and presently the time came when I was able to make some observation firsthand. I was one of the boxers on the card of that first Battle of the Century, the Dempsey-Carpentier fight. I was in the semifinal bout. This place of honor and profit was given to me strictly because of my service title. The ex-doughboys were the heroes of that postwar period, and the light heavyweight championship of the A.E.F. was great for publicity. I was ballyhooed as the "Fighting Marine."

Actually, I had no business in the bout of second importance on that occasion of the first Million Dollar Gate. I was an A.E.F. champ, but we service boxers knew well enough that our style of pugilism was a feeble amateur thing, compared with professional prizefighting in the United States. The best of us were mere former prelim fighters, as I was. There were mighty few prominent boxers in Pershing's A.E.F. In World War II you saw champs and near-champs in uniform, but the draft was not so stern in such matters during the war against the Kaiser's Germany.

In the semifinal bout of the Dempsey-Carpentier extravaganza, I, with my bad hands, fought poorly. Nobody there could have dreamed of me as a possible future conqueror of the devastating champ—least of all Jack himself, if he had taken any notice of the semifinal battlers. I won on a technical K.O. from my opponent, but that was only because he was so bad—Soldier Jones of Canada, who, like myself, was in the big show only because he too had an army title—the war covering a multitude of sins.

After the bout, clad in a bathrobe, I crouched at one corner of the ring, and watched the Manassa Mauler exchange blows with the Orchid Man of France. As prize-ring history records, the bout was utterly one-sided; the frail Carpentier was hopelessly overmatched. But it afforded a good look at the Dempsey style.

The Corporal on the boat sailing down the Rhine had been exact in his description of Dempsey. The Champ was, in every respect, a big Jack Dillon—with all the fury and destruction implied by that. No wonder they called him the Man Killer. But, studying intently, I saw enough to confirm the Corporal's estimate that when Dempsey was defeated it would be by a skillful defensive boxer, a big Mike Gibbons. Correct defense would foil the shattering Dempsey attack.

This estimate was confirmed again and again during subsequent opportunities. I attended Dempsey fights, and studied motion pictures of them. More and more I saw how accurate defense could baffle the Man Killer's assault. The culmination was the Shelby, Montana, meeting of Dempsey and Tom Gibbons, the heavyweight younger brother of Mike. Tom, like Mike, was a consummate boxer, and Dempsey couldn't knock him out. For the first time in his championship and near-championship career, the Man Killer failed to flatten an opponent. The public, which had considered Tom Gibbons an easy mark, was incredulous and thought there must have been something peculiar about it. For me there was nothing peculiar, just final proof that good boxing could thwart the murder in the Dempsey fists. There was a dramatic twist in the fact that the final proof was given by a brother of Mike Gibbons.

2.

AT THE Dempsey-Carpentier fight, I had seen one other thing. Another angle flashed, as at a corner of the ring I watched and studied. Famous in those days was the single dramatic moment, the only moment when the Orchid Man seemed to have a chance. That was when, in the second round, Carpentier lashed out with a right-hand punch. He was renowned for his right, had knocked out English champions with it. He hit Dempsey high on the jaw with all his power.

I was in a position to see the punch clearly and note how Carpentier threw it. He drew back his right like a pitcher with a baseball. The punch was telegraphed all over the place. Yet it landed on a vulnerable spot. How anybody could be hit with a right launched like that was mystifying to one who understood boxing. Dempsey went back on his heels, jarred. Carpentier couldn't follow up, and in a moment Jack was again on the relentless job of wrecking the Orchid Man with body blows. But it was a vivid demonstration that the champion could be hit with a right.

Dempsey was no protective boxer. He couldn't do defensive sparring. He relied on a shifty style, his own kind of defense, and couldn't be hit just any way. His weakness was that he could be nailed with a straight right. Later on, I saw this confirmed in other Dempsey battles. It was dramatized sensationally at the Polo Grounds when the powerful but clumsy Firpo smashed him with a right at the very beginning of the first round, and later blasted Dempsey out of the ring with right-hand punches—the Wild Bull of the Pampas almost winning the championship.

To me it signified that the strategy of defensive boxing might be supplemented by a right-hand punch—everything thrown into a right. It would never do for me to start mixing with the Champ in any knockdown, drag-out exchange of haymakers. He'd knock me out. It would have to be a surprise blow, and it could easily be that. Both Carpentier and Firpo, who had nailed the Champ, were noted for their right—all they had. But Jack would never suspect a Sunday punch from me, stepping in and trying to knock him out with a right.

I was catalogued not only as a defensive boxer but also as a light hitter, no punch. I might wear an opponent down and cut him to pieces, but I couldn't put him to sleep with a knockout slam. That had been true—previously. I had been going along with the handicap of bad hands. I could hit hard enough, but didn't dare for fear of breaking my hands. So I was a comparatively light hitter—and typed as one.

Finally, in desperation, I had to do something about my fragile hands. I went to a lumber camp in Canada for one winter and worked as a woodsman, chopping down trees. The grip of the ax was exercise for my damaged mitts. Months of lumber camp wood chopping and other hand exercises worked a cure. My hands grew strong and hard, my fists rugged enough to take the impact of as powerful a blow as I could land. In subsequent bouts I had little trouble with my hands. This I knew, and others might have been aware of the change, but I was tagged as a feather duster puncher—and that was that. The old philosophy of giving a dog a bad name.

Prizefight publicity often resorts to the ballyhoo of a secret punch, a surprise blow, nearly always a fraud—but I really had the chance. At the beginning of the first round I would step in and put everything I had in a right-hand punch, every ounce of strength. I might score a knockout, or the blow would daze the champion sufficiently to make it easier to outbox him the rest of the way.

I was, meanwhile, fighting my way to the position of challenger. I won the light heavyweight championship from Battling Levinsky and subsequently fought Carpentier, the Orchid Man, and went through a series of savage bouts with Harry Greb, one of the greatest of pugilists. In our first bout, Greb gave me a murderous mauling. In our last, I beat him almost as badly. After a long series of matches with sundry light heavies and heavies I went on to establish myself as heavyweight contender by defeating Tom Gibbons. It was dramatic irony that I earned my shot at the title at the expense of Tom, brother of my model, Mike.

Public opinion of my prospects with Dempsey was loud and summary. The champion is always the favorite, and Dempsey was one of the greatest champions, as destructive a hitter as the prize ring has ever known. He was considered unbeatable, and I was rated as a victim peculiarly doomed to obliteration, pathetic, absurd.

It was argued that I was a synthetic fighter. That was true. As a kid prelim battler, my interest had been in romantic competition and love of boxing, while holding a job as a shipping clerk with a steamship company. As a marine in France, my love of boxing and a distaste for irksome military duties after the armistice brought me back as a competitor in A.E.F. boxing tournaments. We gave our best to entertain our buddies and, incidentally, to avoid guard duty. After the war, when I had grown up, my purpose simply was to develop the sparring ability I had as a means of making money—seeing in the heavyweight championship a proud and profitable eminence.

They said I lacked the killer instinct—which was also true. I found no joy in knocking people unconscious or battering their faces. The lust for battle and massacre was missing. I had a notion that the killer instinct was really founded in fear, that the killer of the ring raged with ruthless brutality because deep down he was afraid.

Synthetic fighter, not a killer! There was a kind of angry resentment in the accusation. People might have reasoned that, to have arrived at the position of challenger, I must have won some fights. They might have noted that, while the champion had failed to flatten Tom Gibbons, I had knocked him out. But then the Dempsey-Gibbons bout was ignored as rather mystifying, one of "those things."

The prizefight "experts" were almost unanimous in not giving me a chance. The sports writers ground out endless descriptions of the doleful things that would happen to me in the ring with Dempsey. There were, so far as I know, only a few persons prominent in sports who thought I might win, and said so. One was Bernard Gimbel, of the famous mercantile family, a formidable amateur boxer and a student of ring strategy. The others included that prince of sports writers, the late W. O. McGeehan, and a few lesser lights in the sports-writing profession. They picked me to win, and were ridiculed. The consensus of the experts was echoed by the public, though with genuine sadness on the part of some.

Suspicion of a hoax started following a visit by a newspaperman to my training camp at Speculator, New York. Associated Press reporter Brian Bell came for an interview. He noticed a book lying on the table next to my bed. Books were unexpected equipment in a prizefight training camp. He was curious and took a look at the volume—*The*

Way of All Flesh. That surprised him. The Samuel Butler opus was, at that time, new in its belated fame, having been hugely praised by George Bernard Shaw as a neglected masterpiece. It was hardly the thing you'd expect a prizefighter to be reading, especially while training for a bout with Jack Dempsey.

Brian Bell knew a story when he saw one. He later became one of the chief editors of the Associated Press. Instead of talking fight, he queried me about books. I told him I liked to read Shakespeare. That was the gag. That was the pay-off. The A.P. flashed the story far and wide—the challenger, training for Jack Dempsey, read books, literature—Shakespeare. It was a sensation. The Shakespeare-Tunney legend was born.

3.

THE STORY behind it all went back to a day in 1917 when a young marine named Gene Tunney was getting ready to embark with his company bound for the war in France. We were stowing things in our kits, when I happened to glance at the fellow next to me. I noticed that among the belongings he was packing were two books. That surprised me.

In the marines you kept the stuff you took to the minimum. You carried your possessions on your back in the long marches favored by the Marine Corps. Every ounce would feel like a ton. Yet here was a leatherneck stowing away two books to add to his burden. I was so curious that I sneaked a look at the two books and saw—Shakespeare. One was *Julius Caesar,* the other, *A Winter's Tale.* He must be a real professor, I thought.

The leatherneck in question was the company clerk. I had known him when in recruit camp—a young lawyer in civilian life, quiet and intelligent. Now, my respect for him went up many notches. He must be educated indeed to be taking two volumes of Shakespeare to carry on his back on the long marches we would have in France.

We sailed in the usual transport style, piled in bunks in a stuffy hold. The weather was rough, and virtually the whole division of marines became seasick. The few good sailors poked unmerciful fun at their

seasick comrades. I happened to be one of the fortunate, and joined
in the ridicule of the miserable sufferers.

Sickest of all was the company clerk. He writhed in misery. He
would lie on deck all day, an object of groaning filth. At night he was
equally disgusting in his bunk. This was the tier next to mine, and I
saw more of him than most. The high respect I had formed for him
went down those many notches. He might be educated, he might take
Shakespeare to war with him, but he was a mess at sea.

We put in at Brest, and promptly the order came—prepare to march.
We were to put on a show at the dock for inspection by the brass hats. I
started to get ready, and then came the appalling discovery. I couldn't
find the tunic of my uniform. I knew I had stowed it in my kit, but it
was gone. I hunted everywhere. In the Marine Corps it was practically
a capital offense for a leatherneck to be without an article of issue, and
here I was without my tunic for the long march upon arrival in France.

I heard a marine asking: "Whose is this?" He was on a cleaning
job, and was holding up a disreputable object that he had fished from
under the bunks. "Somebody's blouse," he announced with a tone of
disgust, "and look at it."

I did—it was my blouse, a mess of seasick filth.

The explanation was easy to guess. The company clerk in the tier of
bunks next to mine had done it. Having befouled all of his clothes, he
had, in his dumb misery, reached into my bunk and taken my blouse.
He had worn it until it was too filthy to wear—after which he had
chucked it under the bunks.

There was nothing I could do. There was no time to get the blouse
cleaned, and there was no use blaming it on the company clerk. It was
strictly up to me to have possession of every article of issue in good
shape. I could only inform our company commander that I didn't have
my tunic—and take the penalty, extra guard duty and kitchen police.

When, ashore, the company clerk came out of his seasickness and
realized what had happened, he was duly remorseful. He was a decent
fellow, his only real offense having been seasickness. He told me how
sorry he was, and asked what he could do to make up for the trouble
he had got me into. What could he give me? That was the way things

were requited among the marines—handing something over to make up for something. What did he have that I might want? He hadn't anything I could take, except those two books. I told him, "Give me one of them and call things square." He did. He retained *Julius Caesar* and gave me *A Winter's Tale.* He knew what he was about, as anyone who knows Shakespeare will attest.

Having the book, I tried to read it but couldn't make any sense of it. I kept on trying. I always had a stubborn streak, and figured the book must mean something. But it didn't, so far as I could make out. I went to the company clerk. He had given me the book, and it might mean something to him. It did, and he proceeded to explain.

He coached me, led me through *A Winter's Tale,* which turned out to be interesting. That was practically my introduction to Shakespeare— the hard way. After training on *A Winter's Tale,* I read such works as *Hamlet, Macbeth, Othello,* with ease.

I had always liked reading—and this had a practical side. I found that books helped in training for boxing bouts. One of the difficulties of the prizefight game is that of relieving tension in training camp, getting one's mind off the fight. The usual training camp devices were jazz phonograph records and the game of pinochle. I didn't like jazz, and the mysteries of pinochle were too deep for me. So I resorted to reading as a way to ease the dangerous mental strain during training. I found that books were something in which I could lose myself and get my mind off the future fight—like *The Way of All Flesh,* which Brian Bell of the Associated Press found me reading while training for Dempsey.

Hitherto, as just another prizefighter, my personal and training camp habits had been of little news interest, and nobody had bothered to find out whether I read books or not. Now, as the challenger for the heavyweight title, I was in a glare of publicity, and the disclosure that I read books, literature, Shakespeare, was a headline. The exquisite twist was when one of Dempsey's principal camp followers saw the newspaper story. He hurried to Jack with a roar of mirth. "It's in the bag, Champ. The so-and-so is up there reading a book!"

The yarn grew with the telling—training for Dempsey on Shakespeare. It simplified itself down to the standing joke—Tunney, the great Shakespearean. This put the finishing touch to the laugh over my prospects in the ring with Dempsey.

It made me angry and resentful. I was an earnest young man with a proper amount of professional pride. The ridicule hurt. It might have injured my chances. To be consigned so unanimously to certain and abject defeat might have been intimidating, might have impaired confidence. What saved me from that was my stubborn belief in the correctness of my logic. The laugh, in fact, helped to defeat itself and bring about the very thing that it ridiculed. It could only tend to make the champion overconfident.

For a boxer there's nothing more dangerous than to underestimate an opponent. Jack Dempsey was not one to underestimate. It was not his habit of mind to belittle an antagonist. He was far too intelligent for that. In fact, Jack rather tended to underestimate himself. With all his superb abilities in the ring, he was never arrogant or cocky, never too sure of himself. But not even Jack Dempsey could escape the influence of opinion so overwhelming, such mockery as "It's in the bag, Champ. The so-and-so is up there reading a book." That could help my strategy of a surprise blow to knock him out or daze him for the rest of the fight.

4.

WHEN WE FINALLY got into the ring at Philadelphia things went so much according to plan that they were almost unexciting to me. During the first minute of sparring, I feinted Dempsey a couple of times, and then lashed out with the right-hand punch, the hardest blow I ever deliberately struck. It failed to knock him out. Jack was tough, a hard man to flatten. His fighting style was such that it was difficult to tag him on the jaw. He fought in a crouch, with his chin tucked down behind his left shoulder. I hit him high, on the cheek. He was shaken, dazed. His strength, speed, and accuracy were reduced. Thereafter it was a methodical matter of outboxing him, foiling his rushes, piling up points, clipping him with repeated, damaging blows, correct sparring.

There was an element of the unexpected—rain. It drizzled and showered intermittently throughout the fight. The ring was wet and slippery, the footing insecure. That was bad for a boxer like me, who depended on speed and sureness of foot for maneuvering. One false step with Jack Dempsey might bring oblivion. On the other hand, the slippery ring also worked to the disadvantage of the champion. A hitter needs secure footing from which to drive his punches, and any small uncertainty underfoot may rob him of his power. So the rain was an even thing except that it might have the therapeutic value of a shower for a dazed man, and Dempsey was somewhat dazed during the ten rounds. Jack was battered and worn out at the end, and I might have knocked him out if the bout had gone a few rounds more. The decision was automatic, and I was heavyweight champion of the world.

The real argument of the decade grew out of my second bout with Dempsey, at Chicago, the following year—the "long count" controversy. It produced endless talk, sense and nonsense, logic and illogic. To this day in any barroom you can work up a wrangle on the subject of the long count. How long was Tunney on the floor after Dempsey knocked him down? Could he have got up if the count had been normal?

To me the mystery has always been how Dempsey contrived to hit me as he did. In a swirl of action, a wild mix-up with things happening fast, Jack might have nailed the most perfect boxer that ever blocked or side-stepped a punch, he was that swift and accurate a hitter. But what happened to me did not occur in any dizzy confusion of flying fists. In an ordinary exchange Dempsey simply stepped in and hit me with a left hook.

It was in the seventh round. I had been outboxing Jack all the way. He hadn't hurt me, hadn't hit me with any effect. I wasn't dazed or tired. I was sparring in my best form, when he lashed out.

For a boxer of any skill to be hit with a left swing in a commonplace maneuver of sparring is sheer disgrace. It was Dempsey's most effective blow, the one thing you'd watch for—you'd better, for the Dempsey left, as prize-ring history relates, was murder. I knew how to evade it, side-step or jab him with a left and beat him to the punch. I had been doing that all along.

I didn't see the left coming. So far as I was concerned, it came out of nowhere. That embarrassed me more than anything else—not to mention the damage done. It was a blow to pride as well as to the jaw. I was vain of my eyesight. My vision in the ring was always excellent. I used to think I could see a punch coming almost before it started. If there was anything I could rely on, it was my sharpness of eye—and I utterly failed to see that left swing.

The only explanation I have ever been able to think of is that in a training bout I had sustained an injury to my right eye. A sparring partner had poked me in the eye with thumb extended. I was rendered completely blind for an instant, and after some medical treatment was left with astigmatism which could easily have caused a blind spot, creating an area in which there was no vision. Our relative positions, when Dempsey hit me, must have been such that the left swing came up into the blind spot, and I never saw it.

With all his accuracy and power Dempsey hit me flush on the jaw, the button. I was knocked dizzy. Whereupon he closed for the kill, and that meant fighting fury at its most destructive. When Dempsey came in for a knockout he came with all his speed and power. I didn't know then how many times he slugged me. I had to look at the motion pictures the next day to find out. There were seven crashing blows, Dempsey battering me with left and right as I fell against the ropes, collapsing to a sitting position on the canvas.

Of what ensued during the next few seconds, I knew nothing. I was oblivious of the most debated incident of the long count and had to be told later on what happened.

The story went back to the Dempsey-Firpo fight, to that wild first round during which Firpo hit the floor in one knock-down after another. This was in New York, where the rule was that a boxer scoring a knock-down must go to a neutral corner and remain there until the referee had completed the count. In the ring with the Wild Bull of the Pampas, Dempsey undoubtedly through excitement of battle violated that rule, as the motion pictures showed clearly afterward.

Jack confesses he remembers nothing that took place during that entire fight. Firpo landed a terrific first blow. Dempsey, after suffering a first-blow knock-down, apparently jumped up to the fray by sheer professional instinct—the fighting heart of a true champion. Instead of going to a corner, Jack would stand over Firpo and slug him as he got up. After one knock-down, Jack stepped over his prostrate opponent to the other side, to get a better shot at him—the referee was in the way. After another knock-down, Dempsey slugged Firpo before the South American had got his hands off the floor, when he was still technically down. The Champ might well have been disqualified for that—not to mention the fact that he was pushed back into the ring when Firpo battered him out. The referee, however, in his confusion permitted all the violations.

The Dempsey-Firpo brawl aroused a storm of protest and brought about a determination that in the future Dempsey should be kept strictly to the rules. In our Chicago bout the regulation applied—go to a neutral corner upon scoring a knock-down. The referee had been especially instructed to enforce this. He was told that, in case of a knock-down, he was not to begin a count until the boxer who had scored the knock-down had gone to a neutral corner.

This was the reason for the long count. Dempsey, having battered me to the canvas, stood over me to hit me the moment I got up—if I did get up. The referee ordered him to a neutral corner. He didn't go. The referee, in accordance with instructions, refrained from giving count until he did go. That imposed on Jack a penalty of four seconds. It was that long before he went to the corner and the referee began the count.

When I regained full consciousness, the count was at two. I knew nothing of what had gone on, was only aware that the referee was counting two over me. What a surprise! I had eight seconds in which to get up. My head was clear. I had trained hard and well, as I always did, and had that invaluable asset—condition. In the proverbial pink, I recovered quickly from the shock of the battering I had taken. I thought—what now? I'd take the full count, of course. Nobody but a fool fails to do that. I felt all right, and had no doubt about being able to get up. The question was what to do when I was back on my feet.

I never had been knocked down before. In all the ring battles and training bouts I had engaged in, I had never previously been on the canvas. But I had always thought about the possibility, and had always planned before each bout what to do if I were knocked down, what strategy to use upon getting up. That depended on the kind of opponent.

I had thought the question out carefully in the case of Jack Dempsey. If he were to knock me down, he would, when I got up, rush me to apply the finisher. He would be swift and headlong about it. Should I try to clinch and thus gain some seconds of breathing space? That's familiar strategy for a boxer after a knock-down. Often it's the correct strategy—but not against Dempsey, I figured. He hit too hard and fast with short punches for it to be at all safe to close for a clinch. He might knock me out.

Another possibility was to get set and hit him as he rushed. That can be effective against a fighter who, having scored a knock-down, comes tearing in wide open, a mark for a heavy blow. If you are strong upon getting to your feet, you can sometimes turn the tables by throwing everything into a punch. Bob Fitzsimmons often did it. But that wouldn't do against Dempsey, I reckoned. He was too tough and hit too hard. He would welcome a slugging match. After having been knocked down, I might not be in any shape to take the risk of stepping in and hitting him.

For my second bout with Dempsey the plan that I decided upon, in case I was knocked down, was based on the thing I had learned about Jack. Word from his training camp had indicated that his legs were none too good. I had learned that his trainers had been giving him special exercises for footwork, because he had slowed down in the legs. That was the cue—match my legs against his, keep away from him, depend on speed of foot, let him chase me until I was sure I had recovered completely from the knock-down.

The plan would work if my own legs were in good shape, after the battering I had taken. That was what I had to think about on the floor in Chicago. My legs felt all right. At the count of nine I got up. My legs felt strong and springy.

Jack came tearing in for the kill. I stepped away from him, moving to my left—circling away from his left hook. As I side-stepped swiftly, my legs had never been better. What I had heard about Dempsey's legs was true. As I circled away from him, he tried doggedly, desperately, to keep up with me—but he was slow. The strategy was okay—keep away from him until I was certain that all the effects of the knockdown had worn off. Once, in sheer desperation, Jack stopped in his tracks and growled at me to stand and fight.

I did—but later, when I knew that my strength, speed, and reflexes were completely normal. I started to close with him and hit him with the encyclopedia of boxing. Presently Dempsey's legs were so heavy that he couldn't move with any agility at all, and I was able to hit him virtually at will. He was almost helpless when the final bell rang—sticking it out with stubborn courage.

5.

I HAVE OFTEN been asked—could I have got up and carried on as I did without those extra four seconds of the long count? I don't know. I can only say that at the count of two I came to, and felt in good shape. I had eight seconds to go. Without the long count, I would have had four seconds to go. Could I, in that space of time, have got up? I'm quite sure that I could have. When I regained consciousness after the brief period of black-out, I felt that I could have jumped up immediately and matched my legs against Jack's, just as I did.

The long count controversy, with all the heated debate, produced a huge public demand for another Dempsey-Tunney fight, number three. Tex Rickard was eager to stage it. He knew, as everybody else did, that it would draw the biggest gate ever. The first Dempsey-Tunney fight grossed over a million seven hundred thousand; the second, over two million and a half. Rickard was sure a third would draw three million. I was willing, eager. I planned to retire after another championship bout, wanted to get all that I could out of it.

But Jack refused. He was afraid of going blind. The battering he had taken around the eyes in his two fights with me alarmed him. The very thing that kept him from being hit on the jaw, his style of holding his chin down behind his shoulder, caused punches to land high. He dreaded the horror that has befallen so many ring fighters and is the terror of them all—the damage that comes from too many punches around the eyes, blindness.

Jack Dempsey was a great fighter—possibly the greatest that ever entered a ring. Looking back objectively, one has to conclude that he was more valuable to the sport or "The Game" than any prizefighter of his time. Whether you consider it from his worth as a gladiator or from the point of view of the box office, he was tops. His name in his most glorious days was magic among his people, and today, twenty years after, the name Jack Dempsey is still magic. This tells a volume in itself. As one who has always had pride in his profession as well as his professional theories, and possessing a fair share of Celtic romanticism, I wish that we could have met when we were both at our unquestionable best. We could have decided many questions, to me the most important of which is whether "a good boxer can always lick a good fighter."

I still say yes.

The Last Days
of Sacco and Vanzetti

BY PHIL STONG

Philip Duffield Stong was a feature writer for the North American
Newspaper Alliance when he went to Boston to interview Nicola
Sacco and Bartolomeo Vanzetti just before their deaths in 1927. He
considers it one of the most important experiences in his life. Later
he worked for the New York *World,* and when that newspaper
died in 1930 he began work on a novel he had been thinking about
for years. Its name was *State Fair* (1932), and it became one of the
most talked about books ever written on an American subject, and
was made into a celebrated moving picture with Will Rogers. Mr.
Stong has written at least a dozen more novels, six books of history
and biography, and a number of juveniles. He was born in Keosau-
qua, Iowa, and still has a home there.

✶ 1.

IF SACCO AND VANZETTI had not been executed in 1927 and
had managed somehow to go on living, they would now be fifty-eight
and sixty-one years old respectively. They would also be forgotten.
They were not important agitators when they were arrested during
the great Red Hunt of 1920; with a short sentence for disturbing the
peace they would probably have never been heard of again. Bart Vanzetti had an exceptional mind, but he was an Italian who spoke mostly
in Italian and was completely unskilled in the methods of American
propaganda. Nicola Sacco did not belong in any political arena. He
was a very happily married man with two children who earned a
hundred dollars or so a week as a shoe workman; his political ideas must
have been vague except as he understood Vanzetti's Tolstoyan notions
of libertarianism.

These notions were difficult to distinguish from anarchy—difficult for Sacco, at any rate, for one of his last cries as he seated himself in the electric chair, according to the Associated Press reporter, was *"Viva anarchia!"* (No one else reported this—the A.P. man was the only representative of the press at the execution, and you may take his word for it if you wish.) The fundamental thesis of Vanzetti's libertarianism was that men are innately capable of spiritual moderation somewhat above the rules of fang and claw, but that this racial self-discipline can be established only when the artificial restraints of law and government are removed.

There was nothing dangerous about this noble nonsense, if only because of its complete impracticality. It has been made quite plain in these later years that without enforced norms of behavior civilization will quickly destroy itself. Sacco and Vanzetti were men of good will, and they considered the normal violence of humanity an unusual accident instead of the ordinary phenomenon it is.

They were philosophers but not pragmatists. The personal and official liberties of Judge Webster Thayer and the prejudices of their fellow citizens destroyed these two men, who were probably not guilty of any serious violation of the codes they deprecated so ineffectively. Certainly the charge of dual murder in a sordid stickup seems utterly fantastic when applied to this unworldly pair.

The events for which they died can be stated very quickly. There is nothing exciting in the business for a connoisseur of crime. A gang holdup was attempted in Bridgewater, Massachusetts, on December 24, 1919. It failed because a streetcar clanged onto the scene and scared the bandits away. No one was hurt and no money was taken.

Nearly four months later, on April 15, 1920, a somewhat similar effort met with more success in near-by South Braintree. On this occasion five men in a stolen car slaughtered a paymaster and a factory guard and got away with a steel box containing a payroll of $15,776.51. This left the police of the area with two unsolved crimes and two unavenged murders on their books.

Bridgewater and South Braintree are part of a network of industrial towns to the south of Boston, centering around the sizable shoe-making city of Brockton. Sacco and Vanzetti landed in the Brockton police station on May 5, twenty days after the murders in South Braintree. They had been picked up with an automobile containing certain propaganda leaflets attacking the United States Government and all other governments. The Brockton police, who had definite plans for them, questioned them closely about their activities on December 24 and April 15. The two prisoners naturally assumed the cops were seeking a line on some of their radical friends, and their answers were confused and evasive. Not until a long time later did they learn what the real charge was going to be.

2.

THE TEMPER of misfortune is to choose special individuals or groups as the source of every wrong. In 1920 America had recently won a war, but a fair number of veterans of that war were disgusted or out of work, and the peace of the world was still in a state of serious disrepair. This, it was generally agreed, was the fault of the "radicals." The wartime Attorney General, a person named A. Mitchell Palmer, encouraged this idea to distract attention from the egregious shortcomings of himself and other members of the administration.

When a dynamite bomb ripped off the front of Mr. Palmer's house in Washington (and incidentally killed the unknown "Red" who planted it), the country really roused to the dangers of radicalism. A thousand hounds began to bark and bay at the heels of a very tiny fox. In the balmiest days of the great Red Scare there were about 150,000 Communists and Anarchists in this country, and the Communists were divided into thirty-two different groups, one of which numbered two members. (These gentlemen lived about ten miles apart in New York City and met once a month.) The whole lot were about as dangerous as a flea on an elephant—or not that dangerous, because they spent their time in biting each other.

Most people, of course, made no distinction between a Communist—who believed in nothing but government—and such philosophical Anarchists as Vanzetti—who believed in no government at all. They were not interested in the ideology of the matter. If a man was a radical he was a radical. It was all right to be a Democrat, though deplorable, but that was about as far as tolerance extended. The benign vacuity of Norman Thomas protected the Socialist party during all this hubbub. Thomas was a preacher and therefore untouchable, but well fitted for his small political harem, without virility and without numbers.

Radicals outside the pale of sanctity were not treated gently. There was a poor Italian named Salsedo who was "questioned" by federal agents high up in a building on Park Row, New York, in May, 1920. He sought to fly fifteen flights or so in the course of the inquiry by Mr. Palmer's G-men, and his crushed body was found on the pavement the next day. At about this time the besieged radicals, including Sacco and Vanzetti, began to carry or accumulate weapons. This was quite in accord with the American way of doing things—most of us would prefer to fight if we are going to be tortured to death anyway. It was the Salsedo case, incidentally, which Sacco and Vanzetti and their Massachusets friends were agitating about when they were picked up by the Brockton police.

They were already marked men, of course. Both were foreigners, and both had evaded the draft. They were brave enough, as it was proved later, but as a mere detail of their libertarian philosophy they did not care to shoot anyone. This, too, was noble and impractical, and by a special quirk of the 1920 mentality it made them logical suspects when a particularly murderous and bloody crime was committed.

The police had other grievances against Vanzetti. He lived an irregular though not an idle life—in the fifteen years or so he had been in the United States he had held a dozen different jobs, ranging from pastry cook (his trade) to bricklayer's helper. He was by no means a vagrant but he was an itinerant: at the time of his arrest he peddled fish from a pushcart in the poorer sections of Boston. The police have always regarded peddlers as being barely within the law. They were not inclined to be patient while Bart endeavored to establish his movements from the testimony of occasional buyers of fish.

Vanzetti had also been a strike leader, which, though not a crime, was certainly an offense in New England in 1920. But his most serious transgression was in being a voluble and somewhat unintelligible radical. Puritan law has always been severe on nuisances of any unconventional type. I am informed—though like Herodotus I make the reservation that it hardly seems credible—that it is still in the Code of Connecticut that when any three citizens complain that a person is a common scold, that party can and must be ducked, per ducking stool.

Nick Sacco very nearly escaped the whole business: he was to have sailed for Italy in a few days, and he would not have been extradited. Mussolini later made a strong protest against the execution of the two men—this probably helped to settle their fate, if it were not already settled. A Latin dictator interfering with the majestic justice of the Codfish State!

Barring his association with Vanzetti as a radical, Sacco had an untouchable record. He was a good and dependable workman with a family and savings account; his son was named Dante, which implies at least a degree of culture. Sacco's employer tried to rescue him and was able to prove to an absolute certainty that he had been at his bench on the day of the first holdup, the one in Bridgewater. On the day of the South Braintree affair, however, Sacco had taken a day off to visit the Italian Consulate in Boston with reference to his forthcoming trip. Both he and the consulate officials gave the most circumstantial accounts of his visit there, but there were other moments during the day which only Sacco himself could vouch for. The coincidence cost him his life.

And of course his plan to go to Italy was held against him, in spite of the fact that his explanation—a very sick mother in the old country—was proved absolutely true. Sacco was lucky or unlucky, according to the way you look at it: except for his friendship with Vanzetti he would probably be a stout, prosperous foreman in a Massachusetts shoe factory at this moment, with four or five *figlie* and a house of his own. No one would have heard of him but the neighbors.

Vanzetti's was the restless spirit. If the murders had been those of Governor Calvin Coolidge and Henry Ford and A. Mitchell Palmer, with Vanzetti somewhere in the neighborhood each time, one might have suspected some unlit depths in that serene and gentle but obstinately crusading soul. I do not believe—and certainly few people ever believed—that he, who opposed all killing, ever committed the railroad track assassination of Frederick Parmenter, an obscure paymaster for Slater and Morrill, and the guard, Alessandro Berardelli. These were the very types of people to whom he gave little printed leaflets as he pushed his cart along the streets, calling, *"Pesce, pesce"* through his thick black mustache. The leaflets did not say anything very new or startling, but perhaps they were more dangerous than bullets after all. The police found one in Sacco's pocket when they arrested him. It read:

Fellow Workers, you have fought all wars. You have worked for all the capitalists. You have wandered over all the countries. Have you harvested the fruits of your labors, the price of your victories? Does the past comfort you? Does the present smile on you? . . . On these questions, on this argument, and on this theme of the struggle for existence, Bartolomeo Vanzetti will speak. Hour——day——Hall. Admission free. Freedom of discussion to all. Take the ladies with you.

3.

THE FIRST INSPECTION by witnesses was absurd. Sacco, aged twenty-nine, who looked a great deal like any other American male aged twenty-nine, was tentatively identified by one of the many witnesses of the South Braintree holdup. Though I myself talked to Sacco for two hours—at a time when he had become much more celebrated—I am sure that I could not have identified him a month later. He was a pleasant little person, not ugly, not handsome, just a face, quiet and decent. He was modest and shy; he effaced himself.

So Sacco, with his ordinary face and figure, more or less like that of any Midwest farmer or Eastern bookkeeper, was tentatively identified as one of the men who killed the paymaster. They had more trouble with Vanzetti. It was difficult *not* to identify a man with an enormous mustache, piercing and intelligent eyes, a hawk-beak nose, an unruly wave of dark hair, and a magnificent forehead.

Yet it took some time to have somebody identify Vanzetti as a person who had been in the murder car, so-called. In this crisis the ambitious District Attorney, one Frederick Katzmann, played his cards under the table. He rushed Vanzetti alone to trial for the botched-up business in Bridgewater and got a conviction on no evidence whatever. By this time there had been so much newspaper agitation against the murderous "Reds" that the chauvinist louts on the jury would have convicted Bart of riding a broomstick if he had had a splinter in his finger. Being a wandering fish peddler, his alibi was worthless.

Sacco, of course, was completely exonerated from the Bridgewater affair by his factory time-card. But now his friend Vanzetti had a "criminal record" which could be used against them both at the forthcoming trial for murder. It was a maneuver—everyone knew it was a maneuver—but Katzmann maintained it was merely the regular order of business. Why kick a man before you kill him, you ask? In this case, to facilitate the killing.

After that the whole business went through smoothly. Every cause needs a crucifixion, and the Communists cheerfully took over that aspect of the case. Vanzetti's thinking was the direct antithesis of Communism, but the various Communist groups were willing to have him crucified in their name. They brought in as attorney a Western lawyer named Frederick Moore, who was not familiar with Yankee people. One can say moderately that he did not conduct his side of the trial with genius. Outside the courtroom the Communists set up a nationwide hullabaloo, but all their uproar simply determined the stubborn Commonwealth of Massachusetts to proceed more firmly on its homicidal way.

After the first peculiar failure to identify the highly identifiable Bart Vanzetti, Prosecutor Katzmann had no more trouble. He was helped along in the identity matter by the fact that many of his witnesses were Italian laborers who had been working in a ditch near the scene of the South Braintree killings. These gentlemen were anxious to avoid trouble and would say "*si*" to anything the prosecutor might ask them.

The double murder trial, which opened May 31, 1921, at Dedham, Massachusetts, was frivolous—and ghastly. A dozen Yankees who had decided on the guilt of the accused before they took their seats listened complacently to harangues on Yankee patriotism from fellow Yankee Katzmann—whose name belied him—and the Honorable Yankee Judge on the bench.

The identification grew more substantial as the trial went on. The burden of proof was shifted heavily to the defendants; nothing but an unassailable alibi would save them. And who has an unassailable alibi for nine-tenths of his life, unless he happens to be in the penitentiary already? The prisoners had unwittingly made things very bad for themselves at the time of their first arrest, before they knew about the murder charge. Sacco, for instance, had been purposely vague about his trip to the Italian Consulate in Boston—he had said he might have made it on April fifth, eighth, or tenth. He had known all along that the fifteenth was the day, but the police questions, which seemed to be aimed at that particular day, had thrown him off and he had tried to cover up.

It was "proved" at the trial that the bullets in Berardelli's body came from Vanzetti's revolver. This meant exactly nothing. Give any police expert the bullet that killed Lincoln and one of the late General Patton's pearl-handled pistols for ten minutes, and some interesting changes could be alleged for history. It would be necessary merely to throw the original bullet out the window and fire a new one from the pistol. I do not assert that this happened here—opinions are not evidence—but to reverse the burden of proof, and in view of the nature of the prosecution, who can prove that it did not?

The speeches of the prosecutor and the charge to the jury of Judge Thayer—who somehow managed to preside at both Vanzetti's earlier trial and the Sacco-Vanzetti murder trial—deserve a place with Herod's pronouncement on John the Baptist. Both of them were designed to nerve the jury up to murder: murder was admirable when it was judicial; murder was patriotic; murder was a duty from which these splendid Americans of old stock would not flinch. Thayer began his charge with a stomach-wrenching torrent of compliments and a lecture on loyalty—no one could have made it plainer that he expected a verdict of "Guilty!" He used the words "beautiful" and "sweet" within three paragraphs and went on to tell the jury:

"I therefore now commit into your sacred keeping the decision of these cases. You will therefore take them with you into yonder jury room, the silent sanctuary where may the Great Dispenser of Justice, wisdom, and sound judgment preside over all your deliberations. 'Let all the ends thou aim'st at be thy country's, thy God's, and truth's.' "

It was some time after this, in point of time, that Judge Webster Thayer remarked to a group of friends, "Did you see what I did to those anarchistic bastards the other day?" The Judge was also accustomed, in the privacy of his country-club locker room, to refer to the two prisoners as "Dagoes" and "sons of bitches" and to state emphatically that he would "get them good and proper." This should give a clearer picture than his charge to the jury of the judico-intellectual processes of the Honorable Webster Thayer.

The jury, which had made up its collective mind about the time it was sworn in, took seven and a half hours to deliberate—thus earning lunch and supper on the state. At any rate, it had to deliberate for a while to lend some suggestion of decency to the whole business. In the immortal words of Nunnally Johnson, "Naw, don't hang him now—let's try him awhile first." But no one had the slightest doubt of what verdict the Great Dispenser of Justice would reach. It was "Guilty," of course. Judge Webster Thayer beamed.

4.

THEREUPON the matter dragged out for seven years. The guilt or innocence of the defendants continued to be debated, but after the obscene spectacle of the trial it was not even the principal issue. The issue was whether there was a Commonwealth in the American Union of States where men could be deprived of their lives without proper hearing or any recourse to obtain such a hearing. Thayer denied an appeal, quite naturally, and as the law of Massachusetts was constituted that put an end to the matter.

A recital of stays and motions would be tedious for anyone but a specialist—it is sufficient that the men were kept in prison, alive, for seven years after they had been pronounced guilty of first-degree murder. This was largely due to the efforts of William G. Thompson, one of the principal lawyers of New England. The case smelled so bad, to use an inelegant figure of speech, that Thompson was moved to investigate it, and when he saw what was happening he went into it with all the power and experience of a very vigorous personality. He was not a criminal lawyer, but he was a lawyer, and—God rest him—he was a scholar and a gentleman. His family was old New England, his clientele conservative, and all he gained from his advocacy of the case of the two Italian "Reds" was his soul's ease. This was more important to Thompson than the fees and friends he lost.

Thompson was a man of medium height, stockily built, with the large, graying cranium of an elderly and oversized Napoleon. He was both benevolent and pugnacious, if that means anything; he could, and did, fight like a bulldog for ethical principles—rather than retainers—when he discovered real injustice. In its beginnings the Sacco-Vanzetti case was obscure and did not come to his attention until it was irretrievably lost.

Again, Thompson was not primarily interested in the evidence of guilt or innocence—he had a basic conviction that neither Sacco nor Vanzetti was capable of an ordinary gangster murder—but he was very much interested in the possibility that an upstart Judge could assassinate people on the basis of prejudicial opinions. After he entered the case he became a partisan of the defendants as people, but his initial interest was stirred by an outrage to the law which was his life's occupation.

It may be reiterated that his part in the case lost Thompson friends, money, and prestige. Publicity may be checked off—it was not useful and it was definitely disagreeable. Thompson was not a "good fellow" of the climber class; he was a patrician, and born that way. My own belief in the innocence of the two prisoners was formed in part from my personal observations but also, to a considerable extent, from what I learned from this cool and astute and practiced attorney.

To my obvious query about his entry into a controversy that had cost him so much, he said simply:

"What else could I do? I went into this case as a man of old American tradition to help two poor aliens who had, I thought, been unjustly treated. I have arrived at a humbler attitude. Not since the martyrdoms of the sixteenth century has such a steadfastness of faith, such self-abnegation as that of these two poor Italians been seen on this earth. Nowhere in *my* soul is to be found such strength and faith and gentility as make the man Bartolomeo Vanzetti."

(Thompson later objected to the "sentimentality" of my write-up of this interview. I took down his remarks in reporter's "doodads," part Gregg shorthand and part abbreviated phonetic script. He did not say that I was inaccurate; I think he was annoyed to find how deeply he had been moved in talking of Vanzetti.)

Thompson later defined to perfection the respective statures of himself and his opponent in a statement to the Lowell Committee:

"I have known Judge Thayer all my life—I could not say that I think Judge Thayer is at all times a bad man or that he is a confirmed wicked man. But I say that he is a narrow-minded man; he is a half-educated man; he is an unintelligent man; he is full of prejudice; he is carried away with his fear of Reds, which captured about 90 per cent of the American people. That is the type of man you are to think about, violent, vain, and egotistical."

This was not a diatribe but a diagnosis, and it did not come from a mere sense of superiority—it came from Olympus. It establishes, inferentially, the vast distance between the rabble-rouser and the dispassionate critic.

5.

FOR SEVEN YEARS Thompson kept Thayer busy denying motions. There is no evidence that the bony-faced little man with a precise mustache and near-set eyes whose mind was full of "Dagoes" and "anarchistic bastards" ever considered these papers for a minute, but their progression in the records took time—a great deal of time. For seven long years Webster Thayer was reminded of his victims as one procedure after another came before him.

Thayer had positively oozed complacency at the trial in 1921, but those seven years changed him. When I telephoned him for an appointment on behalf of one of the largest and most conservative newspaper syndicates in the country, he answered angrily and almost hysterically, "My God, I can't say anything more about that! [This text was slightly altered for the purposes of our member newspapers.] I've made my position clear enough—I did what I had to do. What more can I say? I can only maintain a judicial silence!"

To my mild apology he snapped, "Of course it annoys me! I'd not be human if it didn't annoy me!" And more shouts which it would not be fair to transcribe, because the man seemed mentally confused. Thayer was neither judicial nor judicious. He complained of being "hounded."

Perhaps someone who believes in the furies of Fate can afford to be a trifle sorry for this ambitious little Judge whose last years were so clouded by just one of the hundreds of cases which had come before him. Even criminals helped maintain the pressure. There was Madeiros first, irrevocably condemned for another murder, who generously confessed the killings in South Braintree. Even a believer in the innocence of Sacco and Vanzetti must admit that if all death-cell confessions were credited at face value, one executioner could serve the whole country. Their importance depends on the inclusion of details which only the murderer could know. Madeiros was too foggy about details, but he also fogged the case with new motions and denials for Judge Thayer to attend to.

The question of the "Morelli Gang" and the plunder is by no means so clear. This group of professional thugs was notorious from Boston to their headquarters in Providence. Madeiros was probably a member; he had $2,800 when arrested, which approximated—minus intervening expenses—one-fifth of the $15,766.51 which was taken in the South Braintree holdup. Aside from this possible share, the money had completely vanished, except for one other interesting possibility—the Morellis vanished too until after the conviction of Sacco and Vanzetti, when they reappeared as entrepreneurs of a fairly expensive roadhouse.

Not one cent of the stolen money was or ever has been traced to Sacco or Vanzetti.

Judge Thayer, however, considered all these facts to be irrelevant, inconclusive, and nonevidential. Even he must have noted the fact somewhere in his dry little brain that if Sacco and Vanzetti did commit two murders they were very badly paid for it.

"Thayer is a country-club boy," one of the men on the Boston *Transcript* told me. "He thought he'd get in good with the Cabots and the Lowells and the Lodges by sending these 'Reds' over toot sweet. It backfired on him."

When the day finally came, after all those seven years, to sentence the two "Dagoes" to death, Judge Thayer had trouble looking them in the eye. Vanzetti noticed this and spoke as sternly as though he were the Judge, and Thayer the prisoner at the bar: "What we have suffered," he said, "during these seven years no human tongue can say, and yet you see me before you, not trembling, not changing color, you see me looking in your eyes straight; not blushing, not ashamed or in fear."

Nick Sacco also had something to say in answer to the clerk's time-honored query—"Have you anything to say why sentence of death should not be passed upon you?"

"Yes, sir," said Sacco. "I never knew, never heard, even read in history anything so cruel as this court."

Somehow Thayer got the dirty business over with, looking much of the time at the floor rather than at the men he was killing. On the way out of the courtroom he bumped into some reporters and said with an air of attempted jauntiness, "Well, boys, how did it go?" Not getting any answer he added, "Boys, you know I've often been good to you. Now see what you can do for me." Nobody answered this either.

6.

THE NORTH AMERICAN NEWSPAPER ALLIANCE sent me to Boston in May, 1927, two days before Thayer denied the last possible motions for the defendants within his jurisdiction. Sentence had already been pronounced and the whole business was in the hands of Governor Alvin Fuller.

Fuller was not in town so far as I was concerned—a kind of "Madame is not in" announcement—or perhaps that is an injustice; perhaps he really wasn't in. Fuller was a big, handsome man who started with a bicycle shop and attained to an important automobile agency. His whole education and experience were commercial and he was far out of his depth, and bewildered, by the ruckus of this "Italian radical" case.

Nevertheless, a word should be said for Fuller. He could have settled the matter of a pardon in a minute by saying Yes or No. But he wanted to be fair and he knew his limitations in a controversy which had evoked passionate statements from intellectual giants all over the world. Foreign feeling was almost unanimously in favor of the condemned men, and there was a kind of exultation in the shocked outburst from overseas. So this was the country that claimed a monopoly on democratic institutions! So this was American law and American justice! Barbusse of "J'Accuse" fame protested; so did Romain Rolland and Einstein and Bernard Shaw and scores of others whose names meant something.

In this country the intelligentsia turned out almost to the last man and woman for Sacco and Vanzetti. Heywood Broun was discharged twice from the New York *World* for his bitter statements on the case. John Dos Passos and Edna St. Vincent Millay leaped to their typewriters. Miss Millay presumably had not had much legal education, but Felix Frankfurter, who was and is one of the keenest legal minds in the country, and who now represents Massachusetts on the United States Supreme Court, pronounced Judge Thayer's conduct of the trial contemptible.

The Governor-automobile salesman quite honestly and quite unreasonably selected the most prominent and respectable people he could find to consider the case and report to him on the advisability of a pardon. The three he chose were President A. Lawrence Lowell of Harvard University, President Samuel W. Stratton of the Massachusetts Institute of Technology, and Judge Robert Grant (retired) of the Probate Court. These three Yankee old-timers inquired around and found that there had indeed been a judge and twelve jurors present during the original trial. This being so, they decided that everything was in order and gave the death sentences their blessing.

The opinion of the man on the street in Boston was in complete consonance with that of the big shots on the Lowell Committee. It was painfully evident that the defendants had been tried, in the public mind at least, not for murder, but for political heterodoxy. The curious thing was that the closer one came to the defendants' own stations in society the more virulent was the judgment. The two were merely "Reds" to shop clerks, "damn Reds" in cigar stores, and "God-damn Reds" to taxi drivers.

In thirty or forty inquiries I made I received only two dissenting answers. A minor executive at the Old Corner Book Store who dug up some slightly out-of-the-way volume for me said on the question of the men's guilt, after hesitating for a moment, "My opinion on that case isn't popular—I'd rather not express it." Which was, of course, a very definite way of expressing it.

The other heretic, though he was only half heretic, was one of the most important editors on the Boston *Transcript*. His remarks are approximated below:

"They were fools to put Thayer on that case," he said. "He's conspicuously bigoted, and what is worse, he's maladroit. We have half a dozen men on the bench who could have substituted for Thayer and made that case look pretty good. That charge to the jury! No wonder there's such a howl! They should have made him take a vacation for his health and let Judge Blank or Judge Blank handle it.

"No, of course they weren't guilty. When you're familiar with the transcript, which you can't be through the newspaper reporting of the trial, you'll see that it's more or less an insult to anyone's intelligence to ask that question. This was a gang murder—there were five men in the car. Nobody seems to care much who the other three were. Also, we have a gang that works this territory. They were never even questioned. And so on—read the transcript.

"If they'd been railroaded intelligently it would have saved all this."

I said, "But if a good many men of your influence up here know this and believe as you do, why don't you do something about it?"

He seemed astonished for a moment and then smiled. "My dear man—you're from the West, aren't you?—Yes. None of us knew about it till it was too late to backtrack. For most of us it was just another gang killing with the Reds making capital out of it till Thompson and other people of his caliber got indignant about it. Then when we really went into the matter, it was much too late to do anything."

I asked, "How do you mean, too late? They haven't been electrocuted yet."

He stared for a moment. "This state has, I believe, the oldest legal code built on English foundations in the United States. It worked very well for more than three hundred years. We can't have fingers pointed at it because of two interlopers who are inimical to our social system and take so little interest in our institutions that they avoided the draft.

More than two men gave up their lives to establish our order and maintain it."

"But if the code has developed only to the point where a hanging judge can take the life of an innocent man and deny him any recourse, perhaps it needs some revision."

"Indeed it does, but not under compulsion from outsiders, and particularly not under the kind of compulsions that have been attempted against us. There's nothing that can be done about it. If our courts could be forced to go back on a case like this they could be forced by anyone. I could join the Communist party and go and murder Thayer—which would be a great pleasure—and then yell that I was being framed because I was a radical. We have to insist on the perfection of our codes till we can amend them quietly and voluntarily."

"But perhaps," I suggested, "there could be a commutation and a quiet pardon, later."

He laughed. "Quiet? You know the Dreyfus case—I've seen the name 'Dreyfus' used in connection with this case twenty times. He spent five years in a hellhole, I'll admit, but he got a military promotion he might otherwise never have had. Is that case quiet? Suppose they pardon Mooney, which seems unlikely, probably innocent of the crime alleged but not my dish, at all. But if they did pardon him do you think that case would be quiet? An admission of error merely gives real criminals a new reference to prejudice in perfectly honest trials. And most of them are honest, even to the point of favoring the defendant."

"Better free ten criminals than punish one innocent man, etc."

"That's right, and it usually obtains"—he grinned—"even in the witch-hunting state. You may have seen the word used recently. No, we have to stand by that stupid procedure. It will stink to Heaven, but they'll be forgotten and there'll be a new 'cause' six months after they're dead. Alive—well, look at the Mooney business."

It seemed that he might be slightly in error, and that was the way it turned out. Sacco and Vanzetti seem assured of something nearer immortality than Dreyfus or Mooney. And his statement had some characteristic Bostonian rationalization—Boston invented "pragmatism," or, at least, pragmatically filched it from Schiller.

7.

THE MEN who transcended this moil of convictions and attitudes were confined in prison about an hour out of Boston, at Dedham. It is odd to speak of a prison as pleasant, but this one was, with its old architecture, old brick-bordered lawns and flower beds, and a Warden whose name is forgotten but should be remembered as the model of all Wardens everywhere.* The big central room, with wings of cells thrown off in three directions, was sunny; it was bare and plain, but the sun made up for much of that. There was a faint smell of disinfectant, but it did not reek of the stuff so much as an ordinary schoolroom; there is no need for formaldehyde where enough soap has been used.

I drove out with Herbert Ehrmann, Thompson's assistant defense attorney. The Warden greeted us warmly—he could tell from Ehrmann's presence that I would be friendly to Nick and Bart. When the full tragedy of those last days is written the Warden will not be the least character. He was a big man, without being either tall or fat; he seemed to be one of the typical barrel-chested Irish, with his plump face and wide shoulders—they can be the warmest or the most dangerous of people, as the occasion requires. A warden's business is to ward the people who are put in his charge without any questions. This man did not shed tears when he shook hands with Nick and Bart for the last time, but it was observed that his eyes were shining with them.

When we arrived, Vanzetti was seated at a long oak table—the chairs were kitchen chairs except for arm rests and rounded backs. He had a book which he hastily handed to a warder. It was something about Colonial government in America, but Vanzetti obviously thought it might be suspected as stage property; so it is impossible to gratify its author by further identification.

The Warden said, "I'll go get Nick," and went down the narrow gallery at the left, a kind of catwalk before grated doors.

In spite of his terrific mustache and thinning hair, Bartolomeo Vanzetti was still under forty and as eager for human companionship as a spaniel pup—though he was no spaniel pup. Most of his pictures

* It was William A. Hendry.—Ed.

show the laugh wrinkles about his eyes and cheeks, amused and tolerant and slightly reminiscent of Mark Twain.

Nick Sacco, as he entered, was deep in argument with the Warden about the prison menu. He was an intent, sturdy little chap, amiable and thoughtful to some degree, but he was not Vanzetti—which may, in a way, make him the more heroic of the two persons.

"You say chicken," he told the Warden. "He been chopped up mighty fine since he came from China. That kind of chicken my wife make a pudding with raisins."

"Ah, Nick, you're gaining, aren't you? Go ahead—what do you want for supper? I'll roast a turkey—"

Then there were introductions. Vanzetti had been glancing at a copy of a Boston paper whose margins I meant to use for a notebook. One of the main stories was the sensationalized version of some college students' suicides. The cheap press had decided that the study of Cicero or Xenophon was unnatural and led to self-destruction. (The suicide rate was about normal that year, but a son of prominent parents had hanged himself and it made a good running story.)

"I think Dr. Frood wrong when he says student kill himself to make someone sorry," Vanzetti remarked. "It is when he cannot make someone sorry, he kills himself in anger at world which pays him not attention—in despair—"

"No, no," Nick Sacco said. (He had once tried suicide via a hunger strike.) "I think to die is the best way to free my wife and children. I see her worry and cry. I have no pain—my mind thinks bright and clear. If I die my wife has no more worry—all over after a while. Not tied to me any more."

Vanzetti was thoughtful—he had said, "Only sick mind kill himself," and since Sacco declared that his mind worked "bright and clear" during his tentative suicide there was no use for a gentleman to pursue a subject that might be controversial. Nick was thoughtful for a moment, and then he discussed a prisoner whom he had known during his seven years in the cells.

"He comes home one night and this other man is with his wife, you know. And he shoots at him and kills her. Nine to twelve years. So about two years more they are then turning him free."

"Too long," said Vanzetti, decisively. "You know what he says to me once? 'Vanzetti, you know what I think of all night? My wife—my home. Every night—all time. Now—all gone.' He is the kind of man who love home—he had home, nice home, nice wife—and thees man take all from him—wife, home, freedom—"

Sacco, whose wife, home, children, and freedom had also been taken from him, interrupted emphatically. "I am against these man who break up home—I think such man should not be allow—" and he paused and smiled at Bartolomeo apologetically. "The human being should not be restrained by force—but I am against the man who breaks up home."

It was a problem, of course, which they had posed for themselves. Dante stated it, *"Nel mezzo del cammin di nostra vita, Mi ritrovai per una selva oscura,"* and in the middle of their lives these two found themselves in the same sort of obscure philosophized forest. They were against force—but also against the things it amends.

Dramatically, one regrets to say, a bell rang and presently there was a procession of gray men from the workshops to the cells. Their arms were folded, for some reason, their faces blank, their bodies rigidly erect. The stream divided and disappeared.

"They been working," Sacco said. *"Dio,* when I cannot work I almost go crazy. My fingers want to act. At last, they give me brick to clean. I beg, I argue—give me something to do. You see me now? I gain a pound a day for thirty days."

The Warden nodded.

"First they give me basket to weave, like children. Better than nothing but not much. Then I sit alone—years, years—thousands of days—all to say that man's nature can be perfect—nothing to do— breathe, eat, sit up, lie down—because I think innerly *l'uomo* is noble—"

Vanzetti restrained this speech gently. His own confinement had not been such an ordeal because he had a habit of reading and the seven years had been an opportunity rather than a confinement.

He waved at the departing workers—prisoners under capital sentence are exempted from labor.

"We're capitalists, Nick and me. We have domicile, we eat, we don't do work. We're nonproducers—we live off other men's work outside. When we libertarians make speech, they're calling Nick and me names."

This amused Sacco. But it was late in the day and the deputy who had been left in charge appeared significantly. Suddenly one realized that these pleasant people would die in a month or two in a straight wooden chair, as the country was about to go on its summer vacation.

Vanzetti smiled, gravely and sympathetically, and nodded his fine head. And suddenly his voice was stern.

"If it had not been for this thing, I might have live out my life among scorning men. I might have die, unmarked, unknown, a failure. Now we are not a failure. This is our career and our triumph. Never in our full life can we hope to do such work for tolerance, for joostice, for man's understanding of man, as now we do by an accident.

"Our words—our lives—our pains—nothing! The taking of our lives—lives of a good shoemaker and a poor fish peddler—all!

"The moment that you think of belong to us—that last agony is our triumph!"

There was nothing deliberated or oratorical about this last statement. As Thompson and the *Transcript* man had said, Vanzetti was naturally and quietly eloquent—and disturbing. So he was electrocuted.

8.

THE EXECUTION took place on August 23, 1927. There were picket lines around Dedham Prison at the time, and numbers of the loveliest and the best among the intelligentsia were hauled to jail. The troops were called out to protect the prison and the home of Judge Thayer, who never needed much of a guard because, for the few unhappy years he lived, he was a serviceable red rag for the "Reds." Who judged Dreyfus? Who judged Mooney? A dead judge isn't of any use to the opposition.

Sacco cried, "Live anarchy," in Italian, as he seated himself in the chair, according to the Associated Press reporter. A very discriminating ear—try the same phrase in English or French at thirty feet or so, and try to determine which of the three languages is employed. Sacco had to be an *Italian* criminal.

Vanzetti said:

"I want to thank you for all you have done for me, Warden. I want to tell you that I am innocent and that I have never committed any crime but sometimes some sin. I thank you for everything you have done for me. I am innocent of all crime, not only this, but all. I am an innocent man. I wish to forgive some people for what they are now doing to me."

The Warden, who was in no way responsible, was hardly able to make the prescribed announcement after the execution.

Some time later the front porch was blown off Thayer's house. He probably carried insurance on that, but his later years do not awaken envy. He had hoped to be promoted to a higher court, but he died before the promotion came.

Thompson died, full of years and honor; Lowell died—almost all of the principals died and are only names today. But Bart Vanzetti and Nick Sacco, innocent or guilty, did not die "unmarked, unknown, a failure."

The Lindbergh Legends

BY JOHN LARDNER

John Lardner worked on the Lindbergh kidnap case as a reporter for the New York *Herald Tribune* in 1932. Later he wrote a description for the *New Yorker* of the America First meetings at which Lindbergh was the principal orator and hero. Mr. Lardner believes that—contrary to the popular legend—Colonel Lindbergh has always rather enjoyed being famous and conspicuous, and he believes that the Lindbergh saga has more chapters to come. Mr. Lardner is one of two writing sons of the late Ring Lardner, Sr. He has written two novels and several books on sports, does a weekly sports column for *Newsweek,* and is a frequent contributor of articles and book reviews to the *New Yorker.*

✵ 1.

IN MAY, 1927, a slim, comely man of twenty-five years flew an airplane from New York to Paris all by himself, without stopping. His performance was instantly recognized as the climactic stunt of a time of marvelous stunts: of an epoch of noise, hero worship, and the sort of "individualism" which seems to have meant that people were not disposed to look at themselves, and their lives, in general, and therefore ran gaping and thirsty to look at anything done by one man or woman that was special and apart from the life they knew. The farther the hero went—whether he went upward, downward, sideways, through air, land, or water, or hand over hand on a flagpole— the better, provided he went alone.

The year 1927, which came about two-thirds of the way through this time of escape from mass realities, was the perfect year for the perfect feat. It was the apex of the era, chronologically and emotionally. The young flier, Charles A. Lindbergh, did not know this. He picked his time by chance as far as any ordinary reader of human instincts can say; though then and later he was so repeatedly and so overwhelmingly famous, and showed such a sense, friendly or not, of the rhythms and uses of notoriety, that many newspapermen of his period refuse to lay any part of it to chance. Newspapermen have always felt superstitious, among other things, about Lindbergh.

At any rate, he rang the bell at the top of the range, in that county fair of a setting. I do not want to belittle the skill and cool efficiency of Lindbergh's Paris flight, or his long-standing talent for flying in general, when I liken his deed of that time to such another as, say, Gertrude Ederle's swim across the English Channel a year earlier. With Lindbergh, it was all more so and better—everything was right. He was young, he was photogenic (as they came to say later), he was apparently modest and unaffected by the first wild sweep of fame, and so simple and understandable in what he said and did that the public turned handsprings in delight and self-congratulation. But basically the reaction was the same as to Ederle and the other heroes and heroines of the era. Its flavor was strong and sweet, and people took their time over it, drawing it out. But a one-day wonder can last weeks or months and still be, at bottom, a one-day wonder. Some men said Lindbergh's nonstop leap to Paris was a vital stimulus to aviation; those closest to aviation thought the growth was inevitable, in view of the more studious flights made before and after Lindbergh's, and will tell you today, looking back, that Lindbergh in 1927 had no noticeable, statistical effect on the public's attitude toward flight. In short, he was one for the book . . . a world-wide love affair . . . confetti which cost sixteen thousand dollars to clean off the streets of New York.

And that, by every known precedent, should have been that.

But it wasn't. The end of the story was delayed, spectacularly, time and again. Lindbergh lived on in the world's interest in a recurrent series of reactions—Lindbergh's reactions to the public and the public's reactions to Lindbergh—some violent, some cold, some maudlin. One event which came a few years after the flight to Paris, the kidnaping and murder of Lindbergh's son, calls for no psychological explanation of Lindbergh; it was done to Lindbergh and his wife, brutally and as far as we know objectively, from outside. Yet by and large people have attempted to explain the phenomenon of Lindbergh—the phenomenon of the story that refused to die, that may be smoldering now for another burst into print—in terms of the man's character. I know that the temptation to psychoanalyze Lindbergh has been too much for many men and women in the last ten years. Harold Nicolson, the English writer who rented his home to Lindbergh and his family when they first fled America, later wrote about him as follows, reviewing the years after 1927:

"It was almost with ferocity that he struggled to remain himself. And in the process of that arduous struggle his simplicity became muscle-bound; his virility-ideal became not merely inflexible, but actually rigid; his self-control thickened into arrogance, and his convictions hardened into granite. He became impervious to anything outside his own legend—the legend of the young lad from Minnesota whose head could not be turned."

If that sounds a bit portentous, remember that Nicolson was writing at a time when England was in danger and Lindbergh was openly opposed to saving her. Otherwise, it is a fair specimen of the widespread effort to find the answer to the riddle of Lindbergh in Lindbergh himself, and nowhere else. There is as much truth in it, probably, as in many of the other analyses which rolled off angry lips and pens at the time of Lindbergh's isolationism, when he opened a part of his mind to the world by fighting American intervention in the second World War. Certainly Lindbergh was deliberately responsible to some extent for his continuing fame and notoriety after 1927. Loathing the blatant, contactual phases of publicity, he showed nonetheless one of the truest gifts ever seen on this planet for attracting it—seeming sometimes to go out of his way to get it when it might not have been forthcoming. It almost appeared that he needed fame to subsist, to support his confidence in the role he had won. Here is the paradox that engrosses his analyzers: a man supernormally ingrown and aloof becoming with sure instinct a chronic public figure. Lindbergh once said of "interventionists" and "idealists" before the war that they were "men who were too far separated from fact and life." No man of note was ever further separated from life and fact than Lindbergh. No man could be more reluctant to admit it.

2.

THERE WAS a good deal of glibness, in the heyday of the movement called America First a few years ago, about marking the parallel between Charles A. Lindbergh, Jr., and his "isolationist" father. Possibly Lindbergh wanted to believe that such a parallel existed, but it didn't. His father seems to have been quite another sort of man.

Lindbergh's father was Charles Augustus Lindbergh, Sr., and the father of Charles Augustus Lindbergh, Sr., was Ola Mansson, born in Sweden and for twelve years a member of the Swedish Riksdag, or Parliament. The present Lindbergh, in fact, is the only man of his line in three generations who has not held public office. Ola Mansson went about Sweden crusading against a number of things, including the whipping post, which he helped in the end to abolish. In the 1850's he changed his name to Lindbergh. In 1860, with his new wife and a new son (his first wife had died), he sailed to America, as a great many other people from a great many other nations were then doing. Eighty years later his grandson was to speak with marked disparagement of the immigrant as opposed to the home-grown American.

The Lindberghs went across the land by boat and train as far as St. Anthony Falls, Minnesota, and then by wagon another hundred miles to a homestead near Melrose, in the neighborhood of the Sinclair Lewis town of Sauk Center. The old man is said to have been a robust character who once axed himself in the forest and refused to leave off work. His son Charles went for a few years to a school conducted by a Roman Catholic priest in Sauk Center. In his free time he worked on the railroad cars as a newsboy and candy-butcher, and when he was old enough he entered the Law School of the University of Michigan, earning his way through by washing dishes and waiting on tables. He was practicing law in Detroit when he met and married a schoolteacher, of chemistry and science, Irish by ancestry, the daughter of a Detroit dentist named Dr. Land. Their son was born in Detroit on February 4, 1902. Before he was two months old, his father took the family to Little Falls, Minnesota, and set up a law practice there.

Charles A. Lindbergh, Sr., was known as "C.A." to the people of Little Falls, some of whom are reported to have recognized him early as a soft touch for a loan and to have set in motion maneuvers which forestalled the possibility of his dying wealthy—although he was successful in his work and a rising force in the town, the state, and the region.

"He made money, but he was generous," said his law partner, Walter Eli Quigley. "He seldom refused a farmer a loan."

The farmers liked the elder Lindbergh, and the elder Lindbergh liked the farmers. He lost no time in making them the keystone of his liberal and free-thinking—in fact, socialist—economic theories. C. A. Lindbergh was bookish but gregarious, a thinker and writer but a practicing politician. One of his interests was the creation of an insurance co-operative for farmers, to free them from the big insurance companies of the East. For a time he ran a magazine stumping for co-operatives, which failed, and he became increasingly obsessed by the situation which centered the nation's money in a few hands. He was anti-Morgan, anti-Kuhn Loeb, anti-National City Bank—the champion of workers in farm or factory. His son never shared in all his life, as far as anyone has been able to detect, this anticapitalist bias. On the other hand, C. A., though an affectionate father, never shared his son's growing interest in mechanics, which passed through bicycles and motorcycles and iceboats to jalopies and eventually to planes. C. A. staked his son to eight hundred dollars for his first plane, but he did not, according to Quigley, care much for the notion.

The father and son looked a good deal alike: lean handsome faces with deep eyes and firm mouths. C. A.'s face, however, began in time to take on the lines of maturity and suffering which come, not unnaturally, to those who mature and suffer. One of the men who in later years made a hobby of publicly psychoanalyzing his son said that the latter's face never seemed to age or to reflect grief or any other experience, keeping a sort of cherubic aspect through its fortieth year.

In 1906 C. A. ran for Congress and was elected. He ran, it should be noted, on the Republican ticket. He was as yet a socialist in word and precept only, and the Farmer-Labor party, which he helped to found, was still in the future. His son, five years old, went to Washington with him in 1907 and watched the swearing-in ceremony. C. A. remained in Congress eight years. During much of that time his boy

Charles stayed in Washington too, helping with such office work as running errands and licking envelopes. For a time he went to the Friends School there, along with the children of Theodore Roosevelt, and was part of a "drugstore" gang, led by Quentin Roosevelt, which used to convene at the store and run up mild tabs in confectionery.

There was a panic in 1907, and C. A. Lindbergh swung into action with a campaign for investigation of his great enemy, the "money trust." The newspapers began to work him over. He stored up thousands of clippings denouncing him as a demagogue, a "dangerous radical and dissenter." He fought, fruitlessly, the Federal Reserve Bill of 1913, and published a book called *Banking and Currency* in support of his views. In 1915 he was in at the birth of the Farmers League, a political group which was launched in Minnesota, scored its first successes in North Dakota in 1916, and then turned and drove a wedge into C. A.'s home state with our entry into war. Lindbergh and the League, till then fundamentally progressive, socialistic, and antimoney, at once acquired an antiwar and anti-Britain following—still and always based, in Lindbergh's view, on the suspicion of collusion between British and Wall Street finance. They lined up a heavy farm and labor vote. C. A. Lindbergh ran for Governor of Minnesota on the Farmers League ticket in 1918, and it was a wild, bitter campaign.

He electioneered in his old car, his son driving. Mobs booed him, eggs and garden stock were thrown. This, mark you, was not a prewar campaign, like the younger Lindbergh's before Pearl Harbor. This was actually in wartime, and the elder Lindbergh, called pro-German by his rivals, worked against big pressures and heavy clubs. Department of Justice agents broke the plates of his old book on banking and his new one, *Why Is Your Country at War?*, in which he denounced the sale of Liberty bonds as manipulated and forced by bankers, and said at one point:

"Our purpose is humane; nevertheless I believe I have proved that a certain 'inner circle,' without official authority and for selfish purposes, adroitly maneuvered things to bring about conditions that would make it practically certain that some of the belligerents would violate our international rights and bring us into war with them."

This theory of "maneuver" was in the mouth of the younger Lind-

bergh twenty-two years later, but not "our purpose is humane." Our
purpose had become stupid to him, a waste of supermen and white
Western civilization. There were no "supermen" or "yellow breeds"
in C. A.'s vocabulary. Since we were at war, C. A. favored seizure and
state ownership of mines, trains, plants, and resources to stop profiteer-
ing. He had no personal opposition to Woodrow Wilson, and Wilson
scolded mob tactics against Lindbergh. When C. A. lost the election
he was offered a place on the War Industries Board by Bernard Baruch.
Conservative circles in Minnesota killed this appointment, Baruch
withdrawing the offer politely and C. A. going his way a little more
bitter than before. He was a Farmer-Laborite by 1920, campaigning
for Henrik Shipstead, and in 1923 an author again and for the last
time—with *The Economic Pinch,* which showed him still obsessed by
the evils of big money but brimful, too, of gentle socialist slogans and
advice against such things as the exploitation of children.

His own child was a flier by then. In 1923, in a campaign for a special
Senatorial primary, the young Lindbergh flew campaign literature and
speakers for his father, and once, only once, flew his father too. Afterward C. A. said to his partner Quigley:

"I don't like this flying business. See if you can't get the boy to come
into our office, study law, and join the firm."

Quigley mentioned it to Charles, and the son smiled, shook his head,
and said the law was not for him. C. A. Lindbergh died of a brain
tumor in 1924. His son, then in the Army, was able to visit him once
during his illness, but his leave was up before his father died. Quigley
saw the young man off on his way back to camp in Texas, and recalls:
"I could see he was deeply moved, but outwardly he was stoical."

One day in 1925 Charles A. Lindbergh, Jr., carried out a request his
father had made before he died. From a plane he scattered C. A.'s ashes
over the old Lindbergh homestead near Little Falls, by the Mississippi.

3.

IN A LETTER to the younger Lindbergh when he was training for his
army commission as a flier, an old college classmate asked, among other

things, how Lindbergh's love life was coming along. Lindbergh answered:

"In this respect, I am situated in about the same position that I was in at Madison—i.e., no prospects, past, present, or future."

He was quiet and in-dwelling from early boyhood on. Some who knew him in those years called his manner "grim," and there is no doubt that there was a feeling of withdrawal in him, a discomfort when he came into the world outside planes and mechanics, that made him awkward socially. He seems to have found relief from this social strain and repression chiefly in practical jokes—and they were the sort of practical jokes, complicated, strenuous, and "virile," about which a monograph might be written in connection with American life. The prank called the "snipe hunt," for instance, is apt to cost the jokers themselves a full night of sleep and miles of walking, running, and crawling. Lindbergh arranged a snipe hunt at least once, at the expense of a fellow pilot. Another time he went to great pains to introduce a cow into the neighborhood of an airplane mechanic who had a mortal fear of bulls, and again he filled the ice-water pitcher at the bedside of a roommate, one Bud Gurney, with kerosene. His jokes are what his early comrades remembered best about him; those, and his eating. The young man known to everyone as "Slim" was a spectacular performer with a knife and fork. Apparently he took a shy pleasure in the sociable kidding which he earned by this gift. He would sometimes put away six eggs plus a steak or a chop for breakfast, and later at Curtiss Field on Long Island, when he was waiting to fly to Paris, he hung up local records at the hot dog stand.

If he looked grim, it is pretty certain that Lindbergh was content in his life and work and an amiable enough fellow by his own lights. He lost little time in finding the work, the pleasure, that suited him above everything else. After graduation from high school in Little Falls— where he once wrote an elaborate and not uncomical satire on the finicky methods of his English teacher—he took three semesters in engineering at the University of Wisconsin, where the only thing that seemed to interest him much was shooting (he made the rifle team). Then of his own accord he organized a clean break with the past and enrolled at a flying school in Lincoln, Nebraska. Within four years he was known from Chicago to the West Coast—by the narrow but shrewd circle of men in his own profession—as one of the country's best fliers. Seldom has any man shown a quicker and more natural aptitude for flying a plane.

Lindbergh barnstormed a little at the age of twenty-one, but he needed to know more. The Army was the great practical school of flying at the time, so Lindbergh enlisted in March, 1924, in what was known as the "War Department's Air Service," and was commissioned a Second Lieutenant the following spring. After some more barnstorming he joined the 110th Squadron of the 35th Division, Missouri National Guard, winning the reserve commission of Captain in December, 1925. His flying had already given him associations in St. Louis. He went to work there early in 1926 for Major William B. Robertson, whose company had just been licensed to fly the mail between St. Louis and Chicago.

For this job Lindbergh got $350 a month salary and another $100 a month in flying allowances. He also became the outstanding member of the Caterpillar Club. The Caterpillars were army or army reserve fliers who had parachuted from their planes—strictly of necessity, no daredevil stuff. Lindbergh was never an easy leaper—"he was likely to stick with a plane in trouble longer than the average good flier," said another pilot on the run. Yet Lindbergh made four jumps in the year 1926. Once, jumping near St. Louis when his controls jammed, he dislocated a shoulder. Twice he went over the side when his gas ran out in bad weather, and "walked the mail in"—locating his plane on foot, salvaging the mail, and arranging to have it trucked the rest of the way to its destination. Lindbergh broke into print for the first time, so far as I know, through his Caterpillar Club record. A slightly sob-sisterish story of the time referred to him as "a supple, young, blond giant just past twenty-four."

Then Monsieur Raymond Orteig moved into his life, or, rather, Lindbergh moved into M. Orteig's and the world's.

Writing about the American Middle West recently, an Englishman, Graham Hutton, said that most of the Middle Westerners he talked with thought, among other things, that Lindbergh was the first man to fly the Atlantic. Quite possibly people think so all over the country, and all over the world. Actually, the Atlantic had been flown several times from 1919 through 1926, nonstop or otherwise, by dirigible and plane. There were various transatlantic flights in various stages of preparation in late 1926 and early 1927. This was partly the responsibility of M. Orteig, who had offered twenty-five thousand dollars to the man or men who would fly from New York to Paris or vice versa. Some people spoke unkindly of M. Orteig's offer as homicidal in effect if not in spirit. I know that this elderly landlord burned with desire for Franco-American good will and was so well disposed toward mankind that he once gave me the freedom of the Hotel Lafayette's kitchen, and the best eating in downtown New York, in return for a very small favor. At any rate, his twenty-five thousand dollars was on the line. Talk of flying the Atlantic was in the air. Toward the end of 1926, Lindbergh set out to hustle himself a stake.

He was not ideally equipped for salesmanship. He could not work up interest among the usually farsighted editors of the St. Louis *Post-Dispatch*. The rival *Globe-Democrat,* however, listened to his plans, and eventually, in early 1927, money was forthcoming, mostly from Mrs. Lora Josephine Knight, widow of a St. Louis stockbroker. At San Diego, California, in the spring of the year, Lindbergh was camped at the Ryan aircraft plant supervising the final touches on a silver monoplane built to his order which he named "The Spirit of St. Louis." He had for some time been practicing staying awake for thirty to forty hours at a stretch.

He had never had much to do with newspapermen except for his cash-finding campaign in St. Louis. Now he made proposals to the San Diego reporters which they were to think back on, a few weeks later, with some irritation. He wanted the press to work for him. He asked the reporters to keep quiet about himself and his plans and to keep him posted on what they heard from the East of the moves of his competitors—principally Clarence Chamberlin and Charles A. Levine, in their Bellanca, and Richard E. Byrd and his big, distinguished crew in their Fokker.

The reporters said sure. A few days later they said "So long," and Lindbergh was off. Being the flier he was, he at once made American air history, with the longest nonstop American flight recorded up till then, San Diego to St. Louis, and the fastest over-all time from coast to coast. He arrived at Curtiss Field at 5:33 on the afternoon of May 12, 1927.

The public and the papers were aware of him now, but doubtful. Once, during the week that followed, the *Post-Dispatch* of St. Louis rang up a man at the *Times* of New York to ask if he thought Lindbergh, of St. Louis, was going to amount to anything. The *Times* man could not give a definite answer. Lindbergh himself was not certain how he stood in the matter of news value, but he knew he was going to take off, so he subscribed, in the neat, private, foresighted way in which he did everything else for this flight, to a press clipping service. Then, with no pontoons on the plane to weigh her down, he took off at 7:51 on the morning of May 20 and headed a little north of the sunrise, while his rivals remained on the ground to wait to be sure about weather.

4.

PROBABLY EXCITEMENT never grew with more terrible momentum, from a puff of curiosity to an earth-shaking tension, than it did through the night of May 20 and the morning of May 21. Probably everyone who knew of the flight remembers today where he was, or exactly what he was doing, at some moment in the course of it. There was a fight that night in a baseball park in New York between Jack Sharkey and Jim Maloney; I remember that Joe Humphreys, a little announcer with a bow tie and a voice of brass, arose in the pool of light in the center of the darkness and called for silence and prayer, and his words were maudlin, moving, and eloquent.

It was not a flight that can be spoken of in detail. That was the happy thing about it in the end: nothing happened, except that the plane was sighted now and then, true on its course and making good time. What went on in the flier's mind the flier might have said, but the chances are he could not. He wrote a book afterward, called *We,* in which he told some things about the flight to Paris. He spoke of the preparations he made, the food and water he took along, sandwiches, army concentrated rations for five days, an Armbrust Cup—"which," wrote Lindbergh, "is a device for condensing the moisture from human breath into drinking water. The cup is cloth covered and contains a series of baffle plates through which the breath is blown." In those sentences is the detachment, the cool, scientific preoccupation, the avoidance of bravado or any sense of great adventure, which make *We* the best memento we have of the man who made the flight.

Lindbergh flew 3,610 miles to Paris in 33 hours and 29 minutes, landing cleanly at Le Bourget field on the evening of May 21. A sea of Parisians flowed out to the field, broke down steel fences, swept over the runways. Lindbergh, escaping to some pilots' quarters, "identified" himself—"I am Charles A. Lindbergh"—and showed letters of introduction to Ambassador Herrick and others. He was whisked away from the joyous mob, and the line began to form for more mobs in London, Washington, New York. From that moment, which seemed to be the beginning of the end of the most glorious story of the era of glorious stunts, two forces—circumstance and Lindbergh's character—set to work to prevent such an ending. At the very time he seemed to be trying most desperately to efface himself, Lindbergh unerringly prolonged his fame and shaped himself for new stories to come. At no time in the next fifteen years did circumstance fail to lend a hand in this process when a hand was needed.

5.

EIGHT MONTHS after the Paris flight, a New York editor wired a reporter who was covering Lindbergh on a good-will tour through Latin America:

"No more unless he crashes."

It was the first suggestion—and only one man's suggestion—that the point of surfeit had been reached in the first of the great Lindbergh stories. There is no telling how many tons of newsprint were consecrated to the Lone Eagle (to use the sobriquet which pleased the flier best, or offended him least) in those eight months. His effect on the world had been orgiastic and orgastic. He returned to America to find five hundred thousand letters, seventy-five thousand telegrams, and two freight car loads of press clippings awaiting him. He was decorated in swift succession by the President of France, the King of England, and the President of the United States, who also commissioned him a Colonel. His laundry disappeared every time he sent it out, and he could not write checks because people kept them instead of cashing them. Of the many sentimental songs which were written about him, the most popular, as I recall, was "Lucky Lindy." This was an epithet which Lindbergh hated in each of its parts and *in toto*. He set to work at once to destroy any impression that he was either lucky or that he was "Lindy." It was a sort of battle no other quick celebrity had ever put up, but Lindbergh did not mean to be a quick celebrity. He aimed to perpetuate his fame and what he considered his dignity at one and the same time. His resistance to any other kind of attention was fanatical, skillful, and wholly successful.

Lucky? He promptly flew through all the forty-eight states, through Mexico, Central America, South America, and the West Indies, always alone, touching on sixteen different countries, covering 7,860 miles, without a slip or a flaw.

Lindy? He had been Slim, a good, hard, technician's name, to his old friends. To his new ones—and they were all new now; his social life broke off cleanly, and began along fresh lines, in 1927—he was Charles, a hard man to talk to but a man to be respected at the highest levels. No vaudeville junkets, no movie contracts, no testimonials, no clasping of the hands above the head in response to the yells of the crowd. His new friends were ambassadors, statesmen, high-ranking officers, scientists, executives, almost exclusively men of capital. Lindbergh became a scientist, an executive, and a man of capital himself. But his sense of public relations, unconscious or not, did not fail him. Among the premiums spread before him, he chose the cleanest, the most respectable: a Guggenheim charter, a government prize of twenty-five thousand dollars for his Latin-American flight (the Orteig prize which spawned his Paris trip and his fame was a little more sensational in nature, but, of course, inescapably his), the Woodrow Wilson Medal, writing payments (his articles were staid and objective) from the New York *Times* and the *Saturday Evening Post,* advisory positions and stock in Pan-American and Transcontinental Air Transport, the second of which became "TWA, the Lindbergh Line." He could not keep the masses from calling him Lindy, but he convinced them that he was not the Lindy type. No publicity genius could have charted a campaign better. The public changed its first frank, friendly love for awe and admiration—but Lindbergh stayed in its mind and stayed pre-eminent, instead of dwindling to a line or two of fine type in the *World Almanac*.

Two years after Paris he married Anne Morrow, whom he met in Mexico while her father was American Ambassador there. She was then twenty-one, a year out of Smith College, a dark, shy, quiet girl with a fine mind and a small but pure and valuable gift for putting her thoughts and fancies, about the earth, sky, and sea, on paper. Their first son, Charles, was born in June, 1930. In the next year Lindbergh and his wife flew together to Canada and Alaska, and then to Siberia, Japan, and China. Lindbergh, in his book *We*, preserved for the future a record of what was best and most honest in his own native character. His wife, writing about their flights and adventures in such books as *North to the Orient* and *Listen, the Wind*, set down with a richer literary talent something of the high romance and exaltation that were implicit in Lindbergh's life in the air.

During the years when he was enforcing his resistance to precedent, to the fate of the skyrocket, a small group of men was developing a resistance to Lindbergh—and doing it all alone, in silence. To many people it may not seem important that Lindbergh was antipathetic to newspapermen, and they to him. Yet it is a curious fact, worth noting; for reporters were the key to the fame that sustained him. Knowing the power of his position, Lindbergh seemed to feel that he could point up his hatred of nonprivacy—which is an entirely different thing from publicity—by taking it out on the working press. The working press tried time and again to show him the way to privacy: swallow your medicine, the shouts and the fury, at a quick gulp, like a good patient, and then go off and stop being public. But with strange perversity Lindbergh continued to gag at the medicine and invite the disease.

He once, in the early days of his celebrity, flew coast to coast in record time. The flight was advertised as a record attempt, through the channels Lindbergh thought proper; in short, it deliberately invited reporting. Yet Lindbergh flew into a rage at the men who met him to report its consummation firsthand.

It's hard to say when this cycle of frictions began. It was soon. On his first stop in San Francisco after the Paris flight, Lindbergh took to a hotel room and the press gathered in the corridor outside. Lindbergh sent out word that he would not be available for some time. The reporters waited. Presently a dark and genial face peered out from behind a mustache, through another door in the corridor, and its owner, Señor Álvaro Obregón, of Mexico, said:

"If you're waiting for Colonel Lindbergh, why not wait in here?"

Inside Señor Obregón's room the press got a lively speech on Señor Obregón's plans to be President of Mexico in 1928, and quantities of liquor to wash it down with. When Lindbergh's emissary finally traced the reporters, with the news that the Colonel was ready to talk, he found them agreed that the story was not Lindbergh but Obregón. That is what the papers showed next day.

There are many such episodes accessible for the record, though few of them ended the same way, for, as I said, Lindbergh's position was powerful and the press was seldom able or willing to sacrifice the public's curiosity to its own irritation. To the overwhelming bulk of the public, in the words of a writer commenting on Lindbergh in 1930, he "remained Godlike."

It might be borne in mind, however, that from 1930 on Lindbergh's closest friend was Dr. Alexis Carrel. The doctor was, first, a scientist and technician. But he was also a colorful and persuasive writer, with certain "philosophical" ideas. These ideas, not unheard of before 1930 or since, had to do with the natural supremacy of the white race, the rule of the weak by the strong, and the breeding of supermen.

6.

LINDBERGH'S baby son, Charles, was kidnaped from the flier's home in New Jersey on March 1, 1932. He was found dead seventy-two days later in a patch of woods in the same neighborhood, after Lindbergh, with a plea to the police and the newspapers to help him by keeping their hands off the case, had paid ransom money to the unknown and unseen kidnaper. The crime was at once so cold-blooded and so violent that it would have had nation-wide publicity no matter who the victims were. Since the victims were the Lindberghs, the impact upon the press and public was tremendous; the law of the land itself was affected. Within a few months of the murder, long before the arrest of Bruno Richard Hauptmann, Congress enacted the so-called "Lindbergh Law," which gave federal agents national freedom in the pursuit of kidnapers.

This second Lindbergh story was so "big" that it was seldom out of the newspapers for even a day during the next four years. Nor did the papers see any reason, especially after the baby was found dead, to tone it down or to miss such a sterling chance to play cops-and-robbers. Every manner of reporter and cop, official and unofficial, from Walter Winchell down, or up, took a hand. Naturally enough, a score of newspaper "characters" sprouted in the fringe of Lindbergh's fame and tragedy.

Most of them are forgotten, or at least half forgotten, today. There was Dr. John F. Condon, a mild, sententious old Bronx schoolteacher, nicknamed "Jafsie." Young reporters used to see and hear him at an annual schoolboy reunion party that sometimes made the papers on dull days. Now he enjoyed a front-page run for a while as a far from backward negotiator between Lindbergh and the kidnaper, who lived in Jafsie's neighborhood. There was Ellis Parker, a rural New Jersey detective with a nation-wide reputation for hawkshawing, who involved himself in the case and wound up in the Federal Penetentiary for kidnaping and torturing the wrong "suspect." There were Irving Bitz and Salvy Spitale, New York underworld "operators," who were called in by the police for the not unsympathetic assignment of trying to find out if someone in the "profession" had done the kidnaping. Every reporter in New York worked on some part of the case at some time. I trailed Mr. Bitz through lower East Side tenements, and was one of those eventually summoned to the handsome apartment of Spitale to take a statement. It was plain that the name and prestige of Lindbergh reached far, wide, and deep.

"If it was someone I knew, I'll be God-damned if I wouldn't name him," said Spitale. "I been in touch all around, and I come to the conclusion that this one was pulled by an independent."

Bruno Hauptmann, a Bronx carpenter of German birth, was arrested in 1934. He was convicted of the Lindbergh crime in 1935, after a trial in which the renown of Lindbergh, who was a witness, and the furious public interest in the case had the result of sending those connected with it, lawyers, writers, state executives, and witnesses other than Lindbergh, into a mad spin of histrionics and hysteria.

It has been said by more than one person that the killing of his son and the blatancy of the hunt and the trial which followed not only drove Lindbergh out of his country but formed in his mind the somber ideas which he gave to the world a few years later. That is probably, like so many other easy opinions, the truth but not the whole truth. The details of the crime tell what its effect on the father and mother of the baby must have been, and it is certain that Lindbergh's appearance in court, where his son's clothes were spread before him, brought a shock to his sense of what was private, fitting, and decent. He had another son now, born a month before Charles was found dead. A picture of the second son, Jon, appeared in a newspaper. There is no doubt that the kidnaping and its sequel, including this last detail, were directly responsible for the fact that the Lindberghs sailed secretly for England on December 22, 1935, three months before the execution of Hauptmann.

But Lindbergh had long since shown dissatisfaction with the state of affairs in America and his own relations with it. He had a problem: He could not enjoy the things he wanted, and these included fame and respect as well as work and privacy, in the way he wanted. Even the kidnaping, in the end, seems to have become fused in his mind with dislike for a "state of affairs," not for one man or for any single evil. In the next several years—the years of the clash between fascism and democracy—he spoke of America more than once in private conversation as "immoral" and "disorderly."

7.

ST. JOHN ERVINE wrote a plea for privacy for the Lindberghs in England, when they arrived there. It was not heeded at first by the British press, which put on a pursuit race and a public picnic, but after a few days the English reporters followed the formula which American reporters had so frequently offered for procedure between themselves and Lindbergh, and which Lindbergh himself was so often loath to accept: "Get it over with and the veil is yours." They gave him plenty of privacy—more of it, some who knew him said later, than he wanted. Time appears to have grown heavy on his hands after a few months at Long Barn, the Kentish house rented by him from Harold Nicolson and Victoria Sackville-West.

The villagers answered when he said "Hello," and the Vicar of Weald came to dinner and described him as "a thorough good fellow"; but not long afterward the Lindberghs were dining with the King (later the Duke of Windsor), in company with the Stanley Baldwins and the Ernest Simpsons. Then Lindbergh dropped over to Ireland, where he flew, as was customary, with the highest ranks available, De Valera and the Free State Army Chief. Coming home, he gave England a taste of the whimsy that had sometimes jangled the nerves of American newsmen. Instead of flying to the airport where he was expected, he came down at a small coastal field to spend the afternoon and night, asking the army men there not to report his presence. For a day and a night there were scareheads in the press of the world: "Lindbergh Lost." The government sent word to its ships at sea to be on the lookout, and the ships looked in vain.

The Lindberghs toured Germany, France, Italy, Egypt, and India. They dined or flew with Crown Prince Friedrich, Hugo Eckener, Italo Balbo, the Viceroy of India, and the new King and Queen of England. Balbo and the Crown Prince aroused Lindbergh's deepest suspicion by trying to take snapshots of him. He went to Denmark with Dr. Alexis Carrel to demonstrate the "mechanical heart," or Lindbergh Perfusion Pump, on which the two had worked together in America—a device to promote life and circulation in an organ divorced from the body. By 1937 Lindbergh was calling England "stupid," and by 1938 he had added France, where he lived for a summer and winter, to the now threefold list, with the adjectives "frivolous" and "corrupt." A pair of visits to Hermann Göring had brought him criticism from anti-Nazis in America. Apparently Lindbergh did not realize that such a school of thought existed, until he heard of the criticism. It angered him so much that he told friends he would go to Berlin to live in the following winter, 1938-39. He was dissuaded by the same friends. The Jewish purges of 1938 were at their height in Germany.

Obviously the mere catalogue of Lindbergh's voyages and visits between 1935 and 1939 does not explain what was happening in his mind, what had led him to reject, at any rate to doubt, the future and the character of three nations in rapid succession. Two men influenced him strongly: one, Dr. Carrel, whose association with Lindbergh, as an intimate friend, was now more than half a dozen years old, and the other, Göring, whose knack of salesmanship helped turn Lindbergh's notions about power and war and politics in the same direction as his thoughts about man and society.

"The most highly civilized races, the Scandinavian, for example, are white," wrote Dr. Carrel in 1935, in a book called *Man, the Unknown.*

"Caesar, Napoleon, Mussolini . . ." mused Dr. Carrel in the same book. "All great leaders of nations grown beyond human stature."

It seems a fair inference that the doctor's thoughts and private talk were of a piece with his published philosophy. Born in France, he had been a distinguished physician since 1906 in the fields of suturing blood vessels and transplanting organs. He won the Nobel Prize in 1912, and his scientific work, including that with Lindbergh, was undoubtedly valuable. But in the fields of philosophy and ethnology, which were not his own, the doctor went along with the most superficial, dime-magazine eugenic theories and with the racist cant of the Count de Gobineau and Houston Stewart Chamberlain. These men, whose works have been discredited by every objective technical study and all recorded statistics, are important in that they influenced, among others, Kaiser Wilhelm II and Hitler, and inspired *Mein Kampf.* Their views are reflected in Dr. Carrel's book. Dr. Carrel and Lindbergh summered on adjoining tiny islands off Brittany in 1938, often strolling the beach and talking together, and in the early part of 1939 Lindbergh wrote (in the *Atlantic Monthly*):

"No system of representation can succeed in which the voice of weakness is equal to the voice of strength."

And, speaking of aviation in the *Reader's Digest*: "[It is] one of those priceless possessions which permit the White Race to live at all in a sea of Yellow, Black, and Brown."

Lindbergh, with his wife, first went to Germany in July, 1936, at

Göring's invitation. The German air chief, delighted by the opportunity, dined and feted the Colonel and spread his planes, his plans, and his experiments before Lindbergh's eyes. There was another, more extensive tour in 1938, when Göring escorted Lindbergh through the plants of Messerschmitt, Heinkel, Junkers, and Focke-Wulf and showed him the best of his activated squadrons. At a stag dinner given by Ambassador Hugh Wilson, Lindbergh was assisting in the reception line when Göring, pausing in front of him, deftly and unexpectedly decorated him, "in the name of the Führer," with the Service Cross of the Order of the German Eagle, with Star. Lindbergh never returned it to Göring. His attitude was that he did not care to embarrass any of the parties to the gathering crisis.

The Colonel went in the same year to Russia, for an air fete at Tushino Airport. He saw little except gross and hopeless inefficiency (and he knocked down, at one point in his stay, a police agent who was detailed to guard him and whom he mistook for a newspaperman). Lindbergh still clung at this time to the hope that British stupidity was not so crass as to reject the prudent moral he had drawn from Göring's flashy display of air power. He was every inch the salesman of German strength that Göring thought he might be, when he went to Baldwin, then Prime Minister, with the tip that Germany was strong, Russia inept, and England and France far behind in preparations for air war. The course he then urged on Baldwin, and on anyone who would listen, is no secret; he stated it openly in a speech in 1941:

"I said that war in the west [of Europe] would result in German victory or a devastated and prostrate Europe. I therefore advocated that England and France build . . . their military forces . . . but that they permit Germany to expand eastward into Russia without declaring war."

Baldwin gave Lindbergh a courteous brush-off which, according to his acquaintances, annoyed the Colonel profoundly and reinforced his disgust with British "stupidity." As it happened, he was a better salesman than he knew, for at Munich, France and England followed his prescription almost to the letter, at Russia's expense. But Lindbergh went away—went home to America at last—thinking only of Baldwin's bullheadedness. A year later, again in a public speech, Lindbergh dropped neatly into the same bracket to which he consigned Baldwin when he said, arguing that America was safe from attack:

"An air invasion across the ocean is, I believe, impossible at this time or in any predictable future."

In fact, in the role he now chose to play, Lindbergh exactly opposed his father's published thought: "The world is in constant change." Behind his position he put all of his personal prestige. That prestige was based on skill and foresight in terms of aircraft, and in this very sphere he made what his warmest admirers could only describe, in the light of the record through 1945, as one wrong guess after another. Each guess or prediction involved a denial that any real change was in store for the world through the channels of the air.

8.

LINDBERGH'S home-coming to the United States in April, 1939, was unobtrusive. Shortly after his arrival he made private reports to the War Department and Congress—the factual substance of these could not have been too important, since an American military attaché had accompanied him throughout his inspections in Germany—and embarked on a four-month tour of army duty. When the war began in Europe in September he suddenly—and surprisingly—accepted a suggestion by a radio commentator that he state his views over the air.

It is a curious thing that never before in the twelve years in which the people of the world had known Lindbergh had they seen him open his mind or speak his thoughts. When they did, it was on topics no one had associated with him in 1927 or 1932—international politics and the state of civilization. As always, the reaction of press and public to the name of Lindbergh was immense.

He broke his lifelong public silence from Station WOL in Washington, two weeks after the war's start. Three networks carried the speech, which, written painstakingly by his own hand, favored "strong neutrality" for the United States. Lindbergh said we should make defensive rather than offensive weapons. This form of neutrality, applied to the facts of the moment, markedly favored Germany at the expense

of England and France. Lindbergh spoke of the folly of involving ourselves in the problems of alien "breeds," "yellow" people, "Moors and
Persians."

As one speech followed another—he made five in 1940, and nearly
a dozen in 1941—Lindbergh began to attract criticism both literate and
violent, and as he did so his own talks became less dry and measured,
more bitter, personal, and revealing. Plainly sincere, he was having
trouble dissociating himself and his program from crackpots and ax-
grinders. Lindbergh's embarrassment over such teammates as Joe
McWilliams and Gerald L. K. Smith was intense. He did quite stoutly
share the views of Lawrence Dennis, author of *The Coming American
Fascism,* who wrote to a known German agent, "I saw Lindbergh last
week and will see him often from now on." But Lindbergh offered, on
the platform in Madison Square Garden, to go down and eject the curly
spellbinder McWilliams from the crowd of twenty thousand, which
had shouted, in response to Lindbergh's own remarks, "Hang Roosevelt!" and "Impeach the President!"

He soon satisfied himself with the respectability of America First, a
movement which included several U. S. Senators and the president of
Sears, Roebuck and Company, General Robert Wood. America First,
of course, was hugely pleased to have Lindbergh. But there were phases
of the partnership which pained and annoyed other prominent isolationists. Membership multiplied, but it was noticeable that the crowds
began to leave the hall as soon as Lindbergh's talk was over—and at no
mere trickle. How many came to see the dream prince of 1927, and
how many to save America?

Lindbergh denounced the Presidential election of 1940 as dishonest:
both sides were interventionist. He spoke of "Jewish financing" of the
war. He resigned his army commission when President Roosevelt, in
April, 1941, called him a "copperhead": an allusion to the Northerners
in the Civil War who did not think the South could be beaten. Visibly
stung, Lindbergh retorted:

"A refugee who steps from the gangplank and advocates war is ac-
claimed as a defender of freedom. A native-born American who opposes war is called a fifth columnist."

Translations of his speeches were turning up everywhere in the official propaganda of Germany, Italy, and Spain. Japanese planes dropped them over Chungking. Less than four years before Okinawa, Lindbergh said that "modern aviation made it impractical, if not impossible, for an expeditionary force to cross an ocean and land successfully on a hostile coast against strong enemy air power." He was speaking every two or three weeks now, in St. Louis, Minneapolis, New York, Philadelphia, Hollywood, San Francisco. He had planned a speech in Boston for late December, 1941. But on December 7 America was attacked, and a thick, damp muffler fell upon America First and on Lindbergh.

It is true that ten days after Pearl Harbor, at a private dinner, he made a speech, widely quoted afterward by those present, regretting that the white race was divided in this war instead of banded together against the Mongolian. A little later Henry L. Stimson, the elderly Secretary of War, watched and listened coolly when Lindbergh, in Washington, expressed his willingness to serve the Army in any way he could. Stimson glanced at one of his aides. The aide said carefully that he thought it might be better if Mr. Lindbergh served the Army, or the country, as a civilian. Stimson nodded. Lindbergh also nodded, and left the meeting. In the early spring of 1942 he went to work as a planner and adviser in the Willow Run plant of Henry Ford.

9.

MOST OF THE NEWS STORIES that came between the two great wars can be looked back on with pleasure, amusement, or nostalgia, but certainly with detachment. They are over and done with. Lindbergh's story is not, because it is the story of a man's life and character, and he is still living and his character is still at work. I think it is impossible to write with detachment about Lindbergh at this moment. I don't pretend to have done so.

During the war it was only strict army press censorship that kept Lindbergh off the front page again, when he went along with the P-38 escort on a bombing mission over Borneo and apparently shot down a Japanese plane. General George Kenney, air commander of the area, said later, "I couldn't swear on a stack of Bibles he didn't do it."

Probably he did. There is little that much younger men can do in the air today that Lindbergh at forty-six cannot do. Navy fliers in the Pacific, to whom Lindbergh, as a civilian, gave valuable technical advice in 1944, were cold to Lindbergh at first for his isolationist crusade, but they conceded that no one could untie a mechanical knot more surely. In the summer of 1945 he was in Germany, doing technical work again for the Navy and for the United Aircraft Corporation.

For years, however, Lindbergh's aviation talents have gone hand in hand with a strong compulsion to influence people to see the world as he sees it, and his fame and mechanical gift are the tools he uses to make himself heard. He is still at it. Months after the end of the war Lindbergh was shut in a hotel room with a band of Midwest Congressmen, giving them his recipes: Keep the atom bomb completely secret . . . put no confidence in the United Nations. . . . The war we fought against the Nazis cut directly across Lindbergh's social and racial views, and his feeling of what constitutes civilization. He was never a man to change his mind, and since the flight to Paris in 1927 he has not been a man to undervalue himself or to overvalue obscurity.

There is still time—and there seems to be a growing opportunity—for a fourth Lindbergh Story.

The Crash—
and What It Meant

BY THURMAN ARNOLD

Thurman Wesley Arnold is a product of Laramie, Wyoming, who viewed the Wall Street debacle of 1929 from the philosophical vantage point of a law-college deanship at the University of West Virginia. Later he was appointed visiting professor at the Yale Law School and held a number of posts in the early New Deal. An unabashed "brain truster," he eventually became Assistant Attorney General in charge of the Anti-Trust Division, a terror to monopolists and cartelists, and later Judge of the U. S. Court of Appeals for the District of Columbia. His witty and penetrating book *The Folklore of Capitalism* (1937) has been called the most important stimulus to economic thinking in the United States since Thorstein Veblen. He also wrote *The Bottlenecks of Business* (1940) and *Democracy and Free Enterprise* (1942). He is now practicing law in Washington and keeping a watchful eye on trusts.

✸ 1.

AN EVENT NOW and then reveals a society in crisis. The year 1929 is such a landmark in economic history. It is the year of the stock market crash, of the beginning of the depression, of the great toboggan ride. In the past our economy had experienced other panics; but it had always taken the shock and bounced back. But the crash of 1929 was different. It was not a mere attack of economic indigestion curable by liquidating uneconomic ventures, bringing wild prices down where the consumer could reach them. Instead it turned out to be the first outbreak of a wasting economic fever which, through long years of depression, debilitated an entire nation, deprived it of the use of its productive strength, and created want in the midst of plenty. The public discovered that "sound" business thinking had been mostly superstition. Respectable theories of the functions of the state had to be abandoned. A hesitant Federal Government was forced, step by step, into a dominant role in the operation of our economy, against every American habit and tradition.

In 1928 no one dreamed we were on the verge of a catastrophic depression. It had been a glorious year. Stocks had made a gain of $11,385,993,733. The New York *Times* wrote in its New Year's editorial of January 1, 1929: "But it will go hard to get people to think of 1928 as merely a 'dead past' which we must make haste to bury. It has been a twelvemonth of unprecedented advance, of wonderful prosperity—in this country at least. . . . If there is any way of judging the future by the past, this new year may well be one of felicitation and hopefulness."

The note of hope was sounded everywhere in that New Year edition of the *Times*. Big businessmen made their usual yearly forecasts, all of them rosy, with only here and there a note of skepticism. There were a few stories and comments of an uneasy nature, but only a few. For example, one article told of the disappointing year which England had just gone through. There was a story that the state guarantee of bank deposits in Nebraska was inadequate to meet the pressure of mounting bank failures. But the stock market was up. Most people thought it was up permanently. And anyway sensible conservative people did not believe in guaranteeing bank deposits. It was an assault on free enterprise. It was a penalty put on good bankers for the benefit of poor ones.

There were many reasons for optimism so far as the real wealth of the country was concerned. In the beginning of 1929 national income was still going up in terms of the production of physical goods. It was the end of a ten-year period which had shown the greatest increase in national income this country had ever known. Between 1910 and 1919 the increase in the national income in terms of physical goods was about 10 per cent. During the period from 1920 to 1929 the increase was 93 per cent. We had practically doubled our national production of goods and services. Since in the long run real wealth consists only in ability to produce goods and services, we appeared to the casual observer on New Year's Day of 1929 to be richer by many times than ever before in our history. And the curve of increased production was going up at a more rapid pace than ever before.

We had become more efficient industrially than any other country in the world. Output per man-hour in manufacturing industries had doubled in the twenty years between 1909 and 1929. In coal mining and railroads the increase in output per man-hour had not been so great but it was nevertheless large. As a result, on New Year's Day of 1929 both weekly cash wages and real wages were at the highest point in our economic history. Real wages had more than doubled since 1914.

Mr. Hoover, who was then President, was an engineer with an engineering mind. He shared with everyone else, including our best economists, a lack of vision with respect to the defects in our social organization. But he saw better than most old-fashioned businessmen and bankers the technical possibilities of an industrial revolution in methods of production which had begun in the nineteenth century and was moving toward fruition in the twentieth. During the 1928 election campaign, he had informed the American people that they could expect two chickens in every pot and two cars in every garage as part of the normal standard of living for every family.

Wall Street was fully in accord with such sentiments. During May and June, 1928, stocks wavered, but as Election Day approached, the market advanced. And when Hoover rolled in by twenty-one million votes to Al Smith's fifteen million, the Dow-Jones industrials soared to 300. The "New Era" had arrived. A new school of economists argued that when you buy common stocks, you buy the future, not the present. Imaginative projections of earnings, five and ten years ahead, flourished. Radio went up to 500, was split five for one. Names like Auburn, Grigsby-Grunow, Kolster Radio—names you no longer hear of—flashed across the ticker tape. Blue chips, like U. S. Steel, American Telephone, and Eastman Kodak, reached all-time highs.

Inauguration Day—March 4, 1929—found Wall Street even more ebullient. The Dow-Jones industrials were up another 20 points. When stocks faltered in April, Wall Street seers regarded it as a "buying opportunity." And so it proved for a few months. By August the Dow-Jones industrials hit 380. But somehow, somewhere, the old zip was lacking. Pools worked valiantly, but stocks thrashed about getting nowhere. The first week in September stocks climbed to 381. That high stands to this day.

The break came early in September. There was a mid-month recovery, but it was the last gasp. Liquidation increased. Brokers' clerks worked long hours sending out margin calls. Came Thursday, October 24. Panic. U. S. Steel, which had been as high as $261\frac{3}{4}$, opened at $205\frac{1}{2}$, crashed through 200, and soon was down to $193\frac{1}{2}$. General Electric, which only a few weeks before sold above 400, opened at 315, dropped to 283. About noon, Charles E. Mitchell, head of the National City Bank, slipped into the offices of J. P. Morgan and Company. So did Albert H. Wiggin, head of the Chase National, William Potter, head of the Guaranty Trust, and Seward Prosser, head of the Bankers Trust. They, with Thomas Lamont, of Morgan, and George F. Baker, of the First National Bank, formed a consortium to shore up the market.

Toward 2:00 P.M., Richard Whitney, known as the Morgan broker, bid 205 for Steel. The market rallied. There was in that rally no hint that Whitney, then vice-president of the Exchange and subsequently its president, would ultimately go to Sing Sing for speculations as head of the firm of Richard Whitney and Company—a depression casualty.

Came Black Tuesday, October 28. Buy and sell orders piled into the Stock Exchange faster than human beings could handle them. The ticker ticked long after trading closed. A record 16,410,000 shares changed hands. The climax came November 13, 1929. The Dow-Jones average dropped to 198.7. And how the high and mighty had fallen! American Can was down from $181\frac{7}{8}$ to 86; American Tel. and Tel. from 304 to $197\frac{1}{4}$; General Motors from $72\frac{3}{4}$ to 36; New York Central from $256\frac{3}{8}$ to 160; United States Steel from $261\frac{3}{4}$ to 150. "The Big Bull Market was dead." And Coolidge-Hoover Prosperity was dead with it.

Yet the end of the epoch did not destroy the basic vision. From an engineering point of view Mr. Hoover's guess about the two chickens in every pot was entirely too conservative. In 1929 we had no adequate idea of the industrial revolution of the twentieth century. We did not realize the vast power development which scientific research was to bring forth, or the cheaper transportation, the light metals and chem-

icals, the untold resources of the new age. Almost twenty years later
agricultural experts were saying that, so far as physical capacity is concerned, the world might be raised to an American standard in a matter
of sixty years. And Mr. Charles Luckman, a great American industrial-
ist, was saying:

"My first and only factual statement about the future of your business is that it can and should double during the next generation *if the
leadership of American business is willing to establish as its objective
for 1970 a standard of living for the American wage earners which is
at least 100 per cent higher than the level of today."*

Mr. Luckman made this remark in the year 1946, when industrial
production had doubled that of 1929.

2.

ON THE FOREIGN FRONT in 1929 unrest could be seen, but we watched
it with comfortable indifference. The slogan of the returned soldiers,
"We've paid our debt to Lafayette; who the hell do we owe now?" had
been accepted by the nation. The Senate had turned down the peace
treaty. The people had voted that Europe was not our affair. In a
grandiloquent "return to normalcy" we had turned our back on the
world.

Behind the façade of isolation, however, our commerce was entan-
gled in a world economy that we did not understand. Our ignorance had
been of long standing. In 1919, ten years before the crash, statesmen of
the Big Four had met at Versailles to make the world safe for political
democracy. At the same time a corporate congregation from Britain,
the United States, and Germany assembled at Baden-Baden for a different purpose. The statesmen were busy giving to a quaint and outmoded
nationalism a last fling. The businessmen were concerned with seeing
that their far-flung opportunities for investment were not shut off. As
the statesmen carved out a revised version of the old map of Europe,
the corporate conclave studied ways and means of building vast business empires that ignored political frontiers. When the shooting war
ended, the economic war began.

We know now, as we look back, that Versailles was a foolish sort of thing. It was noble in intent and aspiration. But the little fact that had been overlooked by the big statesmen was that the world of the individual free trader operating under the laws of an independent nation was gone. Large-scale production and mass consumption had changed the world into one in which man could not live alone on isolated farms, in self-sufficient communities, or in independent countries. It took a whole aggregation of closely related industries to supply the wants of a single family. If such an economy were really to work it had to have area, resources, and world markets. The great factory assembly line had created establishments in which the necessities, comforts, and even the frivolities of life were first standardized and then turned into volume by "quantity methods." Such plants to operate successfully had to run at capacity. To run at capacity they needed outlets for their whole output. Political boundaries were not drawn with that kind of market in mind.

Prior to the first World War, the separate national sovereignties had done fairly well, even though some of them were bursting at the seams with the pressure of populations which required more resources than were contained within their boundaries. This was because we had developed the doctrine of complete separation of government and industrial economy. Under this slogan business could jump over national boundaries easily enough. Governments had not interfered with this process to any alarming extent when Britain was developing her empire. In the days of Queen Victoria tariffs that were so high as to stop trade were not tolerated. In the early days of the century America, though it showed evidences of a growing desire for economic isolation, still had a frontier. Tariffs were to encourage infant industry. Some of the infants were pretty big, but the Robber Barons, for all their faults, were gamblers and builders. The least of their worries was the protection of public investment against risk. This may or may not have been hard on the public, but at least wheels turned, railroads and industries were built. Economic expansion went on at a terrific pace. Panics came and went, but never stayed. The process of bankruptcy wiped out the claims of obsolete capital and price lines that were too high. Monopolies were started. Nevertheless, though in an imperfect and disorderly way, the most efficient businesses survived, in both domestic and world trade.

In the twentieth century, the lords of industry had settled down to a more humane and more comfortable bankers' philosophy. Morgan had taken the competitive risk out of the steel industry. He had to pay Andrew Carnegie four hundred million dollars for about eighty million of actual assets. But Andrew Carnegie was a price cutter, and it was worth that to get rid of ruinous competition in the steel industry. Morgan created an industry that could not fail as ordinary industry had failed in the past. It was big enough to protect itself against competition, and to saddle on the American public the vast financial burden of its capital structure forever.

The example of steel was followed in other industries. After World War I this process continued at an increasing tempo. Economists began to preach the advantages of administered prices, controlled by wise businessmen. The idea that industry must be planned by a hierarchy of corporate executives was accepted by the American people. They cheerfully bought stock in bigger and bigger mergers, and happily watched that stock rise. Men began to dream of a new world order in which both panics and wars could be eliminated. Panics would be impossible because all industry was regulated by sound banking houses, which would come to the rescue when danger threatened. Wars would be impossible because international business, which had everything to lose and nothing to gain by war, would prevent any powerful and civilized nation from aggression. Uncivilized nations which bankers did not dominate were too weak to count.

There is an interesting parallel between the great sprawling corporate bureaucracy which had reached its height just before the stock market crash and the medieval Church before the Reformation. Both were institutions that were held together not by political force but by accepted beliefs in established truths. Neither the Church nor the industrial bankers had troops at their command. But each thought they had the power to excommunicate competing organizations. The weapon of the Church was to refuse access to the sacraments. The weapon of international business was to refuse access to financial support. In the nineteenth century the banking power of England ruled the civilized world.

If someone in an undeveloped country wanted to build a factory he took a collection of paper documents to British bankers. If these gentlemen said that the documents represented money he could build. If they thought otherwise he could not.

Since England had both the goods and the control over the seas, her power was real. But it was a power that diminished with industrial development in other countries. Nevertheless, long after the real power was gone, the symbol remained. Many believed that some mysterious economic law made a nation grow weak and infirm if it violated the theories of British bankers. American businessmen believed with a religious faith that the world was composed of independent civilized states, whose function was to keep order at home so that international finance and investment could be free. In 1929 this kind of world no longer existed. But the symbols still remained and were mistaken for the reality.

This faith had been so strong that before the first World War many economists were able to prove that a prolonged war in the twentieth century was impossible because no nation would be able to finance it. When World War I began, articles were written explaining that it could not last longer than a few months because Germany would run out of money. After World War I, men realized that the rules of business did not apply in war. But certainly, the believers in the old religion still maintained, no nation could grow to the industrial strength necessary to fight a modern war if during its periods of peace it disregarded the rules of sound finance!

3.

AND SO, even after the Great Crash of 1929, we were sure that the wisdom of our bankers and industrialists would save us, if we pursued our traditional course and did not yield to the temptation of invoking government controls. Our great businessmen responded nobly. John D. Rockefeller announced to a public eager to follow his leadership, "My son and I are buying sound common stocks." On New Year's Day, 1930, the New York *Times* was still optimistic, relying on the assurance of the leaders of industry and finance. Andrew Mellon, who combined the authority of Secretary of the Treasury with the prestige of controlling the aluminum monopoly, predicted speedy business recovery. Bankers announced their confidence in the industrial future.

However, as one reads the press of that day, one discovers an uneasy note. It recalls the atmosphere of a prayer meeting held to bolster up the wavering faith of a congregation sorely troubled by doubt. Just as the medieval Church in times of trouble stressed the necessity of faith as an end in itself, so our business leaders decided that "lack of business confidence" was the cause of the continued depression. The remedy was to preach business confidence, whether in your heart you believed it or not. This attitude reached a high note in 1932. Men like Nicholas Murray Butler issued statements that "courage will end the slump." The nation, in effect, was called to gather in a giant prayer meeting to reaffirm its faith in business leaders.

In spite of all this, President Hoover was slipping. The stock market refused to respond to his sermons about prosperity being just around the corner. A worried electorate put a Democratic majority in Congress.

The Democrats knew just what to do. They thought they had discovered where the trouble lay. The budget was not balanced. Statistics showed that in 1911 the entire expense of the government had been less than a billion dollars. Hoover had spent over four billion in 1932. And so the Democrats proposed to slash government payrolls and thus restore prosperity. They succeeded to the tune of a few million for a short time. But still the depression continued.

To the actors the drama of the great slump was as strange as it was terrible. It came to them out of the blue; they rode it as they would ride the wind. They were carried along by a course of events they were powerless to direct. Business executives, economists, and the public alike knew little of the industrial system they were operating; they were unable to diagnose the malady; they were unaware of the great forces operating beneath the surface.

The response of the business community was to hope and to go it blind. Its policy—if playing-by-ear is a policy—was to hold fast to familiar landmarks and to hope for the best. Investments had to be protected. Therefore, prices must be maintained. Sales were falling off. So costs were to be reduced at the expense of labor and groups least able to fight back. The case of American Tel. and Tel., no more enlightened and no more foolish than a hundred other corporations, tells the general story. Rates were not lowered to the capacity-to-pay in a depressed economy; instead, they were maintained. Families gave up their phones. The range of service was greatly restricted. Workers were laid off and wages cut, thereby impairing the power of Bell employees to purchase the goods of other industries. Dividends had to be kept at predepression figures to restore business confidence even if surplus had to be dug into. Security was sought for the chosen few; the interests of other groups were neglected; the public interest was utterly forgotten.

The judgment was based not on a realistic or common-sense appraisal of the situation but on values which were inherently moral or religious. The decrease in goods and services impaired the efficiency of the whole economy. Keeping up prices did not protect investments as was intended. Instead, it destroyed the market for goods, because workers who were laid off could not buy. No better policy to keep the depression going could have been devised. Yet any other policy seemed to be an admission of lack of faith in the stability of the system of high prices and sound investments which had been ordained by our industrial priesthood. These men were our leaders. If they wavered and fell we were lost.

When it became clear to President Hoover that government had to do something, it seemed axiomatic, according to the faith of that day, that capital had to be encouraged and stimulated by government aid. To give similar relief to labor would destroy the self-respect of American workmen. On the other hand if the powers at the top, both corporate and individual, were made affluent, prosperity would trickle down through the whole financial structure. Accordingly Hoover put three magic words together, and the Reconstruction Finance Corporation resulted. It seemed impossible that three words of the appeal and potency of these could not lure prosperity from its hiding place around the corner. Yet the depression continued.

The shock of the universal bank failure brought a new group to Washington under the Roosevelt regime. It was composed of men with all sorts of theories. They were united on one thing only: Government must directly intervene and do something to relieve national distress. People had to be fed. The business hierarchy was not up to the task. Government must take over. This program represented a tremendous shift in the objectives of government assistance. The top dog was no longer the chief concern of economic policy. The underdog, the Forgotten Man, had come into his own.

There was wisdom in Roosevelt's "Re-employment Agreement"; for, if assembly lines were to be kept moving, mass purchasing power had to be restored—and only employment and wages could do that. There was a look to the future in his advocacy of the Tennessee Valley Authority. There was help for groups at an economic disadvantage in the Agricultural Adjustment and the Labor Relations Acts. And there was, in the banking and financial measures, quite a bit of tinkering with antique mechanisms which could no longer operate on their own.

But, in general, measures were improvised and hurled at symptoms. There was no probing diagnosis which got beneath the surface of things, no surgery which cut to the root of the disease. There was a magnificent opportunity to do something. Effective measures could not have stirred up more opposition than did the halfway ones which were employed. The cry was for economic reform; the administration settled for a handful of palliatives.

The measures taken did not lack merit, but they did not rise above the plane of expediency. Labor was granted a bill of rights long overdue, but no attempt was made to link its interest with that of the public. An installment of security was provided to the worker for wages against industrial accident, unemployment, old age; but health was timidly omitted, and little was done to reduce these great hazards of life to a minimum. Provision was made for the family to finance and to own its own home; but this did not extend to a continued abundance of jobs, which is the only adequate underwriting of a mass home-ownership. The unemployed, according to their several trades, were gathered into a Works Progress Administration, so broad in its scope as to admit even actors, painters, and musicians. But the sums laid out, for all the cry about their size, were pitiful—far too small to prime the pump of a lethargic economy. At the same time the desire to maintain prices by creating scarcity put its mark on administrative policy. Little pigs were slaughtered that the price of pork might be high in the land. The farmer was to be lifted toward plenty through scarcity. Hoover's R.F.C. was now fitted out like U. S. Steel with a host of subsidiaries, and continued its dole to industry.

4.

THE UNDERLYING IDEA of the Roosevelt New Deal was conservative, not radical. The idea was that people had to be fed while industry got going again; that industry would get going as soon as it believed that prices were stable and investment safe. Nevertheless the program violated two basic tenets of the economic fundamentalists. The first was the one inherited from our Puritan forebears that the life of the poor must be made as uncomfortable and insecure as possible in order to induce them to work. The other was the nineteenth-century doctrine of the separation of business and government. Hence, except for a brief period during the first days of the NRA, the New Deal, instead of reassuring business, literally scared it to death. Class was being aroused against class, was the cry. The government was a peculiarly vicious sort of Santa Claus, because it distributed gifts to the undeserving. And on top of that it was destroying the Constitution, step by step. Property was no longer sacred. Business was being threatened by government competition. Socialism and Communism were on the march in the land of free enterprise.

The faith in old forms was nowhere better illustrated than in the complete confidence of many advisers of the administration that the depression could be cured by the manipulation of currency and credit. Some thought that if the Federal Reserve would only buy enough bonds, all would be well. Others put their faith in abandonment of the gold standard. Looking back at the gold controversy today, we discover how naïve was the thinking of our economists and businessmen on both sides. Professor Warren of Cornell and his followers thought that going off the gold standard would mean the immediate resumption of world trade. Professor Sprague of Harvard headed a group which predicted a disaster from which the country would not recover for years. Dissenting members of the Supreme Court seriously thought that it meant the end of the Constitution, the beginning of an era of lawless anarchy, the end of every conception of government morality and decency.

The trouble with the gold program was that it was only a minor treatment of a symptom. Its advocates and opponents were both wrong. It produced neither disaster nor recovery. Today it seems a sensible step to have taken. Few are now critical. The hysteria which accompanied it appears slightly psychopathic. One also wonders at the basis for the extravagant hopes.

The first frontal attack upon the national economy was the National Recovery Administration. A mandate went out from the White House through all the land that every industry should go up to Washington and be coded. And to Washington they trooped, oil and steel and non-ferrous metals; aluminum, magnesium, and solid fuels; cast-iron soil pipe, paper and pulp; chemicals, heavy and light, ethical drugs and drugs not so ethical, lumber in all forms, sizes, and shapes, carboloy and lead pencils, matches, whether of the book, strike-on-box, or strike-on-pants variety, dog food and waste paper.

Fury, sound, and Hugh Johnson did succeed in establishing hundreds of codes and arresting the tail spin into which price systems had been driven. But as yet business was still too individualistic for such a drastic regimentation. The clash of interests within industry turned codes into compromises; those economists and lawyers who represented the public interest possessed a high nuisance value; against their vigilance codes were not easily instrumented; as times began to improve, businessmen found the necessary discipline onerous. Order, never established in outlying provinces, began to break down. And then, in the case of the dead chicken, the Supreme Court gave a last fatal blow to the crumbling empire of the blue eagle.

After the fall of the NRA in 1935, the economic philosophy of the administration was thrown into reverse. Two events brought a swing in the other direction. Alarmed over the trend toward the concentration of economic wealth and power, the President asked Congress to establish the Temporary National Economic Committee, with Senator Joseph O'Mahoney of Wyoming as chairman. The Department of Justice rediscovered in the statute books an old law against trusts called the Sherman Act, and actually set about enforcing it. The Act, a legacy from Populist days, was plain and strong in its language. It ordered members of an industry to compete with each other and decreed that prices were to be made in the free and open market. Its intent was that big boys were not to get together to fix their own prices and conspire away the rights of the public It went so far as to make "restraint of trade" a crime and to enjoin courts to put a stop to all such antisocial practices. The TNEC revealed large and important areas of the economy in which business was being run in ways of which the law did not approve. The Department of Justice began a vigorous campaign to break up the corporate empires, to restore the free and open market, and to plant the feet of industry firmly on the road to competition.

We were—and are—in everyday contact with these invisible empires. The map of no one of them is to be found in an atlas, but a match, a package of borax, a diamond, a storage battery, a radio set is a link between each American and this series of corporate world estates. You wish to light a cigarette. The match is almost certain to bear the name of the Diamond, Universal, Ohio, or Lion Match Company. But all of these are satellites of Diamond. And Diamond is connected with Bryant and May of London and with the company known as Swedish Match. Diamond, Bryant and May, and Swedish Match each has its own exclusive territory; and rigid rules draw the fangs of competition. Under a gentleman's agreement, several times broken and just as often renewed, Diamond possesses the United States (save for strike-on-box matches, in respect to which it was once compelled to close a factory at Savannah, Georgia), acting as the agent of Swedish Match in this country. Bryant and May supplies 55 per cent and Swedish Match 45 per cent of the sales in the United Kingdom. Bryant and May holds the British possessions. Most of the rest of the world belongs to Swedish Match, which maintains the New York Match Company to handle its interests in the United States.

The electric storage battery is another example. Your range of choice is quite wide. If the old car is slow on the start, you can replace the battery with a product of the Electric Storage Battery Company or of Willard. Or you can import a new one from Exide in Canada or from Chloride, which operates in the United Kingdom. Or, if you must have something unusual, at least before the war, you could secure an A.F.A. product from Germany. That is about all—or rather somewhat more than all. For Willard is wholly owned by Electric Storage Battery; Chloride of London, the British Empire, and the Far East, is dominated by Electric Storage Battery; Exide of Canada is owned by Chloride and Electric Storage Battery; and by a solemn agreement A.F.A. of Germany has always played along. Wars may come and wars may go; but the old united corporation front remains unbroken.

A package of borax reveals a similar corporate empire. The substance has therapeutic properties, serves a wide range of industrial uses, and has wonderful properties for the fusion of metals. At one peak of the borax diagram appears Borax Consolidated, Ltd., of the United Kingdom. It carries on through the Pacific Coast Borax Company, which holds a charter from our own sovereign state of Nevada. It also carries on through United States Borax, a subsidiary incorporated in West Virginia. The other peak is occupied by the American Potash and Chemical Company, a Delaware corporation, owned and controlled by citizens of the German Reich. It, however, is operated by the Gildfields Corporation, a creature of the United Kingdom. Its subsidiaries are Borax and Chemicals, a corporate creature of the United Kingdom and the Three Elephants Company, another Delaware corporation. The industry is regulated by a long-time contract between the two dominant concerns, Borax Consolidated, Ltd., and American Potash and Chemical. Thus it takes a British corporation, with Nevada and West Virginia subsidiaries, and a German-owned American corporation, with Delaware and English subsidiaries, to fix the price of borax.

It is easy to add other examples: tin, luminal, the sulfa drugs, dyestuffs, magnesium, bananas, coffee, molybdenum, cobalt, and a host of commodities which make up the necessities and frivolities of life. Pick up a movie ticket, examine a tin can, take a look at a parking meter, call for an antimalarial compound, send a cable to Mexico City, put your hand to chemicals heavy or light, and you find yourself in personal contact with an invisible *imperium* which transcends the United States.

We have long been a nation where local production and markets have been controlled by absentee owners. In 1909 two hundred industrial corporations owned one-third of the nonbanking corporate assets. By 1929 this was increased to about 50 per cent. By 1939 the share of this group increased to 57 per cent. This trend was observed by Adolf Berle, by the Temporary National Economic Committee, and by the National Resources Committee. The whole situation was described by President Roosevelt in his monopoly message of 1935. He said:

Statistics of the Bureau of Internal Revenue reveal the following amazing figures for 1935:

Ownership of corporate assets: Of all corporations reporting from every part of the nation, one-tenth of 1 per cent of them owned 52 per cent of the assets of all of them.

And to clinch the point: Of all corporations reporting, less than 5 per cent of them owned 87 per cent of all the assets of all of them.

Income and profits of corporations: Of all the corporations reporting from every part of the country, one-tenth of 1 per cent of them earned 50 per cent of the net income of all of them.

And to clinch the point: Of all the manufacturing corporations reporting, less than 4 per cent of them earned 87 per cent of all the net profits of all of them.

The apologists for this system of the concentration of economic wealth insisted even after the crash of 1929 that business had learned its lesson, that competition was wasteful, that great corporate empires were here to stay, and that prices and production would be wisely administered in the future by this financial oligarchy.

Against this philosophy the program of vigorous antitrust enforcement gained great headway. A *Fortune* poll in 1940 showed that it was the only policy of the administration endorsed by a majority of business executives. In the four years following 1939 over 50 per cent of all the antitrust prosecutions brought during the entire fifty years of the

Sherman Act were instituted. There seemed hope at least for a policy
to eliminate absentee corporate control over local industry by inexorable corporate empires.

5.

THE BEGINNING of the movement for industrial decentralization was
suddenly stopped and then put in reverse by World War II. What might
have happened to a government program of decentralization had there
been no war is anyone's guess. The trouble was that war was already
on us as the result of the underlying causes of the great stock market
crash. The political and economic institutions of the nineteenth century
were dying. The cement was falling out of social structures. Peoples
and goods were hemmed in by obsolete national boundaries. When
goods fail to move, armies march.

There was no formal departure from the administration's antitrust
policy. But with military values dominant, all questions of the character
of the economy were postponed. A range of commodities, as varied as
the combined lists in a Sears Roebuck catalogue, had to be obtained—
and in abundance. It seemed to military men easier to place orders—
even if deliveries were not so certain—in large quantities than in small.
It seemed most feasible to deal with the dominant concerns in each
industrial field.

This general program was at least not hindered by the infiltration of
representatives of big business into the War and Navy Departments,
nor by formally recognizing business as a department of government
for war, in the organization which went forward under a number of
alphabetical permutations and came to rest as the War Production
Board. And F.D.R., recognizing that he could have only one war at
a time, was content to declare a truce in the civil struggle. Business gave
him patriotic support—on its own terms. More than 90 per cent of all
war contracts went to a handful of giant empires, many of them formerly linked by strong ties with the corporations of the Reich. The big
fellows got the contracts; the little fellows were dependent upon sub-
contracts with the big boys. Methods of payment and an "accelerated
depreciation" allowed many a concern to reconstruct its plants at the

expense of the government. Though the government kept title, new and old were often so closely fused as to be inseparable; and the only practical disposition of many government plants was to the corporations which operated them during the war. And over all moved the trend to the further concentration of wealth and power—a trend which was given an impetus during the second World War far greater than ever before.

The Radio Priest and His Flock

BY WALLACE STEGNER

Wallace Stegner was born in Iowa, and brought up in several parts
of the farther West, including Utah and California. He encountered
some of the frightening effects of Coughlinism in Boston while
teaching English composition at Harvard, as a Briggs Copeland
instructor. He has written several novels, including the widely
praised *Remembering Laughter* (1937) and *The Big Rock Candy
Mountain* (1943), a book about Utah, *Mormon Country* (1942),
and one about America and its people, *One Nation* (1945). His recent
article for the *New Republic* on Joe Hill, the I.W.W. troubadour,
was a definitive piece of research and writing about one of America's
most fascinating legends. Mr. Stegner is now teaching creative
writing at Stanford University.

✵ 1.

Here is the church, and here the steeple—
Open it up and see all the people!

LET US BEGIN this story on an anxious Sunday afternoon, October
30, 1930, just about a year after the Great Wall Street Crash. Much
water has gone under the bridge in that year; to many it looks as if the
bridge itself were gone. The Little Bull Market of early 1930 has fallen
apart, and is on its way to even deeper lows than those of the previous
October. Inactivity is on its way to becoming paralysis.

For the investor the summaries of the first ten months of 1930 are
a précis of disaster. The value of all listed stocks has dropped almost
23 billion dollars since the hopeful high of April; the profits of 200
leading industrial corporations are down 45.9 per cent; railroad shares
are down 65 points, industrials down 167; steel production is down

40 per cent, automobile production down 60 per cent; stock transactions are off 28 per cent in volume, check transactions are off 25 per cent. The only thing that is up is the suicide rate.

What of the farmer? Even worse, as 1930 wanes into November. The wheat he sold last year for $1.35 a bushel is selling now for $.76. After the blistering drought of the past summer he is lucky if he has any to sell at any price. The bank is getting troublesome about the mortgage. Farm income on the whole is down 16 per cent (it hasn't been really high since the war, even during the Boom). Foreign shipments of agricultural products are the lowest since 1915.

And the workingman? Already there are six million unemployed. Factory employment is down 20 per cent and payrolls are off 29 per cent. The man who still has a job can read the future in his shrinking pay envelope and dwindling bank savings. Even if he doesn't want to look, he can see the breadlines forming, and he is not unmindful that winter is ahead. He is feeling the pinch hard already; he will feel it more.

And all of them—investor, farmer, factory worker—have their eyes uneasily on the banks. Through the first ten months of 1930 the doors have closed on 60, 70, 80 banks a month. In November, though this is not known yet, bank closings will jump to 236. In December they will jump again to 328. As the winter wears on it will be possible for a passer-by in New York, seeing a line forming for Chaplin's *City Lights,* to ask, "What's that, a breadline or a bank?"

In Philadelphia one morning, a middle-aged Italian woman, staring at the little slip of paper tacked to the closed door of a bank, will suddenly double up with her hands clasping her stomach and her stout body rocking back and forth, screaming mindlessly and monotonously until two policemen come to lift her up and take her away.

In Iowa City students at the state university will read the morning papers and go downtown to mill around aimlessly, watching the crowds of the stunned and curious around the doors of all five dead banks. There is not a bank in town open; the thing becomes, after the first shock, almost a joke. Those with food, or with a little cash, share with the utterly strapped until help can be obtained from elsewhere in the state, from home. The mails soon are full of cashiers' checks which have to be taken to Cedar Rapids for cashing. But even in the humorous week of adjustment and reorganization there are Cassandras. Wait, they say, till the "outside" is in the same fix we are. Wait till the whole country is in this fix. It won't be funny then, maybe.

Even when it's funny, it's ominous. Down and down and down goes everything, pitching toward the depression which will be so much deeper and more enduring than anyone now suspects. In bankless Iowa City eggs sell for six cents a dozen. In Chicago the breadlines stretch endlessly along dirty brick walls in windy streets. Women's skirts follow Hoover's prestige on down, and the flapper era ends in grimness and bewilderment and anger. So that thousands of those who are wearily or casually tuning in their radios to Station WJR, Detroit, on this Sunday afternoon of October 30, are plowed and disked and harrowed, ready for the seed the speaker will plant.

2.

PERHAPS, if they had had the habit of listening to WJR for the past four years, they knew something of this speaker—a priest of the parish of Royal Oak, Michigan, born in Canada of Irish-American parents, educated by the Basilian Fathers and the University of Toronto. His name: Charles E. Coughlin. His distinction: a voice of such mellow richness, such manly, heart-warming, confidential intimacy, such emotional and ingratiating charm, that anyone tuning past it almost automatically returned to hear it again. It was without doubt one of the great speaking voices of the twentieth century. Warmed by the touch of Irish brogue, it lingered over words and enriched their emotional content. It was a voice made for promises. For four years the priest had been using it to deliver a Sunday broadcast to children. But on this Sunday of care and fear in America, Father Coughlin elected to address the parents, with a stern denunciation of "money changers" and "subversive socialism."

It is possible that this first socio-economic sermon from Royal Oak was the outburst of a man oppressed with the conditions he saw around him and fearful of the future. It is just as possible that it was the opening lead in the calculated playing of a hand. By the autumn of

1930 a shrewd politician would already have noticed the crowds of shabby men in the reading rooms of public libraries, trying to find from the books what had hit them. Father Coughlin, even then, was a shrewd politician. He took advantage of his Sunday children's hour to tell these men that it was the international bankers who had wrecked the country, and the Communists who were trying to take it over. It was not a memorable speech, especially. What was memorable was the reaction.

Letters poured in. Some wanted to know, as correspondents wanted to know for the next twelve years, what a priest was doing talking on such subjects. Others cheered and wanted more. Taken together, that flood of mail meant that people would listen to anyone who sounded as if he knew answers. Father Coughlin's trial balloon had proved what people wanted to hear, and had shown him how to spread the walls of the Shrine of the Little Flower and bring into one audience thousands upon thousands of listeners. Most of those listeners were angry at the bankers; many were afraid of Communists. Though he added other scapegoats later, Father Coughlin really built his structure on those two. By a miracle of illogic, he eventually combined them.

By the end of 1930 the priest had organized his unseen listeners into the Radio League of the Little Flower, dedicated to the unraveling of the tangled economic web, and was pulling in letters in quantities that amazed WJR and may have amazed Coughlin. Other demagogues in the American tradition have been hay-wagon orators, shirt-sleeve spellbinders from park bandstands and town-hall platforms. But Father Coughlin was the first to discover how he could do the whole job by remote control, be free of hecklers, be just as sure of taking up the collection, and in addition have documentary proof by letter of what his audiences wanted. He boasted many times that he knew American public opinion better than any man alive. In his limited way he was right.

From the beginning he was a master of the art of being several things at once. Speaking as a priest and a hater of Communism, and with the consistent support of Bishop Michael Gallagher of Detroit, Father Coughlin was sure of a large Catholic audience. But as he projected his Little Flower pulpit out into the air waves, he let economics transcend denominationalism. Hillbillies from Kentucky, farmers from Indiana and Iowa and Illinois and Minnesota and the Dakotas, worried clerks in Chicago and Cleveland, unemployed stevedores in Boston and Brooklyn, sweatshop tailors in Rochester and New York, taxi drivers, school teachers, Gentile and Jew and Methodist and Hard-Shell Baptist, listened to the mellow brogue and were swept away. It played upon their dreadful fear of poverty and hunger and insecurity; it said the things their own worries were saying; it turned upon the traitors the whole nation was beginning to turn on, denounced the bankers and industrialists who had ruled and ruined the country, the greedy politicians and the money changers in the temple.

These new listeners cheered the florid Coughlin rhetoric and the roll of the great metaphors, and they followed with angry approval when the voice rose in jeremiads, and they grew solemn when it fell in heavy warning. They wrote letters and they put one-dollar bills in the envelopes and they mailed their approval to Royal Oak. Their pointless unrest was suddenly pointed. There were people to blame, things to be done, and there was a leader to follow. Three months from his opening speech on October 30, Father Coughlin was getting fifty thousand letters a week.

Even on the conservative estimate of one letter writer to each two hundred listeners, that meant an audience of ten million, reached over seventeen CBS stations plus occasional cut-ins. It was an abrupt and heady miracle: the parish priest addressing crowds such as no man had ever regularly addressed before. At first he was cautious; he whipped only dead or dying horses. Poor Mr. Hoover, already politically dead, took a beating. A speech entitled "Hoover Prosperity Means Another War" drew in 1,200,000 letters, an all-time high. The priest attacked prohibition, punch-drunk as it was, and pleased millions. He organized God's Poor Society in Detroit, assisted the indigent, and advertised his work discreetly on the radio. When the 1932 Presidential campaign got under way, he climbed aboard the Roosevelt bandwagon, coined the slogan "Roosevelt or Ruin," was courted by bigwigs and politicos. Without any clear political affiliation he was already a strong political force. His audience was now estimated at anything from 30,000,000 to 45,000,000.

So far the critics were few. On what grounds except bigoted grounds could one mistrust a priestly friend of the poor? What madness would lead anyone to repudiate so substantial a straw in these drowning times? To many, his was the only voice that spoke truth. And others approved. *Commonweal*, the liberal Catholic monthly, had praised him without stint in 1931. Bishop Gallagher beamed upon his protégé. There was reputed to be a letter from the Pope directing thanks to Father Coughlin for spreading the doctrines of social justice first enunciated in the *Rerum Novarum* encyclical of Leo XIII, and amplified by Pius XI himself in 1931.

Yet there were some Catholics who disliked him. Father Coughlin took pride in his Catholic critics, since they proved him an impartial tribune of the people. The rebuke of William Cardinal O'Connell of Boston, that the radio priest was disseminating "demagogic stuff to the poor," had good as well as bad effects for him. When Communists criticized him, he gained Catholic support; when Catholics criticized him, he gained support among Protestants and Jews; when the bankers called him names—as they did in Detroit—his popularity skyrocketed. The game was to play the middle against both ends. Yet it was in the campaign of 1932, because of the rashness of his attacks on individuals, that Father Coughlin first began to acquire an organized opposition. He was too bull-headed, said his enemies; he was guilty of the sin of pride.

Those personal attacks brought on his first radio crisis in 1933. The Columbia Broadcasting System, hearkening to suggestions, refused to renew his contract unless he submitted his sermons in advance for censorship. Father Coughlin refused and was crossed off the air. But he was too much in demand; before long he was back, and on more stations than ever. He bought his own time and created his own network, and the faithful paid the bills—which were large.

During 1933, Father Coughlin was a rabid New Dealer. He supported monetary inflation (from beginning to end of his public career he called for such inflation, and for the return to Congress of the right to issue currency). When Al Smith, in the *Outlook*, dismissed both Father Coughlin and his money theories as "crackpot," Coughlin replied; Smith countered; Coughlin replied again, accusing Smith of undercover dealings with the Morgan interests. His speech was abusive, perhaps libelous, and the response to it was mixed. *Commonweal,* supporting Smith, backed off the Couglin platform and admitted that he was too fond of personal vituperation. But the *Literary Digest* thought his attack on Smith a sign of his integrity: he was pursuing a principle "beyond the gates of creed" in thus attacking a well-known Catholic. (The *Digest* might have come a good deal closer to an accurate statement of the case if it had not looked upon Coughlin as the representative of the political Catholicism so many Americans feared. A good look would have revealed that his demagoguery was a truer profession than his priesthood.)

Through 1934 Father Coughlin's radio receipts often reached twenty thousand dollars a week, most of it in small amounts. Out of these funds he erected a monument to himself and his conception of "Social Justice." He built a seven-story tower with an immense crucified Christ spreadeagled across one side, and he built a new Church of the Little Flower. (For three successive years the AFL formally censured him for using non-union labor, some of it Canadian, and paying less than the union scale.) In the tower were the offices of the Little Flower Radio League and Coughlin's personal headquarters. A large staff of helpers handled the enormous mail and answered requests for the printed sermons, which Father gave away to anyone who wrote in. His radio time was costing him fourteen thousand dollars a week, his secretarial help between three and four thousand dollars. Even so, there was something left over in these plushy years of the deepest depression. Father Coughlin invested the surplus in silver futures—and a little later found himself talking very fast to explain that the investment was made in the name of his secretary for the benefit of the Radio League, and that there was no connection between his investments and his constant public clamor for the remonetization of silver. Because no one, even his enemies, believed him really greedy for money, he talked his way out of that. But the opposition had almost scored a damaging point, and he was steadily getting a worse press. But when he took his case to the people over the air, he got his vote of confidence. The letters continued to come in, the almost pitifully devoted letters, and the dollar bills.

And in Mattapan, Massachusetts, a suburb of Boston, a Russian-Jewish picture framer whom we may call Ben Levin listened on Sunday afternoons, and considered how the picture-frame business had fallen away to nothing, and worried about the rent for the bigger flat he had had to get when the fifth baby was born. He heard Father Coughlin analyze the vicious credit money that the banks created and profited by, and it seemed to him that the priest spoke sense. Levin said part of what he thought to an Irishman who came by on his way from Keohane's Tavern in Codman Square, and the Irishman said, "You're God-damn right. He's the only man jack of 'em with the guts to speak out." Before he went home that night Ben Levin folded a dollar bill in a sheet of paper, and as he went up the street he dropped it in the mailbox for Royal Oak.

It was the Ben Levins who gave Father Coughlin the confidence to make his next moves. He thought he knew who and how many were behind him. He began to criticize the New Deal; to hint that Roosevelt was not moving fast enough or far enough in his reform of the financial structure. And he began to be more open in his criticism of labor unions. In October, 1934, he broke with the AFL, recommending that the government take over the collective-bargaining functions of the unions and administer industrial peace by fiat. Mussolini and Hitler had advocated the same method.

3.

BY BREAKING with the New Deal and organized labor, Father Coughlin started down a road of his own, apparently expecting that he could draw after him many who had up to now followed Roosevelt or the unions. His constant cry, whether he preached woe to the bankers or damned Hoover or credit money or bullyragged Roosevelt or called for a living annual wage or promoted the social-justice program of Leo and Pius, had been, "We are not political." That was still his protestation when in December, 1934, at the very peak of his popularity, he began organizing the National Union for Social Justice.

The National Union for Social Justice, a "non-political" lobby owned and run lock, stock, and barrel by its founder, was not only a sign of

Father Coughlin's growing arrogance: it was a factor in increasing that arrogance. Dedicated to a platform of sixteen points and seven principles, it was clearly designed as the instrument of Father Coughlin's political ambitions. The cards that came in by tens and hundreds of thousands (Ben Levin's was among them) made Coughlin impatient of restraint even from quarters that might have been expected to cow him. When Cardinal O'Connell for the third time rapped his knuckles in public, Coughlin replied. He reminded his hearers that the Cardinal had no jurisdiction outside his archdiocese of Boston; that he could speak only as an individual, not as a prince of the Church; and that he himself might profitably do something about promoting the welfare of the people instead of hobnobbing with the rich so much. A good many people gasped at that impudence, but Father Coughlin was not chastised.

The program of the NUSJ, announced early in 1935, was merely a more formal statement of the ambiguous, vaguely radical-sounding generalities Father Coughlin had been preaching since 1930. It was partly derived from the liberal encyclicals of Leo and Pius, and except where it was insincere, or contradicted itself, or failed to become specific enough to mean anything, it was above reproach. These were the sixteen points:

1. Liberty of conscience and education. (Nothing said of freedom of speech or press.)

2. A "just, living, annual wage for all labor." (But this in the face of an increasingly anti-union policy.)

3. Nationalization of resources too important to be held by individuals. (Yet on occasion Father Coughlin attacked even the TVA as "socialism.")

4. Private ownership of all other property.

5. The *use* of private property to be controlled for the public good. (The implications and the methods were never explored.)

6. Abolition of private banking, and institution of a central government bank.

7. The "return" to Congress of the right to coin and regulate money (which of course had that right all along).

8. Control of the cost of living and the value of money by the central government bank.

9. Cost of production plus a fair profit for the farmer (no methods suggested).

10. "The right of the laboring man to organize in unions . . ." and also "the duty of the government . . . to protect these organizations against the vested interests of wealth and of intellect." (As Raymond Gram Swing pointed out, the vested interests of intellect, if they mean anything at all, must mean labor's own leaders. And since in another context Father Coughlin advocated the control of collective bargaining by the Department of Labor, it seems fairly clear that Coughlin wanted, in Mr. Swing's words, "a fascist solution of the labor problem.")

11. Recall of all non-productive bonds. (Including War Bonds from World War I.)

12. Abolition of tax-exempt bonds.

13. Broadening the base of taxation on the principle of ownership and ability to pay.

14. Simplification of government and lightening taxation on the laboring class. (Father Coughlin never said how these things were to be done while government was at the same time regulating labor, taking over natural resources, and embarking on the vast public works program he advocated.)

15. In time of war, conscription of wealth as well as of men.

16. Human rights to be held above property rights; government's chief concern should be with the poor; the rich can take care of themselves.

The most specific planks in that platform concern the money and banking system. In the collapsing thirties, with the whole banking system paralyzed, reform of the banks was a safe cause. His money theory Father Coughlin got from a Chicago lady named Gertrude

Coogan. He disseminated it in a booklet entitled *Money: Questions and Answers*. (Miss Coogan later charged that he stole it from her, giving her neither credit nor royalties.) Apart from the money issue, however, the program breaks down everywhere into vagueness, slipperiness, yeasty expressions of pseudo good will unimplemented with methods or approaches. On such an issue as the quarrel between production for profit and production for use, the priest coined a typically weasel-worded compromise: "Production for use at a profit." The more one thinks about that phrase, the less it means. But it sounded impressive, and it satisfied the faithful.

With his People's Lobby organized and growing, Father Coughlin undertook to whip some pretty lively horses instead of the dead ones he had been abusing so long. His words of praise were now reserved for Huey Long, Gene Talmadge, Benito Mussolini, and Senators or Congressmen whose position happened to please him. His most violent attacks were on President Roosevelt. The obvious political direction of his ambitions had by now brought him under fairly sharp fire. *Christian Century, Forum, Nation, Atlantic,* all charged him with fascist leanings; several Catholic leaders rejected him. He stirred up angry replies every time he spoke. But Father Coughlin was too deep in his game to heed the warning bell. Under criticism, he posed as the people's friend, loyal only to them and to the two great liberal Popes and God. Let the anti-Christs and the money changers scourge him all they wanted, so long as his message was heard!

How strong was Father Coughlin's crowd? While he boasted an audience in the millions, how many votes could he swing if he chose? How much pressure could his People's Lobby exert? Those who asked those questions had an answer, of a sort, in the result of the World Court vote. With the administration supporting it, with forecasts indicating passage by a good margin of the bill which would require the United States to adhere to the Court, Father Coughlin spoke one Sunday denouncing the Court proposal as "treason," a "conspiracy with the money lenders," and much else. He praised William Randolph Hearst's stand and aligned himself with the isolationist groups. He urged his listeners to wire their Senators and Congressmen. They did. Wires came in by basketfuls, routed around through Baltimore to relieve the strain on the Washington telegraph offices. Raymond Gram Swing gives Coughlin the dubious credit of turning the tide against the Court —and thereby puts him among those who knifed the League of Nations in its crucial year. By now Coughlin was not merely powerful, but was widely feared and widely hated. His Bishop continued to back him, appearing with him on his radio hour to advertise his support. His printed sermons still carried the imprimatur of the Bishop of Detroit. But for the first time, in response to considerable nudging from the radio audience and organized labor, they also bore the union label. The friend of the workingman had printed them for four years in a non-union shop.

Still denying political aims, Father Coughlin prepared for the election year of 1936 by increasing his radio hookup from twenty-nine to thirty-five stations. He also founded a weekly newspaper, *Social Justice*, with himself as editor. No new bogeymen needed to be invented. Money changers, Communists, the League of Nations, Roosevelt, the AAA, the CIO, and William Green sufficed. And for active work there was the job of electing Congressmen who would support the NUSJ, the problem of getting a toehold in the American Reichstag.

4.

THE NUSJ was not a political party; that is, it was not on the ballot in any state. But it had a program, a war chest, a newspaper, an organization which Father Coughlin rearranged by Congressional districts, and a group of candidates whom it labored to elect. True, those candidates were Republicans and Democrats who had discreetly made a noise favoring the aims of the National Union, but Father Coughlin himself said that ultimately the two major parties would both have to be destroyed and a more realistic political system inaugurated. Meanwhile, just to be sure of getting something, the National Union endorsed Republican and Democrat alike, often endorsing several candidates in the same district. Under those circumstances it was pretty hard to lose. The Pennsylvania and Ohio primaries indicated considerable National Union strength. *Social Justice* seethed with non-political organization moves and non-political campaign directions, and in the summer it announced plans for a non-political national convention in Cleveland during August. In June the paper began running a series of articles on parliamentary procedure, and perhaps in preparation for things to come, Father Coughlin removed his name from the masthead as editor in chief.

Then on June 19, on a radio audience estimated at thirty million, Coughlin dropped his blockbuster. He denounced the "promise-breaking" New Deal in more vitriolic terms than he had ever used before; he announced the formation of a new "Union Party," with "Liberty Bill" Lemke of North Dakota as its Presidential candidate and the principles of Social Justice as its platform; and he announced the NUSJ's "endorsement" of Lemke. Stripped of rhetoric and double talk, the speech meant that Father Coughlin had formed his own party. A fortnight later Coughlin announced that Dr. Francis Townsend's hundreds of thousands of would-be pensioners, as well as the remnants of Huey Long's Share-the-Wealthers under Gerald L. K. Smith, had joined with him to support Lemke and O'Brien. It was a thundering coup for Father Coughlin, in a way. He had brought into his own camp, on definitely secondary terms, his two chief rivals among the prophets and the panacea givers, and he had kept a back door open by insisting that his National Union was only endorsing Lemke's party, not creating it. At the same time, if a man is known by the company he keeps, Father Coughlin's dramatic burst into the political arena showed him more clearly than ever before to be a quack, a devious politician, a shifty manipulator of the truth, and a man ambitious for personal power.

And he was in the big leagues now. Against Hoover and prohibition and the NRA and even the World Court he had had victories. Now he was up against not merely Roosevelt and organized labor but both major political parties. Yet unless all the signs are false, he thought he had a chance. His hope seems to have been that Lemke could carry enough states to prevent a majority for either party, thus throwing the election into the House of Representatives. If the Union Party could do that in its first test, it could do more in 1940.

For the purpose of the Lemke campaign, *Social Justice* did a quick about face. Labor baiting died down; labor news increased. The "steel magnates" replaced William Green and the CIO as whipping boys.

The AAA, symbol of New Deal tinkering and mismanagement and "Communism," took a terrible thumping. The page called "The People Speak" was filled with earnestness and enthusiasm. And from Sherlock and Druin and Carter and Ryan and Fitzgerald and Morgan and Clark and Murphy and Kalb and Kuhn and Buckley—and from Ben Levin of Mattapan, Massachusetts—came pledges, contributions, a rising chant from those who had been deep in depression for almost seven years and still knew breadlines, cold rooms, park benches, flophouses, and the virtues of folded newspapers inside worn shoes. In his speeches and editorials Father Coughlin was getting recklessly specific. The NUSJ, he said, would give Lemke five million votes.

Then on July 16 Coughlin addressed ten thousand Townsend Plan delegates at their convention in Cleveland, and for the second time in a month made history. He criticized and threatened and promised. He played the audience like an organ, stroked them and lashed them and flattered and scared and comforted them, and finally he rose on his toes and lifted his fists and denounced that "great betrayer and liar," Franklin Roosevelt. He ripped off his coat and his clerical collar and poured it on, while correspondents dove for the nearest telephone. Coughlin had sassed Cardinals before, but he had never before called the President a liar.

When he was done, the ten thousand Townsendites, in a frenzy of devotion, paraded for an hour in Coughlin's honor. "You had all the throbbing sensation of another great moment in history," said *Social Justice,* "as you watched it go on and on and heard that roaring, unified voice, ten thousand, pouring up from the soul of working class America."

Maybe you had that throbbing sense, but some of the correspondents there had a crawling sense of having heard that unified voice before, in Munich or Berlin, and many radio listeners were bothered by the "betrayer and liar" remark. Ben Levin wrote in from Mattapan saying he hoped Father Coughlin would make some kind of explanation why he called Mr. Roosevelt a liar. There were other pressures besides those of the many Ben Levins. Father Coughlin apologized promptly and publicly, saying in effect that he took back the word "liar," which he had been impelled to use by passion and stress and by the fact that Mr.

Roosevelt hadn't invariably told the truth. Ben Levin read the apology in *Social Justice* and was troubled.

On August 10, just before the Cleveland convention of his National Union of Social Justice, Coughlin wrote his weekly pep talk to the units. His subject was the leadership of the NUSJ. After pointing out that at first he had had to take personal charge, until a permanent organization could be effected, he spoke of the possible changes now coming up: "If they wish to hand this organization over to a group of politicians and chiselers, that will be the business of the convention delegates. If they wish to make of me a Victrola disk, useful only to speak in terms of a master's voice . . . If they wish to make the Congressional district a dukedom or principality, totally independent of the national office . . . In fine, if the delegates wish to adopt a constitution . . . which will relegate me to the graveyard of 'has-beens,' that will be perfectly satisfactory." By such means—by a Hollywood gag, a cheap show of martyred humility: "Of course, if you don't *want* me!" —do the tribunes of the people insure their seats in the saddle.

But he had more strings to his bow than a martyred air. In Cleveland a few days later, before forty-two thousand frantic supporters, he convinced anyone who hadn't been convinced before that he was one of the most effective speakers alive. When he called for clapping as a sign of approval, the sound was deafening; when he called on those who agreed to stand up, the audience rose in one surging wave. And most effective of all devices: seven minutes before the scheduled end of his address he wavered, staggered, collapsed, and was helped off by a group of grim-faced guards. Whether his collapse came from heat, indigestion, or histrionics, it couldn't have been better timed. The lady who had the honor of proposing Father Coughlin's name for the presidency of the National Union almost swooned herself with the enormity of her mission. Her nomination was unanimously approved—or almost unanimously. At the crucial moment a malcontent delegate named O'Donnell rose and bawled, "No!" and was escorted out by the police in imminent danger of his life.

In that same convention, Coughlin made a vow. If Lemke did not get nine million votes, he himself would retire from the radio. But when election night came and returns came in it was clear at once that the Union Party was a bust. In the final count, Lemke got less than a tenth the votes Coughlin had promised him. The radio priest promptly suspended the activities of the NUSJ and retired from the air.

As for Ben Levin, after working for the Union Party almost up to election day, he had undergone a soul-churning change of heart and voted for Roosevelt. So had most of the other nine millions that Coughlin counted on. Roosevelt's personal magnetism had swung them into line—that and the growing doubt of the priest, the way he had turned on The Chief, the way he sometimes talked like a labor baiter, the things he said when he got worked up. He had no business, for example, calling Roosevelt "anti-God" in Cincinnati. Both Archbishop McNicholas and Monsignor Ryan had protested that. And when he advocated the use of bullets "when any upstart dictator in the United States succeeds in making a one-party government and when the ballot becomes useless"—that was pretty dangerous talk. And there was his habit of calling every liberal a Communist, and the way he talked about the CIO as if everybody in it was straight out of Moscow.

And there was also, for Ben Levin, an occasional twinge when he read something in *Social Justice* that seemed to be anti-Jewish—not really and openly, but by implication and innuendo. Ben Levin listened to the rumors that Father Coughlin had been, or would be, silenced by the Pope, and he found that he didn't much care. The NUSJ unit he belonged to wasn't meeting any more. There were no radio speeches. Ben Levin felt a kind of relief, and was glad he hadn't voted for the Coughlin crowd. His son put it aptly enough: "Coughlin loused up his chances by shooting off his mouth too much."

Social Justice went on, once more under Father Coughlin's personal editorship. It licked the priestly wounds, explained the retirement, pointed out how many enemies were after the Father's blood, and printed dozens of grief-stricken letters from the leaderless thousands. Most of them wailed that he couldn't go off the air; he must come back. With so many Communists talking freely, his voice *must* be heard. An Aroused Mother wrote from Stoughton, Massachusetts, exclaiming against a radio speaker she had heard who sounded like a Communist.

"He had a strong foreign accent which he seemed to be trying to control as he talked, but which sneaked out and showed itself unclothed when the speaker became excited."

Father Coughlin had lost much, but he still had a considerable following and he still had Bishop Gallagher. And in a world where speakers were allowed to go around revealing unclothed foreign accents, Coughlin's duty was clear. On January 1, after a retirement of only six weeks, he delivered a radio New Year message. *Social Justice* was already hinting that if members wanted him badly enough, he might return to the air. On January 18 he promised to return if his followers would build up the circulation of *Social Justice* to a million and a quarter. On January 27 he spoke on a nationwide hookup for Red Cross flood relief, and on February 1, without anything like his million and a quarter circulation, he was back with a weekly broadcast. But on that day his strongest support was taken from him: Bishop Gallagher died.

5.

Now FATHER COUGHLIN was non-political perforce. For a while he let his organization rest; then he reconstituted it as a loose confederation of Christian study clubs. If Ben Levin had wanted to go on meeting with the old group from Codman Square where his shop was, he would have been barred. The crowd came around his shop sometimes, but he didn't get the same feeling of marching along up toward something that he had had before. And though he still listened to Coughlin on the radio, he was troubled by what he heard.

Father Coughlin was still bucking the Roosevelt administration, throwing most of his eloquence against the Supreme Court-packing proposal. And he was bucking the unions. The sit-down strikes were a "black plague"; the CIO was run from Moscow. *Social Justice* provided evidence of its friendliness to the dictators when it gave Mayor LaGuardia of New York the weekly "Ill Will Prize" for condemning Hitler and Mussolini and "breeding international bad feeling." The threat of war was no real threat, but a deliberately staged plot of the have nations to force the have-not nations into some kind of violent reaction, and thus justify an aggression against Germany, Italy, and Japan by Britain and the United States. When violence broke out at Republic Steel and the Ford plant, Coughlin's paper blamed labor; a little later he was trying to promote a "Christian" auto union to combat the CIO. He succeeded only in pushing UAW and CIO together.

Political defeat had clarified Father Coughlin as a public figure, made the direction of this thinking clearer. No substantial part of the American press defended him, and when his attacks on the CIO reached a point of frenzy, and he claimed that no Christian could support that instrument of Red Communism, the new Archbishop of Detroit took pains to deny Father Coughlin's words. In an article in the *Michigan Catholic* he deplored Coughlin's remarks about both Roosevelt and the CIO, denied that they represented the attitude of the Church, and denied that the National Union, now posing as a religious organization, had any churchly backing. And he refused to let Coughlin reply.

This was not a rebuke from Baltimore or Boston or Cincinnati, from some Cardinal or Monsignor who could be told to mind his own business. This came from directly upstairs. So Father Coughlin, on October 10, 1937, canceled a contract for a new radio series, and when the ownership of *Social Justice* came under scrutiny, he backed away as editor and publisher. One of his stooges, Walter M. Baertschi, carried on, crying, "My leader is silenced!"

Now, finally, responsible Catholic authorities had done what anti-Coughlin forces had been clamoring for them to do over a period of years. When the Apostolic Delegate, Amleto Cicignani, approved Archbishop Mooney's action, there was a happy uproar from the press. "The Holy See regards as just and timely the correction which the Archbishop of Detroit made in reference to the remarks of Father Coughlin published October 5, 1937," said the Apostolic Delegate on November 29.

Yet on December 27 *Social Justice* was able to announce that in mid-January Father Coughlin would be on the air again over more than sixty stations. It seemed fairly clear that the Church did not want to silence him so long as he promised to stop making remarks that might be interpreted as involving the policy of the Church.

6.

WHATEVER he might have been in 1930, there was no doubt about him as he started his 1938 broadcasts and embarked on a new year of *Social Justice*. He had been caught in too many evasions, too much double-talk; he had been detected in too many misquotations, and his paper had misrepresented too many people by means of the "dot trick." And though he shouted that never had he been unfaithful to the principles of social justice, those principles were too general to hold him; there was too much evidence that he consistently said one thing and did another. A once-defeated demagogue trying for a comeback, he tried what other demagogues abroad had found a useful instrument: terror. His reorganization of the Social Justice Clubs as "Christian" societies had eliminated the Ben Levins and prepared them for the sacrifice. While anti-Semitism boiled to a bloody climax in Germany, Coughlin elected to promote it in America, while piously denying that he was anti-Semitic.

His audience had shrunk. His organized labor followers, both Catholic and Protestant, were pretty well gone; his Jews had been deliberately excluded; the liberals and radicals among middle-class Americans who had followed him at first had long since given him up as a dangerous crackpot; the split in the Catholic hierarchy over his ac-tivities had taken away some of his more thoughtful Catholic listeners; the Townsendites and Share-the-Wealthers might still be with him, but their loyalty was divided. What he had left was mainly the discontented reliefers, the patriotic riffraff, the belligerently "American," the haters of foreigners and Jews, and borderline tough guys, and the hoodlum offspring of broken and disorganized homes. A good proportion of them were Irish and Catholic; some were German and Italian; some were old-line Americans picked up from the ruck of the Black Legion and the KKK, whose normal anti-Catholicism was redirected by the priest against the "Communistic Jews" and the "Jewish International Bankers."

In August, 1938, Father Coughlin began calling for action. He organized the Christian Front in "platoons" of twenty-five. Whatever the avowed purposes, the real purposes were Jew baiting, union baiting, and Communist baiting. The tactics were the tactics of terror: strong-arm methods borrowed from the Brown Shirts. The Christian Front was an American *condottiere* with the same purposes of division and disruption the European models had had. And the tone of *Social Justice,* low enough already as a vituperative smear sheet, bent ominously to the paranoid obsessions of little and violent minds. At the same time it lost whatever claim to journalistic accuracy it had ever possessed. It announced that Kuhn Loeb and "other international Jewish bankers" had financed the Russian Revolution; that twenty-four out of the first twenty-five commissars were Jews; that the Jewish Communists and the Jewish bankers were one and the same crowd, working for Jewish domination of the world. None of this, naturally, was true. It came pretty directly from the World Press Service, a Nazi propaganda agency distributing poison in a half-dozen languages, though Coughlin said he had taken it from a "British White Paper" and an "American Secret Service Report." There never was such a Secret Service Report as he quoted, and the British White Paper did not say what he said it said. The list of commissars was a Nazi fabrication. And an article in *Social Justice* on December 5 proved on examination to have been taken almost paragraph by paragraph from a speech by Joseph Goebbels.

Allied with Nazis and the German-American Bund, fighting Franco's war in Spain, spreading racist lies, leading an organization of militant thugs, Father Coughlin had come a long way. When *Social Justice* reprinted the notorious *Protocols of Zion,* a disreputable anti-Jewish forgery detailing an international Jewish plot, he had reached his own natural level. Every digit of rise in the business index had lost him followers; every attack on unemployment had weaned people away from his slogans; and every loss of prestige, every drop in his influence, had increased his intemperate and arrogant violence. Now, in 1938, with something like good times back again for most of the nation, he was where his logic and his ambitions had led him.

There was hardly a section of even the Catholic press, except the rabid Brooklyn *Tablet,* which defended him. Archbishop Mooney rather grimly said that though he had permitted him to speak he did not necessarily approve of what he said. Cardinal Mundelein of Chicago denounced him. But on street corners in the Bronx or Brooklyn, in saloons in South Boston, in pool halls and beer parlors through the Midwestern cities; among the boys and girls of twelve or thirteen who innocently peddled (and read, and believed) *Social Justice*; among the knot of gray-faced elevator operators gathered under the stairs for their lunch and bull sessions in a New York office building; among the Bundists and Silver Shirts, Father Coughlin had found the true measure of his popularity.

In Mattapan, Ben Levin began to have trouble with the boys from the old NUSJ unit who dropped into his shop. They stuck *Social Justice* under his nose and said, "Here, you're a Jew, Levin. You ought to read about what your pals have been doing lately. Take a look how your investments in Russia are coming." In Mattapan, too, and Dorchester and Roxbury, walls were taking on signs in red paint, and windows were being broken late at night, and Jewish residents were beginning to have trouble with gangs of hooligans who forced them off sidewalks and showered them with insulting remarks. One morning Ben Levin came down to his shop to find it broken open and its contents wrecked.

In New York the Coughlin storm troopers were doing an even more thorough job. The Christian Front vendors of *Social Justice* peddled their papers in front of parish churches, on Times Square, on Fifth Avenue. More often than not their insults directed at passing Jews would start fights, and in these deliberately incited attacks a gang of Fronters would beat up one or two opponents and then vanish. They were a loud, stupid, antisocial lot; Commissioner Herland's investigation, begun in 1942, indicated that the majority of the rowdies engaged in street fights against Jews in the Bronx were from broken or demoralized homes, and had records of sex crimes, incorrigibility, petty theft, or other unsocial behavior. Tommy Gallagher, in James Farrell's story, is a perfect specimen of the type.

In 1939 a "Christian Index" listing non-Jewish shops and advocating boycott of Jewish merchants was circulating in New York. Father Coughlin was cheered to the echo in a Bund meeting in Madison Square Garden. The platoons of the Christian Front were spreading; there were supposed to be twelve thousand Frontists in New York. The New York police blotter showed two hundred and thirty-three criminal prosecutions arising out of racial meetings and sales of racial literature in 1939. Irish hatred of Britain, American hatred of war, middle-class hatred of Communism, all the fears and manias that beset unhappy people were manipulated to create an effective group of terrorists and an even larger group of sympathizers. The *Nation* charged that the police, strongly Irish Catholic, were discriminating in favor of Fronters in street clashes, and inaugurated the movement that was ultimately to bring on an investigation of the police force for Front affiliations.

Other action was afoot, too. The code proposed by the National Association of Broadcasters in July contained a provision that radio time would not be sold for controversial discussions, but would only be given, and to all sides. Father Coughlin was one of the obvious targets; his current campaign on the arms-embargo issue was certainly controversial. In October, just after the outbreak of war in Europe, the NAB adopted the new code and stations began canceling Coughlin off the air. For a while he struggled on, managed to renegotiate contracts for another year, to November, 1940. *Social Justice*'s back cover and sometimes other whole pages were devoted to appeals for funds. Ten thousand dollars a week, a total of two hundred thousand dollars, had to come in before the year's broadcasts would be assured. The radio talks went on until April, and then Coughlin quietly withdrew. Presumably he had found his public no longer willing to support so expensive a luxury. The voice that had been golden with promises and vital with hope in 1930 went dead at the beginning of the forties. The Coughlin program, which with varying interpretations could have meant anything, had proved to mean rioting and race hatred.

7.

IT WOULD MEAN those things for more than two years longer. In January, 1940, the FBI picked up seventeen Brooklyn Fronters and confiscated a formidable arsenal, along with evidence of a plot for an armed coup. Coughlin, spiritual father of the prisoners, blew hot and cold. One week he denied having anything to do with the Christian Front. The next he said his connection was with a "genuine" Christian

Front. The next he "took his stand" belligerently beside the defendants, guilty or innocent. When the seventeen were acquitted, *Social Justice* gave the decision triumphant space.

Though the magic had gone out of Father Coughlin's activities with the closing of the airwaves, he could still make speeches to mass meetings and testimonial dinners. As war feelings intensified, the dinners and other celebrations had a tendency to go underground; admittance came to be by card and ticket only, and the pro-Nazi, anti-British character of the speeches became pronounced. In Boston, Francis Moran, the local Christian Front führer, twice showed the Nazi propaganda film *Victory in the West* and advocated resistance to the draft. In Codman Square, Ben Levin's frame shop, catching the overflow from the Front meetings at Hibernian Hall in Roxbury, was broken open and wrecked a second time. In New York Jews were knifed in brawls and beaten. The riots and fist fights on Times Square, on Fifth Avenue, in the Bronx, multiplied and grew in violence. Women and girls were often used as *agents provocateurs,* and when the insulted Jews replied, the brass-knuckle boys moved in. Their technique was smooth and well practiced, and the cops often looked the other way or arrested the wrong parties while the hoodlums blew. The elevator operators who had listened to Father Coughlin in their rooms under the stairs developed a habit of slamming the doors viciously behind Jewish passengers. *Social Justice* rang all the changes, all the varieties of possible sneer and insult, upon the word "Jew."

Father Coughlin was now, and would remain until several months after Pearl Harbor, the center and sparkplug of the nationalist, isolationist, pro-Nazi groups. His program through 1940 and 1941 looked considerably different from his sixteen principles of social justice—a defense of a sort could have been made for the sixteen points. His preachments now said (1) that a British-Jewish-Roosevelt conspiracy had caused the war; (2) that Germany and Italy were have-not nations forced into struggle with the anti-Christs, the big haves; (3) that the United States was fighting to save the British Empire; (4) that the increased taxes were not for defense but for solidifying the bureaucracy; (5) that Great Britain was going Communist; (6) that Russia was the aggressor against Germany; (7) that Britain was likely to deal to save her Empire, leaving us holding the bag; and (8) that Roosevelt was run by the Jews, whose war it was.

Sense and objectivity and positiveness had all departed; these were the preachments of a divisive frenzy. On their face, some of them would seem to be clearly seditious. But the constantly called-for arrest was never made, and the priest went on with his program of anti-Semitic terror, anti-British propaganda, anti-war harangues. His position brought him some new allies: by now, whenever he made a speech, Hearst papers had begun a curious habit of reprinting it verbatim. And though Coughlin had failed to unite the depression-struck millions behind him in 1936, he apparently still felt that the emotional and goonish fringe could be welded into a formidable organization. Until the bitter end he went along his fascist line, with three quarters of America yelling for his scalp and his reputation for any sort of integrity or honesty utterly gone. Many people believed, and still do, that he was taking Nazi money to run his machine. Whether he took money or not, he took Nazi ideas and Nazi methods, and evidence at the Nuremburg war-guilt trials later attested Germany's intense interest in promoting Father Coughlin's activities. His gangs were on the loose in a dozen cities; Jewish mothers were afraid to send their children to school for fear of the young hoodlums, influenced by their Christian Front elders and companions, who made a practice of beating up every Jewish boy they could catch alone.

The men who hung around Codman Square had quit joking with Ben Levin and sticking *Social Justice* under his nose. Their kidding had dwindled away into hostile silence; they didn't recognize him on the street. In the fall of 1941 his shop was wrecked for the third time, and he reluctantly closed it up and took a job in downtown Boston.

Coughlin's activities were clearly, after Pearl Harbor, intolerable. There was a point, at least in wartime, where division and disruption had to be stopped. In April, 1942, Attorney General Biddle charged *Social Justice* with violation of the Espionage Act, and Postmaster General Walker simultaneously barred it from the mails. For a few days there was defiance among the Fronters. In Boston a *Social Justice* truck went out to distribute the paper without benefit of the mails. When a Boston *Traveler* photographer tried for a picture, the truck driver kicked his camera apart while a friendly cop held the photographer's arms. But these were dying flurries. Father Coughlin did not show up to defend his paper in court, and finally agreed with the court decision that *Social Justice* cease publication.

Even then, silenced over the air and with his newspaper dead, Father Coughlin showed an ugly, sinister vitality. The testimonial dinners to "the greatest priest in America" went on; the faithful still met and talked and encouraged each other's hatred; the dirty and malicious jokes about Jews still circulated on mimeographed sheets and printed cards through war plants; the threats about what the boys in the Army were going to do to the Jews when the war was over kept cropping up, and Christian Fronters unwillingly in uniform carried them to ends of the earth. The beatings of Jewish children in Dorchester and Mattapan and the Bronx and Brooklyn and Philadelphia went on. Ben Levin's oldest son raised up on a patrol on Guadalcanal and took a Japanese rifle bullet between the eyes; a few months later his youngest brother was run off a South Boston beach by a gang of Irish kids who taunted him with what would happen to the cowardly Jews as soon as the war was over. And this was not a propaganda story devised by a do-good organization to show the evils of race feeling. This was sober truth. This happened to real people. I have talked a good deal with Ben Levin and Ben Levin's youngest son, and I have inspected the official announcement of the oldest son's death and fingered his Purple Heart.

The taproot of Coughlin-inspired hatred lives on, though to all appearances the radio priest has been politically and publicly dead since April, 1942. The other fascist demagogues, more successful for a time, fell further when they fell, and instead of retirement to the duties of a simple parish priest, found their end in a burning city, or hung by their heels in a public square. Farther Coughlin was lucky in that he didn't have a real and enduring desperation to play with; the depression was brutal and hard and long, but it did not go deep enough to give a demagogue real anguish to manipulate. Discomfort, want, hunger, but not quite anguish, not quite hopelessness or despair. And Father Coughlin was fortunate, too, that Franklin D. Roosevelt was his contemporary. The presence of a leader with all the personal magnetism of the führers, but without their venality or their vanity or their incurable lust for a white horse, robbed Coughlin of his chance to hang himself and possibly ruin the nation in the process.

But it would be well to ponder the enormous following he had at his peak. It would be well to consider how vague, misty, unformed, contradictory, and insincere his program was, and yet how it won the unstinting belief of hundreds of thousands, even millions. It would be well to remember that even a people like the Americans, supposedly politically mature and with a long tradition of very great personal liberty, can be brought to the point where millions of them will beg to be led, and will blindly follow when a leader steps forward. It would be well to mark, too, the reputed four hundred thousand names which have been sent in to Father Coughlin by wives and mothers of service men, so that he may pray for them to St. Sebastian. That "St. Sebastian Brigade," so called, is being closely watched as an incipient veterans' organization of some strength.

It is not likely that Father Coughlin or any of his American imitators can ever again be more than public nuisances, vermin in the national woodwork. But let conditions again become as bad as they did in the deep thirties, and the vermin will reappear.

On the other hand, there will be thousands of Americans, burned by this one experience with fascism under an American and Christian label, who will be warier when the next demagogue arises. The last ironic act of Ben Levin's real-life drama was symbolic, and like the death of his son it had almost too pat a moral. When the contents of his dead son's pockets were sent him by the War Department, he donated the money not to any golden-tongued radio orator or any leader with a panacea, but to a Good Neighbor Association formed to resist the racial hatreds that the leader had brought on.

The Mysterious Death of Starr Faithfull

BY MORRIS MARKEY

Morris Markey went calling on Starr Faithfull's family shortly after that unfortunate young lady's body was found in 1931, and he was lastingly intrigued by their reactions. He was also intrigued by the strange manner of Miss Faithfull's death, and in the article which follows he suggests an explanation for that event which seems highly plausible, but which no one seems to have thought of at the time. Mr. Markey was the original "Reporter At Large" for the New Yorker, and many of his articles for that magazine have become classics in the schools of journalism.

✵ 1.

THE HEAT WAVE was subsiding. All over the country the committee of American mayors who had been visiting in France were returning to their respective constituents, and these, except in a few churlish instances, greeted them with flags and whistles and even listened to their speeches. Mr. Hoover's offices in Washington were pleasantly devoid of news. And Mr. Daniel Moriarty, up with the dawn to meet the tide, was strolling the sands of Long Beach—some twenty miles out from New York—searching for drift that he might turn to a profit. The flotsam that he came upon, finally, was of a fabulous nature indeed. It was the body of a young woman, really a beautiful young woman, clothed in a silk dress and nothing else, and quite dead. Within half a dozen hours the front pages of the country's newspapers, on that eighth day of June, 1931, had a new name to fit into their headlines. It was a singularly poetic name. Starr Faithfull.

It lies within the very nature of a mystery story that it must be told backward. The only possible beginning is the corpse. And then things are learned and told about the corpse and the creature that existed before it became a corpse, until at last we do not have a corpse at all, but a living and very human being to remember, with friends and enemies, with hopes and defeats, with sins, and passions, and now and again a few nobilities.

Now be it observed that the District Attorney of Nassau County, the county in which Long Beach is situated, was a man named Elvin N. Edwards. Mr. Edwards was just dusting his hands after sending a prominent thug named "Two-Gun" Crowley to the electric chair when this new sensation, this mystery with the wonderful name, came within his jurisdiction. He had discovered already that publicity was no dainty drink but wine with delight in every bubble. We are indebted to his muscular management of the events that ensued, almost as much as we are indebted to the newspapers, for the strange and fascinating story that was unfolded in the weeks to follow—weeks when nothing much was happening except heat, and an occasional thunderstorm, and President Hoover speaking peevishly to the Emperor of Japan about certain dull happenings in a place called Manchuria.

Starr was not born Faithfull. She was the daughter of Frank W. Wyman, occupation unknown, and of a Boston woman who possessed what once were called good social connections. Ten years before our story opens, the mother had divorced Wyman and married Stanley E. Faithfull, a retired manufacturing chemist and occasional inventor of devices that never seemed to work. The Faithfull ménage, in the spring of 1931, consisted of the mother and the stepfather—whose name had been eagerly adopted by all hands—of Starr, who was now twenty-five, and her sister Tucker, younger by two or three years.

The first, hurried reports characterized the dead girl as an heiress, "the brown-haired, brown-eyed product of a Boston finishing school, who preferred to be alone, reading volumes on philosophy and kindred subjects."

But that impression did not survive the first twenty-four hours of journalistic labor. As always in such circumstances, there were friends eager to talk, and they told the tale of an elusive and difficult young woman, devoted to the proprieties and yet capable of the most bizarre escapades, racing at full throttle to escape from the role into which existence had cast her, and from herself.

This urge to escape inevitably guided her toward the sea. She had made two trips to England. But in this, her last spring, she had no money for another voyage. So she haunted the liners at their berths, reveling with the tourists as they prepared to sail and then, with such painful reluctance as we may imagine, stepping back ashore at the last minute.

On May 29, ten days before her dead body was found, she had been overcome at the last moment by that reluctance. She went aboard the Cunard liner *Franconia* to see the ship's surgeon, Dr. George Jameson-Carr. She was madly in love with him. Her emotion was not reciprocated, and for several months Dr. Jameson-Carr had been embarrassed by her eager attentions, her incessant confessions of devotion. On this day, she was pretty drunk when she went aboard the ship. Drinking was not her vice, ordinarily. Those were, of course, the bootleg days, and because he was terrified of speakeasy gin her stepfather, Faithfull, often mixed a flask of Martinis for Starr to take with her. As often as not she came home altogether sober, the flask still full. But on this day of waning May she was tight—volubly and almost boisterously tight.

Dr. Jameson-Carr sent her away from his sitting room some time before the ship's sailing hour. But she did not go ashore. She mingled with the passengers, and the *Franconia* was well down the bay before her presence became known to the ship's officers. The vessel was stopped, and she was put ashore by a tugboat after a scene in which the doctor's embarrassment was made public property. The ship, with Jameson-Carr still aboard, of course, sailed on for England.

The next day, May 30, she wrote a letter to him.

On June 2, she wrote another one.

On June 4, she wrote still a third.

These letters will appear somewhat later on in our narrative.

June 4, a Thursday, was the day she disappeared from home. She had been, apparently, in normal spirits—which is to say, irritated by her incessant febrile depression, and trying to compensate that emotion with little bursts of gaiety and generosity. The family was low in funds. Only three dollars could be spared for her purse. Nobody in the house asked where she was going or when she would be back, and she did not volunteer the information.

2.

THIS IS THE TIME for our first glimpse at the Faithfull home. (We shall, before the end, visit it again.) Nobody ever was able to find out, not even the strong-minded District Attorney, Mr. Edwards, the source of the Faithfull family's income. There were theories, beginning with blackmail and ending with an international drug ring, but they were mere flights in the tabloids, and nobody ever took them seriously. There is a fairly sound assumption that we are able to make about the family finances, but that, again, belongs somewhat further on.

However—

The family lived in a second-floor walk-up apartment at No. 12 St. Luke's Place, in Greenwich Village, three doors away from the home of Mayor Jimmy Walker. The building itself was almost identical with the Walker home, an early New York façade with a high front stoop, not without its attraction to the passer-by. The flat cost eighty-five dollars a month to rent, and it was distinctly not roomy enough for four people. But in it there was more than fifteen thousand dollars' worth of very beautiful antique furniture—Empire and Chippendale chests, a buffet by Sheraton. Such things.

There were, to be sure, manifestations of eccentricity in great abundance in this family. But Stanley Faithfull, according to his lights, was a devoted father even to a bewildering girl who was not his own daughter. When Starr did not come home on the night of June 4, he was worried. And by nine-thirty the next morning he was at Police Headquarters. There he gave a confidential report to the Missing Persons Bureau—which meant that his wish to avoid publicity would be respected. He also telephoned numerous friends and acquaintances, asking if they had seen Starr, and even wrote notes to certain of the girl's acquaintances whom he had not met.

The Police Department put in motion its routine confidential search. It got nowhere. The next news of Starr Faithfull was telephoned by an excited Mr. Daniel Moriarty to the Long Beach police station.

Late in the afternoon an assistant medical examiner reported upon the findings of the first autopsy (there were to be two more). Starr Faithfull had died by drowning, he reported, and her body had been in the water at least forty-eight hours. There were no traces of alcohol, but she had taken from one to two grains of veronal—possibly enough to cause unconsciousness but certainly not enough to cause death. She had also eaten a large meal. There was much sand in the lungs, suggesting that she had still been breathing as she lay in the shallow water at the edge of the beach. There were many bruises, resembling finger marks, on her upper arms. And she had been criminally assaulted. The last phrase was the euphemism of the day for rape.

Within a very short time, however, the diagnosis of rape began to lose its validity, as other doctors insisted they could find no evidence at all to support it.

District Attorney Edwards issued the first of his many hundreds of interviews: There was no question whatever but that the girl had been murdered, and he was hot on the trail of the villain who did it.

Now in order to understand the theory which leaped at once to the minds of detectives and newspapermen, you must be familiar with the geography of the scene. The 130-mile-long, narrow strip of sand called Long Island lies almost due east and west, immediately off the coast of New York and Connecticut. Steamships sailing from New York pass along the length of it as they set their easterly course, and often are in plain sight from the beaches.

An immediate investigation showed that two big liners, the *Mauretania* and the *Ile de France,* had sailed for Europe in the late afternoon or early evening of June 5 (and presently we shall examine evidence tending to show rather clearly that this was the day on which Starr Faithfull died). During the late afternoon, she certainly went aboard the *Mauretania.* And, just as certainly, she left it well before sailing time. There were numerous witnesses to both of these facts. Certain other evidence, not nearly so convincing, indicated that she also went aboard the *Ile de France,* lying at her pier a short distance from the *Mauretania.* This could never be definitely proved. But, supposing that she did go aboard the *Ile de France,* there is no evidence whatever that she left it before sailing time—10 P.M.

An immediate assumption was almost unanimously agreed upon: the girl had remained aboard one of the ships, secretly, and while the vessel was passing Long Island she had jumped or fallen overboard. The most emphatic dissent from this opinion was delivered in a muted bellow by Mr. Edwards. Starr Faithfull had been murdered. No doubt about it. He was promptly joined in this position by Stanley Faithfull. It was an outrage upon the memory of his daughter, he said, to suggest that she had done away with herself. Somebody had killed her. Her death must be avenged.

Well, naturally, the newspapers were eager to throw away their own theories and subscribe to the theory of murder—the more foul and revolting, the better. A suicide is perishable news indeed. A murder mystery is durable goods, front-page stuff for weeks.

But even as they cast a solid vote for murder, the newspapers clung to the romance of the ocean liners. Somebody had thrown her overboard. Had Starr Faithfull ever been to Long Beach before in her life? Did she know anybody there? The answer was a reasonably accurate no.

3.

MEANTIME the past of the unhappy girl began to emerge. The first item was simple scandal. Just a year before her death she had been in trouble with the police. People heard screams coming from a room in an uptown hotel, and called a patrolman. When he entered the room he found Starr lying naked on the bed, and a vigorous-looking young man in an undershirt regarding her with angry eyes. There was a half-empty bottle of gin on a table.

The man said he was Joseph Collins, and showed his army discharge papers to prove it. He either did not know or would not tell Starr Faithfull's name.

The police officer seemed more than usually dense. Despite the fact that Starr was rather seriously beaten up by fists, he told Collins to get out—make himself scarce—which he did, permanently, never being heard of again. Starr was revived and taken to Bellevue, where she spent the night. The hospital record was brief and to the point:

"Brought to hospital by Flower Hospital ambulance. Noisy and unsteady. Acute alcoholism. Contusions face, jaw, and upper lip. Given medication. Went to sleep. Next A.M. noisy, crying. People came. Discharged."

Her own statement to the hospital people reads: "I was drinking gin as far as I know. This is the first time I have had anything to drink for six months. I don't know how many I had. I don't remember. I suppose somebody knocked me around a bit."

But the first hint of something darker and more appalling than mere scandal came now with a series of rumors and half hints. It was learned that Starr had been under the care of one or more psychoanalysts. It was also learned that there was something unusual in her approach to the problems of sex. Could it be that Mr. Joseph Collins had been deliberately employed to take her to the hotel, not to beat her up, to be sure, but to give her, if possible, a normal sexual experience? And had her reluctance so infuriated him that he completely lost his temper? No proof of that, at any time. Because nobody ever heard of Mr. Collins again.

Now her diary, which she called her "Mem Book," was picked up by a policeman prowling among the hundreds of books in the little flat (good books they were, too—solid and thoughtful works for the most part). It was written in a sort of shorthand—no names of anybody, only initials—but even its fragmentary nature told clearly enough of a bitter, and frustrated, and indeed a ruined life. Its most interesting feature, to the tabloids, was that it contained passages of eroticism which even they did not feel disposed to print. But a set of initials cropped up persistently: AJP. Sometimes she hated AJP and sometimes she was affectionate in her references, but always she was frightened sick of him. "Spent night AJP Providence. Oh, Horror, Horror, Horror!!!"

It became news, for a day, that when she was nineteen she spent nine days under mental observation in a Boston sanitarium, and the record showed upon her release that she was "much improved."

And there were some revealing dispatches from London. On one of her recent trips there she had been accompanied by her mother and her sister, Tucker. They had lived in cheap lodgings while Starr cut a swath in the town, wearing beautiful clothes, sharing the champagne and jollities of the giddier fringes of aristocracy. On her second trip, alone, she tried to commit suicide. She swallowed twenty-four grains of allonal, but somebody found her and she was revived.

Even the most cynical of the horde of men and women prying and picking into the brief twenty-five years of her existence knew, by now, that Starr Faithfull was not just another tramp. She was not just another by-blow of the speakeasies, nor a demimondaine like the celebrated Dot King and Louise Lawson who, also, had gone down to violent and early death in those treacherous times. Something about her was pitiful rather than sordid—perhaps even tragic. But what was it?

4.

AT THIS JUNCTURE of the affair I went calling one night on the Faithfulls. Thirty-five or forty reporters and photographers were gathered about the stoop, and I asked how one went about getting upstairs to the flat.

The only answer was, "You can walk, can't you? But it's hot as hell up there."

Mr. Faithfull was standing thoughtfully in the doorway of his living room, a big pipe in one hand and a volume of the *Encyclopedia Britannica* in the other.

"Come in," he said. "I was just trying to determine the normal weight of the human liver. There are some things about that last autopsy report I don't like, and I'd like to satisfy myself. Do you know how to translate grams into pounds and ounces?"

A very large photograph of Starr stood in a leather frame on a table, with a vase of peonies drooping over it. On the table, too, were several volumes on criminology and one on anatomy, and a pad of yellow foolscap with much writing upon its top sheet.

"The answer to everything lies in that veronal," said Faithfull. "We've got to know exactly how much was given her."

"You think she did not take it herself?"

"Nonsense!" He wrote more figures on his pad.

Mrs. Faithfull came in—a thin woman with what we used to call the touch of good breeding upon her, wearing a nervous smile and offering hospitality in words that tumbled over each other.

"I'm quite relieved it is just you," she said. "We thought it might be the police to take Tucker away. One of the reporters told us an hour ago that they were coming to arrest her. We thought he was just saying that to see what reaction he would get, but we were a little upset anyway. That man Edwards out there is likely to do anything to keep his name in the papers. So Tucker went back and got into bed. She was going to say she was too ill to move."

"Would it be possible for me to meet Tucker?"

"Why, certainly."

(Remember that I had never been in the Faithfull home before, never met one member of the family before.)

She led me back through a dark little passageway to the room the two girls had shared until the week before. Tucker was propped up in bed reading a book—not the newspapers—and she was very steady in the nerves.

"What can I do about these?" she began, and threw a handful of telegrams out upon the pink counterpane. The telegrams were from Broadway, from agents and movie scouts, from night-club owners and vaudeville people. All of them begged for luncheon appointments, and all of them talked of wonderful contracts that were waiting to be signed. Tucker did not wait for my answer.

"I can't take any of them," she said. "It's terrible I can't take any of them up, because I'd do almost anything for that much money. I haven't got a dime."

Mrs. Faithfull laughed gaily. "And we are the family of blackmailers the papers are talking about! They've told us in the papers how shabbily we live, how much rent we pay, how many bills are in the mailbox downstairs, and that we can't even afford a telephone. Not very competent blackmailers, I would say—wouldn't you?"

With the utmost coolness, Tucker began to talk about the newspapers. "Why is it, really, that they print all of that stuff? One of them said today that we were pals with Legs Diamond. I never heard of the man except in headlines, and neither have any of us. Do they really make up stuff like that? And half the things they print about Starr are perfectly ridiculous."

I said, "Mr. Faithfull talks too much to the newspapers. You ought to have a lawyer who could protect you a little."

Tucker said, "We couldn't pay a lawyer."

Feet tramped on the stairs, and Tucker said wearily, "Well, I guess those police are coming after all." But it was only a new detachment of reporters, who settled around Faithfull in the living room, and puffed pipes, and discussed his theories with him.

I stayed there in the back room for an hour, chatting with them. And our talk drifted far from the mystery and the dead girl who was the center of it—about books, about Europe and travel in general, finally about the theater. They were very fond of the theater.

"How did you like *Wonder Bar?*" Mrs. Faithfull asked.

I confessed that I had found it dull.

"Well, now!" she exclaimed brightly. "Isn't that an interesting reaction? It was the last show Starr saw, and we loved it but she thought just as you do. She said it was dull, too."

Tucker asked, "What's going to happen to all of us when the excitement dies down? Will they let us alone? Will we take up living again just like we lived before?"

Mrs. Faithfull said, "There's one thing you can say for all the excitement. It keeps you so worked up you don't have much time to think that Starr is really gone, and isn't coming back."

Tucker looked up with a peculiar expression.

"Starr!" she said. And she did not smile.

The apartment was suddenly cleared of all such intruders as myself. A dapper young newspaper reporter arrived, and he was a very special visitor who required privacy within the family circle. He had been engaged to write Mr. Faithfull's own personal narrative for a press association—a literary undertaking in which Faithfull declined to share the profits.

As its chapters began to appear, the confusing character and actions of Starr Faithfull were clearly explained at last. She had been seduced at the age of eleven by a middle-aged Bostonian of wealth and prominence, with whose children she was accustomed to play at the beach and in the parks. Her seduction had been accomplished by the use of ether, and thereafter she had become something of an ether addict. The relationship with this man had persisted for a number of years and it had obviously had a profound effect upon her. She went through periods of "queerness" which her family could not understand at all—periods when she refused to go swimming because she would not expose herself in a bathing suit, indeed insisting upon ankle-length skirts and even upon boys' clothes—periods when she would not associate with any of her young friends and spent days at a time alone in her room.

At last, after two nights in a New York hotel with this man, when she was still in her teens, she told her mother all about it.

The villain of the piece was identified by Faithfull in his story as "Mr. X." But it did not take long for those who had read the girl's diary to associate this individual with the "AJP" so often referred to in its pages. And, almost as quickly, a man was located whose name fitted the initials. He was Andrew J. Peters, former Congressman, former Mayor of Boston, and a distant relative of Mrs. Faithfull's.

It was certainly true that Starr had played with his children, that the two families had seen a good deal of each other, and that he had been alone with Starr on many occasions. Next it developed that the Faithfull family had been paid a considerable sum of money for signing a formal release to some unnamed individual, quitting him in lengthy terms of all liabilities for damage done to Starr. Faithfull said that the sum was twenty thousand dollars, and that all of it was spent on medical and psychiatric care for the girl. Other reports indicated that the sum was about eighty thousand dollars, and that it had been the source of the Faithfull family's income for years. The firm of Boston lawyers which negotiated the payment and release had only one comment: "If Faithfull wants to say that it was only twenty thousand dollars, then we're satisfied to let it rest at that."

No official representations were ever made to Peters. His only comment was a formal denial, issued to the press, that he had ever indulged in improper relations with Starr Faithfull.

5.

WHILE THESE MATTERS were occupying the public attention, the family received permission to cremate the body. Frank Wyman, the girl's real father, had now appeared on the scene, and with the three Faithfulls he attended the funeral service. The four were kneeling before the candle-lit bier in a Long Island mortuary when men from the office of District Attorney Edwards rushed in.

"Stop the funeral!" they cried. "The D.A. has ordered another postmortem examination. New evidence!"

Volunteers from the gathering of newspapermen lifted the coffin into a wagon and the body was taken off for a new hour or two of scrutiny.

The next day, Edwards made his announcement: "I know the identity of the two men who killed Starr Faithfull. One of them is a prominent New York politician. They took her to Long Beach, drugged her, and held her head under the water until she was drowned. I will arrest both of them wthin thirty-six hours."

That was the last of that.

Nobody was paying much attention to Edwards anyway, by now.

On June 23, Dr. Jameson-Carr returned from England. He had been in Belgium on vacation when news of the girl's death reached him, and he had made his way to New York, voluntarily of course, with all dispatch. He was a pleasant fellow, cast in a difficult and highly embarrassing role. It would have been altogether impossible for him to be involved in the girl's actual death. But English sense of propriety being what it is, the Cunard Line was annoyed with him for getting his name into the papers at all. Privately (and a little ruefully) he confessed that they had taken him off pay for his trip to New York— a trip which he thought would certainly clear up the whole mystery, for he brought with him the three letters he had received from Starr.

The first one, written on May 30 (the day after she had been put ashore from his outbound ship), was on hotel stationery. The envelope was marked for the *Berengaria,* and the letter began without saluation:

I am going (definitely now—I've been thinking of it for a long time) to end my worthless, disorderly bore of an existence—before I ruin anyone else's life as well. I certainly have made a sordid, futureless mess of it all. I am dead, dead sick of it. It is no one's fault but my own—I hate everything so—life is horrible. Being a sane person you may not understand—I take dope to forget and drink to try and like people, but it is of no use.

I am mad and insane over you. I hold my breath to try to stand it—take allonal in the hope of waking happier, but that homesick feeling never leaves me. I have, strangely enough, more of a feeling of peace or whatever you call it now that I know it will soon be over. The half hour before I die will, I imagine, be quite blissful.

You promised to come to see me. I realize absolutely that it will be the one and only time. There is no earthly reason why you should come. If you do it will be what I call an act of marvelous generosity and kindness. What I did yesterday was very horrible, although I don't see how you could lose your job, as it must have been clearly seen what a nuisance you thought me.

If I don't see you again—good-by. Sorry to so lose all sense of humor, but I am suffering so that all I want is to have it over with. It's become such a hell as I couldn't have imagined.

If you come to see me when you are in this time you will be a sport— you are assured by this letter of no more bother from me. My dear—

Starr

The second letter, that of June 2, was simply a formal note of apology, obviously written for the record or for him to show to his employers if the occasion arose. It was addressed stiffly to "Dr. George Jameson-Carr, Dear Sir," and said that she regretted her conduct on the ship, that he had not invited her to come aboard or served her any refreshment—she had brought her own liquor and drunk it too hastily. It gave formal assurance that she would never embarrass him again, and was signed, "Yours very sincerely, Starr Faithfull."

The third letter was written on June 4, the day she disappeared from home. It was posted at 4:30 P.M., written on the stationery of a department-store writing room, and addressed to Dr. Jameson-Carr, and marked "Via USS *Olympic*":

Hello, Bill, Old Thing:

It's all up with me now. This is something I am going to put through. The only thing that bothers me about it—the only thing I dread—is being outwitted and prevented from doing this, which is the only possible thing for me to do. If one wants to get away with murder one has to jolly well keep one's wits about one. It's the same way with suicide. If I don't watch out I will wake up in a psychopathic ward, but I intend to watch out and accomplish my end this time. No ether, allonal, or window jumping. I don't want to be maimed. I want oblivion. If there is an after life it would be a dirty trick—but I am sure fifty million priests are wrong. That is one of those things one knows.

Nothing makes any difference now. I love to eat and can have one delicious meal with no worry over gaining. I adore music and am going to hear some good music. I believe I love music more than anything. I am going to drink slowly, keeping aware every second. Also I am going to enjoy my last cigarettes. I won't worry because men flirt with me in the streets—I shall encourage them—I don't care who they are. I'm afraid I've always been a rotten "sleeper"; it's the preliminaries that count with me. It doesn't matter, though.

It's a great life when one has twenty-four hours to live. I can be rude to people. I can tell them they are too fat or that I don't like their clothes, and I don't have to dread being a lonely old woman, or poverty, obscurity, or boredom. I don't have to dread living on without ever seeing you, or hearing rumors such as "the women all fall for him" and "he entertains charmingly." Why in hell shouldn't you! But it's more than I can cope with—this feeling I have for you. I have tried to pose as clever and intellectual, thereby to attract you, but it was not successful, and I couldn't go on writing those long, studied letters. I don't have to worry, because there are no words in which to describe this feeling I have for you. The words love, adore, worship have become meaningless. There is nothing I can do but what I am going to do. I shall never see you again. That is extraordinary. Although I can't comprehend it any more than I can comprehend the words "always"—or "time." They produce a very merciful numbness.

Starr

District Attorney Edwards was quietly nonplussed as his murder theory evaporated. Stanley Faithfull promptly cried to the press that the letters were forgeries, trembling with indignation as he talked to the reporters. But half a dozen handwriting experts said there was no doubt at all that the hand which wrote the diary also wrote the letters.

There can certainly be no doubt that Starr Faithfull intended to commit suicide. But there may be more than a fragment of doubt that she succeeded in her purpose. Two or three things pique the curiosity:

She had her last big meal, yes. It was one of the few things about the autopsy that everybody agreed upon.

But the autopsy surgeons agreed upon something else, too: There were no traces of alcohol in her system, though she had written, "I am going to drink slowly, keeping aware every second."

She had made her secret plans, and specified in her last letter, "no allonal," yet allonal or veronal—they are both barbiturates and very similar chemically—was found in her body.

More provocative, perhaps, are several other things she dropped into her last letter, written about twenty-four hours before she died. You will observe that she says two things which might very well be taken in conjunction: she will not worry about flirts, indeed will encourage them; and she can be rude to people, tell them exactly what she thinks of them. Furthermore, she confesses that she is a "rotten sleeper."

Now let us remember back for a moment to her adventure with Mr. Joseph Collins. Is it too far-fetched to suggest in connection with that episode: That Mr. Collins (however he fell in with her) found himself in a room with a beautiful and naked girl; that her poor qualities as a "sleeper," her insistence upon those "preliminaries" which counted so greatly with her, made her appear to him as simply a tease; that his anger and frustration drove his emotions out of control, and he gave her the beating which neighbors and the police stopped before it went too far.

Perhaps, then, it is not too fantastic to suggest that on the final day of her life she allowed herself to be picked up by an attractive stranger, that she agreed to his suggestion that they go to Long Beach. (Long Beach was by the sea, was it not? You could see the liners sailing out from there, could you not?—all brilliantly lit and crowded with gay people escaping from the humdrum. She had seen Long Beach from the outbound ships, but never the ships from Long Beach.)

They had a good dinner and she decided not to drink after all. Here, at the very end, she could be more certain of enjoying every moment if she remained quite sober. Every moment of what? Of putting a panting male in his place—a male who lay eternally in her mind as the male who had hurt and frightened her and savagely disillusioned her, so long ago in Boston. She would get him excited. That was easy. And then she could ridicule his excitement, laugh unrestrained in her contempt for him.

The veronal comes in here somewhere. I shall not dare to imagine where, but I think she always had it with her. It is to be remembered that drugs, preferably ether but one of the barbiturates if ether was not handy, were essential to her whenever she approached the realm of sex. They were the signal element in that first, haunting experience, the element from which she could never thereafter escape.

I think they did not go to a room, but found a lonely spot on that almost endless stretch of shadowed sand. The *Ile de France* would make her way past soon. She discarded all her clothing except the thin silk dress—her coat and shoes and underclothing. And then, I think, she teased this unknown man beyond endurance. He mauled her, perhaps into unconsciousness. Then he was frightened because he had mauled her, and decided that she would never tell of it. So he took her down to the water's edge and held her head under for a while.

And so, reading over all the old documents in the perspective of time, I think that Starr Faithfull was foiled of her final purpose as she had been foiled of everything else in life. She was not even able to accomplish her own end, which she had been so determined to do. That quantity of sand, heavy in her lungs, tells rather plainly that she did not go over the rail of a ship in the open sea. She was a good swimmer, it is true; but what swimmer, even an expert, full of veronal, could dive fifty feet into the swells from the deck of a liner and swim five miles through surf to reach the sand-filled water close inshore, still alive and breathing?

No single item of her clothing ever was found. It may easily be argued that even had she stripped herself down on the *Ile de France* or any other ship, the owners would not be very eager about producing the clothes she left behind. Public-relations officers are jealous of the good names of their charges. But such matters are rather hard to keep secret. And it is rather more difficult than you might think to go off the deck of a well-ordered ship, rather early in the evening, without being seen.

Again, you may ask, "If this unpremeditated murder were accomplished on Friday night, why was the body not seen by the crowds which swarmed the beach over the hot week end?" The answer to that is the movement of the tides. It has happened often enough that the bodies of bathers, drowned close inshore, have drifted out and not been cast ashore again for days.

It is even possible that District Attorney Edwards had somewhere in his thoughts an approximation of this theory of mine. At any rate, he had the Coast Guard make an elaborate study of the tides and currents at Long Beach. He never published the result of his findings, however. And at last the sounds of his voice subsided. Within a month of that June week end, the tale was done. Detectives turned to other misfeasances of the human race. And city editors, looking a little sourly at the suicide notes, decided that the story was about over.

The First Hundred Days
of the New Deal

BY ARTHUR M. SCHLESINGER, JR.

When Arthur M. Schlesinger, Jr., published *The Age of Jackson* in 1945, he stepped immediately—and at the precocious age of twenty-seven—into the front rank of American historians and publicists. The book won a Pulitzer prize and a much wider reading public than any recent work of history. Since the end of the war, in which he served abroad with the Office of Strategic Services, Mr. Schlesinger has been collecting material for a book on the age of Franklin D. Roosevelt, and has written many articles for magazines and newspapers. He is also the author of *Orestes A. Brownson: A Pilgrim's Progress* (1939). He is an active member of the Americans for Democratic Action, and is now an associate professor of history at Harvard, where his father has been professor of history since 1924.

✹ 1.

THE WHITE HOUSE, midnight, Friday, March 3, 1933. Across the country banks had shuttered their windows and closed their doors. The machinery of American capitalism had broken down; the great depression had reached its symbolic climax. "We are at the end of our string," the retiring President, weary and red-eyed, said to his friends as the striking clock announced the day of his retirement. "There is nothing more we can do."

Saturday dawned gray and bleak. Winter clouds hung over the Capitol, where a huge crowd, quiet, somber, drawn almost by curiosity rather than by hope, gathered to watch the new President. The colorless light of the granite skies merged with the emotionless faces of the people who stood in huddled groups, sat on benches, climbed on trees and rooftops in front of the Capitol. "What are those things that look like little cages?" asked someone in the waiting crowd. "Machine guns," replied a woman with a giggle.

On the drive to the Capitol the President-to-be was sociable and talkative. Herbert Hoover, his face heavy and sullen, could not conceal his bitterness. They separated inside the Capitol. The new President, waiting nervously in the Military Affairs Committee Room, started down the corridor toward the Senate ten minutes before noon. He was stopped; it was too early. "All right," he laughed, "we'll go back and wait some more."

The bugle blew at noon. Franklin Roosevelt, leaning on the arm of his son James, walked down a special maroon-carpeted ramp to the platform. Charles Evans Hughes, erect in the chilly gusts of wind, administered the oath on a Dutch Bible which had been in the Roosevelt family for three hundred years.

Then the new President turned to the crowd, and microphones carried his words to millions across the land. "Let me assert my firm belief that the only thing we have to fear is fear itself—nameless, unreasoning, unjustified terror which paralyzes needed efforts to convert retreat into advance." The crowd stirred as if with hope. "In every dark hour of our national life a leadership of frankness and vigor has met with that understanding and support of the people themselves which is essential to victory."

The firm, resonant tone itself brought a measure of confidence. "This nation asks for action, and action now. . . . We must act and act quickly. . . . It may be that an unprecedented demand and need for undelayed action may call for temporary departure from that normal balance of public procedure.

"We do not distrust the future of essential democracy," he said in summation. "The people of the United States have not failed. In their need they have registered a mandate that they want direct, vigorous action. They have asked for discipline and direction under leadership. They have made me the present instrument of their wishes." Herbert Hoover stared glumly at the ground.

There was a diffused roar of applause, quickly dying away. The crowd began to break up, curiously excited as it had not been an hour earlier. Some saw dismal portents in the eloquent but ambiguous phrases. "The thing that emerges most clearly," wrote Edmund Wilson, down from New York to report the occasion for the *New Republic*, "is the warning of a dictatorship." But the people as a whole welcomed the promise of action—action to exorcise the dark spell that lay over the nation's economy, to break through the magic circle which benumbed the powers of government.

2.

THE NATIONAL GOVERNMENT never followed the desires of the business community so faithfully as it did in the years from 1921 to 1933. American business had convinced the American people that it had discovered the philosopher's stone which would transmute the uncertainties of the capitalist system into permanent prosperity. The crash of 1929 thus came on a people intellectually and morally unprepared to take swift action.

1929 gave way to 1930, and 1930 to 1931, as the bewilderment deepened. By 1932 twelve to fifteen million persons were out of work (some Freudian resistance deterred the government from taking a census). An estimated thirty million depended on public or private charity. Millions more stayed alive by drawing on the savings of years. Farm prices caved in, leaving farmers to stagger under a savage burden of debt. Local and state governments, railroads, and much of business in general similarly were weighed down by debts on which they were increasingly unable to meet the carrying charges.

Hoover in his first reaction appeared to regard the depression as psychological in its origins and hence to be cured by exhortation and pep talk. In January, 1930, he pronounced the trend of business to be upward; as late as December he observed, with his gift for phrase, that the nation had weathered the worst of the storm.

Later the gravity of the situation compelled him to go further than his original remedies, which included such measures as the reduction of individual and corporate income taxes. Hoover reluctantly accepted Eugene Meyer's proposal for a Reconstruction Finance Corporation and thus sanctioned direct federal relief for corporations, though he continued to draw the line at direct federal relief for people. He worked at all times with a terrible and driving earnestness. Someone told him he should occasionally relax. "I have other things to do when a nation is on fire," Hoover replied.

But he was hampered by theory: in a time when it has been fashionable to denounce starry-eyed visionaries, few men have more systematically and honorably sacrificed actuality to doctrines than Herbert Hoover. One theory set up rigid limitations on the action of the Federal Government; in the service of this theory he vetoed bills designed to cushion in various ways the impact of the crash. Another theory declared the depression to be international in its origin; this theory shunted responsibility and action away from the American business community. Hoover was hampered basically by his profound and doctrinaire conviction that the forces which brought the depression would bring the revival. "Economic depression," he said, "cannot be cured by legislative action or executive pronouncement. Economic wounds must be healed by the action of the cells of the economic body—the producers and consumers themselves."

However lofty the grounds for Hoover's inhibitions, they added up to one thing in the minds of the people: impotence. The government was helpless before the crisis.

3.

BY THE BEGINNING OF 1932, the depression was settling into a way of life. The nation knew too well the bitter symptoms: the slammed doors, the endless walks, the shoes lined with newspapers; the straggling, sullen breadlines, the brief comfort of the soup kitchen; the hands warmed before gloomy fires in city dumps; the intense, hate-filled apathy of the Hoovervilles—everywhere the dull contagion of helplessness and fear.

These were the requirements for revolution; the gunpowder was loosely trailed across the land. But the spark was lacking. The theory of permanent prosperity had somehow pierced the confidence even of the radicals. Revolutionary vigor had died in the labor movement with the IWW. Who would lead a revolution? Not the unemployed, without organization, leadership, or political conviction, still confused by the collapse of permanent prosperity. Not the Communist party, which had more formidable backing from the intellectuals than from the workers.

For a moment in the spring and summer of 1932 fears focused on a minority which did have organization, leadership, and, beyond that, military experience. The Bonus Army marched on Washington, fifteen thousand strong, and settled in makeshift huts and ragged tents on the unsanitary lowlands of the Anacostia Flats. On the last day of Congress, as the June sun steamed on Washington, the B.E.F. seized the broad center steps of the Capitol. One leader, his voice high and bitter, shouted to the surging thousands, "Comrades . . . you must keep a pathway clear down the center so the white-collar gentlemen upstairs can get out without brushing into us rats." The government lay at their mercy. But the moment passed; the revolution was postponed. Twelve days later General Douglas MacArthur mobilized his tanks and bayonets, drove the veterans off the flats, and burned the miserable cantonments down.

For a few days panic had transformed doughboy griping into a revolutionary menace. As General MacArthur put it (his rhetoric would develop, but he already swung a mean subjunctive), "Had the President not acted today, had he permitted this thing to go on for twenty-four hours more, he would have been faced with a grave situation which would have caused a real battle. Had he let it go on another week, I believe that the institutions of our government would have been severely threatened."

So the republic was saved. But meanwhile the fires of a real revolution were beginning to burn—not in the gray cheerlessness of Union Square, not in the swamps of Anacostia, but in the middle-class heart of the nation, in the most prosperous farm lands of the Middle West.

The farmers had never shared in the prosperity of the twenties. After 1929, when the bottom fell out of food prices, the farmer carried debt obligations incurred when wheat and corn sold for four times as much. In Iowa, the most heavily mortgaged state, nearly one third of the farm value was in thrall. Notices of mortgage foreclosures and sales for taxes began to appear on the sides of barns and in county courthouses.

In the spring of 1932 grim-faced farmers banded together to fight dispossession. Desperation bred violence; their warnings, sometimes underlined by action, frightened the agents of banks and insurance companies out of the bidding, and the farms, knocked down to friends, were returned to the owners. Milo Reno ushered in a new militance during the Iowa milk strikes, and in the late summer the Farmer's Holiday movement began to spread. The action was in an honorable American tradition: "Raise less corn and more hell," Mary Ellen Lease had shouted to the Kansas Populists in the 1890's.

4.

"FRANKLIN D. ROOSEVELT is no crusader," Walter Lippmann wrote. "He is no tribune of the people. He is no enemy of entrenched privilege. He is an amiable man who, without any important qualifications for the office, would very much like to be President." Yet there was a warmth and energy about the new man which contrasted favorably with the clammy hauteur of President Hoover. Some observers, moreover, could detect the contours of a new and bolder philosophy of government lurking behind the generalities of his speech at the Commonwealth Club in San Francisco and behind such phrases as "the forgotten man" and "the New Deal."

The people thus decided in the elections to postpone revolution. But they had no real faith in the incoming administration. Four uneasy months of interregnum increased the anxieties. Unrest flared through the farm belt. At Malinto, Ohio, a banker's man saw a noose dangling from the barn of a farmer whose property he was about to foreclose. At Deshler, Ohio, a $400 debt was settled before a silent crowd for $2.15. At Logan, Iowa, Farmers' Holiday forces halted the projected sale for non-payment of taxes of two thousand pieces of property. At Le Mars, Iowa, a coldly angry group mobbed the agent of the New York Life Insurance Company and forced him to send a desperate wire pleading for authority to increase the company's bid.

Everywhere there were louder demands for debt moratorium, for currency inflation, for stays of judgment. John Simpson, head of the Farmers Union, warned the Senate Agricultural Committee: "The biggest and finest crop of revolutions you ever saw is sprouting all over this country right now." Ed O'Neal, head of the conservative Farm Bureau Federation, declared that unless something was done for the American farmer, "We'll have revolution in the countryside in less than twelve months."

Even the cities were shaken by strange fears. Pat Hurley, Hoover's Secretary of War, ordered troops transferred from a small Texas post to Kentucky. Tom Connally rose in the Senate to accuse the War Department of deliberately concentrating its troops near the larger cities. "The Secretary of War, with a glitter of fear in his eye," Connally reported, "referred to Reds and possible Communists that may be abroad in the land."

John P. O'Brien, New York's vaudeville mayor, reassured his city. "You're going to have a mayor with a chin and fight in him. I'll preserve the metropolis from the Red Army." But the next week a group of Communists pushed their way through a police line before the brownstone house on East Sixty-fifth Street where Franklin Roosevelt was laying his plans. Eleven Democratic Congressional leaders (among them two future Secretaries of State) were having their picture taken on the front steps; they fled into the house as the Communists shouted, "When do we eat? We want action!"

The lame-duck President in Washington tried to deal with a succession of crises. Various devices were suggested to bridge the four months' gap, but all dwindled to periodic and fruitless conferences with the President-elect. The two men met first in November. Like duelists, each brought his second: Hoover, Ogden Mills, his Secretary of the Treasury; and Roosevelt, Professor Raymond Moley, who headed his "brain trust." Roosevelt and Mills indulged in a passage of urbane kidding about their Hudson estates and about the campaign, while Hoover sat in gloomy silence. Then the discussion began.

Nothing flowed between the old President and the new: Hoover, sternly convinced that he knew the policies to solve the economic crisis, could not make out this flippant and evasive man, while Roosevelt had no intention of accepting responsibility for measures in which he had no confidence. "He did not get it at all," Hoover was heard to remark after the President-elect had departed. In the end, consultation was effective only concerning foreign affairs, where Roosevelt and Secretary of State Stimson discovered a common ground.

In February the Senate Finance Committee called on a procession of leading businessmen for their ideas on the crisis. It was a cruel exposure of the bankruptcy of business leadership. John W. Davis said, "I have nothing to offer, either of fact or theory." W. W. Atterbury of the Pennsylvania Railroad: "The only way to beat the depression is to hit the bottom and then slowly build up." Most endorsed the formula advanced by that perpetual elder statesman Bernard Baruch: "Put federal credit beyond peradventure of a doubt. . . . The suspicion is growing that we do not really intend to balance the budget." This was the business recipe for salvation—cut relief, public works, government expenditures, cut everything, balance the budget.

And the President-elect's plans? Visitor after visitor filed into the study of his house on East Sixty-fifth Street. Huey Long, the irrepressible Louisianian, had his own version of the interviews. "When I talk to him, he says, 'Fine! Fine! Fine!' But Joe Robinson goes to see him the next day and again he says, 'Fine! Fine! Fine!' Maybe he says, 'Fine!' to everybody." Roosevelt saw them all, left each with the feeling that they had his fundamental sympathy, and kept his own counsel.

In late January he went to Warm Springs. The deputations continued, but Washington noted that liberals came back more cheerful than conservatives. Someone asked George Norris, "Is he really with you?" "He is more than with me," the veteran fighter replied, "because he plans to go even further than I did, but in the same direction." Off-the-record press conferences disclosed some of the President-elect's far-reaching ideas about public power, communications, transport.

5.

THE OLD PRESIDENT and the new were far apart—a whole half century. But circumstances forced one more attempt at collaboration. On February 14 the Governor of Michigan decreed an eight-day bank "holiday." An ominous crack was widening in the nation's banking structure. The people could not but wonder if the impassivity of the new President would be any improvement over the impotence of the old.

On February 15 an unemployed bricklayer named **Joe Zangara,** armed with a revolver he had bought for eight dollars at a pawnshop, clambered on a bench amidst a crowd watching Roosevelt at Miami, Florida. Zangara sprayed bullets wildly at the official car thirty-five feet away. He wounded five people, one of whom, Mayor "Tony" Cermak of Chicago, later died. Roosevelt's strong voice rang out above the panic: "I'm all right! I'm all right!" The magnificent courage, the sure reflexes, the calm voice of confidence went through the nation like an electric current. The people had a rush of faith in their new leader.

Meanwhile the clock ticked closer to midnight on the banking system. Investigations by Ferdinand Pecora disclosed each day new facts about the unsound foundations on which the nation's credit was based. Federal Reserve figures reflected the rise in hoarding.

Hoover made one more attempt to persuade Roosevelt to join him in announcing long-range policies—though, as usual, they were to be Hoover's policies. (The retiring President had no illusions about the nature of what he persisted in calling co-operation. "I realize that if these declarations be made by the President-elect," he wrote secretly to Senator Reed of Pennsylvania on February 19, "he will have ratified the whole major program of the Republican administration; that is, it means the abandonment of ninety per cent of the so-called new deal.") With one eye fixed nervously on future historians, he already began to persuade himself that not his own administration but apprehensions over the incoming one had been the cause of all economic calamities since the election. His never-failing gift for phrase continued. "Gentlemen," he wrote to the Federal Reserve Board on February 22, "I wish to leave no stone unturned."

Still the panic spread. On February 24 the banks of Maryland went under. On February 26 Charles E. Mitchell, symbol of an era of unrestrained banking, resigned as head of the National City Bank. Across the country individual institutions were limiting payments or shutting their doors. By March 2 one state after another was enacting or contemplating bank holidays, while depositors stood wearily in line in the hope of filling brief cases and satchels with gold. The bolder spirits around Hoover pressed for action. Secretary Mills and Eugene Meyer, chairman of the RFC, urged him to declare a banking holiday, for which certain unrepealed war powers provided legal basis. Hoover refused to believe that the situation required such a drastic measure.

On the day of inauguration the clock struck twelve, every bank in the nation was closed, and the irony of the situation was perfect. "Our entire banking system," cried former Secretary of the Treasury McAdoo, "does credit to a collection of imbeciles."

6.

"THIS NATION asks for action and action now. . . . We must act, and act quickly." That night the new cabinet was sworn in quietly at the White House. The next day the President convened a special session for March 9 and, late in the evening, proclaimed a four-day bank holiday.

Yet, for all the audacity of his long-range plans, the President's intentions toward the banks were strictly conservative. His advisers were intent on restoring business confidence. Roosevelt himself had been impressed by the deathbed repentances. When Senator LaFollette gave him a plan of drastic reform, Roosevelt declared it wasn't necessary at all: "I've just had every assurance of co-operation from the bankers."

The problem, as he saw it, was to reopen the banks as quickly as possible. The Republican holdovers at the Treasury stood by. Leading bankers, frightened and panicky, converged on Washington. Phones rang incessantly with calls from distant cities. Four days of tense, weary, and endless conferences began. In the prevailing near-hysteria, only the President, who seemed to be exhilarated by crisis, and Secretary of the Treasury Woodin, who moved through turbulence in his own serene way, strumming his guitar in moments of perplexity, remained calm. As day was breaking on Thursday, March 8, Woodin left the White House with the emergency banking bill. "Yes, it's finished," he told newspapermen. "Both bills are finished. You know my name is Bill [he hated the more popular Willie], and I'm finished too."

Congress met. The House passed the bill in thirty-eight minutes; most of the Representatives had only the sketchiest idea what it was all about. The Senate took three hours. In the evening the President signed the act in the Oval Room. The tired men at the Treasury took showers, shaved, and turned to the frantic twenty-four-hour task of deciding what banks should reopen.

Later that same evening Roosevelt handed party leaders his economy bill, aimed at reducing government expenses and cutting veterans' compensation. On March 12 he called for the legalization of beer. With Republican support and progressive opposition, Congress passed the economy bill on March 15, 3.2 beer on March 16. By now the banks were reopening; a surge of deposits showed that the people were regaining their faith in the banking system. On March 15 the Stock Exchange resumed.

The President had rejected the opportunity to overhaul the banking system. He had struck out for a balanced budget. Lewis Douglas, a good sound money man, was at his right hand as Director of the Budget. The business community relaxed with relief.

Then, on March 16, came the message calling for the Agricultural Adjustment Administration, and the revolution which had begun in Iowa finally reached Capitol Hill.

7.

THE NEW DEAL was now beginning; it was a new era of American government. And with the New Deal came the New Dealers. Like circles beyond circles, the academic network was limitless; so too was the law-school network; and, with each prominent New Dealer acting as his own employment agency, Washington was deluged with an endless stream of bright young men. Government had never before been so eager to hire men of analytical competence, and the depression, by cutting off normal outlets in the universities or in law practice, enormously expanded the resources upon which government could draw.

They brought with them an alertness, an excitement, an appetite for power, and a never-failing instinct for crisis which became during the 1930's the essence of Washington: the interminable meetings, the chains of cigarettes, the lunches at the Carlton or the hasty sandwich at the desk, the call from the White House, the ominous rumor passed on with relish, the postponed dinner, the neglected wife, the office lights burning into the night, the selflessness, the vanity, the mistakes, the achievement. Rex Tugwell's youthful verse, written nearly twenty years before, still caught a good deal of the sense of challenge, along with a good deal of the slightly theatrical response:

> *I have gathered my tools and my charts;*
> *My plans are fashioned and practical;*
> *I shall roll up my sleeves—make America over!*

At his worst, the New Dealer became an arrant sentimentalist or a cynical manipulator. At his best, he was the ablest, most intelligent and disinterested public servant the United States ever had.

Sam Rosenman, anticipating the need for a program committee in the Roosevelt campaign, had brought Ray Moley and Rex Tugwell into the inner circle early in 1932. The circle slowly grew; trial-and-error eliminated the intellectually unsympathetic or socially uncongenial; and on weekly trips to Albany the "brain trusters" conveyed their own sense of excitement and opportunity to Roosevelt, whose antennae had been stretching out for policies of an imaginative boldness and technical ingenuity proportionate to the crisis. Tugwell took over broad responsibility for agriculture; Adolf Berle for the credit system; Hugh Johnson joined the group with a holding brief from Bernard Baruch; and Moley became the co-ordinator and the chief liaison with Roosevelt.

Partisan recrimination gave them a reputation for radicalism, but in a basic sense they were more to the right than the people who succeeded them in Roosevelt's confidence. "I am essentially a conservative fellow," Moley used to say. "I tilt at no windmills." They believed in the necessity of collaboration with the business community, either because, like Moley and Johnson, they were fundamentally pro-business, or because, like Tugwell and Berle, their far-ranging economic views required the transformation of business rather than its isolation and terrorization.

The "brain trust" stopped functioning as a single committee after the 1932 campaign—just about the time the quarrel was getting heated between those who wanted, in the phrase of the day, to trust the brain trust and those who wanted to brain the brain trust. By March, 1933, "brain trust" had become a generic term, designating any branch from the original tree, and the branches soon intertwined and hung lattice-like over Washington. But it still roughly described the source of considerable legislation, the agency of plot and counterplot within the bureaucracy, the reservoir of a passionate and honest concern for the underprivileged, and the running forum where the problems of the day were subjected to continuous, unrelenting, and extremely acute analysis.

8.

THE AAA ushered in the New Deal. Rexford G. Tugwell, a handsome, hard-fighting, somewhat arrogant professor, with substantial confidence in his own capacity to solve almost any complex social question, had conferred during the campaign on farm problems with rural leaders, among them an earnest ex-Republican editor named Henry A. Wallace. After Wallace was appointed Secretary of Agriculture, he brought pressure on the reluctant Tugwell to come down as Assistant Secretary. Talks among Wallace, Tugwell, Mordecai Ezekiel, M. L. Wilson, Beardsley Ruml, and a protégé of Bernard Baruch's named George Peek resulted in the outlines of a bill designed to increase the price of farm products. The bill delegated wide powers to the Secretary (Wallace and Tugwell were supposed to have worked this out as a solution of constitutional difficulties while strolling one night around the Lincoln Memorial) authorizing him to pay benefits to the farmers in exchange for a reduction of output.

Government, under the Agricultural Adjustment Act, would play an active and continuing role in managing the economy. The conception shocked conservatives of both parties. Marvin Jones, chairman of the House Agricultural Committee, refused to sponsor the bill. The business community in general recoiled from its sinister collectivism. But the big farm organizations went down the line for AAA. After amendments to satisfy the inflationists (and further to horrify Lewis Douglas, who saw in them "the end of Western civilization"), Congress passed the bill in April.

The pressure continued for weeks; Congress barely had time to come up for air. Throughout the confusion of Washington, small groups of men, their mandates vague, their lines of authority obscure, their composition often accidental, even their office space insecure and fluctuating, drafted, tore up, redrafted, wrangled over proposed bills, worked until dawn in quiet government buildings or shabby George-town houses.

Somewhere the commotion had a center. Perhaps it was the President's bedroom, where every morning Moley, Douglas, and one or two other reigning favorites discussed the urgencies of the next twenty-four hours. Somehow Roosevelt kept all the balls in the air. He cracked jokes, stroked egos, mixed politics and professors, and came out with policy. He saw agitated Congressmen, frightened businessmen, jealous bureaucrats, and had energy left over for arguments into the night. His press conferences crystallized the excitement for the reporters. And, on occasion, the whirl would come to full stop, and that confident, mellow, friendly voice would explain necessities to the common people across the land.

In quick succession he sent his messages to the Congress: the Civilian Conservation Corps, the $500,000,000 relief appropriation, the Farm Credit Administration, securities legislation, railroad legislation, farm and home mortgage relief. On April 10 he committed the nation to one of its bravest and most fruitful experiments. "I . . . suggest to the Congress legislation to create a Tennessee Valley Authority, a corporation clothed with the power of Government but possessed of the flexibility and initiative of private enterprise . . . charged with the broadest duty of planning for the proper use, conservation, and development of the natural resources of the Tennessee River drainage basin and its adjoining territory for the general social and economic welfare of the nation." Senator Norris's dream was about to be realized in concrete and steel.

Yet none of these measures attacked directly the basic fact of industrial standstill and widespread unemployment. On this problem (and on others in years to come) Congress took the initiative; the New Dealers forced the hand of their President. LaFollette, Costigan, and Cutting had long urged a public-works program. Wagner had been studying schemes for industrial recovery. Hugo Black, the able Senator from Alabama, now reintroduced his bill to spread work and purchasing power by establishing a thirty-hour week. Organized labor backed the bill; the public cheered it on. The Senate passed it on April 6.

Roosevelt thought the bill too rigid. "There have to be hours adapted to the rhythm of the cow," he said, and he sent Frances Perkins down to the House to do what she could to make it workable. Her more flexible substitute, with its provisions for minimum wages, alarmed business almost as much as the original. The President had wished to delay a comprehensive recovery program until his advisers could agree among themselves, but now the heat was on.

Several groups had been working independently on the recovery program. Moley, Tugwell, and Hugh Johnson had talked the problems over often during the campaign. In late April, as Johnson was returning from a hunting trip with Baruch in South Carolina, he met Moley at the Carlton Hotel. Flooded with other responsibilities, Moley felt he could no longer function as the President's clearing house on recovery plans. He persuaded Johnson to stay and take a desk in his outside office in the State Department. With his usual wild energy, Johnson dug in for eighteen-hour stretches. Tugwell and a labor lawyer named Donald Richberg helped, and before long they had a bill. Senator Wagner in the meantime was trying to get agreement on a plan from an ill-assorted group, including businessmen, lawyers for trade associations, government officials like John Dickinson of the Commerce Department, and young New Dealers like Jerome Frank and Leon Keyserling.

Johnson, Tugwell, and Wagner reflected in different ways the widespread revulsion against a competitive system which competed at the expense of the very life blood of the economy. Businessmen felt an urgent need, reflected in Gerard Swope's proposals of 1931 and the Chamber of Commerce recommendations, to co-ordinate their efforts by industry planning through trade associations. Liberals felt an urgent need to substitute co-operation for cutthroat competition and to safeguard wages, hours, and working conditions; and the business demand for a suspension of the antitrust laws suggested corresponding guarantees for labor to organize in unions of its own choosing.

The President, calling the proponents of the main bills together, appointed a subcommittee to be locked up somewhere until it could pro-

duce a single brief bill. The active members were Lewis Douglas,
Wagner, Johnson, Richberg, and John Dickinson. They settled down
in Douglas's office and worked continuously until they agreed on a
draft. On May 17 Roosevelt sent a message to Congress recommending
the passage of the National Industrial Recovery Act, of which Title I
provided for industrial self-government through codes of fair competition, and Title II provided for a public-works program. On June 16
this was signed into law.

And so the first hundred days of the New Deal came to a dramatic
and somewhat uneasy end. In the last weeks, Congress, driven perhaps
by some instinct toward self-preservation, staged sporadic small revolts
against the executive whirlwind. But the President had rallied the
people, had infused them with his own buoyant and courageous spirit,
and Congress knew they would not be denied. Still observers could see
in the seeds of conflict a portent for the future.

9.

FOREIGN AFFAIRS took a back seat in these breathless days. The brain
trust regarded American recovery as an independent problem which
should not be sacrificed to abstract conceptions of international economic welfare. As Assistant Secretary of State, charged with the preparation of data for the impending World Economic conference, Ray
Moley was in a position to advance this point of view. But Secretary of
State Cordell Hull, doctrinaire free trader, regarded the destruction of
trade barriers as the solution of all economic problems.

The conference opened in London in June with Hull as chief of the
American delegation. World attention had detected the schizophrenia
in American policy, and Moley's conferences with the President and
subsequent mission to London undercut Hull's authority. Personal
tensions engulfed the American delegation. With intermittent spasms
of tact, Moley sought to appease Hull, but the ex-mountaineer's vanity
was involved and his feuding instincts were roused. Roosevelt's message
breaking up the conference confirmed Hull's determination to get at
least personal vindication. With cold implacability he set out to destroy Moley, as he would later move to destroy Sumner Welles. His

hold on the Southern Democrats was an actuality; the President could see no choice. He greeted Hull with open arms on his return, and shifted Moley to making a survey of the federal anti-racketeering program. The Southern Democrats had triumphed in their first clash with the New Deal.

10.

THREE MAJOR EMERGENCY AGENCIES emerged from the hundred-day riot of legislation—AAA, NRA, and PWA. Their organization and experience contained omens for the future.

Politics dictated a conservative appointment to the directorship of so novel an agency as AAA; and the job went to George Peek, a manufacturer of farm equipment and a Baruch man. Peek brought along his old associate Chester Davis, and the two men went into uneasy harness with Tugwell and with Jerome Frank, who became AAA's general counsel. The central purpose of AAA—the increase in farm prices— was achieved, in part because drought assisted government efforts to curtail production.

The movement of events soon became too much for Peek, who got out, trailing invective about "collectivists," "internationalists," and "mystic idealists." In the meantime, as farm prices rose, new questions emerged. Should the increased income go just to farmers, or should the processors and distributors also get a large cut? And, among the farmers, should the increased income go just to the large farmers, or should tenants and sharecroppers get some share of benefit payments? Davis led those who favored the processors and the large farmers—that is, a restoration of the agricultural status quo--while Tugwell and Frank favored utilizing the opportunity to make some enduring changes in the distribution of farm income. The tension flared intermittently until the AAA purge of 1935, when Henry Wallace decided in favor of Davis and decreed that the Department of Agriculture continue as the agency of the large farmer.

The obvious choice for head of NRA was another Baruch man, the strange, vivid, and arresting figure of General Hugh S. Johnson. Johnson had been the driving force behind the bill. Indeed, the whole scheme of business self-regulation through trade associations had been in the back of his mind since the experience of the War Industries Board in 1918. He was associated with Baruch in the twenties, but he had obscure and powerful ambitions of his own. "I think he's a good number-three man, maybe a number-two man, but he's not a number-one man," Baruch remarked before the appointment was made. "He's dangerous and unstable. He gets nervous and goes away for days without notice. . . . Hugh needs a firm hand."

"It will be red fire at first and dead cats afterward," Johnson said on his appointment. He had a cavalryman's speech, rich and colorful (George Patton had been his tentmate on the Mexican border), and a cavalryman's confidence in his own physical endurance. He worked without rest and swept the American people behind him in his torrential conviction that they must unite to whip the crisis.

Johnson looked on public works as an essential part of the recovery program, which would revive the capital goods industries while the codes of fair competition would control consumers' goods and distribution; and he assumed that both functions would be in his charge. But his driving personality had roused misgivings. The performance of Peek in AAA also had provoked a suspicion of Baruch men in some New Deal circles.

Just before Roosevelt left for a cruise after the adjournment of Congress, he called Johnson over to the White House at the tail end of a cabinet meeting. As Johnson beamed, the President announced his appointment as administrator of NRA, then added that this job would be tough enough, so that he was slicing off the public-works project and giving it to Harold Ickes. Johnson's smile vanished; his face grew red and then purple; he finally said, his tones low and strangled, "I don't see why. I don't see why."

Roosevelt called Frances Perkins over as the group was dismissed and told her to watch Johnson. Almost in a daze Johnson walked to the door, muttering to himself, "I've got to get out. I can't stay." Miss Perkins took his arm and led him to her car. They drove for miles around Washington as she tried to calm him down. "Don't pull out," she would say. "It's terrible, it's terrible," would be his broken reply. Years later Johnson rationalized the experience: Miss Perkins was "so understanding, friendly, kindly, and persuasive that there was hardly a choice but to agree with her and . . . very fatuously, I did."

As head of the Public Works Administration, "Honest Harold" Ickes, the old-time Bull Mooser, who feared above all the possibility of graft and corruption, made it his first mission to spend money honestly. The result was that he spent slowly—too slowly to have any immediate effect on recovery, or to provide the co-ordination with NRA which the planners—and especially Johnson—had intended.

11.

PROBABLY no one but Hugh Johnson could have pushed through the codes so quickly or could have so charged the whole enterprise of code making with excitement. Henry Wallace told him about thunderbirds, and Johnson quickly sketched the Blue Eagle on a piece of paper. The new emblem became the focus of moral and civic pressure. Parades celebrated it; speeches praised it; throughout the land stores put it in their windows and stamped it on their products. For a time it gave the nation almost a sense of wartime unity. The colorful General and his NRA shouldered the rest of the recovery program out of the picture. One day, as Johnson and other top NRA officials were lunching at the Occidental, Frances Robinson, Johnson's assistant, came in, her face plunged in gloom. "This is the first day since NRA began when it hasn't made the front pages," she said.

But Johnson overestimated his physical strength as well as his capacity to hold all the reins in a single hand. Power reacted ominously on him. Fatigue, overwork, and the intoxication of authority stretched taut his nerves. He worked too hard; he drank too much; the omnipresent "Robbie" assumed an increasingly large role in his decisions. At first, he had thought of NRA as an emergency agency, but his dreams expanded. He read Raffaello Viglione on *The Corporate State* and began to see NRA as a permanent function of government which would absorb the Departments of Labor and of Commerce. Frances Perkins, who knew this restless, dictatorial, neurotic figure well, began to wonder "whether he might be moving by emotion and indirection toward a dangerous pattern."

Yet Johnson's unconscious motion toward dictatorship was in part an inescapable reflection of the central dilemma of NRA. By its nature NRA was an unstable mechanism which would work only so long as a sense of emergency gave the public interest a chance to win out over special interests. The businessmen who staffed NRA had a natural tendency to resolve doubts in favor of business. The trade-association theory, moreover, played into the hands of the large corporations; and the exemption from antitrust prosecution led to the joyful public indulgence in such formerly secret vices as price fixing and production quotas. While Section 7a promoted considerable trade-union organization, labor did not tend to associate these gains with NRA, especially as the NRA leadership attempted to dilute or obstruct 7a. A business-dominated NRA looked more and more like the halfway house to the corporate state. If, on the other hand, NRA decisions were to be made against the business community, a political storm would either overthrow NRA or cause the government itself in self-defense to march much faster on the road to statism.

Johnson's tense intuitions sensed the NRA dilemma, and his own thirst for power drove him along statist lines. He favored larger coverage, stricter enforcement, more coercion, at a time when much of business itself, now that it was slightly revived, wanted the government out of the picture. The administrative problems of NRA became intolerable as the good will on which it subsisted declined. The Supreme Court's unanimous decision against its constitutionality in 1935 relieved the administration of an unprofitable burden.

The experiment in business self-government had failed. The failure produced a growing bitterness in the White House toward business and thus a basic redirection of the New Deal. Experience was teaching Roosevelt what instinct and doctrine taught Jefferson and Jackson: that, to reform capitalism, you must fight the capitalists tooth and nail.

12.

THE MAN whose mastery emerged most clearly out of the excitement and anxiety of 1933 was, of course, the President. He thrived on crisis. Where his associates grew haggard or irritable, Franklin Roosevelt preserved his remarkable gift for relaxation. His wit would flash into gray and gloomy conferences, and that hearty, infectious laugh would provide a release from the inescapable tensions. His fireside chats transmuted the complex problems of government into simplicities for the forgotten man, and this new rapport between the White House and the citizen enabled him to rally support for his program as no president ever had before him.

With this support and with his own tactical brilliance, he could handle all political challenges. He surrendered to Hull on what seemed at the time a minor point, and that surrender would have unhappy consequences in later years; but even the Southern Democrats for the time being were under control. The Republicans were feeble and helpless.

Huey Long represented another and more dangerous challenge. On a hot summer morning in June, 1933, he came to the White House for a showdown with Roosevelt; the issue was whether federal patronage in Louisiana should be dedicated to building up the Long machine. The Senator breezed in, wearing a light summer suit and a jaunty straw hat with a garish band. He sat down, opened the conversation, but did not take off his hat. It was a test of wills. The President leaned back in his chair with a broad smile on his face and refused to be annoyed. After a time Long appeared to realize that he was getting nowhere; he could not break through the ring of cool and gracious phrases. Later he remarked to Jim Farley, "What the hell is the use of coming down to see this fellow? I can't win any decision over him." He never came again.

Roosevelt's superb confidence radiated through the nation. "When Andrew Jackson, 'Old Hickory,' died," he said in July, "someone asked, 'Will he go to Heaven?' and the answer was, 'He will if he wants to.' If I am asked whether the American people will pull themselves out of this depression, I answer, 'They will if they want to.' "

The recovery program of 1933 made no basic changes in the American economy. In its frenzied way it started wheels of industry turning again; with the aid of drought, it raised agricultural prices. The business situation achieved a measure of stability, and basic social rights won a measure of government guarantee. NRA in particular had a considerable educational impact. It accustomed the country to the feasibility of government regulation, and it trained personnel for the responsibilities of government service.

Roosevelt's basic pragmatism verged at times on improvisation for the sake of improvisation, an addiction to playing by ear in the nervous conviction that any kind of noise is better than silence. The great administrative innovation of the hundred days was the Tennessee Valley Authority. Yet this brilliant conception of an independent public corporation has remained in lonely magnificence.

But the legislative achievements of the hundred days were perhaps unimportant next to the moral achievements. They were brave days— days of desperation and of hope, of drama and of triumph. For many of the people who lived them, they were more exciting than anything they have known since. Here, for a moment, the clouds of inertia and selfishness lifted. A broken and despairing land had a glimpse of America as it might become. The clouds rolled back, as they always do. But in that moment the American people threw off a sick conviction of defeat and recovered an old faith in their capacity to manage their own destiny.

Full House:
My Life with the Dionnes

BY KEITH MUNRO

When Keith Munro arrived at Callander, Ontario, to report the birth of the Dionne quintuplets for the Toronto *Daily Star,* he brought with him a very suitable friendship offering in the form of twelve dozen diapers. The very next day he saw a considerable number of them hanging on the Dionne clothesline. In 1937, Mr. Munro resigned his newspaper job to become the full-time "manager" and publicity representative of the Quints, which provided, he says, "a very exciting, not to say hectic, seven years." He also did considerable ghost writing for the famous "little Doc" Dafoe, including his widely syndicated daily medical column, "which meant 365 columns a year, no holidays." The only book he ever had anything to do with, he adds, was a compilation of those columns which was printed without his knowledge, and of which he does not have a copy. He left the Dionnes in 1944 and is now operating his own public-relations office in New York City.

☆ 1.

IT WAS a crisp, bright May morning in 1934. Things were just beginning to get under way for the day in the city room of the North Bay *Nugget* when an early call came for Eddie Bunyan, the city editor. A voice came over the wire: "Say, Eddie, does it cost any more to print the notice of the birth of five babies than it does one?"

"Do you mean five babies to one mother?" the editor demanded incredulously.

"Yup, a young French woman over near Corbeil had five this morning. And they're all living—or were when I left there a little while ago."

"Well, Doc, we'll run this one free for you," laughed Eddie as he hung up. Then he beckoned to one of his reporters. "Doc Dafoe tells me that he attended a woman who gave birth to five babies this morning. Get Dick Railton, go over there, and get a story and pictures."

Then Eddie sat down at his typewriter and tapped out a forty-four-word dispatch for the Canadian Press wire:

North Bay, May 28:—Mrs. Oliva Dionne, residing within a few miles of Callander, nine miles south of here, gave birth to five girls today. All are healthy, said Dr. A. R. Dafoe, Callander attending physician. Mrs. Dionne is twenty-four and had previously given birth to six children.

These forty-four words were the first of millions that would go out over those same wires about those same babies. I know because in the ensuing two weeks I sent out a good many thousand words myself and I was only one of a dozen or more reporters on the job.

2.

I LIKE TO SAY that I was the first out-of-town newspaperman on the scene, but that claim has always been challenged by Charlie Blake of the Chicago *American*, so let us call it a tie. We arrived almost at the same time, but Fred Davis, the photographer, and I, both from the Toronto *Daily Star,* stopped in Callander to talk to the little doctor who was already becoming world famous. Charlie went straight out to the lonely Dionne farmhouse where the miracle of fertility had happened.

Neither Charlie nor I came to Callander empty-handed. But here again he shaded me a bit. I brought nearly three hundred dollars' worth of things small babies are supposed to need, including twelve dozen diapers, Brecht feeders, gauze, cotton, flannelette, even a bathtub. But Charlie was the hero of the hour. He had managed to dig up an old-fashioned baby incubator that was heated by hot water. It was almost a museum piece, yet there is little doubt but that it kept Marie's tiny spark of life aglow during that first incredible week. And there is a good chance that Emilie, too, owes her life to that funny little black box. For Dr. Dafoe and other experts who subsequently examined the babies estimate that they were "prematures" of even less than seven months. The weakest of them required a temperature of at least 85° and so incubators were a necessity. They had to be of special construction because no electric current was available at the Dionne farmhouse. Down in Toronto the *Star* was having special incubators made by men who were working day and night to get them finished. But Marie couldn't have waited for them to arrive. She had far too little to wait with.

An attempt to make up for this lack of incubators almost put an end to the lives of the children their second night on earth. The kitchen stove was kept roaring all night and toward morning the ceiling of the room became overheated. Flames didn't break out, but Nurse Yvonne Leroux had to call Oliva Dionne, the father, to throw water on it.

When Fred Davis and I reached Callander, we rang the bell of a modest brick house that bore the sign "Dr. A. R. Dafoe." We had no idea then just how world famous that name would become in the next few days.

The Little Doc, as we soon dubbed him, answered the door himself. When he heard we were from the *Star,* we were more than welcome. It was the paper he'd read all his life. He was pathetically grateful for the load of supplies we'd brought him.

That May evening as he greeted us at his door, Dr. Dafoe looked anything but a world figure. He was short, not much over five feet, and roly-poly. His head was enormous. One time when I asked him why he always wore caps he said that local stores never carried hats big enough to fit him. He was dressed in baggy gray pants innocent of crease, and a sweater coat. He had his pipe in his mouth. I've often thought that he must have been born with a pipe in his mouth.

We talked with him until far into the night; got from him the details of his fight for the lives of babies and their mother that epochal Monday morning.

Doc was humble. He gave credit for the babies' lives to the nursing they were getting, to the healthy blood stream they had been born with. Him? Oh, he'd done nothing much, he insisted. Afterward, in conversation with baby specialists, I found that it was this "do-nothingness" that saved the babies' lives those early days. The spark of life was so weak that if they had been handled as normal babies are they would have died. The doctor's order to his nurses was: "Do not take them up more than once a day."

After our talk we hurried to North Bay, where another *Star* man, Gordon Sinclair, and I got our stories on the wire. We had a big argument about what to call them, for nobody had yet figured out the generic term "quintuplets."

3.

THE NEXT DAY we got up about 4 A.M. and hurried out to the Dionne home, for Dr. Dafoe had told us that he wasn't any too hopeful about Marie. In fact he wasn't hopeful about any of them.

"I don't see how they can live, but they're living," he said, and added that they were the smallest babies he'd ever seen. He was something of an expert too, because he'd delivered around fifteen hundred babies in the twenty-five years he'd been in Callander. In fact he delivered half a dozen "singles" that first week while I was there covering the story. It was spring, and that is always baby season in that prolific land. One of his mothers had given birth to no less than twenty-four children.

The Little Doc was a newspaperman's dream. He just told you everything and relied on your sense of decency not to let him down. I don't think we ever did.

The Dionne homestead was about two and a half miles off the highway and the road was little better than a lumber trail. Our car was low-slung and we dragged the chassis over rugged rocks until I was afraid we'd wreck it.

Appropriately enough, our first impression of the place was of lines and lines of diapers hung out to dry. I guess some of them were the ones we'd brought up because Dr. Dafoe had gotten them out to the Dionnes the night before. The diapers almost obscured the tiny, unpainted, clapboard house where the Dionne family had lived for a couple of generations. The United States papers almost unanimously labeled it a log cabin. I guess it had more significance that way. In fact, the desk at the *Star* began changing my copy to make it read "log cabin."

At the house we learned from Nurse Leroux that the babies were still alive. Marie had had a crisis. Her tiny heart had seemed about to quit. Finally on doctor's instructions the nurse had given her a couple of drops of rum, and the mite had rallied. That was our lead for the day.

Finally Dr. Dafoe drove up and went in. We waited outside and plotted how to get in and take some pictures. In a few minutes he came out and even before we asked him he said, "Do you want to see the babies?"

We piled into the house and got one of the big thrills of a lifetime. There, propped up in bed, was the pretty mother, smiling, as friendly as only country people can be. Beside her, in a basket that had been their cradle since the first day, were four heads—only they looked more like oranges, they were so small, so wrinkled, so dark in color. Marie, the fifth baby, was tucked away in Charlie Blake's incubator.

There was something terribly exciting about those babies that made thrills run up and down my spine. I can't explain it. But I've seen it happen to other people. I've seen crowds go on wild stampede at the sight of the five little girls.

With some hesitation I asked Doc if we could take pictures. We knew that any minute other reporters and photographers would arrive in droves. We wanted to get our pictures and be away before the dam broke.

Doc said it was all right with him, and Olivier Dionne, the grandfather, translated our request to his daughter-in-law. She smiled gracious consent. Davis was one of the fastest men with a camera that I ever saw, but he exceeded even his own speed record getting set up and ready.

I held the flash for him and he started shooting. The first picture went fine; so did the second. At the third shot my first gray hair burst into full bloom. In those days flash bulbs weren't perfected as they are now. Sometimes they exploded with the flash. That's what happened this time, and the shattered glass flew all around the little room. It seemed to me that a whole shower descended right on the basket with the tiny heads. In a flash I could see the headlines: " 'STAR' FLASH-BULB BLINDS QUINTUPLETS," or worse still: "MARIE DIES FROM SHOCK OF EXPLODED FLASHBULB." At very least I expected that we would be thrown bodily out of the house by an irate doctor, nurse, and family.

Again I was astounded at the friendliness and hospitality of these

simple people, for no one seemed in the least disturbed but us. The doctor even made some little joke about it. But the most unperturbed of all
were the tiny babies. You'd think they liked being showered with glass.
We went ahead and took more pictures, but we took no more chances
with those tricky bulbs, for we wrapped each one in a handkerchief.

As we were leaving, up drove Charlie Blake and his photographer.
They went in and took pictures too, but they were the last. When
other photographers appeared later the same day, the Doc's patience
gave out. "No more pictures," was his order. It made us rather happy
because the ones we had taken were now invaluable. Months later the
Dionne Quint pictures mushroomed into a million-dollar business.

4.

I DON'T THINK that it was altogether because the Doc's patience was exhausted that he forbade pictures. For the first couple of days he didn't
give the babies any chance to survive. Then about the third or fourth
day it suddenly was borne in on him that they could be pulled through.
At that moment the world's greatest "no" man was born. And when
that happened the babies' chances of living increased from one in a
million to about one in half a million.

That day too a supply of mother's milk arrived from Chicago, sent
by Dr. Herman L. Bundesen. Again the babies' chances of survival were
doubled.

The next morning when we arrived at the Dionne home we were
greeted by "No Admittance" signs. Of course that couldn't mean us, we
argued. We had had the run of the place for the first couple of days on the
strength of the diapers and things we'd brought. Blake, by reason of his
precious incubator, shared this favored position and he was with us.
But when we tried to get in the gate Grandfather Dionne appeared,
pitchfork in hand, and sternly bade us scram. We were hurt. We tried
to work on the old man's sympathy, asked him to recall all we had done
for them. You could see that holding us at bay was outraging his native
courtesy and sense of hospitality. But, he said, Dr. Dafoe had given
him his orders.

That made us feel better. The Little Doc was just putty in our hands.

We would soon get that order rescinded. As we waited we attempted to establish communications with Nurse Leroux, the girl we'd been calling "Yvonne" for days. But all we got from her was a stony stare.

The Doc drove up and I thought there was a different flavor to his "Good morning, boys" as he hurried in. When he came out he gave us the morning report. Marie had had her usual crisis and of course had been saved by rum. Then he let us in on a little joke. Several prominent doctors had called him to ask why he used rum instead of brandy. His reply was simple: "I can't afford brandy. Rum is cheap and besides it works." The Doc was relenting, we thought. Now was the time to ask him to let us go in the house, talk with the nurses, and make general nuisances of ourselves. Newspapermen seem to think this is their God-given right.

That was when we got our first look at the new and different Doc Dafoe. He looked us right in the eye and said quietly, "These babies need quiet. I value their lives ahead of anything else in this world." Then he walked away, leaving us all feeling as cheap as hell.

I must say he did relent a little bit. He did let us inside the fence and he did let the nurses talk with us. But get inside that house? Over someone's dead body!

All day Thursday and Friday we searched for Oliva Dionne, the young father. But he was nowhere to be seen. Then we discovered the deal. He and his priest, who acted as his adviser, had stolen away to a near-by town to meet with promoters who wanted to take the babies to the World's Fair in Chicago.

On Thursday they were back in Callander, very secretive about their trip. But their secrecy did no good because the promoters were anxious to tell the world that the father of the Quints had signed a contract which called for the babies' appearance in Chicago on the World's Greatest Midway. They would, no doubt, be sandwiched in between the fat lady and the India rubber man. "Right this way, ladeez and gentlemen—"

Of course, screams of protest went up all over Canada. Oliva Dionne was pilloried as an inhuman father, a monster. While Dr. Dafoe was fighting for his babies' lives, the father was pictured as selling them down the river to the circus.

Nothing could have been further from the truth. It was just that Oliva listened to bad advisers. This little French-Canadian *habitant* was beside himself. He had scratched a precarious living from the few tillable acres of his rocky farm. He had always paid his way. Then a miracle struck and there were five more mouths to feed; there were doctors' bills, nurses to be paid. What would he do? The three-thousand-dollar mortgage on his farm was about due.

When the Chicago offer came, Dionne went first to his priest. For in these small *habitant* communities, the priest was often the only man with education. After all, who could he turn to if not his priest? Dionne then went to Dr. Dafoe. The promoters were offering money for the babies to come to Chicago. What should he do?

At that time the babies were a couple of days old. Almost every hour brought a crisis in at least one of their lives. Dr. Dafoe himself just couldn't believe that the children would live. So he told Oliva to go ahead and make any money he could before the bubble burst.

Dionne wouldn't talk about the contract so I went over to Corbeil to see the priest. He was a voluble, roosterish little man. He defended the signing of the contract as a financial necessity for the Dionnes. Then he showed me the contract. Dionne was to get a hundred dollars per week until the babies were set up in the Midway, then two hundred and fifty dollars per week, plus expenses and thirty per cent of the "take." (They were pikers, those Chicago boys. Just four and a half years later New York interests were offering one million dollars in cash for an appearance of the little girls out at the home of the Trylon and Perisphere.) I examined the contract further and discovered that the priest was also mentioned in the document. He was to get seven per cent. His argument all along had been that he was completely disinterested except insofar as the Dionnes were members of his flock. When I asked him about this he had a ready answer. In two of his previous parishes he had had the great privilege of raising enough money to build churches. His Corbeil services were held in a basement and so he yearned to keep up the good work and build a church here too.

5.

PAPA DIONNE was no sooner back home in Callander than he deeply regretted signing that contract. Criticisms were coming at him from all quarters. Neither his doctor nor his priest who had advised him to take the step came to his rescue. He was left out there on the firing line all by himself. This was the beginning of Dionne's bad press. It was also the beginning of his distrust of newsmen, and that didn't help him either.

He tried to void the contract on grounds that it wasn't a legal document because his wife hadn't signed. But he had made the mistake of taking money from the promoters. He announced that he was sending the money back and that neither he nor his daughters would appear at the Chicago Fair. The promoters later sued for a million dollars, but their suit didn't get very far.

By Friday, the Quints' fifth day, Callander had become a madhouse. Reporters, feature writers, sob sisters were arriving by plane, by train, by car. Lack of snow was all that ruled out the dog teams. To tell the truth I was more than a little frightened. Big newspaper names I had read for years were thick around the place. I felt sure that when their stories began to appear I would be recalled to Toronto in disgrace.

Thank God for Charlie Blake. He was a real movie-type reporter, well-dressed, blasé, self-confident. He had been trained in the tough Chicago school of journalism, probably the most competitive in the country. He had dined with Al Capone. He had covered the St. Valentine's Day massacre of the anti-Capone mob. He carried a wallet that had been taken from the body of a slain gangster.

When I expressed my fears, he just laughed. "Don't let them scare you." Certainly they never scared him. I felt much better about it a few days later when I got a swell telegram from my very tough editor urging me to keep up the good work. I've kept that telegram all these years.

But it wasn't only the swarm of reporters that made the place hectic. The promoters were coming in droves and they hounded Dionne day and night. Finally Dr. Dafoe lost his temper, and got a policeman to stand guard and keep them away from the little unpainted house, where the fight for five little lives was being waged so sternly.

There was another incident that made that fifth day hectic. Charlie and I didn't learn of it until evening, when we made our regular visit to the Little Doc's. He liked us both and he loved to have us come down in the evening, bring a bottle, and sit and gossip. He loved to gossip and he had no objections to sharing the contents of the bottle. That night he told us what had happened out in the crowded little make-shift nursery.

All five babies were losing ground. They were all constipated. He advised that a few drops of magnesia be added to their formula. Three of the babies responded to the treatment. The other two didn't. And, of course, it would have to be the smallest and the weakest of the lot, Marie and Emilie.

The two of them were kept in the precious incubator. He went out to the little home that day, wondering what to do. When he got there, Nurse Leroux, with tears in her eyes, told him she thought the pair were dying. He lifted the glass cover of the incubator, looked at them, put the tips of his fingers on their foreheads, and agreed. If something wasn't done, and done soon, they would die. They had absolutely no reserve to fall back on. They only lived from minute to minute. This crisis called for an enema. An enema for two mites whose combined weight was three pounds ten ounces and whose bodies just fitted in the cupped hands of the nurse! Certainly the ordinary instruments for giving enemas wouldn't do. Looking for something to make do, he picked up a hypodermic syringe, fitted the end with a small rubber tube.

The nurse watched with fascination. She had fought without sleep all week for these lives. Now they were slipping away.

"Doctor, it will kill them," she whimpered.

"If I don't do it, they will die for sure," he replied simply. Deftly he performed the simple operation. Then he put them back in the incubator.

"I think they deserve a little rum for that," he said with a feeble attempt at humor. The babies were given their drops of liquor and the nurse and doctor stood and watched as minutes dragged like hours. Gradually the flickering flame of life in the dying pair revived; the furious panting ceased, and they rested easily. For the umpteenth time he had driven the old man with the scythe out of that little farmhouse.

That night, too, he gave us the fantastic weights and measurements of the five. Marie weighed one pound, thirteen ounces; Emilie was the same. Cecile was two pounds, three ounces; Annette two pounds, six. Yvonne was the heavyweight: she was two pounds, nine ounces. All five together weighed a fraction over ten pounds. A few days later they had shrunk to less than ten pounds.

6.

THOSE EVENINGS in the Little Doc's homey living room were a high point in each day for us chosen few. They were entertaining, and besides we picked up good stories for our papers. But during that first week end the fun came to an end. We went out to see our little friend, but he was aloof and uncommunicative. Finally we wheedled out of him what the trouble was.

A few prominent doctors down in Toronto were "annoyed" because he was getting so much publicity. It was undignified; it was unethical, a reflection on the profession. If it continued the world's most powerful union, the Medical Association, might have to "take steps." This disturbing news had been communicated to him by his brother, who was himself a Toronto doctor of note. Then I saw how Chicago reporters operate.

Charlie stormed out of the doctor's house, flaming mad. We drove back to North Bay and there he got the Doc's brother on the telephone. First he asked if anything could be done to straighten out matters so the Little Doc could continue to talk to us. The Toronto brother was worried. The Toronto medicos had made up their minds.

Then Charlie struck. When he had first come into Canada with his incubator, efforts had been made to keep him from bringing it in. Certain doctors were piqued to see a "foreigner" stealing the limelight away from them. They even went so far as to telephone the Little Doc and learn from him that he needed the incubator desperately before they gave in. Even so, Blake was soaked for a good deal of duty on it. Charlie had told me this before, but he hadn't written anything about it for he was practicing his own good-neighbor policy. Now, over the long-distance phone, he threatened to write this story, plus the story of how certain interests were seeking to force the Little Doc to keep his mouth shut. It would make a beautiful story for the United States press. I remember Charlie's closing words: "It's a story that is just crying to be told. And if the Little Doc doesn't get a message in half an hour telling him he can talk to us, I'm going to write it."

Fifteen minutes later the phone rang. It was the Little Doc inviting us to come down and chat with him. He was chuckling as he shook our hands.

"I guess I know now what they mean by the power of the press," he said.

7.

LATE ON SATURDAY a big incubator arrived by train as the gift of the *Star* and finally the basket was discarded. I've often wondered about that basket and how it reproduced itself. A couple of years later, no less than three of the curio stores that sprang up around Callander displayed the "authentic and original basket" that held the Quints. The Doc swore he destroyed it.

Their first Sunday on earth the quintuplets were the subject of at least one sermon. The priest at Corbeil made them the theme of his discourse. Their birth, he declared, constituted a challenge, a rebuke to everyone in the whole world who advocated or practiced birth control.

Sunday was a big day around the Dionne home too. Newsreel cameramen arrived, set up, took pictures of the Little Doc arriving in his car and entering the home. He was beaming with good humor and even brought Nurse Leroux and Nurse Louise de Kiriline out on the veranda to be photographed with him. De Kiriline was his special trouble shooter, imported by the Doc to take over and make sure things were done his way.

Being Sunday, the curious for miles around, some from as far as Toronto, flocked to the little shrine. The police had a busy day.

And Sunday was an especially big day for the Little Doc. His young brother, one of Toronto's most famous obstetricians, drove up to see what it was all about. He visited the nursery, examined the babies, and was loud in his praise. You could see that he was very, very proud of his older brother and he expressed regret that their doctor-father could not be alive to witness what his boy had done.

On Monday the Quints completed their first week of life. Living had become a habit with them and they seemed to like it. Also, Monday was one of the banner days of my life. I will never forget it. I went out to the home early as usual. Grandpère Dionne wasn't on hand to keep us at a distance, so we stood and looked in the window as the nurses gave the babies their once-a-day going over. I wrote a story about it for the *Star* and a lot of people liked it. By some strange chance I have a copy of it here in my pocket. Would you like to read it? Fine. Here it is:

Corbeil, June 4:—But a handful of persons in the world have seen quintuplets a week old receiving their oil bath, but this reporter witnessed that sight today—through the Dionnes' cabin window. While the bath was in progress no one but Madame Louise de Kiriline and Miss Yvonne Leroux, the nurses in charge, were permitted in the room.

Madame de Kiriline walked over to the incubator in which four of the premature babies are kept. She lifted the glass top, reached down, and with one hand lifted out a tiny roll of white. She laid it on the table by the window and then for the first time a tiny wrinkled face, no larger than an orange, could be seen.

The eyes were closed and there was no movement. The face was wrinkled like that of an old, old man. Madame de Kiriline first washed the face and eyes with a boracic acid solution.

"This is Emilie," she called through the window with a smile. This awakened Emilie. For the first time she exhibited signs of life. As she lay there in the sunlight that came streaming through the window, the eyes opened just a little, then closed again.

The nurse undid the swaddling cloth that wrapped the tiny form and there she lay, all thirteen inches of her, the color of dark mahogany. Through the flesh, ribs that looked like delicate tracings could be seen. The tiniest bit of femininity in the world was breathing.

Emilie liked that sunlight. All of a sudden she opened her mouth and yawned prodigiously. Then she stretched. Actually stretched. Arms the size of your little finger went out straight, and her tiny legs did the same. Even the minute fingers and toes wriggled.

The olive oil kept at blood heat was then applied by the nurse with a bit of absorbent cotton. Emilie lay with her eyes half open like a kitten just about to purr. Sunlight was a new sensation to her and she found it good.

On the pan of the scales that stood on the table was a bit of absorbent cotton scarcely bigger than your hand. On it lay a hot-water bottle and when the oil bath was finished the baby was lifted up and laid on the scales atop the bit of cotton. The nurse bent down, adjusted the weights, and smiled. "Emilie weighs one pound, thirteen ounces," she announced. Then she wrapped the mite up. Yes, wrapped her up so that only the tiny head was visible; then she put her back in the incubator.

While Madame de Kiriline had been doing this, Miss Leroux was doing the same for Cecile, who seemed a trifle lighter in color than her sister. She, too, enjoyed the sunlight. She seemed even more active, for her arms waved and she kicked those unbelievably small legs.

Little black eyes opened wide, gazed aghast at the Peeping Tom who was looking through the window into her boudoir. Her hand went to her head in a seemingly aimless way and rumpled her hair.

"Cecile weighs two pounds, one ounce," announced Miss Leroux.

Annette came next and she too was the same rich, dark brown as her sisters. She was the color of a lifeguard at the beach after he has spent months in the blazing sun. She opened her eyes, looked around once. Then with an air of utter boredom she yawned and went back to sleep.

"Annette weighs two pounds, four ounces."

Yvonne, the largest and perhaps lustiest of the quintet, was a bit cross when her nap was disturbed. But she was lifted out of the warm incubator and put in the sun. Through the window you could hear kitten-like sounds that told how Miss Yvonne was protesting.

Her arms waved in the air; her legs kicked. Even her fingers and toes telegraphed indignant protest against such treatment.

Then the warm oil soothed her and she forgot to cry any more but lay there breathing prodigiously.

"Yvonne weighs two pounds, six and a quarter ounces."

That left only Marie, the tiniest, weakest of the whole lot to be attended.

Marie has passed through crisis after crisis with her heart until the nurses always approach her with fear and trembling. She was in the extra incubator so the attention paid her would not disturb her stronger sisters. The nurse lifted up the glass top of her home and bent down. How would she look? She was allegedly smaller than the others, but that seemed impossible. The tiny bundle was brought forth and laid on the table with even greater care than the others.

The head was dark, sun-tanned just like the others, but there weren't the same lusty signs of life. Madame de Kiriline undid the pin that held the diaper in which she was rolled and held it up. It bore a tag which read "Marie."

The clothing was unwrapped and there she lay, absolutely motionless and oh so small. Her sisters were small, but this mite was tinier. All her body was wrinkled.

There wasn't a movement in the body as the nurse bathed the face and eyes. Even the nurse seemed disturbed by her lack of movement.

"Marie, Marie," Madame de Kiriline called. Movement began in one of the arms which was drawn up to the face as though to shield her eyes from the sun. A leg kicked. Both legs kicked, and there was a wail so weak as to be almost inaudible.

Marie is alive. In fact, she is livelier than usual, the nurse states softly as she bathes her. As she holds her up, the little body comes between the watcher and the sunlight. One could almost swear that she is transparent. If she is livelier now than she has been any morning it is easy to see why the nurses have been watching her for twenty-four hours at a time.

As she is laid on the scales she opens her eyes for just an instant and her cry is hushed.

"Marie weighs one pound, ten ounces."

The boudoir scene is over and the babes all back in their incubators.

8.

So ENDED the most exciting week of my life. I've only given a sketchy idea of all that went on. I averaged two hours' sleep a night that week. I sent out thirty-five thousand words about the kids. It proved to be one of those turning points in my life because three years later, almost to the day, I left the newspaper business and went north to manage all the affairs of the quintuplets.

I was in the middle of the fight as Dr. Dafoe and the parents struggled for power. I saw the Little Doc gradually lose control as forces too great for even him to control developed and I was a shocked spectator one sunny day, May 29, 1941, when the quintuplets turned their backs on him and refused to have anything to do with the man who had saved their lives. It was his fifty-eighth birthday. He was just out of the hospital after a very serious operation. He pretended that what happened didn't hurt him. But I knew different.

He died two years later, almost to the day. Oliva and I drove down to Toronto for the funeral. I sort of hoped to be one of the pallbearers, but nobody asked me.

The Peculiar Fate
of the *Morro Castle*

BY WILLIAM MCFEE

William McFee, one of the great modern writers of sea stories, was
born, appropriately enough, on a ship homeward bound from India
to Liverpool in 1881. Like Joseph Conrad, he got his experience at
first hand, as chief engineer of British vessels plying to every part of
the world. At the age of thirty he changed his base to the United
States, though he returned to serve in the British Navy during World
War I. His first book was *Letters from an Ocean Tramp* (1908), and
he has written more than a score of others, mostly novels, but including a scholarly life of Sir Martin Frobisher, the great Elizabethan sea
dog. Readers of the following article will discover that Mr. McFee
has some definite and authoritative ideas regarding the cause and
probable blame for the most famous sea disaster of the early 1930's,
which uselessly destroyed 134 lives.

☼ 1.

"It is not enough, to exonerate all persons who are interested in the boat from
all just blame, to say they have no direct agency in any accident that may
happen. They should be considered as tied together by the cord of a common
interest—as sharers in the profits and losses—and as moral participants in
all acts pertaining to the business in which she may be used, and the law
should hold them accountable."

Senate report, in the State of New York,
on the loss of the steamboat Swallow, *1845.*

SATURDAY, September 8, 1934, was a blustery autumn day along
the Atlantic coast. There was some rain, the leaves were falling, and so
was the barometer. It was the kind of day on shore which indicates
dirty weather at sea. September is the hurricane month.

Three days earlier, September 5, the twin-screw turbo-electric liner *Morro Castle,* of the Ward Line, sailed from Havana on her homeward run to New York. September 8, in a storm of wind and rain, she was three miles east of Barnegat, heading for the Ambrose Channel, where she would pick up her pilot. It was nearly three o'clock in the morning. Her 318 passengers and most of her crew of 231 men and women were asleep.

The usual Friday night conviviality, the "farewell dinner," the paper hats and toy balloons, the drinking, dancing, and love-making, the traditional culmination of a pleasure cruise in the West Indies, had been clouded by an unusual event. Captain R. Willmott was taken ill at dinner and died within a few hours.

It was a grave psychological strain for the chief officer, Mr. William F. Warms, who had come off watch at eight o'clock. He was about to turn in, for he had a strenuous day ahead of him in New York, when he made the discovery. To find his captain dead in his bunk, to face the sudden responsibility of taking over the command of the ship, would impose a burden on the strongest of men.

Mr. Warms, moreover, had another anxiety.

The gap between chief officer and master of any ship is wide enough, but in this particular case much of the executive authority usually assumed by a chief officer by custom and tradition had been retained in his own hands by the dead captain. We have to keep this in mind when we come to the actions of Captain Warms, suddenly confronted with the most terrifying emergency to be faced by the master of a vessel crowded with helpless, sleeping passengers.

At five minutes to three Mr. Hackney, acting second officer, saw smoke issuing from the stokehole fiddley. He called down from the bridge to the engine room to know "if there was a fire in the engine room." Cadet Engineer William F. Tripp, an eighteen-year-old Massachusetts Institute of Technology student, who was on duty near the telegraph and telephone, for they were about to pick up the pilot, replied in the negative. He knew of no fire. This is a highly important detail which, for some reason, was not emphasized by the experts. One minute later, at 2:56, Mr. Hackney pulled the fire alarm, which would be relayed all over the ship.

By this time, of course, Captain Warms was on the bridge. Accepting the above official record, confirmed by Mr. Tripp's log sheet, we face the extraordinary facts that (1) some eighteen minutes elapsed before the captain ordered a radio call for assistance; (2) the radio operator, Mr. Rogers, whose cabin, fifty feet aft of the navigating bridge, was on fire, sent three times to ask for instructions; (3) other ships near by saw the fire and sent calls before the *Morro Castle* call went out; (4) the ship was kept at nineteen knots, into a twenty-mile wind, in darkness, pouring rain, and pounding seas, before being stopped.

By that time, around half past three, the fire had made such headway that the ship's upper structure, from the forward funnel to the mizzenmast, which rose abaft the deck ballroom and the veranda, was a furnace. The passengers were crowding to the tourist section of the ship, right on the stern rails, on B and C decks. They were pouring through the passageways. Some, who were later seen at portholes, screaming for help, had been trapped in their cabins and were to die horribly there. Six young ladies, who had been carried by stewardesses from the bar to their cabins at the end of the evening's festivities, were not seen again. Some, of course, probably less fuddled, more athletic, and more enterprising, squirmed their way through their portholes and dropped into the sea, and were lucky enough to be picked up by the boats.

Most of the passengers, however, suddenly awakened by the raucous loud-speakers, frightened by the roaring of the flames and the running of men who had lost their wits and had no one to command them, surged aft through the smoke-filled passages. In such a case the word "panic" is inadequate. It conveys nothing of the actuality. These people, running through corridors of a burning ship, half-clothed and many of them half-demented, were in a bad way. When they came out on the after rail it was raining in torrents. There was no light save the lurid flames leaping at them from the superstructure. Below them was the dark turbulence of the sea, dotted with crying people in life belts, calling to the boats dimly seen, standing off fearfully from the heat of the burning ship. Desperation came to these people, and a measure of courage too. Down they went, jumping, or sliding down ropes, and, being inexpert at such business, scorching their soft hands, so that some of them were forever incapacitated for their professional work. There were many women there too, and they threw off their flimsy shoes by the rail, discarding their lipsticks and compacts, their lighters and cigarettes and girdles, as though, when faced with the final, grim, eternal verities of the sea, they instinctively abandoned the nonessentials.

2.

IT IS LOGICAL and even inevitable now to regard the events of that fatal morning off Barnegat, in a storm of wind and rain, as the classic modern example of a marine disaster. Nothing was wanting to complete the picture. There was incompetence, panic, evasion, ignorance, credulity, and avarice. And from the first moment of alarm, when the C.Q. signal went out (the radio call for immediate assistance), legend and myth began to crystallize around the stark facts of the tragedy.

There was, for instance, the rumor which inland radio listeners heard early on Saturday, that the *Morro Castle* had been struck by lightning and had blown up, with a loss of five hundred lives. So incredible did it appear to the ordinary landsman for a fast modern liner, known to thousands who had made the cruise to Havana and to many more who hoped to make it, a liner with 173 voyages successfully and joyously completed, a liner often described as the safest ship afloat, to be destroyed by fire at sea, within sight of land, and surrounded by ships rushing to her assistance, that many people instinctively credited the disaster to natural causes and an "act of God." They thought it must be due to an unavoidable malignancy of the elements, or to sabotage, to spontaneous combustion of cargo—to anything, in fact, but what it was, panic and incompetence.

There was nothing remarkable about so many ships being on hand on this occasion. Every ship south-bound from New York, every ship coming up from the Americas, is on this course, to or from Ambrose Channel. What was remarkable was their inability to get a clear notion of what was going on, on board the *Morro Castle*. It must have seemed to some of those commanders, peering through the rain, that there were lunatics on board. How otherwise explain a ship in flames driv-

ing full speed into a twenty-mile gale? How explain the delay in sending out a call?

How explain the inexplicable?

There were the boats, which were rendered largely useless by the
delay in getting them swung out, because they were all amidships or
nearly so, and were burning on their chocks. There was the speed with
which the fire, discovered in a locker in the writing room, upstairs on B
deck, abeam of the forward funnel, became a roaring furnace. This
speed the New York *Times* on the following Monday morning described as "a mystery." It remains a mystery if we accept the official
contention that the fire started between two and three o'clock. There is
reason to believe it began long before that, and did not originate in the
locker. And when Mr. Hackney asked Mr. Tripp, down at the engine-
room telegraph, if there was a fire down there, he may not have been
so far off the track after all.

3.

SOON AFTER, then, with his ship in flames twenty miles south of Scotland Light, where the voyage officially ends, Captain Warms authorized C.Q. signals to all ships. He was only fifty feet away from Mr.
Rogers in his wireless cabin, but they might as well have been strangers
who had not been introduced. Captain Warms, who had not had a command before, and whose predecessor lay dead in the master's cabin,
was under a strain. You can go to sea in command for forty years and
never face a crisis such as he confronted inside forty minutes, almost,
from the time he took charge. For a while he was rattled. He took too
long to make his decisions. For many years it has been an unwritten
law that a ship in trouble should avoid at all costs calling for assistance
to outside ships. She should, if possible, get help from another ship of
the company. It was a cruel predicament for Captain Warms. He seems
never to have had the executive authority and responsibility a chief
officer should possess. And his bosun was reported drunk at 2:30 A.M.

Among those who have had experience of ships like the *Morro
Castle,* the natural reaction to the extraordinary lethargy of the personnel would be, Where was the watchman? What was he doing all

this time? Why was "a fire in the writing room," a public space on B deck, only a few feet away from the bridge, not reported? And why did not the automatic fire-detection system warn the officer of the watch?

Shrewd questions, but they have the simplest answers. The watchman, it was revealed at the inquiry, had so many other duties he had little time to watch. In ships under discipline the watchman makes his rounds, as in a factory or store on land. He has a key which he plugs into the system at various points on his itinerary, to record his vigilance. This is his duty, and he has no others. But on the *Morro Castle*, he said, he had many other duties, so that he was not really a watchman at all, in the legal sense.

The writing room, where the watchman, if he made his rounds, had noticed nothing unusual, had no fire-detection apparatus. Nor had any of the public rooms on the ship. The Darby system was installed in the private cabins, where fires sometimes start because women plug in electric toilet appliances and forget them, or drop cigarette butts into wastebaskets full of tissues, and these conflagrations would have given a warning in the wheelhouse. But writing letters, however passionate or inflammatory, was not considered by the builders or the naval architect to be a fire hazard. Moreover, although the United States signed the 1929 Convention for Safety at Sea in London, the august United States Senate had not ratified that Convention in 1930, when the *Morro Castle* was launched. So she was neither built nor operated in compliance with the Convention. Yet she was publicized as "the safest ship afloat."

So we have the picture of a splendid, modern ship, of fifteen thousand tons' displacement, steaming at nineteen knots toward the Ambrose Channel, to pick up her pilot, and dock early on Saturday morning, suddenly bursting into flames which roar along the alleyways and trap sleepers in their beds, and nobody seems to know what to do. The stories told by passengers sound like fiction of an unusually lurid type, yet they were corroborated so often, and they fit so closely into each other, that there can be no controversy. For a short time the ship had no direction at all. Members of the crew declared that the fire alarm in the crew quarters was feeble, "like an alarm clock." When the fire pumps were going and the hoses were brought into operation, we have the evidence of a passenger, an expert professional fire fighter, that the crew did not know how to lay them out. He had other things to say, this particular passenger, of great importance. He will be quoted again.

One of the wireless operators of the *Morro Castle*, having come out of the affair with credit, went on a barnstorming tour as a hero. Anyone on that ship who did his simple duty was hailed as a hero by an uncritical press and public. But not Captain Warms. It was an appalling crisis, but shipmasters have been facing appalling crises for centuries, and many of them have left records of greater glory than Captain Warms. Why was this? Why did his chief engineer, Mr. Eben S. Abbott, instead of staying with his commander, go off in Lifeboat 1? Why did Boat 3 get away with sixteen of the crew but no passengers? A boat certified to carry seventy persons!

These questions are not so personal and particular as they may seem at first glance. The *Morro Castle* affair was part of the general picture of the United States Merchant Marine. "The Ward Liner *Morro Castle*" and "the Ward Liner *Oriente*," her sister ship, were phrases which gave a misleading impression. So did "the Ward Liner *Mohawk*." All were part of a picture which had been getting darker and gloomier for a number of years.

More than one Congress had been bedeviled by the problem of how to have an American Merchant Marine without emptying the Treasury. It had been tried over and over again. Millions of dollars had been poured into the industry, and the industry had sooner or later reached a state of receivership and disintegration. Forty-five years ago a member of Congress declared, "The moment a man invests his capital, or any portion of it, in ships or ship-building interests, he blossoms into a full-grown patriot and insists on having the Treasury of the United States opened for his benefit." Thirty years ago William Gibbs McAdoo, Secretary of the Treasury, complained that "every shipowner and every ship monopolist wants subsidies." The Shipping Board became the greatest pork barrel in the history of the country. And still there was no Merchant Marine. In spite of a closely protected coastwise service, in spite of the denial of American registry to foreign-built ships, in spite of high wages (100 per cent more than Great Britain), in spite of long-term building loans at small interest and generous operational subsidies, in spite of mail contracts which could hardly be distinguished from charitable bequests, there was no Merchant Marine, and almost no shipbuilding. Capitalists were no longer interested in risking their capital in American ships. Shippers did not permit their patriotism to interfere with their business. They patronized any firm under any flag —British, German, Dutch, Danish, Norwegian, Swedish, or Japanese—which delivered cargoes on fast, dependable schedules.

Something had to be done and something was done, but not what the shipping interests were asking. They had grandiose schemes for competing in the transatlantic trade by inaugurating four-day crossings. Congress decided on a more balanced Merchant Marine. The Jones-White Bill of 1928, as the new Merchant Marine Act was called, authorized a construction fund of $250,000,000. Approved companies could get twenty-year loans covering 75 per cent of the cost of a ship. Mail subsidies were based on tonnage and speed. For example, a six-teen-thousand-ton vessel doing twenty knots earned a subsidy of ten dollars a mile on the outward voyage.

This legislation authorized the construction of, among others, the Ward Line sister ships *Morro Castle* and *Oriente*. They were designed by Theodore F. Ferris of New York, an eminent naval architect, and built by the Newport News Shipbuilding Company, one of the largest and best yards in America. The firm applying for the loan was the Atlantic, Gulf, and West Indies Steamship Lines, a merger of a number of smaller companies, including the Ward Line, under whose house flag the ships sailed. They were cruise ships. They carried mails and cargo. They maintained a fast service for bona-fide passengers between New York and Cuba, but their primary function, the function which made them pay, was taking round-trip cruise passengers from New York. Their cost was around four millions apiece. The United States Government held a first mortgage of $3,422,181 on each ship, with very low interest charges.

4.

THE *Morro Castle,* then, was a first-class ship of the most modern design, and in spite of the fact that certain requirements of the 1929 Convention for Safety at Sea were not included, it is reasonable to accept her as one of the safest ships of her day as to structural design. The defects of the *Morro Castle* lay in her personnel, afloat and ashore.

She was of 11,520 tons register, 6,449 tons net. She was 508 feet in length between perpendiculars, 70.9 feet beam and 39 feet draft. She was a twin-screw, oil-fired ship with six Babcock and Wilcox water-tube boilers, General Electric turbo-electric generators driving electric motors on the two shafts. She developed 16,000-shaft horsepower, and her service speed was 20 knots. She was built to the highest classification of the American Bureau of Shipping, and she had been approved by the United States Navy as a naval auxiliary. It seems strange we should have heard that talk, after the disaster, of her "faulty construction."

She had nine water-tight, transverse bulkheads extending to the shelter deck, and her water-tight doors were electrically operated. Her superstructure was three decks in depth, with a combined forecastle and bridge. All decks were of steel and laid with teak.

Her fire-fighting equipment was the best of its kind in 1930. The Darby system was installed everywhere except in the public rooms, as we have noted. Down below the cargo space was equipped with the Rich smoke-detecting apparatus. Twenty-seven lines of piping connected the holds to a box on the bridge, where the officer of the watch could at once detect the origin of smoke. There was also a Lux carbon-dioxide system for smothering fires in the engine room and boiler rooms. There were nearly a hundred fire extinguishers on brackets all over the ship. There were 2,100 feet of canvas fire hose.

There was criticism in some quarters because no sprinklers were installed. Sprinklers, as we find them on shore, are not the answer to marine risks. In any case they would have been useless in the *Morro Castle* fire.

What more was needed? What more could any steamship owner provide for the protection of his patrons? The answer is, Nothing except personnel of the same quality as his ship. There was nothing the matter with the *Morro Castle* that night except personnel.

By comparing, in *Lloyd's Register of Shipping*, the *Morro Castle* and *Oriente* with the company's other vessels, such as the *Mohawk* (5,896

tons, single-screw freighter with some passengers, 387 feet in length),
we get the impression that there had not been a development of discipline on board and organization in the office to cope with liners of the
Morro Castle class, ships carrying several hundred passengers and a
crew of 230. The voyage was short; the turnover in personnel 20 per
cent, which would have given any management with intelligence uneasy nights. The ship was of course adequately serviced in New York
by shore staffs, but the time at sea was so short that it was almost impossible, remembering that 20-per-cent turnover, to develop any sense
of solidarity. It was not, in a seaman's sense, a voyage at all, but a
high-speed junket to a tropical port, where liquor was plentiful, potent,
and cheap. The ship was a constant headache to the Narcotics Squad,
Havana being what it was. Andrew Furuseth, then head of the Seaman's Union, said that *Morro Castle* "seamen" actually paid for their
jobs instead of receiving wages, their profits on smuggled dope were
so high.

There was, then, a musty odor of slackness in running the ship. According to Section 2 of the Seaman's Act, the crew should have been
divided into day and night watches. There were only seven men on
duty at night, out of a total of 231 on board, when the fire started. If
Captain Willmott tolerated this arrangement for his own reasons, nobody else was likely to make complaint.

Another astonishing feature of the way the ship was operated
was that there was no list of rules, no book of company regulations, to which an officer could turn (if he did not already know them
from long service) for guidance. This was so extraordinary that the
question was put to the vice-president in charge of operations more
than once. No, there were no printed regulations.

Now here was something which might be listed under the heading
"faulty construction." In all first-class lines the traditions, experience,
and policy, accumulated by generations of management, are crystallized,
distilled, condensed, reduced to a set of rules and regulations, which
have the authenticity and prestige of Holy Writ. In one company in
which the writer served it was actually known as "the Bible," without
any intention of being irreverent. The captain and his heads of departments each had a numbered copy. In the hands of a literal-minded and

possibly malevolent commander such a code of laws could be used to further his own ends, exactly as other codes on land have been misapplied. The point is that a company of any quality almost inevitably evolves such a code, and prints it, and insists on its observance at sea.

But on the *Morro Castle,* according to the first vice-president, there was nothing of this at all.

Allusion has already been made to the suspicion that Captain Warms, as chief officer, lacked the usual authority of that rank. Captain Willmott, in fact, had been a long time in the company, and he seems to have run the ship by rule of thumb and word of mouth. It worked all right from his point of view. He was able to keep down expenses. Printed rules would have had to adhere to the law regarding ships, so perhaps it was better to have no such hard-and-fast instructions issued. Captain Willmott told his chief mate what to do. But when Captain Willmott suddenly was not there, the defects of his system became obvious enough. Right on down the line, to the stewards and bellhops who swarmed into a boat and rowed away, there was no company "principle" at work.

So, the skeptics may say, the ship caught fire because there was no principle, no discipline? They could not handle the fire because there was a lack of discipline? You want us to believe that?

Let us go back a little. We have it from Andrew Furuseth, a man not given to reckless libeling of seamen, that the crew on these New York–Havana runs paid for their jobs, to smuggle narcotics. This writer has been at his breakfast in the messroom after such a run, and the messman, an intensely respectable, pious, efficient, and (to us) valuable person, in the very act of serving our ham and eggs, has been taken away by government agents, under arrest, to be seen no more by us. Nothing unusual in this. It was going on all the time. They had found narcotics in his bunk.

We have, moreover, the statement of the night watchman that he had so many other duties he could not do much watching. There were not enough men on duty to comply with the law. We may ask here, What sort of men? Who chose them for their work? What were their qualifications?

Here we come to grips with the relations between the shipowners and the Bureau of Navigation and Steamboat Inspection. The *Morro Castle* had been inspected for Voyage 174, which was her last, in May, 1934. She was reinspected on August 4, a month before the disaster. This meant, probably, that the May inspection had not been completed before she sailed. Anyway, she was inspected, just as the ill-fated *Vestris* was inspected, and the excursion steamer *Mackinac,* whose boilers were inspected in New York not long before they blew up and killed forty-seven people.

These inspections had become largely routine, formal, and in the nature of gentlemen's agreements. It was assumed that the master and his officers would not knowingly go to sea with defects likely to jeopardize their own lives and ships, or at any rate their professional reputations. With a ship like the *Morro Castle* the inspection was perfunctory. She was new; she was a first-class job; she was approved by the Navy, and she was underwritten by Lloyd's of London.

Another thing. The Inspection Service was the Cinderella of the government services bureaus. To quote Mr. Howard S. Cullman, who in 1936 was on President Roosevelt's Committee for Safety of Life at Sea, and who was becoming a thorn in the side of the Department of Commerce, "The Bureau was shockingly undermanned and underpaid. There were not enough clerks or surveyors. . . . Innumerable reports by competent investigators were quietly buried." Mr. Cullman and the Committee were also quietly buried soon after, so far as any results could be discerned, and Mr. Cullman, whose interests ranged from tobacco wrappers to financing Broadway shows, from New York hospitals to the receivership of the Roxy Theater, decided that reform of the American Merchant Marine was not his destiny.

The Bureau was part of the Department of Commerce, whose Secretary at the time of the *Morro Castle* disaster was a smooth, Southern lawyer-politician, Mr. Daniel Roper. His grasp of realities, incredible as it seems today, was such that, when the *Morro Castle* suddenly revealed the stagnation and obsolescence of his regime, he appointed a *naval* officer to sail on each merchant ship, to prevent accidents. At no time did Mr. Roper become aware of the Gilbert-and-Sullivan situation of his Bureau when accidents did happen. If the Bureau was negligent, the Bureau investigated itself, and of course the Bureau discovered that the Bureau had no flaw.

The Bureau, for instance, had been issuing what were called lifeboat certificates to seamen, as well as certifying those seamen as "able" or otherwise. These documents were pieces of paper, quite small; easily lost or stolen; easily sold, like the official American discharges. In the new legislation of 1936 discharge-books for seamen were authorized. Every other maritime nation on earth used these books. The continuous-discharge-book corresponded to the passports carried by passengers. But American seamen would have none of it. To have their records permanent and inviolable was, in their view, "un-American."

In 1934, however, it was common knowledge that these paper discharges and certificates were sold outside the Seamen's Institute on South Street to any who wanted to ship out. No chief officer or first assistant regarded them as having any meaning. He took what he could get, and if the men were no good he fired them and tried again. Or, in the case of the *Morro Castle,* the crew were engaged by the Ward Line's shipping master.

Here again we float off into cloud-cuckoo-land. The United States Government, through the Bureau of Navigation and Steamboat Inspection, was trying to lift some of the curse on American shipping. Part of that curse was the large number of native and alien incompetents who were buying their credentials in South Street. Another was the peril involved in so many aliens, unidentifiable and unable to speak, write, or read English. Many of them could not read or write any language. It was highly desirable, to say the least, that the official responsible for engaging seamen should scrutinize their credentials before hiring.

But the Ward Line shipping master, a Greek gentleman, could neither read nor write English. If the American discharges had been printed in Greek it may be doubted whether this modern Ulysses would have been any the wiser. Perhaps he spoke Cuban Spanish, for many of the deck hands were Cubans. We do not know. What we do know is that he was the employee of the Ward Line appointed to select the crews for American-flag ships, and the law of the land, to put it mildly, was interpreted in an elastic manner.

5.

So MUCH for the crew. There could not have been much "inspection" of *them,* and they acted very much as an uninspected crew would act. What about the boats?

Lifeboats are for saving life, though there have been times in recent years when American shipowners gave the impression that they were designed for rowing races and publicity. To chief officers lifeboats are a headache, a clumsy apparatus for painting the ship's sides and boot-topping.

The *Morro Castle's* steel boats would have been adequate if kept in condition. Like the ship, they were only four years old, yet it was stated by crew members that Boats 3, 9, and 10 had buoyancy tanks rusted into holes. Boat 1 had a motor which would not work, and the boat had to be rowed.

The general public is ill informed on the subject of lifeboats. Indignation surges up white hot when it transpires that lifeboats are not regularly lowered, operated, inspected, revictualed, and maintained. If you ask, When is this to be done? there is a certain lack of unanimity in the answers. The ship ties up at her pier in New York. The boats on the dock side cannot be lowered. Often neither can those on the off side, for the dock, as often as not, is full of lighters. The crew are mostly off their articles and will not rejoin until sailing morning. Is the chief officer supposed to do this job single-handed?

At the other end of the voyage it is not much better. You say, the law demands it. The ship should lie off in the river or the harbor, and go through boat inspection and drill.

It sounds quite simple. But in a world where ships are run to make money and keep schedules, and government subsidies are earned only on the number of sea-miles they cover, a world in which wages go on all the time and passengers are irked over an hour's delay, these are counsels of perfection. Lifeboats are heavy. Motor lifeboats are extremely heavy. The present writer, taking over as engineer on a New York-Havana liner twenty-five years ago, discovered that the motor of the lifeboat (Number 1) had never worked in all the ten years of the ship's running. The valves were rusted solid in their seats and the timing had never been adjusted. On arrival in Havana it took several quarrels with the chief officer and an interview with the master to get the boat into the water for a test. Suppose we had needed that motorboat in a crisis!

Steel boats, moreover, are the very devil to keep in good condition. Sea air and water corrode mild steel like magic. The average clinker-built wooden lifeboat costs around $250 a year to maintain in condition, but it can be so kept. The steel boat is rusting internally all the time. It is fair without, but within it is full of minute corrosions. You cannot have copper buoyancy tanks, as in a wooden boat, for the salt water sets up electrolytic action between the steel hull and the copper tank.

But boats are only part of the story. Those members of the crew, with their lifeboat certificates, are the main thing. With that personnel turnover of 20 per cent, what chance had the *Morro Castle* of boat crews trained and experienced? The answer is, She had no chance at all.

This accounts for the bizarre fact that Boat 3 (with her rusted tanks) got away with sixteen of the crew, but no passengers. She was certified to carry seventy persons. Boat 1 went off with three passengers (evidently resourceful and agile fellows) and twenty-nine of the crew. The general impression we gather from these facts is that the crew had only one thought in mind, which was to save their own skins, and there seemed to be nobody in command to correct that thought. At last, off Sea Girt, all power having failed, the anchor was dropped by the new acting chief officer, Mr. Freeman, and the *Morro Castle* lay swathed in dense smoke and fumes, shot by the flames consuming the interior of the upper decks, while passengers, huddled by the after rail, dropped into the sea or shinned down ropes. They saw the more resourceful members of the crew rowing away as hard as they could. This is one of the most terrible features of a terrible disaster. Nothing impresses the student of this marine casualty more than the complete distintegration of all conscience in the crew of the ship. Many of the passengers were in a panic, a fact which we can sympathize with and condone. But the crew exhibited an ignoble panic which deprives them of all human forgiveness. Many of them were, quite simply, despicable in their behavior.

Captain Warms, who was to be master for the shortest time on record, followed the immemorial tradition of the sea by being the last man to leave the doomed ship. He and fourteen of the crew of two hundred and thirty remained on the forecastle, which was untouched by the fire. When the Coast Guard cutter *Tampa* arrived it was decided to tow the burning hulk to New York. Two tugs were also in attendance, and the dreary procession, moving slowly through heavy seas, reached Asbury Park, when the hawsers parted. The *Morro Castle* drifted broadside on a sand bar, a few yards off the huge, lacustrine Convention Hall, at the foot of Sixth Avenue. Here she stuck fast. The two powerful salvage tugs failed to shift her. This was Saturday evening.

6.

THEN BEGAN one of the most amazing episodes in American maritime history. It was a Saturday in early September, and Asbury Park is a "resort." It lives on tourists, week-enders, conventions, beauty contests of bathing girls, and suchlike "attractions." And here was the nation's latest sensation, a glittering cruise liner, full of exactly the kind of people who patronized Asbury Park, catching fire at sea and coming to rest right off Convention Hall Pier. Dead bodies were already washing ashore on the beach. Lifeboats were coming in. Authorities were coming down posthaste from New York. It was an incredible, a stupendous, a miraculous "attraction."

Asbury Park had a commission government headed by a city manager, a gentleman named Carl Bischoff. Mr. Bischoff saw the smoldering *Morro Castle* from one point of view and one only. To him she was an "attraction," a gold mine for Asbury Park. As thousands of cars streamed through the September night on all the roads of New Jersey, heading for Asbury Park, Mr. Bischoff decided to cash in. Beach and Convention Hall were fenced off and a charge of twenty-five cents a head was made for admission, to stand on the outer galleries of the structure and gape at the still-burning vessel, where people like themselves had been caught in luxurious cabins and burned alive as in furnaces, while the ship fled through the night.

This was understandable enough. Showmanship is part of the American scene. But Mr. Bischoff had other ideas. It struck his forward-looking but simple mind with great force that, since Providence had brought the *Morro Castle* to beach herself in his front yard, so to speak, finders were keepers. To him she was no tragedy at all, but a gold mine, and he saw no reason why, as city manager, or mayor, of Asbury Park, he should not take possession of her. He was a humane man and a public-spirited citizen. He would have been angry and outraged if he had seen the ghouls that night dragging the bodies of the dead ashore and hacking off their fingers to get the rings. He was sorry for those who had lost their lives or their loved ones in the disaster. But it was hardly likely that another burning liner would ever come ashore in Asbury Park and lie in such a miraculously good location for commercial exploitation. He saw the jam of cars in the streets, the land-office business at the pier, and he wanted to keep the *Morro Castle* where she was, as a permanent "attraction," a museum as well as a mausoleum for the charred dead.

This attitude of Asbury Park's leading citizen was a symptom. It expressed in dramatic form the prevailing lack of understanding in the public mind concerning ships. When Frank B. Conover, of the New York Board of Underwriters, arrived on the scene, he found Mr. Bischoff in possession. The Board of the Steamboat Inspection Bureau, headed by Mr. Dickerson N. Hoover, and the United States Attorney, all had urgent business on board the *Morro Castle*. Mr. Bischoff had never heard of such people. He claimed—and this is perhaps the oddest note in a very odd affair—"riparian rights" over the ship. He even threatened to arrest Mr. Conover, the representative of the Federal Government, for disorderly conduct, unlawful entry, and (note this) insubordination. Mr. Bischoff became so much of a deterrent to official business that it was necessary to remove him from the scene. He would have found a kindred spirit in the mortician who joined the crowd of anxious relatives outside the Ward Line offices and handed around his business cards.

7.

THE INQUIRY which sought to discover the cause of this terrible disaster afforded a field day for cranks and headline hunters. Captain Willmott was pictured as a commander afraid of and suspicious of his second wireless operator, Mr. George Alagna. Shipmasters are traditionally conservative. To Captain Willmott, Alagna was a "radical" because he had the fortitude to head a protest against conditions of labor on the ship. Mr. Alagna was promptly arrested and handcuffed to a deputy United States marshal as a material witness. Later he was released with what was almost an apology, and then immediately rearrested and released on bail.

All through the inquiry there ran a vein of hysteria, and another vein of stubborn though clandestine wishful thinking, to ascribe the *Morro Castle* fire to arson. There are four hundred pages of maritime laws in the federal statute book, and one of them, the Harter Act, defines arson on a ship as "an act of God," thereby releasing the owners from civil liability.

Captain Warms, asked what motive would inspire anyone to sabotage the *Morro Castle* by arson, replied, "God knows what the motive was."

Others, however, were less modest. Not only God, but they, knew. It was all due to "Reds." Major Cayetano Fraga, head of the Havana detective force, announced his conviction that a liquid-fire bomb was planted on the *Morro Castle* by Communists, members of a secret international maritime sabotage ring who shipped as members of the crews. These fiends in human form, the Major insisted, received direct instructions from the Third International in Moscow. And Captain Oscar Hernandez, chief of Havana harbor police was convinced that "Communists and terrorists," directed by "the Caribbean Bureau" of the Third International, had set fire to the ship.

Reading through the evidence, the arson note is like a refrain. Most of it is hearsay, conjecture, prejudice, and downright lunacy. Nobody, for instance, asked these people what motive Moscow would have in destroying a cruise liner. It could not even be agreed on that the labor troubles in Havana had any bearing on the disaster. Scores of ships entered and left Havana unscathed. But a "Red" scare was the universal explanation of anything unusual at that time. For a while, after the *Morro Castle* fire, every fire in a ship's hold was blamed on "Reds" or sabotage, as though ships had never had any fires in their holds before the Russian Revolution.

There were some witnesses, however, who were sane and contributed useful evidence. Mr. William M. Tripp, the young M.I.T. student already mentioned, impressed everybody with the clarity and honesty of his statements. There was no getting away from the bell sheet, the log he kept of the orders coming down from the bridge. But he could let no light into the darkness surrounding the main question—What set the ship on fire?

It was discovered, you will recall, in a locker in the writing room, on B deck, a locker which normally held stationery, ink, and suchlike equipment for writing. This is the classic official explanation of where the fire originated. Nobody seems to have questioned it for a moment. So far as can be determined from the blueprints, the writing room extended across the ship, part of it being known as the library. In any case the funnel passed up through B deck at that point. Just forward of the funnel were the main first-class staircase and elevator, both of which were to act as flues for the fire. Above the boilers was the first-class dining room, with its mezzanine, then the lounge and ballroom, also with a mezzanine, and then the writing room and library. Above these public rooms were staterooms on either side, on A deck. The fact that the funnel carrying the gases from six oil-fired boilers passed through this passenger structure was not mentioned by anybody.

But it started in the locker, we are assured, and Captain Warms knew of it shortly before 3 A.M. The call went out at 3:15. At 3:29 the lights went out in the engine room, which was filling with smoke. Nobody inquired how smoke was getting through steel bulkheads from the writing room. Second Officer Hackney, promoted from third when Captain Willmott died, saw smoke coming *out* of the ventilators in the fiddley at 2:55. These must have been the fire-room ventilators, but Mr. Tripp assured him at that time that there was no fire in the engine room. Here is a point which should have been narrowly cross-examined by the board of inquiry.

Unsatisfactory as most of the witnesses were, there were two who not only agreed, and who were innocent of collusion, but whose evidence disposed of the sedulously cultivated fiction that the ship took fire with miraculous suddenness and was as quickly destroyed as if she were constructed of celluloid. One was a cruise passenger, Mr. John Kempf, by profession a city fireman of Maspeth, Long Island, who was on vacation. He was presumably an expert witness as regards fires. The other was Harriet B. Brown, a stewardess. Mr. Kempf stated that he smelled smoke *soon after midnight*. Mrs. Brown confirmed this.

Mr. Kempf had a number of uncomplimentary things to say about the skill, discipline, and courage of the ship's crew. He made a special point of the fact that there was no officer visible anywhere to tell the crew what to do or where to go. If it were possible to attribute the fire to arson, the crew rendered first aid to the arsonists by knowing nothing about their duty in an emergency. So did Captain Warms, for that matter, when he kept the ship at 19 knots into a twenty-mile gale. Of course there were exceptions. In several hundred men and women we are bound to find exceptions. Third Engineer Arthur Stamper remained on watch until driven from his post by smoke and fumes. Dr. DeWitt Van Zyle, the ship's surgeon, died with the women and children he attempted to save. His body was picked up by a fishing boat.

8.

WHO, then, was to blame? It is a tradition in American transportation, deriving from the bad old days, when American railroads were less safe than now, to blame the dead engineer. The engineer was generally dead. The Ward Line, however, did not have this consolation. Their engineer, Mr. Eben S. Abbott, was very much alive. He left in Number 1 boat. Captain Warms stated that the engineer appeared on the bridge, suffering from smoke and fumes, and said he could do no more and was leaving the ship. What Captain Warms, who sorely needed sustaining at such a moment, must have thought of his engineer we have no means of learning, but those of us who have been to sea can hazard a guess. We are told, by members of the crew in the boat, that the engineer tore off the braid from his sleeves, with a view to preserving his anonymity when he got ashore.

Obviously such a tragic figure did not create a very favorable impression at the inquiry. His good fortune was that there was no one conducting the interrogations technically competent to ask leading questions.

There was no one, for instance, to correct the public notion that the chief engineer should have been "at his post" in the engine room. His post was on deck. So far as we know, he was doing what he was supposed to do, supervising the fire-fighting equipment. We are told that he was ordered by the captain to abandon the ship, which might have a number of differing interpretations, but they would all be conjectures now.

What did emerge from the sorry business was that neither Warms as master nor Abbott as engineer was an inspiring figure. While Warms was chief officer, the reigning authority was evidently Willmott, who by long service, and possibly financial interest in the Line, kept everything in his own hands, including fire and boat drills.

Now, if you take from a lieutenant the authority which properly belongs to his rank, you injure his self-respect and render him indifferent to discipline and efficiency. This point was not made by anyone at the inquiry. The point was not made that a shipmaster of immense seniority and with stock in the company usually keeps things in his own hands. It used to be a commonplace in the old British Mercantile Marine, when shipmasters invested in shipping. But in the frenzied hunt for sabotage and arson, in the attempt to detect the sinister hand of the Third International, vital questions such as the above were never raised.

Mr. Martin Conboy, United States Attorney, complained that the Ward Line's officials and lawyers did all they could to frustrate and interfere with the inquiry. The Ward Line's legal representatives denied the charge. In the opinion of the present writer the charge is not sustained. A defendant is not supposed to assist in his own indictment, and the Ward Line knew very well that they were, in the eyes of the public at any rate, defendants. The lawyers of a steamship line in trouble are perfectly justified in coaching the crew, not in what to say under oath, but in what not to say to reporters. Men who have just escaped a horrible death, who are under mental and physical strain from shock and exposure, are not fit subjects for newspaper interviews.

The aim of the Ward Line was, of course, to evade responsibility for a most shocking disaster. They did not succeed, because negligence was nakedly exposed. All we can be sure of now is that they would have created a better impression in the public mind if they had revealed even common humanity toward the victims of that disaster. But while they were collecting $4,186,000 hull insurance from Lloyd's, $263,000 more than the ship's book value, they attempted to limit their liability to the value of the freight and passenger fares—around $13,000—plus the value of the ship, which was nothing. A year after the tragedy the claims of over four hundred survivors were still pending. Another Ward Liner, the *Mohawk,* had by that time made history by going mysteriously haywire while passing the tanker *Talisman,* and had been rammed and sunk. By September, 1936, the Ward Line had experienced a change of heart. The sum of $890,000 was allocated to the *Morro Castle* case, and most of the claimants accepted the settlement.

9.

IT WOULD BE EASY to lay undue stress, in a history of this character, on the trial, conviction, and sentences imposed on the captain, chief engineer, and the vice-president in charge of operations in the office. Four years in prison for Chief Engineer Abbott and suspension of his license, two years for Captain Warms, and temporary suspension of his master's license, and one year's suspended sentence, with a fine of five thousand dollars, for Mr. Cabaud. In addition a fine of ten thousand dollars was imposed on the Line. Warms and Abbott appealed, and the United States Circuit Court of Appeals, after wading through nearly five thousand pages of "transcript of record," reversed the judgment against them.

The whole business was a gesture. It is difficult to believe that the judge who imposed the prison sentences, or the defendants, believed that any time would be served behind bars. It was simply that, when it became obvious that Moscow was not responsible for the destruction of the *Morro Castle,* public opinion demanded scapegoats. The gesture was made of sending the ship's officers to jail. The Secretary of Commerce made the gesture of placing naval officers on merchant ships, to render them safe. Less spectacular but more important, Congress made the gesture of improving the obsolete, understaffed, underpaid Bureau of Navigation and Steamboat Inspection. It could no longer be permitted to imperil human lives. The incompetence of the Bureau was dramatized by appointing Captain George Fried, who had made some highly publicized rescues at sea, as head of a new department of inspection. But by the middle of 1937 the United States Senate reported that "it seems clear . . . no further activity may be expected in connection with the *Morro Castle* fire."

By that time the captain and engineer had regained their licenses and were again at sea. The name "Ward Line" was permitted to fade from the public memory, and the *Morro Castle*'s sister ship, the *Oriente,* continued a successful career as a cruise liner.

The historian is left groping through the records for an answer to the original conundrum—What caused the fire? Why did a modern ship burn with such inconceivable rapidity? The reply at first was "arson." We were asked to believe that the criminal, with fiendish ingenuity, after poisoning the master, selected the locker in the writing room (1) because the writing room had no electric fire alarm, (2) he knew the stewards kept illegal and inflammable polishing liquid in the locker (this was never established as a fact), and (3) he chose the hour for his crime when most people on board were either drunk or asleep, or both.

This was the sensational yarn elaborated after the Red scare passed. Nobody asked the simple question, What was behind the writing room locker?

The present writer was at one time chief engineer of oil-fired steamers. The popular notion that fuel oil is a dangerous element is incorrect. Fuel oil is about as volatile and inflammable at room temperature as the oil spread on roads in the fall and spring. It has its hazards, chief of which is explosive gas given off from the oil, gas which is heavy and hangs around in bilges and tanks. Another is the danger of overheating the long uptakes which lead from the furnaces to the funnel, if the burners are neglected.

Like most modern, medium-sized, medium-speed steamers, the *Morro Castle* had only one real funnel. The after funnel was partly ornament, partly a ventilator. If, through neglect of the burners in the furnaces, the funnel base had become overheated, the heat would have been most intense where the funnel passed through the writing room, behind the cupboard. The writer once discovered his funnel red-hot just above the uptakes, owing to negligence. The ship was a freighter. There was a wide space between the funnel and the accommodation, and only minor damage ensued.

The validity of a theory is based on the number of observed facts it can account for. Most of the theories advanced for the *Morro Castle* fire were merely fantastic. They flourished on the obvious unfamiliarity of the interrogators with the actual operation of modern oil-fired turbo-electric ships. The present hypothesis assumes that parts of the steel structure around the funnel had been red-hot for hours and were charring the woodwork, disintegrating the insulation, giving off that smell of smoke which Mr. John Kempf and Mrs. Brown, the stewardess, declared they smelled soon after midnight. Remember that Mr. Hackney, the second officer, saw smoke coming up from the fiddley grating and inquired if there was a fire in the engine room, receiving a negative reply from Mr. Tripp. Then, at three o'clock, according to Mr. Hackney, smoke was seen in the writing room, and the door of the locker burst open, belching flames. And from then on they could do nothing to stem the conflagration.

Does anyone believe that a fire generated in a locker with steel bulkheads behind it could be of such fierceness, even if it had contained a "time bomb"? Does anyone believe that such a source could consume a large part of the ship with such speed? The flames roared up stairways and elevator shafts. It made the passageways impassable. But if you assume that the interior structure of the funnel casing, passing up through the ship behind the writing room walls, had been reddening for hours (through negligence), sending the heat along the steel deck beams, plates, and stanchions, all was set for the holocaust, while the ship drove on through the night.

Only a hypothesis, but it does attempt to explain something, which the fumbling, prejudiced conjectures of the day did not.

Who, then, was to blame? As regards the particular instance, we shall never know. As regards the general picture of the American Merchant Marine, of which the *Morro Castle* fire was the incandescent center, we may apportion the responsibility. There was the haphazard system of permitting, without adequate supervision, the amalgamation of numerous small lines, each with its special traditions and loyalties, and consigning their operation to an impersonal office management, without sea experience, and controlled by a "holding company." There was the slow ossification of the Bureau of Navigation, whose inspections were in such low repute that underwriters ignored them. And there was the complete absence, among legislators, of any interest in the integrity and character of the men who demanded such lavish generosity when they proposed to build and operate a merchant marine.

Another factor, less immediate but of great importance in the long, lugubrious deterioration of the industry, was the attitude of the American Federation of Labor toward marine unions. The A.F.L. had and has a tradition of craft unionism, but instead of fostering that tradition in seafaring, the A.F.L., through ignorance, indolence, and unintelligence, ignored the great champion of the seamen, Andrew Furuseth, and allowed the craft of the sailor to slide into the depths. Going to sea became the last resource of the dregs of the waterfront, the vicious, the improvident, the incompetent, and the irresponsible.

A further indictment can be made against the American public in general. Until disaster followed disaster, and bludgeoned it into paying attention to realities, that public had consistently failed to take any interest at all in its own merchant marine. Capital would not invest in it, the average citizen would not sail in it, and the working, native-born American would not accept employment in it. Not even the first World War, when American troops had to be ferried to France in British transports and defended by British warships, made any lasting impression on the inland populations. American newspapers, from coast to coast, placed all possible emphasis on such trivia as "the Blue Riband of the Atlantic," so that their readers were conditioned to believe that a merchant marine consisted of very large, very fast, very luxurious passenger vessels. Those same newspapers, moreover, publicized and overemphasized every mishap and accident to an American ship. The wages of able seamen and junior officers, and the social prestige of the calling, were so low that parents shied away from the sea as a possible profession for their sons.

It took another great war to change all that. The United States now has an enormous merchant marine. Nothing like the *Morro Castle* tragedy can ever happen again—ships will take fire on occasion, but there will never recur the staggering incompetence of that fatal Saturday in September, 1934. Or so we hope. It depends on the public, which in the past has been quick to anger, quick to forgive, quick to forget, but slow to do anything about it. The lesson of the *Morro Castle* is so simple that it may quite possibly be misunderstood. It is that the price of a merchant marine, like the price of liberty, is eternal vigilance.

Huey Long:
American Dictator

BY HODDING CARTER

When Hodding Carter lay in a roadside ditch with a shotgun in his hands, ready to open fire on Huey Long's state troopers, he wasn't especially proud of himself. Nor was his self-esteem increased when he helped burn ballot boxes and handed out WPA work orders as political bribes, in a desperate effort to lick the hillbilly dictator in one small parish of Louisiana. "Fascism makes men do some pretty strange and pretty terrible things in their efforts to stay free," he explains. Mr. Carter was born in Louisiana in 1907, attended Bowdoin College, the Columbia University School of Journalism, and Harvard University as a Neiman Fellow. He worked as a reporter in New Orleans, ran his own anti-Long newspaper in Hammond, Louisiana, for a time, helped start *PM* in New York City, and in 1939 acquired the Greenville Delta *Democrat-Times,* which he now edits and publishes. In 1946 he was awarded a Pulitzer Prize for his courageous and liberal editorial writing. He has also published two novels and a book about the lower Mississippi River.

✭ 1.

FOR NEWSPAPERMEN, those were Gargantuan, memorable days. You stood beside his hotel dining table, as he slopped up great tablespoonfuls of cereal with a sidewinding sweep or tore broiled chicken to pieces with his fingers, and you jotted down the incessant harangues against the lying newspapers, the city machine, and the battered enemy politicians, while the bodyguards glowered protectively near by. You didn't like him, if only because the slugging of newspapermen didn't seem justifiable even for vote getting, and especially when the strongarming became personal. You were chased by militiamen across the parade grounds of Jackson Barracks in New Orleans and held a prisoner after you had sneaked in to discover whether the Governor was calling out the troops on the eve of the Senatorial election—in which the Governor was a candidate.

In a corridor of the garish Roosevelt Hotel, managed by an oily former shoe clerk who was now his paymaster and treasurer, you watched a fellow reporter being hustled out of the Governor's suite. Inside the suite the reporter had struck the Governor in retaliation for being cursed, and the Governor had struck back, but only after his bodyguards had pinioned his attacker.

You interviewed him after he had precipitated a silly international incident by receiving a German admiral in disheveled green pajamas, and you laughed in spite of yourself at his shrewdly appealing account of his gaucherie. You heard a pale-faced man, thrust before a microphone, identify himself as Sam Irby, who had been kidnaped by state police on the eve of an election because he had threatened to tell what he knew about his daughter and the Governor, who employed her as his secretary. And after Irby had told who he was, in front of the microphone in the hotel headquarters, you marveled at his exoneration of the Governor, and speculated upon the reasons therefor.

Afterwards, in the corridor, a fellow reporter was to have a gun thrust into his stomach as he sought to enter the elevator on which the mysterious Mr. Irby was being whisked away.

And then you testified in United States District Court that a telegram, also absolving the Governor and purportedly coming from the mother of another kidnaping victim—the secretary's ex-husband—was signed with the name she had borne before her second marriage. Counterfeit, neither pure nor simple, was this telegram which you had seen and read on a speaker's stand in New Orleans on one of the last heated nights before election. And so, endlessly, through brawling campaigns, brawling legislative sessions, brawls . . .

2.

SUCH GOINGS-ON made of Louisiana a reportorial heaven. But in the spring of 1932 I turned from reporting to start a small daily newspaper in Hammond, Louisiana. By then, Huey Long was immovably established as Louisiana's junior Senator in Washington and Louisiana's Kingfish at home. From the first issue of our newspaper I editorially criticized his tightening grip upon the state and the corruption which accompanied it. The initial reaction of his district lieutenants was a fairly mild annoyance. Ours was a puny, insecure newspaper. Doubtless it would welcome help. A man whom I had known since childhood, a friend of my family, came to me with the suggestion that I get right. Surely I needed better equipment for my newspaper, and better equipment could be procured for the friends of the administration. There were constitutional amendments to be printed, political advertising, security, permanence. Just get right.

Later the approach was to change. I still have the threatening, unsigned letters. Get out of town, you lying bastard, if you know what's good for you. Intermittently, for four years, I received threats by letter and telephone, and twice in person. I carried a pistol, kept it in my desk during the day and by my bed at night.

But violence and the threat of violence were not always one-sided. In 1934 the Congressman from our district died. The district had been consistently antagonistic to Long, although the dead Congressman had chosen to play safe with the Senator. Long did not believe that a friendly successor could be elected. So, instead of having the district Democratic Executive Committee call the mandatory Democratic primary for the election of the party nominee, he ordered this controlled group to declare the Congressman's widow the nominee, and to call a perfunctory general election with her name the only one to be printed on the ballot as Democracy's choice against any Republican, Communist, or Prohibitionist foolhardy enough to seek the office. It was a simple if illegal way to avoid a showdown in the district.

A young anti-Long judge named Nat Tycer enjoined the general election in his own judicial district, composed of four of the Congressional district's twelve parishes. Declaring, "It's a poor judge who can't enforce his own ruling," he began swearing in deputies to enforce his injunction. I became one of the deputies and wrote an angry, intemperate editorial which ended, "If ever there was need for shotgun government, that time is now."

In each of the parishes of our judicial district, deputies and unsworn volunteers took the election ballots, election boxes, and other voting paraphernalia out of the courthouses where they were stored and burned them. The Long-controlled state administration scattered thousands of leaflets throughout the district, warning of the jail sentences and fines in store for anyone interfering with elections. We kept burning ballots, adding effigies of Long to the bonfires. The administration sent in more ballots.

The night before the election was to have been held our deputies, considerably smaller in number than the hundreds who had originally been sworn in, assembled at assigned points throughout the judicial district. Some were posted at Pass Manchac, where a drawbridge links the district with the southward continuation of the New Orleans highway. They were to raise the bridge and try to fend off the militia, which, according to rumor, was being dispatched from New Orleans to insure the holding of the election. Other deputies waited in the ditch beside the highway at the border line between our district and East Baton Rouge Parish, in which the state capitol is situated. During the night, state police in trucks loaded with ballots were fired upon and forced to retire to Baton Rouge. The militia from New Orleans weren't ordered out.

All night long, scared witless, and armed with a sawed-off shotgun and a .38 revolver, I was one of a roving patrol which visited all the election booths in our parish in search of signs of political life. But not a vote was cast in our judicial district and only a comparative handful in the Congressional district itself.

Nonetheless, Long's district Democratic Executive Committee declared the widow the elected representative. In Washington, the House of Representatives eventually refused to seat her as well as our own candidate, whom we selected in a rump election a few weeks after the fiasco, in order to make a contest in Washington. And when the administration finally called a legitimate election, we defeated Huey's candidate, the Commissioner of Agriculture, a popular and perennial officeholder who had served for years before Long's advent.

Except for one victory by the Old Regular machine in New Orleans in a mayoralty campaign, this was the only major political setback suffered by Long from 1930 until his death. But the real importance of the episode is its indication of the desperation to which his tactics could drive otherwise law-abiding men. Our roles as special deputies were specious. And it was no fun to feel like an outlaw, especially when the other side had the militia, the state police, most of the judges, and a majority of the voters in the state at large.

3.

BY THE SPRING of 1935, Huey Long owned Louisiana. And in that spring another and lesser man, except for his honesty, gave a fey, lonely warning.

His name was Mason Spencer. Young, big-boned, unafraid, he was relatively unimportant, almost the last member of the legislature not to acquiesce in profitably or accept silently the final substitution of government by personal dictatorship for government by ballot. The Louisiana legislature had granted Senator Long, through his administrative and judicial proxies, incontestable control of all elections, including the appointment of commissioners, the power to disqualify unfriendly voters, and the privilege of padding the voting lists wherever and whenever necessary. Already he possessed the courts, the municipal police forces, the school teachers, the taxing authorities, the Governor, the state government, even the banks. Now, the vote itself.

And Mason Spencer, an unimportant, honest man, rose in the legislature and said this:

"When this ugly thing is boiled down in its own juices, it disenfranchises the white people of Louisiana. I am not gifted with second sight. Nor did I see a spot of blood on the moon last night. But I can see blood on the polished floor of this Capitol. For if you ride this thing through, you will travel with the white horse of death. White men have ever made poor slaves."

Representative Spencer was a better prophet than historian. In September of that year, the Capitol's marble floors were soiled with blood. Huey Long's blood, and the blood of the quiet, studious young doctor who shot him.

But the prophet of tragedy had overlooked the history of his state. Most Louisianians, for two hundred years, had been docile political

slaves. Few knew enough about their state to recognize this almost un-
interrupted and hitherto gently managed servitude. Nor was it something which those who did know want to be bruited about.

This historical truth must first be comprehended if the success of
fascism in one American state is to be understood.

4.

THE LOUISIANA of the eighteenth century was not the America of the
Eastern seaboard. Its people were not Englishmen or the sons of Englishmen, protesting because the privileges of free men at home were
too skimpily granted to the colonial free.

Instead, the Louisianians were successively the vassals of two deca-
dent and dying monarchies. The brothers Le Moyne had come in the
name of the French King to colonize the lower Mississippi. To popu-
late the colony there had followed an impotent conglomerate to be
gutted by the elect: Canadian *coureurs de bois* and their Indian women;
professional soldiers of short life expectancy; a few adventurous or
disappointed members of the French aristocracy; and a pitiful succession of immigrants, peasants and artisans, sewer-scourings and exiled
whores, having in common only poverty, hopelessness, and neglect.

Among such settlers there was scant thought of self-government.
They were monstrously exploited. In 1763 France presented the vexa-
tious colony to Spain; and a handful of rebels who plotted a free nation
on the Mississippi discovered before a Spanish firing squad that political liberty was not for Louisianians. Not until a quarter of a century
after the American colonies proclaimed themselves free did the Louisiana Purchase bring the promise of freedom. But even afterwards there
was no democracy in Louisiana. From the first, government was directed
by the entrenched few. Creole gentry and American merchant and
planter perpetuated a basic agreement. Only gentlemen and politicians
managed by gentlemen should direct the backwoodsmen who spilled
over into the new territory and the descendants of the French and Spanish riffraff.

So, almost uninterruptedly, Louisiana politics from the Purchase
until the Civil War was a story of genteel corruption, of steady political

degeneration, of venality, of a studied neglect of civic advancement. Reconstruction further debilitated self-government; and where Reconstruction ended, rule under the gold-directed manipulation of the Louisiana Lottery began. At the beginning of the twentieth century, Louisianians could count on the fingers of one hand those major public servants who in all Louisiana history had been honest and progressive, active in behalf of the small people, and given to implementing campaign promises with administrative performance.

Throughout the years the same political pattern prevailed. The city dominated the state: New Orleans, the nation's mecca of the fleshpots, smiling in not altogether Latin indifference at its moral deformities, and, like a cankered prostitute, covering those deformities with paint and lace and capitalizing upon them with a lewd beckoning to the stranger. Beyond New Orleans, in the south, French Louisiana, devoutly Catholic, easygoing, following complacently its backward-glancing patriarchs, suspicious of the Protestants to the north. And in central and northern Louisiana, the small farmers, principally Anglo-Saxon; bitter, fundamentalist Protestants, hating the city and all its evil works, leaderless in their disquiet and only vaguely aware that much of what they lacked was in some way coupled with the like-as-like office seekers whom they alternately voted into and out of public life.

Diversity was not so pronounced among the political leaders of these divided groups. They were, for the most part, conservative stereotypes; and even in New Orleans the machine politicians were guided in the things that mattered. They co-operated with the bankers, the large merchants, the oil and sugar and cotton interests, the affluent votaries of the *status quo*. A wise statesman didn't antagonize the railroads, the banks, the refiners, the lumbermen, the enterprising developers—or exploiters—of the great and noble State of Louisiana. A wise statesman dressed and acted like one. He orated, with elocutionary fire, about the glories of the past and the wonders of the future, about the dark days of Reconstruction, about white supremacy and black threats, God's mercy and the rightness of the established order. A wise statesman steered a safe course between the Scylla of Standard Oil and the Charybdis of the poor man's yearnings. He promised good roads and occasionally produced a few. He predicted the beautiful but tantaliz-

ingly distant day when Louisiana would come into its own. And among
his own kind he made deals that kept his own kind in office. This is
not to say that all were politically immoral or amoral, though most of
them were. They resembled atavistic mastodons, towering above and
unknowingly becoming trapped in a surging human slough. In this
they were not unlike their fellow politicians elsewhere. The difference was that for two hundred years Louisiana had been so very safe
for the mastodons.

5.

SUCH was the political Louisiana in which Huey Pierce Long was born
in 1893, in impoverished Winn Parish in north Louisiana, a breeding
ground of economic and political dissenters. His background was tailor-
made for a politician. A log cabin, albeit a substantial one, was his
birthplace. His father was a farmer of small means but with considerable ambition, who managed to send six of his nine children—but not
Huey—to college.

Young Huey hated both farm work and conformity. In high school
he discovered his talent for spell-binding oratory, and the power of
a vocabulary enriched by Biblical allusion and directness, acquired
naturally in a devout Baptist home. This gift was useful in school
politics, and soon thereafter in the art of the traveling salesman, an
occupation which he chose upon graduation because his father was not
able to send him, the eighth child, to college.

The years between his graduation and his becoming a member of the
Louisiana Bar at twenty-one tested to the limit his extraordinary physical energy and driving mental discipline—the only discipline which
he ever perfected in himself. He married before he reached the voting
age, and supported himself and his wife by peddling Cottolene, a cooking compound, throughout north Louisiana, meeting thereby and
making friends of many farm folk who were to become the core of his
political organization. He attended Oklahoma University Law school
for one tempestuous term. Then, incredibly, he completed the three-
year law course at Tulane University in eight months and, securing a
special examination from the Louisiana Supreme Court, became a

lawyer at twenty-one. No other student at Tulane has ever matched this record.

As Huey Long put it in his autobiography, he "came out of that courtroom running for office."

He hung out his shingle in Winnfield, county seat of Winn Parish. And here he received his first lessons in an economic-social philosophy that would later burgeon into a gaudy, national movement. His first benefactor in Winnfield was a state Senator named Harper, a prosperous man for the locality, but a "radical" who proposed a redistribution of national income as the only cure-all for the country's ills. During the first World War, Harper published a pamphlet calling for conscription of the nation's wealth as well as its manpower. A Federal Grand Jury indicted him. He was defended by his young disciple, Huey, who was deferred in the draft because he had a wife and child. (Huey also tried to gain exemption as a public official. He was a notary public.) Huey, through questionable strategy, won Harper's acquittal.

Most of his other early cases were minor ones, the only kind available to a beginner in a crowded profession. But at twenty-four Huey sought the one state office open to one of his age, a state railroad commissionership. The Railroad Commission was Louisiana's three-man utilities regulating body. He won. In the campaign he gained another ally, an older Winnfield man named O. K. Allen, who lent him five hundred dollars to help finance his campaign. Later, when Long was elected United States Senator, he rewarded O. K. by making him his Governor, stooge, and errand boy.

As Railroad Commissioner, Huey was something uncomfortably new and strange. Some regarded him as a radical menace; others saw only a coarse publicity-seeking clown, a thickening, comical-looking youngster with a face that was a puffy caricature of a cherub, with its dimpled chin, snub nose, and unruly, curling reddish hair. But among the masses there were multiplying thousands who saw a champion, a new Great Commoner. He damned and insulted Bigness in all its Louisiana manifestations: Standard Oil, the state's dominant and frequently domineering industry; the large corporations; the corporation lawyers. He clamored for a common carrier pipe-line law—Standard had denied the use of its own to the independents, among them a company in which Huey owned stock—and for a higher severance tax on oil. He won a telephone rate reduction.

In 1920 he supported, for Governor, John M. Parker, a one-time Bull Moose, because he believed the comparatively liberal Parker would deal strongly with Standard Oil. But Parker, to Huey's thinking, was too lenient after he became Governor. Huey broke with him, was indicted and convicted of libeling the Governor, and was fined a dollar and given a thirty-day suspended sentence. He refused to pay the fine, so the judge and opposing counsel made up the dollar themselves.

But he was winning friends and influencing voters. In 1924, at the height of the bitter Klan fight in Louisiana, Huey Long, now thirty, announced for Governor. He tried to go down the middle on the Klan issue. He almost succeeded. Before Election Day he predicted that he would win if rain didn't keep the mud-farmers away from the polls. It rained. Yet, in a three-cornered race, he polled seventy-three thousand votes against eighty-four thousand and eighty-one thousand for the other two candidates. His day had not yet dawned. But already the uneasy feeling had arisen among his opponents that he would be unbeatable the next time.

6.

FROM 1925 to 1928 Huey mended political fences, kept himself in the headlines, and built up a large and lucrative practice as attorney for some of the vested interests against which he ranted. He explained it in his autobiography this way: "When the millionaires and corporations fell out with each other, I was able to accept highly remunerative employment from one of the powerful to fight several others who were even more powerful. I made some big fees with which I built a modern house in the best residential section of Shreveport at a cost of forty thousand dollars." There were other and less charitable explanations of his affluence.

The 1928 campaign was more like a cyclonic disturbance than another three-way race for the Governorship. Huey was probably the most indefatigable campaigner and best catch-as-catch-can stumper the demagogically fertile South has yet produced. He belabored and promised and defamed, speaking in the harsh, bitter language of the poor man, eighteen and twenty hours a day. His promises were bright ones, long overdue: good roads for the farmer, lower utility rates, free bridges, free school books. He mixed filthy imputations with rhapsodic pleading. Beneath the erroneously named Evangeline oak, he drove his program home to open-mouthed, whooping Cajuns:

"And it is here that Evangeline waited for her lover Gabriel who never came. This oak is an immortal spot, made so by Longfellow's poem. But Evangeline is not the only one who has waited here in disappointment. Where are the schools that you have waited for your children to have that have never come? Where are the roads and the highways that you spent your money to build, that are no nearer now than ever before? Where are the institutions to care for the sick and disabled? Evangeline wept bitter tears in her disappointment. But they lasted through only one lifetime. Your tears in this country, around this oak, have lasted for generations. Give me the chance to dry the tears of those who still weep here."

No rain fell on Election Day this time. The evil city again rejected him, but Catholic and Protestant farmers united to give him a lead, though not a clear majority. His two opponents wouldn't join forces; and at thirty-five Huey Long sat in the Governor's chair that he was to transform into a throne. Louisiana's poor whites had come into their own. "Every man a king, but no man wears a crown," Huey's campaign banners had proclaimed. No man, that is, but Huey himself. And already he was boasting, "I'm going to be President someday."

The campaign had been only a movie trailer, teasingly heralding what was to come. Long summarily discharged every state job holder under executive control who had not actively supported him. Loyal lads from the bayous and burnt stump lands began to replace the town and city slickers. Lacking a majority at the first session of the legislature, he swapped patronage for concessions, and in both House and Senate placed his own men in the chair. The legislature approved his proposal for a thirty-million-dollar bond issue to provide farm roads, increased hospital and other institutional support, and free school books, levying a severance tax and higher gasoline taxes to pay for the program. Behind Huey were the people, and the people wanted these things.

And with the people behind him, Huey expanded ominously. Defying rule and convention, he personally directed strategy from the floors of the House and Senate. Once he bragged that he was the state constitution now, and again that he had bought a legislator like a sack of potatoes. He coerced banks which hesitated to make the state a tide-over loan. When the legality of his free textbook law was challenged because it included parochial schools among the recipients, he argued his own case before the United States Supreme Court and won brilliantly. Without constitutional authority, he ordered the state militia into the unfriendly, wide-open parishes adjoining New Orleans, and closed the casinos until the gamblers co-operated.

All this was shocking enough to those Louisianians who favorably recalled less troublesome days and ways. But when Huey summoned the legislature into special session to enact a five-cent occupational tax on oil to aid "the sick, the halt, the blind, and the children," all hell broke loose. A barrel-house free-for-all took place on the floor of the House when Long's Speaker, smelling impeachment in the air, declared the House adjourned *sine die*. Bloody-faced legislators groped blindly for assailants who had struck them from behind. Men were felled by inkwells, canes, bare fists. A protesting representative hopped from desk to desk like a mountain goat, vainly trying to reach the Speaker and wreak personal vengeance on him. Men were cursing, screaming, some sobbing in anger.

The next day the Speaker decided that the House had not adjourned, and the House proceeded to impeach Huey Long. The charges ranged from the grave to the ridiculous. Huey had sought to bribe legislators. He had plotted the murder of an opposition Senator. He had misused, misapplied, and misappropriated state funds. He had squandered monies allocated to a national governors' conference in New Orleans on a riotous, bosomy party, testimony concerning which left some Governors red-faced. He had acted unbecomingly in public places, even to the extent of getting cockeyed drunk. Without authority he had ordered the classical old Governor's mansion torn down to make way for a new one. He habitually used unquotable profanity, required signed, undated resignations from his political appointees, made illegal loans. The House impeached.

Huey fought back with promises, intimidation, and circulars, distributed by the hundreds of thousands by state employees to the faithful. Again he barnstormed Louisiana. His primary targets, not altogether without justification, were Standard Oil, the newspapers—particularly the New Orleans newspapers—and the old political guard.

To most of the state it looked as if Huey was finished. Then, dramatically, he produced a round robin, signed by fifteen Senators, who declared that no matter what evidence was submitted to the Senate they would not vote to convict the Governor because they believed the charges against him were invalid. The number was one more than enough to prevent the two-thirds majority necessary for conviction. The deserving fifteen reaped earthly rewards, and never again was Huey in dire political danger.

From this fiasco emerged the dictator, vindictive and intent upon a domination that could not again be challenged. No holds had been barred by either side in the impeachment fight. From now on there were to be no holds except those in which Huey was master. The impeachment fight technique would be improved upon later, but never radically altered. Frighten the wavering legislator by appealing over his head to the voters. Woo him with certain gratuities to be arranged on the side. What was the legislature, anyway? Just a hodgepodge of ward heelers from New Orleans, a scattering of lawyers, a couple of wagonfuls of simple-minded and simpleton farmers, most of them alike in that they had a price. Own them. Fashion them into a ready blade with which to carve empire.

7.

LOUISIANA'S FRIGHTENED, vengeful Governor surrounded himself with a half-dozen gun-ready, slugging bodyguards. He established a weekly newspaper, the *Louisiana Progress,* staffed it principally with skillful, conscienceless young newspapermen, and sicked it on his enemies. State employees found it good insurance to subscribe to the *Progress,* the number of subscriptions depending upon the size of their salaries, but with a minimum of ten to be sold, eaten, or used as wallpaper. No opponent big enough to be worthy of notice escaped its

libeling. The voters of the nation's most illiterate state could understand its cartoon obscenities even when they couldn't spell out the text.

The public-works program went into high gear. The depression was
rocking Louisiana. Public works meant needed jobs. And the administration could count on at least five votes for each employee; the votes
of the aunts and uncles and cousins and wives and children of job
holders who made it clear to their relatives that their fifteen to thirty
dollars a week was secure only so long as they could prove their loyalty
with political performance.

The first program was followed by a second and more ambitious one:
a sixty-eight-million-dollar highway construction project, a five-mil-
lion-dollar skyscraper capitol, and another twenty million dollars in
assorted projects, all to be financed by an additional three-cent hike in
the gasoline tax. With a year and a half yet to serve as Governor, and
with the opposition organizing against the program, Huey decided to
run for the United States Senate with the state program as his platform.

The use of the sound truck and the financial strangulation of the
enemy city of New Orleans were the principal innovations of the campaign. Conservative, goateed, seventy-year-old Joseph Ransdall, the
incumbent whom Huey dubbed "Feather Duster," burbled unavailingly. Huey won hands down; and when his inimical Lieutenant Governor claimed the Governorship because of Long's election to the
Senate, Huey called out the state police and the National Guard, read
the Lieutenant Governor out of office, and put in the president *pro
tempore* of the Senate as acting Governor. He designated his old benefactor, O. K. Allen of Winnfield, as the apostolic choice for the next
full term.

Meanwhile he concocted what might have been a good if desperate
expedient for the cotton South. With Biblical precedent to back him up,
he proposed that in protest against ruinous five-cent cotton the South
should let its cotton fields lie fallow for a year. But Huey managed to
insult Texas, the South's principal cotton producer, and the Texas legislature, thumbing its nose at "the arrogant jackass who brays from
Louisiana . . . ignoramus, buffoon, meddler, and liar," would have
none of the plan. So it died.

The wider horizon beckoned. In January, 1932, the Kingfish from

Louisiana breezed into Washington. For the next three and one-half years he performed simultaneously in two rings of a dazzling political circus, the capital of Louisiana and the capital of the nation. He soon broke with President Roosevelt, each sensing in the other a challenge, and from the Senate floor ridiculed "Prince Franklin, Knight of the Nourmahal," and his New Deal, unconcernedly violating the Senate's rules of personal decorum by lampooning such administration stalwarts as Carter Glass, Henry Wallace (Lord Corn Wallace), Ickes (the Chicago Chinch Bug), Hugh Johnson (Sitting Bull), Joe Robinson, and Pat Harrison. No Senator could match him in debate or in monopolizing the front page. Day after day Huey made news. Sometimes amusing news, as in the controversy over whether corn bread should be dunked or crumbled in turnip-greens potlikker. Sometimes bad news for Huey, as when an unidentified guest at a Sands Point, Long Island, club resented with hammering fists the Kingfish's impatient and misdirected attempt to make use of a urinal before the other had moved aside. On another occasion his national and state prestige sagged momentarily when the Old Regular machine in New Orleans rebelled, returned its mayor, T. Semmes Walmsley, to office, and Walmsley followed up his victory by journeying to Washington and waiting around unavailingly to thrash the well-guarded "yellow coward."

In 1934 Long formalized the program which he hoped would eventually win him the Presidency. The hazy concept of a national redistribution of wealth, presented fifteen years before by the obscure state Senator from Winn Parish, took definable shape in a national "Share Our Wealth" organization. No dues were necessary. Huey produced the expense money as easily as the nation disgorged the followers, both by the hundreds of thousands. No matter that the Share Our Wealth program was demonstrably impracticable as presented. It *was* believable: a limitation of fortunes to $5,000,000; an annual income minimum of $2,000 to $2,500 and a maximum of $1,800,000; a homestead grant of $6,000 for every family; free education from kindergarten through college; bonuses for veterans; old-age pensions, radios, automobiles, an abundance of cheap food through governmental purchase and storage of surpluses. The Share Our Wealth members had their own catchy song, "Every Man a King," their own newspaper, the mud-slinging *Louisiana Progress,* expanded now to the *American Progress.*

The movement was nothing less than a new political party, heir to the yearnings and frustrations of the Populists, the Whiskey Rebels, the Know-Nothings, the Free Silverites, of all the have-nots of capitalism. Almost single-handed, Long won the election of Hattie Caraway of Arkansas to her deceased husband's Senate seat. The Share Our Wealth clubs began cutting across old lines in Mississippi, Alabama, Georgia. The New Deal became worried and began to use its Louisiana patronage accordingly.

By legislative action Long made sure that no federal relief money could be obtained by any Louisiana municipality or county except with the approval and supervision of an agency of his own. The administration retaliated by withholding PWA project funds. Revenue agents roved through Louisiana from 1932 until long after Long's death, and with eventually decisive results. A Senatorial committee timorously held hearings in New Orleans relative to the corruption which accompanied the election to the Senate of a Long ally, John Overton; and, after being defied, browbeaten, and ridiculed by Huey and his jibing lieutenants, exonerated Overton with a weak-kneed finding that he "had not personally participated in or instigated any fraud."

As the Share Our Wealth chorus swelled, Huey, like a wise military tactician, took care to protect his rear. In a spectacular, degenerative series of special sessions in 1934 and 1935, his legislature reduced Louisianians almost literally to the status of Indian wards. Together with this final elimination of the actualities of democratic self-government—to the unconcern of a majority of the unconsulted electorate—came new benefits: homestead tax exemption, theoretically up to two thousand dollars; abolition of the one-dollar poll tax; a debt moratorium act; and new taxes—an income tax, a public utilities receipts tax, an attempted "two cents a lie" tax on the advertising receipts of the larger newspapers, which the United States Supreme Court pronounced unconstitutional.

Perhaps it seems inconceivable that any legislature, no matter how great the material rewards for its complaisant majority, could have so completely surrendered a people's political powers and economic and personal safety to one man. But Louisiana's legislature did. Administration-designated election supervisors were given the sole right of select-ing voting commissioners, sole custody over the ballot boxes themselves, and the privilege of designating as many "special deputies" as might be necessary to guard the polls. Huey's figurehead Governor, O. K. Allen, was given the power to call out the militia whenever he—or Huey—wished. The Governor could—and did—expand the state police force into a swarm of private agents, some uniformed and some not, their number and the identity of the ununiformed alike a secret. The State Attorney General was empowered to supersede any district attorney in any trial. The State Tax Commission was given the right to change any city or county tax assessment, so that a misbehaving cor-poration or individual might know just who held the economic strangle-hold. An ironically designated civil service board was created, with appointive control over all fire and police chiefs, and a school budget committee with the right to review the appointments of every school teacher and school employee. The Governor was even enabled to re-place the entire city administration of Alexandria, a recalcitrant munici-pality in which Huey had once been rotten-egged. There were other repressive measures, many others. But these are sufficient to indicate what had happened to self-government in Louisiana.

8.

IT IS PERHAPS a corollary that in the last year of his life Long became obsessed with a fear of assassination. He increased his armed body-guard, and took other unusual precautions to insure his personal safety. In July, 1935, he charged on the floor of the Senate that enemies had planned his death with "one man, one gun, and one bullet" as the medium, and with the promise of a Presidential pardon as the slayer's reward. This plot, he said, was hatched in a New Orleans hotel at a gathering of his enemies. A dictograph, concealed in the meeting room, had recorded the murderous conversation. I was at that meeting. It was a caucus of die-hard oppositionists, dolefully trying to decide what to do for the next state campaign. And the "plotting" was limited to such hopefully expressed comments as "Good God, I wish somebody would kill the son of a bitch."

And somebody did. That July, the white horse of death, foreseen by Mason Spencer earlier in the year, was but two months distant. On the night of September 8, a slender, bespectacled man in a white suit stepped from behind a marble pillar in the capitol as Long, accompanied by his closest aides and bodyguard, hurried to the Governor's office. Dr. Carl Austin Weiss, the man in the white suit, drew a small pistol and fired once. Seconds later, the assassin lay dead, his body and head riddled by sixty-one shots. Huey Long staggered away with one bullet wound, perhaps a second, in his stomach. Thirty hours later he died.

9.

FOR FOUR YEARS, from 1932 to 1936, I published my paper. It was good for neither the nervous system nor the pocketbook. Together with the repeated inducements to change sides, there were the continuing threatening letters and telephone warnings, the subscription cancellations, the refusal of some—but not a majority—of the Hammond advertisers to do business with a newspaper that fought Long. But Huey didn't get around properly to those smaller newspapers which opposed him until the summer before he was killed. Then, in a special legislative session devoted to tightening the state's straitjacket, he enacted a law for our especial undoing.

This law created a State Printing Board and empowered it to determine the eligibility of any newspaper in the state for the position of official journal. Each town and city, each school district and each parish had hitherto selected their official journals themselves for the printing of minutes, tax delinquent lists, ordinances, proceedings, and other official matters required by law to be published. For many small newspapers this legal printing meant the difference between survival and failure; and, in our case, our newspaper's selection a year before as official journal of the parish potentially added several thousand needed dollars to our revenues.

As its first act, the State Printing Board declared that our newspaper could not serve the parish as official journal. No reasons were given, just the decision. It was useless to seek redress for breach of contract in the state courts. So we sought to prove that our contract with the parish had been impaired rather than violated when the parish's governing body, the police jury, had been forced to select another journal.

Impairment of contract is a federal offense. We won our case in the United States District Court in New Orleans. The state, using a battery of lawyers from the Attorney General's office, won a reversal in the United States Circuit Court of Appeals. We appealed to the Supreme Court, which held that our contract had not been impaired but breached and that the state courts must decide the case. And it was futile to go into Huey's courts.

But months before this decision was handed down, Huey had been assassinated. And the 1936 state campaign had begun. I ran for the state legislature. It was something like a one-legged man's running a race with Panama Limited.

The principal legatees of the kingdom effected an uneasy peace among ourselves, a settling upon one Richard Leche, a fat, easygoing minor henchman who held a judgeship, as a compromise candidate for Governor. They had a limitless war chest and the election machinery. The Share Our Wealth Clubs were out to avenge their martyr. The repeal of the poll tax had almost doubled the voting lists, and the overwhelming majority of the new voters were remembering the man who had given them this free privilege and their roads and school books and a wonderful circus besides.

On our side we had only the federal patronage. In a vote-getting sense, this consisted mainly of WPA work orders which were distributed by the thousands to the anti-Long organizations. They didn't help much. The poor jobless devils took the work orders readily enough, but they didn't vote WPA.

Few among us could have won even in an honestly conducted election. In the eyes of too many old and new voters, the hands of the opposition were stained with Huey's blood. And we had nothing to offer except the promise that self-government would be returned to a people apparently content without it. Adopting as best we could the Long techniques, we spoke from makeshift sound trucks, distributed blackguarding handbills by the hundreds of thousands, printed our own state and district political weeklies. The campaign was macabre. The heirs of Long did almost everything in his memory except display his body on the platform. And by the thousands upon thousands the Louisiana electorate voted vengeance for their martyr against the mythical "bloody murderers" whose indictments and convictions were a Leche campaign pledge. The newly enfranchised voters, almost doubling any previous vote total, gave the administration a greater majority than Huey himself had ever won. We would have been defeated even in an honest election; yet it was a bitter thing to stand by helplessly while the pre-marking of ballots through the endless chain device insured machine majorities in most of the boxes where the issue might otherwise have been in doubt. Less than a dozen anti-Long men were elected to more than three hundred state, parish, and local offices. And Dick Leche, his morals as flaccid as his body, ascended to the throne of the Kingfish.

No wealth-sharing ideologist or political rough-and-tumbler, Leche ushered in an era of comparably good feeling and incomparably good pickings. He took things easy, and his fellow freebooters took almost everything easily. "When I took the Governor's oath I didn't take the vows of poverty," quipped fat Dick. No rough stuff, boys. There's plenty for all of us. Good old Dick. Good old George. Good old Jimmy. Good old graft. Good old world.

With an eye on Louisiana's electoral votes in the 1936 Democratic National Convention, the more practical politicians of the New Deal made a special kind of deal with Louisiana. Income tax prosecutions were dropped. Dick visited Washington, where he called upon and was photographed with President Roosevelt and some of the lesser figures of the administration. He was visited in turn in Louisiana by the President and Attorney General Murphy. When he revived the *Progress,* and through forced subscriptions and forced advertising made it as nearly a 100-per-cent profit venture as is possible in business, the first issue carried a photostat of a letter from the President glowingly paying tribute to the virtues and glory of a free press and the Governor.

And then in 1939 the haunted, graft-debased house of Long began to fall apart. President James Monroe Smith of Louisiana State University went to the penitentiary for stealing state bonds. Dick Leche went to federal prison. So did Seymour Weiss, the treasurer, Abe Shushan, one of the earliest Louisianians to support Long and to profit from that support, and several others. One grafter killed himself. Too many escaped. And, measured by their loot, the penalties paid by those who were caught were small indeed.

Earl Long, the flamboyant, politically unsuccessful brother of the Kingfish, tried to carry the flickering torch. Running for a full term, he was opposed by James Noe, a wealthy oilman and ally of Huey, whom the gang had shunted aside and who made it pay for the snub; Sam Jones, a young, incorruptible attorney who had spent most of his mature years fighting Longism; and James H. Morrison, a brass-voiced newcomer who in platform technique was another Long. Earl Long led in the first primary, with Sam Jones second, Noe third, and Morrison a poor fourth. Noe's support in the second primary would determine the winner. He got even with Earl Long by supporting Sam Jones.

An overdue housecleaning and the rescinding of the legislative acts which had enslaved and made politically impotent the Louisiana electorate were the objectives and primary accomplishments of the Jones administration. But even in 1943 the ghost of Huey Long was not laid. A Long man was almost elected Governor. He was defeated not by a forthright crusader against machine politics but by a mild and pleasant composer and singer of hillbilly ballads, a former professor and public service commissioner, who campaigned with his band and said nothing against any opponent. Perhaps because they were tired of invective and hate, Louisianians elected Jimmie Davis Governor. His administration was uneventful, untroubled by corruption and perhaps too colorless for a state grown accustomed to bread, thieves, and circuses. And early in 1948 the ghost of Huey Long rose out of his grave and stalked across Louisiana again, when his brother Earl was finally chosen Governor on nothing more than the magic name of Long.

10.

No, the ghost is not yet laid, although Huey Long is dead these many long years. Nor will it be for many years to come. For this hideous thing that we remember as the rough-shod reign of the Kingfish was not hideous in its beginnings. Whether or not Huey Long himself was ever sincere in his protestations for the poor and downtrodden is, basically, beside the point. For he led a social-economic revolution in Louisiana; and after his death the entire South was debated ground.

It was not his political genius and ruthlessness alone that made him possible. There were two other factors equally important.

The first factor was that, after two hundred years, the people of Louisiana were ready and waiting for a messiah who would translate their needs into accomplishments. Theirs was the ground swell of the little people, a people undisturbed by his tactics as long as they got the roads, the free bridges, the hospitals, the free school books, the public works; as long as the men whom he pilloried and broke and banished were identified with the leaders of the past, bumbling representatives of an indifferent, negative ruling class. The little people shrugged at graft because of their certainty that there always had been graft of a kind. This time, whatever the politicians skimmed off the top, they were getting theirs too. And they were getting something else. Revenge. A fantastic vengeance upon the Sodom and Gomorrah that was called New Orleans. A squaring of accounts with the big shots, the Standard Oil and the bankers, the big planters, the entrenched interests everywhere. Huey Long was in the image of these little people. He talked their language. He had lived their lives. He had taken them up to the mountaintop and shown them the world which the meek would inherit.

The second factor was the make-up of the forces actively opposed to Long. His disunited enemies had difficulty from beginning to end to maintain an alliance that had its base in military necessity alone. We were strange bedfellows: cynical spoils politicians of the Old Regular ring in New Orleans; ardent, idealistic New Dealers; inept leaders of the country parishes, turned out in short grass; nonpolitical gentility awakened from their slumbers by rude knocking; the hitherto secure representatives of Big Business; honestly disturbed, solid bourgeoisie. Our combined cries for good government made a dissonant chorus. Huey bowled us over like ten-pins, with rare misses, from the time of the failure of the impeachment proceedings to his assassination.

Looking back, I know now that part of our failure arose from an unwillingness to approve any Long-sponsored proposal for change, regardless of its merits. We offered none of our own except a plea for democratic rule, and that sounded hollow in contrast. Yet, at the end, it became the one thing of importance to Louisiana.

And Long triumphed over men far wiser politically than we. President Roosevelt and his pulse-feeler, Jim Farley, became uneasy about Long's threat soon after the Share Our Wealth movement overran the borders of Louisiana. On the Senate floor he made the most adroit, belligerent, and fluent opponent look and sound like a political freshman.

Even had Huey Long relied only upon his mesmeric appeal to Louisiana's masses and his ability to make promised delivery of the material things those masses wanted, it is probable that he could have dominated his state as completely and for at least as long as he did. But he was not content to rely upon these weapons alone. His compelling lust for power as such—a primary, animating force in his political life —and the intense vindictiveness which from the start characterized his public career lured him to a morally indefensible position.

When impeachment seemed a certainty in those early months as Governor, he simply bought and paid for enough legislators "like sacks of potatoes" to prevent the majority vote necessary for conviction. From then on, Long bought those whom he needed and could buy, and crushed those who had no purchase price or whose price was too high.

Nor was the control of a governor, a majority of legislators, a court majority enough. It should be repeated that no public officeholder, no teacher, no fire chief or fireman, no police chief or policeman, no day laborer on state projects held his job except in fee simple to the machine. Except among the political job holders, he used this economic power sparingly. Yet even private citizens made their living by his sufferance. Long could have taxed to extinction any business, large or small, and business knew it. Men could be—and were—arrested by unidentified men, the members of his secret police, held incommunicado, tried, and found guilty on trumped-up charges. A majority of the State Supreme Court became unabashedly his. Through his State Printing Board he cracked an economic whip over the rural and small-town press, lashing all but a few into sullen silence. A thug, making a premeditated skull-crushing attack upon a Long opponent, could draw from his pocket in court a pre-signed pardon from the figurehead Governor. Entire city administrations could be removed, not by the electorate but by legislative action.

In the end, these things indirectly destroyed Huey Long himself. There are many conflicting tales as to why and how he was killed. This much is a certainty: His assassination was not plotted. It is not probable that Dr. Weiss went to the capitol the night of September 8, 1935, deliberately to kill Long. But he must have intended to protest a grave injury, the double-barreled kind of injury Long delighted in inflicting. Dr. Weiss's father-in-law, an implacable enemy of Long, had been gerrymandered out of his judgeship. Two of the judge's daughters had been dismissed from their teaching positions in further retaliation. And worse, Long had circulated noisome rumors about the family's ancestry.

Political punishment compounded with savage slander—an old, tested formula for reducing enemies to impotence. But this time the formula distilled a deadly reaction. Those who knew young Dr. Weiss best say that he could have sought Long only to protest verbally or with his fists this grave slander. They say that he could have drawn his gun only because the bodyguards threatened him. Few people in Louisiana believe that the full, true story has been told, for Long's henchmen were the only spectators. Perhaps the single bullet, fired from Weiss's small pistol, fatally wounded Long. Perhaps there was a second wound, as many Louisianians believe, caused by a ricocheting bullet from a bodyguard's gun. One bullet, two bullets. It is unimportant now; it was unimportant even then. Out of the terror he created, out of the driving passion to destroy other men, out of the futility that warped the minds of the Louisianians who opposed him, Huey Long himself forged the weapon which felled him.

11.

AND it need not have been so. He might have served Louisiana and the South as had no other political leader. Before the numbed thousands of his followers, the worn and credulous who milled across the grounds of the Capitol, Gerald L. K. Smith, the grasping opportunist who directed the Share Our Wealth clubs, spoke an epitaph deserving to have been said of a better man by a better man:

"His body shall never rest as long as hungry bodies cry for food, as long as lean human frames stand naked, as long as homeless wretches haunt this land of plenty."

Close beside the bier crowded the thieves and sycophants of the inner circle. Beyond wept the poor.

Toward what was this man thrusting? The political goal is discernible. It was the Presidency of the United States. But what of the goal as President? Was the Share Our Wealth movement only a cynical vote-getting scheme? Or did the attractive packaging decorate a basic belief in a redistribution of the national income and national benefits, implanted in the mind of a poor farmer's son in Winn Parish fifteen years before?

My own conviction is that Huey Long was no true revolutionary. Power for power's sake was his mastering god. No revolutionary but —the word is used not loosely but gingerly—a dictator. A dictator, *sui generis*, the first truly such out of the soil of America. Had all Americans lived some of those years under him, democracy would be more secure today, because democracy would have come to have a more precious meaning.

The King
and the Girl from Baltimore

BY MARGARET CASE HARRIMAN

Margaret Case Harriman, who here writes so knowingly of the ways of high international society, began her education in the mores of that special world by being born into it. She is most celebrated for the many "Profiles" she has written for the *New Yorker,* in both amusing and enlightening fashion, about such personages as Clare Boothe Luce, Gilbert Miller, Moss Hart, Helen Hayes, and many others. Several of these were published in book form as *Take Them Up Tenderly* (1944). Mrs. Harriman is now at work on a book about the Algonquin Round Table, to be published in the fall.

✶ 1.

POSSIBLY no man except some diver tangling with an octopus has had livelier troubles than Edward, Duke of Windsor, in the eighteen years that have passed since he first met the Mrs. Simpson who is now his Duchess; and the Duchess has shared all his problems except those, such as being King of England, which she eliminated simply by existing. When Edward abdicated and became the Duke of Windsor in 1936 in order to marry Mrs. Simpson, the Windsors, ironically enough, exchanged the tangible burden of ruling the British Empire for a responsibility that was both frailer and tougher. They became at once the trademark for the last really great romance likely to be known in a world that loves romance and loves kings too, and has efficiently been deprived of both. If ever two lovers had to *stay* in love, or else get the whole world mad at them, the Windsors were those two.

The reaction of one American businesswoman vacationing in Nassau soon after the Windsors took up residence there as Governor-General and First Lady of the Bahamas partly expresses the sentiment that flowed toward the runaway King and his bride. This tourist, a stout, sensible party relaxing from the wholesale garment trade, was strolling along a Nassau road when she saw a blue coupé, which had been pointed out to her as one of the Windsors' cars, coming down the road with a chauffeur driving and two people in the back seat. She got off the road and sat on a rock, breathlessly. As the car drew nearer it seemed to bulge and tremble from some inner pressure, and strange noises came from it. Noises that sounded (the American lady said later) like cows dying. These sounds were broken by a feminine voice crying, "No, darling! No more, no *more*!" The coupé swept by the lady tourist and she had a brief but definite glimpse of what was going on in the back seat. The Duchess of Windsor was pleading with the Duke, who, with rolling eyes and cheeks distended, was stubbornly serenading her on a bagpipe.

"I do not say," the lady tourist afterward remarked to friends, "that it was not interesting to see a former King of England play the bagpipes in a coup. But that wasn't what I thought about that day. I just stepped out onto the road again and walked along in the ex-King's tire tracks, and pretty soon I found I was humming a tune called 'Here's to Romance'—remember it? Nice tune. It used to be on a record, about 1936. On the other side of 'These Foolish Things.' "

A certain radio executive, a tough kind of man, has also been tossed by the tide of sentiment and romance that surrounds the Windsors, and for him, the most mellowing blow came from the Duchess herself. This radio man, an American, called on the Windsors in Nassau with an idea for some broadcasts by the Duke, on an international hookup. He had met the Windsors, and he knew that, although the Duke had requested that the Duchess be addressed as "Your Royal Highness," a form usually reserved in England for princes and princesses of royal blood, most Americans in Nassau took the even safer course of addressing her as "Ma'am," a form generally reserved for the Queen. While the Duke sat thinking over the broadcasting proposal, the radio man approached the Duchess, who had crossed the room and stood looking out of a window. "What do you think of it, Ma'am?" he asked her.

"The Duke can be extremely moving on the radio," she said quietly.

"I heard him, Ma'am—once," said the radio man, and (he now declares) wiped away a tear.

Friends of the King who were with Mrs. Simpson on that December day in 1936 when, as Edward VIII of England, he broadcast the announcement of his abdication from the throne, say that Mrs. Simpson wept along with the rest of us. Americans remember that day as a rainy late afternoon with crowds pushing into radio shops, hotel lobbies, and bars, or standing on street corners in the rain, their unabashed tears falling on their wet raincoats as they listened to that infinitely sad yet determined English voice saying, "At long last I am able to say a few words of my own. . . . I have found it impossible to carry on the heavy burden of responsibility and to discharge the duties of King as I would wish to do, without the help and support of the woman I love."

Mrs. Simpson, in fact, did more than weep. Six days earlier, on December 6, she had fled to France as darkly and dangerously as any Dumas heroine, although under the sturdy escort of Lord Brownlow, aide-de-camp to the King. Her London house in Cumberland Terrace had been stoned in November by a mob of angry Britishers, and even though the King had then posted a guard of men around the house who solidly blocked all doorways, inspected the mail, and searched the ashcans, she continued to get threatening letters and an occasional rock through a window. It seemed wise for her to go quickly to her friends, Mr. and Mrs. Herman Rogers, who had a villa at Cannes.

On the way, however, she made one notable and sincere gesture; she stopped at Lyons and telephoned the King. She had won him by her charm, but now she had no time to be charming. She even forgot to call him "Sir," as she had always graciously done. All she said, in that brief telephone call, was, "*Don't* abdicate!" and there are people who insist that she desperately added, "You *fool!*"

2.

ONE OF the interesting things about the former Wallis Warfield that seems to have escaped attention is the fact that her ancestry considerably excels that of her husband, who was once a King. The Warfields are one of the oldest families in Maryland, having originally settled in

Howard County on land granted to Richard Warfield by Charles II in 1662—fifty-two years before the Duke of Windsor's forebears, the House of Hanover, acceded to the British throne, and two hundred and fifty-five years before they changed their name to Windsor. In Maryland the Warfield men included lawyers, professors, merchants, and one president of the Sons of the American Revolution, and Wallis's favorite relative, when she was growing up in Baltimore, was her Uncle Saul, S. Davies Warfield, one-time president of the Seaboard Airlines Railroad, who reciprocated by leaving her a trust fund of fifteen thousand dollars when he died in 1927. The family was not rich, and Wallis's aunt, Mrs. Bessie Merryman, sometimes took paying guests into her house on East Biddle Street, where Wallis also lived during most of her youth.

Bessie Wallis Warfield, now the Duchess of Windsor, was born at Blue Ridge Summit, Pennsylvania, in 1896, the only child of Teackle Wallis Warfield and the former Alice Montague, a Virginia beauty. Teackle Warfield died a few weeks before his daughter's birth, and Mrs. Warfield married twice again before her own death in the late twenties, becoming successively Mrs. John Freeman Raisin and Mrs. Charles G. Allen. Wallis, as she was always called, was not a pretty child but she began at an early age to glow with a certain spark. Once, when her mother had made her a new white dress to wear to a party, Wallis stamped up and down and roared with disappointment. "I want a *red* dress, so the boys will notice me!" she shrieked explicitly. While she was still in socks and hair ribbons she took such a fancy to the choirboys of St. Paul's Cathedral that, with her short starched skirts and stiff ribbons flying, she would run down the street in pursuit of the full choir every time it appeared on its way to rehearsal or Sunday service. When she entered the near-by Oldsfield School for Girls the headmistress usually had to punish her for the twin crimes of "writing to boys" and keeping jam and cheese hidden in her clothes closet. The school had two basketball teams, one—with ineffable Southern charm —called "Gentleness" and the other called "Courtesy." Wallis played on the Gentleness team, and she was so good that Gentleness was often able to lick the stuffing out of Courtesy.

Wallis came out in society in 1914, at the Bachelors' Cotillion in

Philadelphia, and after three crowded years as a debutante married
Lieutenant E. Winfield Spencer, Jr., a navy man who was then an instructor of aviation at Pensacola, Florida. They were divorced in 1927,
and the following year Wallis Warfield Spencer married Ernest Simpson, in London. Simpson, the son of an American, was English born
and bred, a member of the Coldstream Guards (the Prince of Wales's
own regiment), and, it is safe to say, a man with positively no idea
of what was eventually going to happen to him.

3.

EDWARD ALBERT CHRISTIAN GEORGE ANDREW PATRICK DAVID, the first
and only Duke of Windsor, was born to the Duke and Duchess of York
—later King George V and Queen Mary—at White Lodge, Richmond
Park, on Midsummer's Eve, 1894. The ex-King's career is well known,
and all that will be recounted here are certain highlights that indicate
the kind of man he was when he met Wallis Simpson in London, in
1931. This meeting occurred at a party given by Thelma, Lady Furness,
another American beauty whose friendship with the then Prince of
Wales was warm and of long standing. Lady Furness was, of course,
one of the illustrious Morgan twins, and her sister Gloria had married
Reginald Vanderbilt. Until the evening of her party in 1931, Lady
Furness was also a good friend of Mr. and Mrs. Ernest Simpson.

The young Prince had been given the kind of education required by
any heir to a throne, but with a rather dashing emphasis on the Navy.
At the age of fifteen he was sent to the Royal Naval College at Dart-
mouth, where he was so strikingly democratic that he punched several
schoolmates in the nose because they snobbishly insisted on addressing
him as "Your Royal Highness." He was happier when he entered
Magdalen College, at Oxford, since his fellow students there instantly
translated his title of Prince of Wales into Oxford slang, and referred
to him affectionately as "the Pragger-Wagger." His best friends and
family always called him David—never Edward.

At Oxford, Wales was addicted to cigars and apples, and Compton
Mackenzie has quoted a rather charming discussion between Wales's
visiting parents, the King and Queen, and one of the Oxford masters,

on the subject of expenses for these items. "Good gracious, Mr. Gunstone," said the Queen, according to this account, "I never knew before that cigars had different prices. I thought all cigars were the same price." ("Fancy her thinking that," Mr. Gunstone remarked later to Mr. Mackenzie. "I must say I was very surprised. She can't know much about smoking.") At this point the King asked about a daily entry of three halfpence. "Oh, that's his apple," said Mr. Gunstone. "What?" said the King, laughing. "Does he still eat his apple every morning? He's always done that." Mr. Gunstone answered this gravely. "Yes, every morning regularly," he said, "and you ought to speak to him, Sir, about the way he *will* start peeling it as soon as he comes out of the Common Room. He'll slip on the stone stairs one of these days and give his head a nasty bump, and perhaps cut himself with his penknife. I've spoken to him about it myself several times, but he won't listen to me. He'll pay more attention to you, Sir."

Wales's Oxford career was cut short after two years by the first World War and his own eager effort to get into it and let the Germans have a chance to give him possibly more than a nasty bump on the head. He was appointed liaison officer to one or two field marshals, and then aide-de-camp to Sir John French, but in spite of all Britain's desire to protect him from danger he became celebrated for his gift of disappearing for days at a time and turning up eventually, covered with mud, in a front-line trench. He was a good soldier, as any Englishman who fought in that war will tell you, and as one of them puts it, "He was almost as much of a worry to us as the Germans." After the war, the Prince came to America on one of his journeys as "the Empire's salesman," and most of us needn't be reminded that he instantly became our synonym for romance. He set all American girls to dreaming of dancing with him, and he made all American young men begin wearing Burgundy carnations on their lapels. He was slim, fair-haired, and gay, and at parties he liked to be allowed to take over the drums in the dance band. Sometimes he ducked a dowager's ball to sit on a back staircase and sing songs with the Duncan sisters, and upon hearing this, we all exclaimed in great surprise, "Why, he's democratic!"

The Prince of Wales's democratic ways got him into trouble soon after his return to England. In 1927 he toured the British mining districts during the General Strike, and made the first of his public comments on conditions in the mines and the miners' homes. The comments amounted to "This sort of thing stinks, and I shall do something about it!" and he was to repeat them some ten years later with even more troublesome results to himself. He was Prince Charming, and the British Government, in their striped pants and bowler hats, did not want him to go poking his nose into coal-pits. In 1928 the Government gave him a private plane in the unexpressed hope that, high in the clouds with this new toy, he might forget the miseries of the miners underground. Wales learned to fly the plane, but he could not fly high enough to forget the miners or to escape the complications of his life below. For the first time, the Happy Prince was beginning to feel unhappy.

His family life was not very satisfactory. He and his mother were fond of each other, but miles apart emotionally and intellectually. His father, George V, was a mild-mannered man with the usual mild man's inner toughness, and he and his son had never understood each other. "My father doesn't *like* me," Wales sometimes told his closest friends with an air of gentle sorrow. "Not at all sure I particularly like *him,*" he would occasionally add, perhaps after a second brandy. It was a thing that was on his mind. Besides, his family and the Government and the British people in general were beginning to nag him a little, in the late twenties, about getting married, and marrying was one thing Wales definitely did not want to do, until he met Mrs. Simpson. Altogether, it would have been hard to find a man more emotionally insecure than the Prince of Wales was on that June evening in 1931 when he met Wallis Simpson and her husband at Lady Furness's party in her London house.

4.

WALES had known Ernest Simpson slightly but had never met his wife, and he was enchanted with her on the spot. She was slighter and shorter than he—five feet four inches to his five feet six or so—so that she had to look up to him, which he enjoyed. She was the most exquisitely groomed, *cleanest*-looking woman in the room (as she always is), and she had on a little blue thing of a frock that exactly matched her cornflower-blue eyes, and her eyes had laughter lines around them and looked as though they were laughing all the time, even when she was quite grave. And she had a delightful way of bossing him around without being boring or coy about it. *"Don't* eat that, Sir!" she would say smiling and taking a caviar canapé out of his hand. "Have this instead?" and she would give him a bit of cream cheese on toast, best possible thing for a tired and overworked man.

Once she even quietly took a drink out of his hand and set it down beyond reach, and Wales, who had never been looked after except officially, blossomed and beamed under this fond supervision. From that time he was a fairly constant guest at the Simpsons' dinner table, and all of Mrs. Simpson's menus were planned with a view to his nervous stomach, which became less and less nervous as one calm meal after another vanished within it. Wales, like his father, was essentially a domestic man.

(The home life of the Duke and Duchess of Windsor is still, after almost twelve years of marriage, domestic to the point of coziness even when they travel and have to live in hotels.

"Darling, don't forget to order your spinach!" the Duchess will carol from her Waldorf Towers bedroom when the waiter comes up to take a luncheon or dinner order.

"I hate spinach," growls the Duke, hunched over a menu in the next room.

The Duchess appears in the doorway, calm and shining. "But you must have *some* vegetable, dear. Asparagus? . . . [to the waiter] Asparagus, please, *vinaigrette.* And now—where is Pookie?"

The Windsors travel with five dogs, a Jones terrier, two Cairns, and two Lhasa terriers, whom they have named so whimsically that the dogs might be better suited to a cottage called "Idlewild" or "U-an'-Me" than to the Waldorf Towers or a villa in southern France. These pets are named Pookie, Preezie, Gremlin, Bundles, and Yackie, and certain dog lovers who know the Windsors declare that every one of the dogs refuses, quite properly, to answer to its name.)

However, in 1931, all such cozy domestic bliss seemed far away. The Prince of Wales was thirty-seven years old, and he had just met a lovely American lady who sometimes, in the evening, wore a diamond in her hair. Here is the groundwork for high romance and deep tragedy. Unfortunately, there is an interlude of pure, shrieking farce.

Lady Furness, through whom Wales first met Mrs. Simpson, had been well known in London as the Prince's favorite dinner and dancing companion. But she had another suitor, one Ali Khan, a son of the Aga Khan. She had an engagement to dine with him in Paris on the very evening, as it happened, that Syrie Maugham, Somerset Maugham's ex-wife, had asked her to dine in London. After Lady Furness had wired Mrs. Maugham her regrets from Paris, the dinner date with Ali Khan somehow fell through, so Lady Furness took the next plane back to London and turned up at Mrs. Maugham's party after all. "Where is David?" she asked the moment she swept through the front door. "I'll find him for you," said Mrs. Maugham quickly, but not quickly enough. Lady Furness hurried past her down a corridor, threw open a door she seemed to know well, and sure enough, David, Prince of Wales, was in the *small* library quite alone, except for Mrs. Simpson. Sensation!

The anguish of Lady Furness was soon dwarfed by the events that followed, including the anguish of Prime Minister Baldwin and the Archbishop of Canterbury. In June, 1931, Mrs. Simpson was presented at the Court of King George V and Queen Mary, in defiance of the tradition which forbids a divorced woman to be presented. According to the court grapevine, the ceremony was the result of a fiery session between the Prince of Wales and his parents, to whom he gave some kind of ultimatum or other. From that time, Wales and Mr. and Mrs. Simpson rapidly became the best-known threesome in London. They went everywhere together, and Mr. Simpson's deadpan demeanor on these outings inspired the inevitable sad gags about the Importance of Being Ernest.

The Government had long wanted Wales to marry a suitable wife, and government officials soon began getting such lines in their faces over Mrs. Simpson that the London *Times* finally came out with a veiled editorial describing the official state of mind, with true British understatement, as "uneasy." The working classes were on the Prince's side, however, and they stayed that way until he became King. The creed of the working-class Englishman is both indulgent and severe:

a Prince may have his fun, and Lord love him for it, but once he becomes a King, he'd better behave himself properly. One thing that is said to have turned the tide of popular feeling against the King and Mrs. Simpson, later, was the King's generosity to Mr. Simpson. Simpson had had a fairly good position in London society, but when Edward became King it improved to a startling degree, and when Edward proposed him for membership in the King's own chapter of the Knights Templar, Englishmen in general blew up.

5.

THE FIVE YEARS between 1931 and the death of George V in 1936 were probably the happiest that Wallis and her Prince have ever known. They cruised with light-hearted friends on the royal yacht *Nahlin*, they stayed at house parties in the south of France and gave house parties at Wales's own Belvedere Lodge in England. Mrs. Simpson became the most famous hostess in London, and not only because of her royal dinner guest. She served good food, introducing succulent Southern dishes to a people long paralyzed internally by boiled meat and suet pudding. She had made her house lovely with old mirrors, new colors, and fresh flowers. And she had the true charm of a woman who seems to be genuinely interested in everyone who talks to her. Besides, she had the puzzling kind of good looks that are unconnected with beauty and are much more interesting. She was so neat that she glistened, and she had a way of perking herself up with something unexpected long before anyone else thought of it—such as wearing her hair in a braided coronet with a bright ribbon woven through the braids. Her clothes were so wonderful that Englishwomen spent hours over teacups discussing which was better dressed, Mrs. Simpson or Princess Marina, the Duke of Kent's wife. This question naturally led to violent competition between Mainbocher, who dressed Mrs. Simpson, and Molyneux, the Duchess of Kent's dressmaker, and the rivalry between these two gifted gentlemen produced such quantities of heavenly clothes that both women kept on looking better and better, and people began going out of an evening in London simply to see what Marina and Wallis were wearing that night.

Intellectually Mrs. Simpson had it slightly over the Duchess of Kent, because Mrs. Simpson had become known in London as a "wit." This astonished everyone, because no one expected so charming and restful a lady to be witty as well, and when examples of her repartee began to cross the Atlantic Americans were astonished too. For instance, it seems that Mrs. Simpson, soon after she became Duchess of Windsor, was playing bridge with Somerset Maugham, and Mr. Maugham said to her, "You had a king, why didn't you take that trick?" The Duchess replied, "Oh, my kings never take tricks, they just abdicate." (That's the end of that witty saying.) Another time, the Duchess happened to be a fellow passenger of Noel Coward's on a plane, and Coward asked her what she would feel like if she ever became Queen of England. "Exactly like a crash landing," said the Duchess. (End of second *mot*.)

Whether or not we understand the hidden sparkle of these remarks, it is welcome news that the Duchess doesn't take herself too seriously, and that the Duke must obviously be a man who is easily amused. Although the Duchess's cracks might never make a radio comedy program, she has a way of saying things, with laughter behind her ultra-blue eyes, that is extremely contagious and that gives her least remark a pungency it seldom turns out, on examination, to possess. She is far too clever, anyway, to be brilliant when men are around; and that may be one of the reasons men usually *are* around the Duchess.

The friends who surrounded Wales and Mrs. Simpson belonged to the international set—the people who flocked in season, like birds to the sun or sheep to the slaughter, to London, Paris, Vienna, the Dalmatian coast, the Lido, and the Riviera, with Elsa Maxwell as their First Robin or Judas Goat, depending on how you look at it. The Prince and Mrs. Simpson were both cheerfully gregarious and they made inevitable mistakes of judgment in choosing their friends. They made no more mistakes than most of us did in those heedless days that led to the second World War, and their judgment could hardly have been shakier than that of all the various Governments put together. But they were two people in a unique position and at least three of their errors were serious. They became chummy with Charles Bedaux, Axel Wenner-Gren, and Count von Ribbentrop. It was difficult for anyone who was not physically repulsive, poverty-stricken, or socially dead *not* to be friendly with those three gentlemen immediately before World War II; they were everywhere, they were hospitable and insistent, and in contrasting ways they were all attractive. Bedaux was an American go-getter, Wenner-Gren a shy, blue-eyed Swede, and Ribbentrop was a Nazi smoothie. Since no one else knew then that they were all working hand-in-hand for Hitler, it seems unfair to blame Wales and Mrs. Simpson for not having guessed it.

The charges of pro-Germanism which have been made against Wales as Prince, King, and Duke of Windsor are mainly his own fault, however, and might be traced to the terrible sincerity of a man who truly believed he could do business with Hitler to the benefit of his own country and possibly the world. Edward had always been pleased by his German blood, directly inherited from his great-great-grandmother (Victoria's mother, a German princess) and his great-grandfather, Prince Albert of Saxe-Coburg Gotha, as well as from the House of Hanover in general. "You forget I am three-quarters German myself," he once sternly reminded an acquaintance who was criticizing the Boches. He twice visited Hitler at Berchtesgaden, once as Prince of Wales and again, in 1938, as Duke of Windsor with his wife, the Duchess. Eyewitnesses to the last visit say (and it's not hard to believe) that Hitler stood at the top of a long staircase and made the former King of England climb the full flight of stairs to shake his hand. Edward's defenders insist that his purpose in visiting Hitler was a wholehearted desire to bring about an understanding between the two Anglo-Saxon countries, England and Germany, and to avert a war. The British Government took a more skeptical view of Hitler's hospitality. It seemed to them that what the Führer was after was a friend like Edward installed on the British throne as a puppet King, susceptible to German orders.

6.

WHEN George V died, on January 20, 1936, and the Prince of Wales became Edward VIII, he already had two strikes against him—his friendship with Mrs. Simpson and his first visit to Hitler. He proceeded at once to do himself in the eye a third and a fourth time.

First, on a trip to the East Coast he publicly repeated his statement of ten years earlier, that the living conditions of the miners there were "a shame," and, stopping off in Wales, he promised the Welsh jobless that "something would be done" about their plight. Prime Minister Baldwin, a rocklike member of the Old Guard, felt that all this was entirely too much for the head of a constitutional monarchy to take upon himself without consulting his Government. Returning to London, the new King once more electrified the Government by asking Parliament to set aside for his wife, in the eventuality of his marriage, the sum customarily allotted to the Queen of England. This would have been welcome news, except that the King was still constantly seen in the company of Mrs. Simpson.

The Queen's allotment amounts, in American money, to $200,000 a year, plus $125,000 set aside for a potential Prince of Wales. These incomes are administered by the Privy Purse and cannot be touched by the King himself. The King, it may be said, doesn't need them. As Prince of Wales Edward received an income of $500,000 a year. As a bachelor King he was granted $2,500,000 annually—some $300,000 less than his father, a married man, had received. As King he also drew $425,000 a year from the Duchy of Lancaster and $330,000 from the Duchy of Cornwall, in addition to other profitable properties, and he had a personal bequest from Queen Victoria, who left all of her descendants well fixed. During the short year that Edward was King, his income tax amounted to about $215,000, and it is safe to say that he gave up an income of some nine or ten million dollars when he abdicated. (As Governor-General of the Bahamas he was paid a salary of $12,000 a year.)

In October, 1936, Mrs. Simpson, after a summer of cruising with the King and visiting him at Belvedere Lodge, divorced Ernest Simpson, and matters rapidly came to a head. After Mrs. Simpson was granted a decree *nisi,* which meant that the divorce would become final in six months, she hurried straight from the divorce hearing to Belvedere Lodge, and the British public could no longer close its eyes to the fact that the King was in love with Wallis Simpson and intended to make her Queen of England. The masses were sentimentally all in favor of the match at first, and crowds gathered in every street with cries of "Let 'im 'ave the gel 'e wants, Gord love 'im!" The early enthusiasm of the people was due largely to the fact that the British press, out of deference to the royal family, had published little about Mrs. Simpson except that she was an American. The newspapers never mentioned her divorce proceedings, and all references to her were so carefully censored that Miss Ellen Wilkinson, Labor Member of Parliament, finally rose in the House to inquire why American papers and magazines arriving in England had so many paragraphs and pages clipped out.

The British press had also refrained from reporting many meetings between the King and Prime Minister Baldwin behind closed doors at the King's bachelor quarters in St. James's Palace or at Belvedere Lodge. But late in November, 1936, the reverberations of these interviews grew too loud to be ignored, and at the same time the Bishop of Bradford administered a public rebuke to the King, saying that he hoped His Majesty was "aware of his need of God's grace." British newspapers abandoned their censorship—which had been partly voluntary and partly by request from Buckingham Palace—and published everything they knew about Mrs. Simpson. The British workingman, learning with a shock that she was a woman twice divorced, promptly withdrew his approval of her as England's future Queen.

Mrs. Simpson's divorces were also the source of the Government's disapproval, and the Church of England's. Neither Government nor Church would have objected to Edward's marrying an American; the marriage might have brought the two countries closer, and England wanted that. There was no objection, either, to his marrying a commoner. His sister, Princess Mary, had married a commoner, Lord Lascelles; and his brother, now King George VI, had married another —the present Queen, formerly Lady Elizabeth Bowes-Lyon, being of noble but not of royal blood. Mrs. Simpson was wellborn and charming, and might have made an admirable Queen. Her two divorces were the only obstacles to her marriage with Edward VIII, but they were insurmountable.

The Church of England does not recognize divorce, and therefore Edward and Mrs. Simpson could not have been married by any representative of that Church. If they were married elsewhere the Church of England would not recognize the marriage and would refuse to participate in the subsequent coronation ceremonies. This would amount to excommunicating the King. Ironically enough, it was this same Church of England that was established by Henry VIII in order that he might be granted a divorce which the then-existing Catholic Church of England would not give him. Unlike Henry VIII, Edward VIII could not disestablish the existing Church except by Act of Parliament, and Parliament, in 1936, was clearly not disposed to throw out the Church of England even if Edward and Mrs. Simpson had wanted it done, which is unlikely.

Friends of theirs who saw them at that time will tell you now that the Prince and Mrs. Simpson never acted like people who wanted to overthrow the Church of England. They acted, their friends say, like a couple in love who wanted to get married, and who were plainly horrified by the momentous events this simple desire had set in motion. "They seemed to think you could leave the throne of England the way you get up out of a chair," one pal said, lately, "and you couldn't help loving them for it, they were honestly so damn naïve." Another friend, questioned about this remark, made a more incisive comment. "People always act simple when they're tired out," she said, "and this naïveté you mention was probably just physical exhaustion. I saw the King and Wallis during that time, and I never saw two people so *tired*. He was tired from his long battle to make Wallis Queen, which he was absolutely determined to do, and she was tired from trying to please him and please everybody else too. They both acted like zombies when other people were around, and the only time they ever showed a spark of the old liveliness was when they were alone together. I know, because I looked out of a window once and happened to see them alone. I give you my word, they looked like *kids*."

In his battle to marry the woman he loved, the King was opposed by the Government, headed by Prime Minister Stanley Baldwin, and by the Church, headed by the Archbishop of Canterbury. He was supported by Winston Churchill, who was not in public office at the time, and by the "press Lords," Lord Rothermere and Lord Beaverbrook, but it was a losing battle. A morganatic marriage (the only possible compromise) was out of the question, first because British law had

long declared morganatic marriages unconstitutional and insisted that
the wife of a reigning monarch become Queen and nothing less, and
second because Edward felt exactly the same way and was determined
that Wallis Simpson be nothing less than Queen as long as he occupied
the throne. On this point Edward agreed with the Government and the
Church.

A footnote to the problem was the eventuality of children born to
Edward and Wallis, who would, by British law, become direct succes-
sors to the throne. On December 5, 1936, the Prime Minister told the
House of Commons, "The only possible way in which this result could
be avoided would be by legislation dealing with a particular case. His
Majesty's Government are not prepared to introduce such legislation."
This speech caused the British to blow up again, in their own quiet way,
and all England became a battleground between the people who were
in favor of the King and his lady and the people who were not. Lon-
don newspapers carried their usual constipated headlines, such as
"Crisis in House," and "King Dissents," but in New York the digni-
fied *Herald Tribune* was moved to livelier headings that read, "Public
Rallies to King, Baldwin Yielding: Crowd Boos Cabinet, Hustles
Archbishop of Canterbury as He Quits Residence of Premier. Mrs.
Simpson," the *Herald Tribune* added, "Remains Secluded with New
York Hosts on Riviera."

7.

THE KING stayed at Belvedere Lodge during most of this crisis, and a
man who was with him—it may have been Colonel Piers Leigh, his
equerry—has said that the King showed his nervousness only by the
way he constantly changed the carnation in his buttonhole. "He just
kept putting one in, ripping it out ten minutes later and putting a fresh
one in," this observer has said. "Nearly drove me crazy, but of course
he obviously didn't know he was doing it." Prime Minister Baldwin,
possibly treading on old carnations, constantly visited the King at
Belvedere that week end to urge him to give up Mrs. Simpson, and the
King's voice was heard to ring out time after time from the room
where he received the Prime Minister. "No, and again no, and no

again!'' he was heard to say. The King was strengthened in his refusals by his still unquenched hope that Winston Churchill could carry through a plan he had confided to the King. Churchill wanted to form a new government, with himself as Prime Minister, which would enact a law permitting Edward to marry Wallis and make her, at least, a morganatic Queen. This coup would have had a certain political value to Churchill, a semi-retired statesman who was getting pretty tired of bricklaying for the rotogravures, and the fact that it never came to pass now seems more of a misfortune for England than for Mr. Churchill, who eventually came into his own anyhow.

Its failure was, however, a tragedy for Edward and Mrs. Simpson. On December 6, the day after Prime Minister Baldwin's decisive speech in the House of Commons, Mrs. Simpson fled to the south of France. The King, after the last of several painful sessions with his mother, Queen Mary, whose feelings can readily be guessed at, summoned Premier Baldwin and spoke the historic words, "I am determined to marry Mrs. Simpson, and I am ready to go."

"That, Sir," said Baldwin, "is most grievous news."

On December 11 the Speaker of the House of Commons read the King's message to a hushed chamber: "I, Edward, do hereby declare my irrevocable determination to renounce the throne for myself and my descendants." The next day Edward broadcast the news of his abdication, and that night, wearing a heavy black ulster and accompanied only by his equerry, Colonel Piers Leigh, a private detective, a valet, a police car, and a station wagon to carry his luggage, he drove to Portsmouth, where he took ship for the Continent, to stay with his friends, Baron Eugene Rothschild and his wife, in Vienna. The name of the ship that took him forever from England was the *Enchantress*.

On June 3, Edward of England, newly created Duke of Windsor by his brother, King George VI, married Wallis Simpson at Monts, France. The bride wore blue and, as usual, painted her mouth but not her nails. England soon forgot them, but they spent the next three years happily enough, mostly in the villa at Antibes which they rented from Sir Pomeroy Burton. When the war broke out, the Duke offered his services to Great Britain and was appointed liaison officer to the British and French High Commands, with headquarters carefully restricted, however, to France. Once more the Duke displayed his talent for turning up in the thick of battle in spite of everything, and although there may have been no connection, King George in 1940 appointed him Governor-General of the Bahamas, one of Great Britain's most distant possessions. On August first of that year the Duke and Duchess sailed from Lisbon aboard the American liner *Excalibur*. They were traveling light, they told reporters. Besides their dogs, they took only three truckloads of baggage, a Buick car, a trailer, a sewing-machine, two golf bags with clubs, two cases of champagne, two cases of gin, and two cases of port.

The Windsors did a good job in the Bahamas. They were both up and dressed by eight-thirty every morning to tackle their daily chores. The Duke got the natives interested in agriculture rather than in their habitual industry of seasonally gypping tourists, and also worked hard in co-operation with the United States Government in establishing air and naval bases in the Bahamas. The Duchess did prodigious war work, and excited the local ladies by the way she redecorated Government House—she did the living room, for example, all in different shades of beige, from grayish beige to rosy pink. "Like stockings!" one visitor exclaimed. The Windsors were enchanting hosts, and the Duke sometimes pleased his guests by turning up at dinner in full Scottish regalia, wearing the dark green jacket, the kilt, the sporran, the gillies, and the little dagger thrust in the side of one long wool sock. "Only damn nuisance about this costume is no pockets," he would say, slapping his thighs in vain. "Just look what I'm forced to do if I want a cigarette or a shilling or something." And with an air of disgust he would unsnap his sporran, extract the cigarette or shilling or something, and snap it shut again like an old lady fussing with her purse. Watching his charm and gaiety, more than one thoughtful guest went away feeling sad that this man who had once been sovereign over six hundred million people and one-quarter of the earth's surface should be reduced to governing sixty-eight thousand people and a handful of islands.

8.

IN 1945 the Duke resigned his post in Nassau and, with his Duchess, returned to France and to the villa at Antibes which they thought of as their actual home. They stopped off in Paris for a few days, for the Duchess to buy some clothes and the Duke to make a couple of the shopping expeditions he likes best—buying kitchen and household utensils. He conducts these deals almost entirely in pantomime, his French being fluent but not always intelligible to Frenchmen, and when he describes them later to friends, his descriptions depend more on gestures than on words. "I found the most terrific egg beater," he will say, whirling his hand around like an egg beater in violent motion, "and then I bought a tray . . ." and here his hand rises abruptly, palm upward, representing a tray. The house at Antibes had been lived in by Rommel and his staff during the German occupation, but they had done little harm and to the Duchess's delight had never been able to find her gold-plated bathtub, which the caretaker had cannily hidden away. The gold bathtub now stands once more in the Duchess's pink-tiled bathroom, and things at the villa are almost the same as they always were.

Not quite the same, however. The Germans mined the grounds, and when the Windsors went to walk through their gardens and park during the first summer they had to keep to narrow paths rigidly roped off for safety. This seemed a rather symbolic thing to happen to two nice people who have had to spend the last eighteen years remembering, in one way or another, that they had better watch their step.

An Occurrence at Republic Steel

BY HOWARD FAST

Since the publication of his first novel, *Two Valleys,* in 1932, Howard Fast has produced a steady stream of historical fiction and biography—fifteen books in all. The most noted of these are probably *Citizen Tom Paine* (1943), the story of the Revolutionary War pamphleteer, and *Freedom Road* (1944); the most recent is *My Glorious Brothers* (1948). During World War II he served overseas with the OWI, and as a correspondent. He has been a frequent contributor to *New Masses* and is generally regarded as a spokesman for the militant left-wing segment of the American labor movement.

✵ 1.

MEMORIAL DAY in Chicago in 1937 was hot, humid, and sunny; it was the right kind of day for the parade and the holiday, the kind of day that takes the soreness out of a Civil War veteran's back and allows him to amble along with the youngsters a quarter his age. It was a day for picnics, for boating, for the beach or a long ride into the country. It was a day when patriotic sentiments could be washed down comfortably with Coca-Cola or a bottle of beer, as you preferred. And there's no doubt but that a good deal of that holiday feeling was present in the strikers who gathered on the prairie outside and around Republic Steel's Chicago plant.

Most of the strikers felt good. Tom Girdler, who ran Republic, had said that he would go back to hoeing potatoes before he would meet the strikers' demands, and the word went around that old Tom could do worse than earn an honest living hoeing potatoes. The strike was less than a week old; the strikers had not yet felt the pinch of hunger, and there was a good sense of solidarity everywhere. Because it was such a fine summer day, many of the strikers brought their children out onto the prairie to attend the first big mass meeting; and wherever you looked, you saw two-year-olds and three-year-olds riding pick-a-back on the heavy-muscled shoulders of steelworkers. And because it was in the way of being their special occasion as well as a patriotic holiday, the women wore their best and brightest.

In knots and clusters, the younger folks two by two, the older people in family groups, they drifted toward Sam's Place on South Green Bay Avenue. Once, Sam's Place had been a ten-cents-a-dance hall; now it was strike headquarters, which meant, in terms of the strike, just about everything. There, the women had set up their soup kitchen, and there the Union Strategy Board planned the day-to-day work; food was collected at Sam's Place, and pickets used it as their barracks and headquarters.

Today, several thousand people gathered around the improvised platform set up at Sam's Place, to listen to the speakers and to take part in the mass demonstration. How serious an occasion it was, they knew well enough; rumors circulated that the police were going to attempt something special, something out of the run of clubbing and gassing which had marked the strike from the very first day; rumors too that a mass picket line was going to be established today. It was a serious occasion, but somehow something in the day, the holiday, the sunshine, and the warm summer weather made the festive air persist. Vendors wheeled wagons of cold pop, and brick ice cream, three flavors in one, was to be had at a nickel a cake.

For the young folks, it was the first strike; they sat under the trees with the girls, grinning at the way the strike committee worked and poured sweat; and the women, cooking inside the hall, reflected, as a hundred generations of women had reflected before, that man's work is from sun to sun, but women's work—

A group of girls sang. Strike songs were around, a new turn in the folk literature of the nation. First shyly, hesitantly, then with more vigor, then with a rising volume, augmented by the deep bass and rich baritone of men, they sang the mournful tale of Joe Hill, the song-maker and organizer whom the cops had killed; they sang, "Solidarity forever! The union makes us strong. . . ." They sang of the nameless

I.W.W. worker, tortured into treason, who pleaded, "Comrades, slay me, for the coppers took my soul; close my eyes, good comrades, for I played a traitor's role."

The meeting started and came down to business. The chairman was Joe Weber, who represented the Steel Workers Organizing Committee. Outlining the purpose of the mass meeting, he flung an arm at the Republic plant, a third of a mile down the road. Twenty-five thousand men were on strike; their purpose was to picket peacefully, to win a decent raise in wages, so that they might exist like human beings. But there had been constant, brutal provocation by the police. Well, they were gathered here, as was their constitutional right, to protest that interference.

Dozens of strikers had been arrested, beaten, waylaid; strikers' property, as for example a sound truck, had been smashed and destroyed. Even women had been beaten, dragged off to jail, treated obscenely. The National Labor Relations Act guaranteed them their rights; today they were going to demonstrate in support of those rights.

Other speakers backed up Weber. When the audience cheered some point, the children present gurgled with delight and clapped their hands. As soon as the meeting had finished, the strikers, wives, children too, began to form their picket line. After all, this was Memorial Day; the thing took on a parade air. Some of the strikers had made their own placards; also, a whole forest of them appeared from inside the Union Hall, made by committees. The slogans were simple and direct. "REPUBLIC STEEL VIOLATES LABOR DISPUTES ACT." "WIN WITH THE C.I.O." "NO FASCISM IN AMERICA." "REPUBLIC STEEL SHALL SIGN A UNION CONTRACT." The signs were handed out, many of them to boys and girls who carried them proudly. At the head of the column that was forming, two men took their place with American flags. The news reporters, who had come up by car only a short while before, were hopping about now, snapping everything. For some reason that has never been analyzed, news photographers and strikers get along very well, even when the photographers come from McCormick's Chicago *Tribune*. Now there was a lot of good-natured give-and-take. When the column began to march, down the road from Sam's Place first, and then across the prairie toward the Republic Steel plant, the news photographers moved with it, some walking, some by car. This fact later turned into a vital part of American labor history; the equivalent would be a battalion of photographers leading a battalion of troops into battle.

2.

REPUBLIC STEEL stood abrupt out of the flat prairie. Snakelike, the line of pickets crossed the meadowland, singing at first: "Solidarity forever! The union makes us strong," but then the song died, as the sundrenched plain turned ominous, as five hundred blue-coated policemen took up stations between the strikers and the plant. The strikers' march slowed, but they came on. The police ranks closed and tightened. It brought to mind how other Americans had faced the uniformed force of so-called law and order so long ago on Lexington Green in 1775; but whereas then the redcoat leader had said, "Disperse, you rebel bastards!" to armed minutemen, now it was to unarmed men and women and children that a police captain said, "You dirty sons of bitches, this is as far as you go!"

Once there was an illusion somewhere that the police were gentle souls who helped lost children, but a striker put it afterwards: "A cop is a cop, that's all. He's got no soul and no heart for a guy who works for a living. They learned us good."

About two hundred and fifty yards from the plant, the police closed in on the strikers. Billies and clubs were out already, prodding, striking, nightsticks edging into women's breasts and groins. But the cops were also somewhat afraid, and they began to jerk guns out of holsters.

"Stand fast! Stand fast!" the line leaders cried. "We got our rights! We got our legal rights to picket!"

The cops said, "You got no rights. You red bastards, you got no rights."

Even if a modern man's a steelworker, with muscles as close to iron bands as human flesh gets, a pistol equalizes him with a fat-bellied weakling—and more than equalizes. Grenades began to sail now; tear gas settled like an ugly cloud. Children suddenly cried with panic, and the whole picket line gave back, men stumbling, cursing, gasping for breath. Here and there a cop tore out his pistol and began to fire;

it was pop, pop, pop at first, like toy favors at some horrible party, and then, as the strikers broke under the gunfire and began to run, the contagion of killing ran like fire through the police.

They began to shoot in volleys at these unarmed men and women and children who could not strike back or fight back. The cops squealed with excitement. They ran after fleeing pickets, pressed revolvers to their backs, shot them down, and then continued to shoot as the victims lay on their faces, retching blood. When a woman tripped and fell, four cops gathered above her, smashing her flesh and bones and face.

And so it went, on and on, until seven were dead and more than a hundred wounded. And the field a bloodstained field of battle. World War veterans there said that never in France had they seen anything like this.

Now, of course, this brief account might be passed off as a complete exaggeration, one-sided and so forth. It might be said, as the Chicago *Tribune* said the next day, that this was the doing of reds who were plotting to take over the plant, and the police had only done their duty.

But, as we noted before, the photographers were on the spot, and everything I have described here and a good deal more of the same was taken down with both newsreel cameras and still cameras. The stills and the moving pictures were placed on exhibit during the hearing on Republic Steel, held by the Subcommittee of the Committee on Education and Labor, United States Senate; and I recommend to the special attention of anyone interested in checking this bit of labor history Exhibit 1418, Exhibit 1414, Exhibit 1351, and the morbid chart of gunshot wounds—in the back—known as Exhibit 1463.

That, in brief, is a summary of what happened in Chicago on Memorial Day of 1937. These events, which came to be known as the Memorial Day Massacre, shook the nation as nothing else had since the Haymarket Affair of the 1880's. Later, the Senate Committee's investigation highlighted them, and brought home to the American people the full savagery of the police and the men who ran Republic Steel. But then the war washed the memory out for a time, and to understand fully today what happened then in Chicago, certain other facts must be noted.

3.

IT REQUIRES, to begin, a brief review of the time between the two wars, in connection with the labor movement. We might remark that the immediate aftermath of the first World War saw the notorious Palmer raids—ostensibly conducted by the government, through Attorney General Palmer, against the infant Communist movement of the time, but actually a full-fledged offensive against all militant labor leaders. It drove the Communists underground; it waged bitter warfare against the I.W.W.; and it gave management freedom to dive headlong into the depression of the early twenties.

The battle cry of the I.W.W. (International Workers of the World), perhaps the most militant and native of all our labor movements, had been *industrial unionism,* as opposed to the narrow *craft unionism* of the American Federation of Labor. Craft unionism takes a specific craft as a line cutting through many industries and organizes it: for instance, the carpenters, one of the old A. F. of L. Unions, has members in over a hundred industries. Thus, a plant which employs a hundred thousand men, of whom one hundred are carpenters, would have those few carpenters as members of a separate union—and so with many of the other crafts down the line.

There were many effects of this kind of organization. For one thing, it had to concentrate on the skilled trades to have any kind of stability: floor-sweepers were too easily replaced to ever form into such a craft union; for another, it made a successful strike most difficult, since even if the hundred carpenters walked out, in most cases the plant could continue to operate. It left the bulk of the working class unorganized— and as long as it remained the only form of unionism, the American working class was prevented from taking any real mass steps forward.

The I.W.W.'s slogan was: "One big industrial union." They set out to organize whole industries into single unions embracing all crafts within those industries. And before World War I, in lumbering and in mining in western America, they were remarkably successful.

The early twenties marked savage raids against these organizers and as we climbed out of the depression into the shaky prosperity that lasted until 1929, labor made very few gains. Industrial unionism fought an erratic battle, here and there, but gained no very firm foothold.

It was not until the great depression of the thirties wiped out the puffball prosperity of the twenties that industrial unionism began to make itself felt as a really important factor in American life. It is an old saying, and a very true one, that depression benefits no one. Labor and capital both suffer; but labor's suffering is more acute, more personal, and more tragic. In times of depression, labor faces the very essential matter of staying alive, and starvation and cold are both good teachers. Labor learned basic lessons in the early thirties; and as American business slowly took a turn upwards, labor girded itself for a struggle for a decent level of subsistence and for an organization that really represented it. Out of that need and that consciousness arose the Committee for Industrial Organization, headed, in the steel industry, by Philip Murray, who was elected chairman of the Steel Workers Organizing Committee.

Steel is the industry of industries, the most basic of all industries. In modern times, steel is the barometer of a nation's freedom; without steel industries, a nation is dependent on other nations. Steel is also a barometer of a nation's strength; all other modern industries pyramid up on the base of steel. When depression hits a nation, steel is the first to suffer; when the wheels start to move again, nothing can be started without steel.

Steel, also, has the longest tradition of both violence and organization of any American industry. The oldest American union of any strength and importance was William Sylvus's National Iron Molders Union.

And over a period of almost a hundred years, the record of labor's struggle in the steel industry reads like front-line reporting from a battlefield. It takes strong men to make steel, and their very work is constant close contact with mechanical violence. But it should be recorded that any careful study of the situation will prove that in almost all cases, the violence came originally from management, either by instigation or by provocation—not from organized labor. This statement will be further demonstrated.

Now let us look at the situation of steel after the worst part of the depression. Taking United States Steel as an example, we find that by

1935 the firm was well on the way over the hump, with a net profit of $6,106,488. Wheels had begun to turn again in America, and the next year's profit took an enormous jump upwards, a net of $55,501,787 in 1936. Then the graph rose even more sharply, and in the first three months of 1937 the company recorded a net profit of $28,561,533.

This was "Big Steel." Republic, a light steel concern, was a part of what was known as "Little Steel," and while the profits there were smaller—$4,000,000 in 1935 and $9,500,000 in 1936—they were part of the upward spiral.

It was within this framework of hot furnaces and mounting profits that the C.I.O. began to organize. In 1936 the C.I.O. began to make real progress in organizing the steel industry, and by the middle of 1937 half a million steelworkers had joined the union. Over 750 union lodges were formed, and by now most of the steel manufacturers realized that it was a most destructive kind of insanity to fight organization. Again, by June, 1937, some 125 companies had signed union contracts. Among these firms, which employed 310,000 workers, were Carnegie-Illinois and several other subsidiaries of U. S. Steel.

But the big independents, the so-called "Little Steel" combine, still held out. Let us name them, as they stood on that Memorial Day of 1937. There was Tom Girdler's Republic Steel, employing 53,000 workers. There was Bethlehem Steel, employing 82,000 workers. There was Youngstown Sheet and Tube Company, which employed 27,000 workers. Then there were the smaller firms, National Steel, American Rolling Mills, and Inland Steel. All together, these firms employed almost 200,000 workers and they accounted for almost 40 per cent of the steel produced in America.

They were lined up for a knock-down, drag-out fight, no quarter asked, no quarter given. Tom Girdler was granted nominal leadership; a latter-day "robber baron," to use Matthew Josephson's phrase, he was a natural for such a position, and we shall see later how his tactics led to the Memorial Day Massacre.

But he did not introduce the concept of violence; it was not necessary for him to do so. As far back as 1933, the steel companies were arming themselves for the coming struggle. For example, the following order was shipped to Bethlehem Steel. The invoice, entered on the books of Federal Laboratories and signed by A. G. Bergman, is dated September 30, 1933:

12 blast type billies
100 blast type billies, cartridges
24 Jumbo CN grenades lot No. X820
24 military bouchons
48 1½″ cal. projectile shells (CN)
24 1½″ cal. short range shells (CN)
4 1½″ cal. riot guns, style 201 sr. No. 337, 386, 390, 403
4 riot gun cases

That makes for quite a sizable armament, but Youngstown Sheet and Tube went in for more and deadlier protection against unarmed strikers and their dangerous wives and children. On June 6, 1934, this firm was billed for the following order:

10 1½″ cal. riot guns 201, $60 ea.
10 riot gun cases 211, $7.50 ea.
60 1½″ cal. long range projectiles, $7.50 ea.
60 1½″ cal. short range projectiles, $4.50 ea.
60 M-39 billies std. barrel no disc, $22.50 ea.
600 M-39 billy cartridges, $1.50 ea.
200 grenades 106M, 10% disc., $12 ea.

These are only two examples of widespread gun-toting by the steel companies. Nor were these the only techniques they used. They hired spies and special agents. They organized "goon squads," composed of thugs, professional gangsters, and assorted degenerates. They bribed police chiefs and sheriffs. And under their natural leader, Tom Girdler, they set themselves for violence.

That was part of the background to the Memorial Day Massacre. Another part was Tom Girdler himself, and it is worth while to look into that gentleman's history.

4.

MATTHEW JOSEPHSON's fine book, *The Robber Barons*, should be read as background to any study of Tom Girdler. Girdler is a latter-day

Morgan, a Jim Fisk, a John D. Rockefeller—but operating at a time when the tactics of these financial pirates were supposed to be outdated and hopeless. Perhaps in some new edition of Josephson's book, Girdler will be included, along with a few other of his worthy contemporaries, as a sort of appendix.

Girdler is a farm boy, and he likes to think of himself as a part and a little more than a part of the good old log-cabin tradition. He was fond of saying, in those days of steel trouble, that he liked a good rough-and-tumble fight; and he talked tough and tried to look and act tough. But his toughness was the toughness of the rear-echelon general, the armchair two-gun man. It was never his lot to face even a small reflection of the violence he created.

In the 1920's, Cyrus Eaton, a Middle-Western manipulator, formed Republic out of four small steel companies. Eaton, too, had dreams of becoming an Andrew Carnegie; but his skill did not measure up to his ambition. He tangled with a very hard-boiled customer, Bethlehem Steel, and in the ensuing struggle Republic's shares fell from 80 to 2. At that time, Girdler was making a very local name for himself in Jones and Laughlin Steel; Eaton pulled him out, promised him an arm and a leg, and told him to save Republic. In that case, anyway, Eaton's judgment was not at fault, for not only did Tom Girdler save Republic: he turned it into the most up-and-coming steel company in the land— and in doing so, he took just a little more than the arm and the leg; he eased Eaton entirely out of the picture.

There is no doubting that Girdler made the most of what he stepped into. Republic was light steel, specializing in steel for furniture, boilers, automobiles, light trains, various types of metal containers. Nor could this kind of production be changed; the plants, too, were specialized. Reluctantly, Girdler worked with what he had. His own fancy was for heavy stuff, girders, plates for warships—the kind of work Bethlehem did. He looked to a future alliance with Bethlehem, but in the meantime he worked with what he had. He hired scientists and picked their brains in the traditional fashion. He forced the development of more and better alloys, until his stainless steel had gained a national reputation.

The plants were old and inefficient, so he began to replace them.

Cyclical depression usually winds up with a replacement of fixed capital which has become outdated, and the fact that Girdler's action was being duplicated all over the nation in the middle thirties set at least a part of the wheels of industry in motion. At this point, Girdler was not too interested in profits; profits could be assured for a later period if he was successful in replacement and in mergers.

He worked for control of Republic by chasing down small holdings of shares wherever he could locate them. He begged proxies. Because his Ohio plants were a good distance from the ore deposits of Minnesota, he planned and executed a merger with Corrigan-McKinney of Cleveland. When this went through, he had a lake port to operate from, and a modern steel plant to add to his growing empire. For four years he worked to get proxies and control, until at last he was sitting firmly in the driver's seat, with plant after plant coming into the growing orbit of Republic. He went after Truscon Steel, the largest fabricator of building-shapes, doors, lockers, and window frames in the Middle West, effected a merger, and built up Truscon until it was the largest plant of its kind in the world. All this cost money, and from 1930 to 1935 Republic lost somewhere around $30,000,000. This did not affect Girdler; he drew his income from his own huge salary. He did not own the combine; he merely had control. No single stockholder held more than 6 per cent of the total stock, but by 1935 Girdler was so firmly in the saddle that no one could challenge his rule—and since the financial-industrial empire was growing, in spite of some 2,000,000 additional shares of watered stock, no stockholder or group of stockholders made serious efforts to challenge or unseat him.

For all of his drive and his large talk about free enterprise, Girdler demonstrated in action that he not only did not believe in what American business calls "free enterprise," but that he personally was working night and day to destroy it in the steel industry. His tactics were toward monopoly. He interlocked with Youngstown Sheet and Tube; he interlocked with Jones and Laughlin. He thought and talked combine—and he operated in that direction with a ruthlessness that bowled over his competitors like tenpins.

And when it came to dealing with his 50,000 workers, he chose the same tactics of ruthlessness and direct aggression.

He liked to refer to himself as a worker, but that was an out-and-out fiction; from his very beginnings in the industry, he had been an ally of management, and then, very soon, he became a part of management.

He entered the industry as a salesman for Buffalo Forge. Then he was employed by the Oliver Iron and Steel Company. He was an assistant superintendent with Colorado Fuel and Iron Company, and he held similar jobs elsewhere. But always it was over labor or apart from labor. It was Tom Girdler getting ahead and using his brains in the best Horatio Alger tradition, while all around him heavy-set, heavy-muscled men by the thousands worked long hours to turn the ore into metal and to shape it, forge it, tool it. One would surmise from his later actions that he had never held anything but contempt for those who worked with their hands.

He was schooled well for the battles of 1937. Jones and Laughlin's Aliquippa Works was known as the "Siberia of America." Their company town was a place where the few brave union organizers who dared to enter faced death, literally, tar and feathers, or some of the more gruesome and less printable fates that goon squads specialize in. The town was also called "Little Hell," a most descriptive name.

Apparently, it was a place that suited Girdler excellently, for in a space of four years he rose from an assistant to president. And after that, he continued to climb steadily on the irreproachable ladder of success. As he climbed, his technique of dealing with the men he employed became progressively more ruthless. When the Memorial Day slaughter occurred, he was earning $130,000 a year. One might consider his statement that he would go back to hoeing potatoes before he bargained collectively with his employees as a piece of not too original verbiage. At the same time, he never gave any indication that the dead men and wounded women and children strewn over the Chicago prairie disturbed either his sleep or his equanimity.

5.

YET it would give a very false picture of the industrial situation in the second half of the third decade to single out Tom Girdler as industry's bad boy. Nor could the dreadful occurrence of Memorial Day be understood from that point of view. From that point of view alone, the Chicago incident becomes an isolated instance of one man's callousness—but it was by no means such an isolated instance.

Half a century before, the Haymarket Affair, also in Chicago, became the labor *cause célèbre* of the nation and the world. The four labor leaders who were then framed and put to death in Chicago became martyrs or devils, according to the reaction of one class or another. But they could not have been so framed and murdered had there not been complete accord on the part of the most powerful forces in American finance. The same accord operated in the case of Girdler and the Chicago bloodshed.

Girdler was the front, the testing ground, the trial balloon of the most reactionary forces in American capitalism. This is not a matter for speculation. Keen economic observers of the time analyzed the situation of Republic Steel in terms of the shareholders as well as the Wall Street moguls.

I pointed out before that Girdler never owned even a tiny fraction of Republic's stock. The big stockholders in Republic—and among them were some of the most powerful finance blocks in America— willingly allowed him to climb into the saddle and, once there, made no effort to unseat him. It should be historically noted that the Chicago dead did not arouse either the ire or the disgust of these same shareholders. Their attitude was that of smiling behind their palms, and quietly letting Girdler bear the brunt of the storm. Also, Girdler all during that period was responsible to a board of directors. This board represented, in its composition, far-reaching and important interests; but at no point is there any record of their reprimanding Girdler or disagreeing with his action. Other factors can be cited. A handful of key men in Wall Street could have picked up their phones, called Girdler, and called a quick halt to the bloody, senseless battle with labor which he was promoting; they did not, and there is every reason to believe that they silently backed Girdler in his policy.

Following this line of thought, it is interesting to observe the general press reaction to the Memorial Day Massacre. Although brief, the description of events on that day given earlier in this account makes a fairly good picture of what happened in the meadows outside of Re-

public. Further documentation, hundreds of pages of detailed testimony, is included in the Senate Report, S. Res. 266, 74th Congress,
Part 14, U.S. Government Printing Office, 1937. Exhibits presented
also run into the hundreds. The testimony is explicit; it goes into
minutiae, as may be gathered from the following extract, page 4939.
John William Lotito, one of the strikers, is being examined by Senator
La Follette:

Senator La Follette: All right. Did you see Captain Mooney while you stood
there in front of the police?

Mr. Lotito: I think Captain Mooney was standing on the side where the other
flag was—that is, to my left.

Senator La Follette: Did you see what he was doing?

Mr. Lotito: Well, he had his hands up like this here. He was talking to the
strikers. His lips were moving anyway. I couldn't hear what he was saying.

Senator La Follette: You could not hear what he was saying?

Mr. Lotito: No.

Senator La Follette: About how long would you say you stood there?

Mr. Lotito: Oh, maybe five minutes.

Senator La Follette: All right. Now, tell me exactly, from your own knowledge, what happened at the end of this five-minute period.

Mr. Lotito: At the end of the five-minute period? Well, I was talking to this
policeman there, and the first thing I knew I got clubbed, while I was talking
to him.

Senator La Follette: And then what happened?

Mr. Lotito: I got clubbed and I went down, and my flag fell down, and I
went to pick up the flag again, to get up, and I got clubbed the second time.
I was like a top, you know, spinning. I was dizzy. So I put my hand to my
head, and there was blood all over. I started to crawl away, and half running
and half crawling, and I didn't know what I was doing, to tell you the truth.

After I got up, why there was shots, and everything I heard, I didn't know which way to run. Anyway, I retreated back that way.

Senator La Follette: You mean back toward Sam's Place?

Mr. Lotito: And then I got shot in the leg.

Senator La Follette: How far away were you from the place where you had been standing talking to the police when you were shot in the leg, would you say?

Mr. Lotito: Oh, I got quite a ways from there, all right.

Senator La Follette: Can you approximate how far?

Mr. Lotito: Maybe 30 or 40 yards away I got.

This is just a page of testimony, chosen at random; there are far more harrowing details that might be listed; but the point is this: all the details necessary are there. They are reports of thousands of eye-witnesses who saw what happened. Newspaper reporters on the scene saw what happened. And if that were not enough, in addition to the still photographers, the Paramount News people took down a detailed photographic record of the whole affair.

In other words, the newspapers knew the facts of the case. They could not plead ignorance, even the carefully conditioned ignorance which allows them to interpret events precisely as they please. With all that, they too acted, with very few exceptions, very much as if they were part of the combine behind Tom Girdler. They lied about what had occurred outside the Republic Steel plant. They lied hugely and in unison, although they departed from the truth on many different levels.

The Chicago *Tribune,* for example, was overt and completely un-abashed. It described the men and women and children who composed the picket line—none of whom were ever proved to possess a firearm during the march—as "lusting for blood." It raised a red scare, which scare was sedulously promoted by the Hearst and the McCormick interests and their fellow hatemongers. The more conservative journals doubted that the police had indulged in provocation and pointed out that force was a necessary ingredient to the preservation of law and order. One looked in vain in such papers as the New York *Times* and New York *Herald Tribune* for editorials reproaching Tom Girdler, or his private police, in even the mildest terms. No criminal action was even taken to seek justice for the men who had died in Chicago. Only the few independent newspapers and the labor press kept the issue alive and fought for justice—and there too is a remarkable parallel to what happened before in the Haymarket Affair.

6.

YOU MAY WONDER how it was that you do not recall seeing the newsreel which so graphically describes all that happened, and which was shown at the La Follette investigation. The following editorial from the *New Masses* of June 29, 1937, sheds a good deal of light on that:

The reason given by Paramount News for suppressing its newsreel of the Chicago Memorial Day steel-strike massacre is an obvious sham. Audiences trained on the Hollywood school of gangster films are not likely to stage a "riotous demonstration" in the theater upon seeing cops beating people into insensibility, and worse. Against whom would the riot be directed anyway? The Board of Directors of Republic Steel and the Chicago municipal authorities are hardly likely to be found in the immediate vicinity.

The real reason behind the film suppression is its decisive evidence that virtually every newspaper in the country lied, and continues to lie, about the responsibility for violence in the strike areas. The myth that the steel strikers have resorted to violence to gain their just ends is now the basis for the whole campaign of slander and misrepresentation against them. That is why Tom Girdler of Republic Steel refuses to confer with the Steel Workers Organizing Committee, and that is why 95 per cent of the press carries on a publicity pogrom against the strikers.

Even after the St. Louis *Post Dispatch* performed a genuine service to the American people in breaking the story of the film (for which, though it is Pulitzer owned, it is very unlikely to get the Pulitzer award), the venal press still continued to blast away at the strikers with the same old legend. Not a comma has been changed in the editorials which, day after day, have defended the steel tycoons on the ground that there can be no compromise with labor violence.

And all this time, the film record exists—and has been described—which would enable the public to make up its own mind on this very crucial point!

At this point, with the added emphasis of the above editorial, we begin to have a very different picture of the Memorial Day Massacre than that which popularly surrounds it. Not that Tom Girdler's responsibility is lessened, not that the brutality of his agents is mitigated one iota, not that the Chicago police bear any less the responsibility for murder; but the incident in whole becomes broader and more inclusive. We find that far from being an isolated case of managerial violence, it was a focal point for the theory and the technique of reactionary capitalism in the organizational struggles of the thirties. It was a test case; it was symptomatic. Steel is, as was said, the industry of industries, and in 1937 steel was chosen by the entrenched forces of the open shop as the battleground for the open shop—against industrial unionism.

7.

IT IS the difficult and tedious task of the labor historian to document every statement he makes. There is a good reason for this, of course; the body of knowledge (press, magazines, most books, etc.) presented to the public, both currently and contemporaneously to the times of which he writes, contradicts almost every premise and almost every fact which he brings forth. Only the labor press, which has a limited readership compared to the commercial press, bears him out. This is not the case with other historians. For example, one could start a story about Lincoln with the accepted premise that he was a great and good man; in the case of Eugene Debs, one would first have to document his actions and prove his intentions.

In connection with that, the charge that labor promotes almost all industrial violence cannot be dismissed as a lie; it must be proved to be a lie—and once proved, this small account of the Memorial Day Massacre can be closed. I have shown some of the facts in the arms orders of the steel companies. After our account of what happened in Chicago, it might do to cite the New York *Times* headline for May 31, 1937:

4 Killed, 84 Hurt As Strikers Fight Police In Chicago. Steel Mob Halted.

Technically, that is not a lie. Only four men had died then; eventually five more succumbed from wounds. If you called the picket line a mob, then there is no doubt but that it was halted—although some might prefer the word "slaughtered." And some of the strikers did fight for their lives against the police. But this is pettifogging; the sense and intent of the headline, which very much set the pattern for nonsensational headlines all over the country, is more than apparent for anyone.

Let's go on with the record. Monroe, Michigan—ten days after Chicago. There is a Republic plant which employs about 1,350 persons. The strike is called; the workers go out, and for two weeks picket lines are maintained in a disciplined fashion. There is absolutely no disorder.

Then, suddenly, there appears on the scene what we know familiarly as "the bloodthirsty mob of strikers," and the hospital wards are full, and the damage is reckoned in lives as well as thousands of dollars. But the records show that after due deliberation and planning, Police Chief Jesse Fisher swore in enough special police to form a small army —at an expense of $9,000 to the little town. Leonidas McDonald, a Negro C.I.O. organizer, was attacked by a mob and severely beaten. This incident, which members of the mob assured reporters was carefully planned, touched off the riot. Then Chief Fisher ordered his men to attack the picket line. They went to work with tear-gas shells and grenades. The next day, the hospital wards were full, but Chief Fisher, bursting with pride, set about organizing a shotgun brigade of six hundred men.

It had worked in Chicago. Why not Monroe?

Newspapers told us that in Beaver Falls, Pennsylvania, the same pattern of violence was being inaugurated by strikers of the Moltrop Steel Products Company. But George Mike was not a picket and not a striker. He was a crippled war veteran, who stood on a corner in Beaver Falls, selling tickets to a C.I.O. dance. A deputy sheriff leveled his gas gun at him and fired. The shell smashed his skull, and he died the next day.

Our newspapers, during the same weeks, described the frightful riot provoked in Youngstown by—not the strikers, but their wives. Women too can be a frightful menace to society, if you only see them in the proper perspective. Many of these women carried their small children on this particular day, and no doubt that added to their potential menace. They were coming home from a meeting of the Ladies' Auxiliary, and a few of them paused to rest on an embankment that was a part of Republic's property. The deputies on guard ordered them off. The women and children responded too slowly, and the deputies helped them along with gas shells. As the women fled, their screams brought men to the scene, and when the men appeared, the deputies switched to repeating rifles.

Result: two dead, thirty injured.

Massillon, July 11, and strikers holding a meeting outside C.I.O. headquarters. Again, the firing starts, and in a little while there are three dead strikers and five more on their way to the hospital. Then C.I.O. headquarters is surrounded, and for an hour lead is poured into the building. And in the building, there is *not one* firearm.

But the newspapers said, the next day: "STRIKING MOB ATTACKS MASSILLON POLICE." That was a Middle-Western paper, but most others bore variations of the same.

This sort of record could be continued indefinitely. One labor historian estimates that casualties suffered by the working class in organizational struggles outnumber total casualties suffered by United States Armed Forces in all of this country's wars up to World War II. Though the violence of Tom Girdler's Republic Steel was sharp and dramatic, it could be matched by the violence of any one of a hundred other corporations, over a period of half a century.

8.

SOME OF THE BACKGROUND to the Memorial Day Massacre has been presented here. It was shown that the incident itself was both a part and a focal point in the pattern of closed-shop violence. The strange, wild, tragic, and disordered years of the third decade of the twentieth century, here in America, were not unproductive. Out of depression and despair came the greatest organization of labor this country has ever known—the industrial unionism of the C.I.O. Out of the broad united front against fascism, led by the C.I.O. and other organizations, came the strength and desire to resist Hitlerite Germany and to carry the world through its sharpest crisis.

The America of today is not and cannot ever be the America of a decade ago. History does not stage repeat performances. It is very likely that there will be violence in connection with future strikes; but the American people have learned a good deal. And if such an incident as that in Chicago occurs again, it is wholly possible that those responsible will have to face the anger of millions instead of thousands.

The Man on the Ledge

BY JOEL SAYRE

Joel Sayre has been a connoisseur of the more lively aspects of American life for a number of years. His first book, *Rackety-Rax* (1932), was a fantasy about a mob of racketeers who went into college football and really made it pay. Critics hailed it as one of the most effective satires on the age of jazz and gin. Mr. Sayre was a reporter for City Editor Stanley Walker on the New York *Herald Tribune,* later wrote movie scripts in Hollywood, and worked in the radio department of Time, Inc. During the war he was a correspondent for the *New Yorker.* His other books are *Hizzoner the Mayor, Persian Gulf Command,* and *The House Without a Roof.*

☼ 1.

IT WAS HOT and cloudy in New York City on the morning of Thursday, July 26, 1938. Patrolman Charles V. Glasco, of the Traffic Division's Summons Squad, began his tour of duty at 8 A.M., his duty being to serve summonses on persons who had been guilty of traffic violations. An amiable, rather rotund man of better than average height, with sharp brown eyes and black hair almost gone on top, Glasco, aged thirty-five, had been in the Police Department for fourteen years and was highly regarded by the other members of Traffic C, the unit he was attached to, as a teller of dialect stories. Glasco was very proud of his Irish ancestry and very sensitive to his surname's being mistaken for a non-Irish one. Whenever this mistake was made in his presence, he would do a brief slow burn and then produce his membership card in the Ancient Order of Hibernians, which he always carried for just such emergencies. "If the name was Costello, nobody'd ever question it for a second," he used to remark somewhat bitterly on these occasions.

Having begun his tour of duty at 8 A.M., Glasco was due to finish it at 4 P.M. When he had left his home at Woodhaven in the Borough of Queens, his wife, Margaret, had told him that for dinner that night there would be liver and bacon, one of his favorite dishes. Glasco spent the morning serving summonses around the West Side of Manhattan. He was not feeling too spry: his sacroiliac had been paining him lately, and his back was strapped with adhesive tape. On making his routine telephone check-in with his office at noon from a street corner call-box, he was ordered to report at once to Sergeant Murphy at Fifth Avenue and Fifty-fifth Street and lend a hand in a big traffic tie-up there.

As Glasco approached Fifth Avenue and Fifty-fifth Street, which is in a district devoted mostly to luxury shops and expensive hotels, he thought that there must be a fire somewhere in the immediate neighborhood, for, in addition to staring crowds gathered on the sidewalks, he saw two hook-and-ladder trucks, a rescue truck from the police Emergency Division, three police radio cars, and an ambulance. The traffic tie-up at the intersection was indeed big. Glasco soon found Sergeant Murphy, who was standing on the south steps of the Fifth Avenue Presbyterian Church at the intersection's northwest corner, and reported to him. The sergeant was mopping his brow. "Take a look up there," he said, pointing at the Hotel Gotham, directly across Fifty-fifth Street.

The Gotham's roof rises 202 feet above the sidewalk. On a façade ledge four floors below the roof, Glasco saw the hatless, coatless figure of a man standing outside an open window. He was leaning with his back against the edge of an oval architectural ornament of floral design, about a yard wide and almost shoulder high, that protruded from the building's wall. The man was facing westward, toward Sixth Avenue. Immediately to the east of this ornament, in the direction of Fifth Avenue, was another open window, and suddenly through it appeared the blond head of a woman, who lay with her right side resting on the sill and beckoned to the standing man with her left arm. At her appearance the man whirled eastward in her direction, then crouched swiftly, holding on to the architectural ornament with one hand and raising his other arm to his head, as though to ward off a blow.

"That'd be his sister, I guess," the sergeant said. "He's been on that ledge about half an hour now, come out around eleven-forty. I wish the hell they'd get him in before he louses up all the traffic on Manhattan Island."

"Well, if they don't jump the first hour, they never jump," Glasco said. "At least that's what I've heard many a time from Emergency Division guys that spent years working on ledge-walkers. Why don't they grab him?"

"Can't get at him. He threatens to jump every time a cop comes near that window."

"I'd get at him," Glasco said. The sergeant lowered his gaze and stared. "I'd stop being a cop for a while. I'd get at him."

The sergeant thought it over. "Well, maybe you would, at that. You always was a pretty good actor. It's worth trying anyhow. Go on up to room 1714 and tell the lieutenant I sent you. See if you can get that poor loopy in off of that ledge, Charlie. They tell me he's only a kid. Con him in off of that ledge, and maybe we can have a little peace down here."

2.

THE MAN on the ledge was John William Warde, aged twenty-six, who lived with his parents at Southampton, Long Island. His father, John A. Warde, was an employee of the American Railway Express Company in Southampton, which has a population of about four thousand and is best known as a summer resort for the rich. Young Warde had been graduated from high school just in time for the Great Depression. He was a quiet, slender, good-looking boy with thick, curly, black hair. He was fond of sports, music, and poetry. In high school he had had the reputation of being moody. For some years he was a clerk in a local bank, where he was known as an intelligent worker though a bit peculiar at times. In July, 1937, John tried to kill himself with a knife. After he had recovered from his wounds, he was committed to the State Hospital at Central Islip, Long Island, for observation. The following November he was released from the institution with a note on his discharge papers, "The patient's manic-depressive psychosis seems to have arrested itself."

Mr. and Mrs. Patrick A. Valentine, Jr., a kind-hearted couple in their mid-thirties who had spent many summers in Southampton and were well acquainted with the Warde family, employed John after his discharge from the hospital as a companion to their two small children and as a sort of casual chauffeur and handy man. It was their hope that a job in pleasant surroundings and under friendly conditions might help him conquer his depression and recover his self-confidence. The Valentines were people of wealth. Mr. Valentine's father, Patrick A. Valentine, Sr., came to this country from Scotland as a young man, went to work for the Chicago packing firm of Armour and Company, rose to be its financial director, and married the widow of Philip D. Armour, Jr. In 1910 he paid a steel baron half a million dollars for a mansion off Fifth Avenue and moved his family to New York. He died in 1916. Patrick Valentine, Jr., married a first cousin of his, Miss May Valentine. Their summer place at Southampton was called Valmay. Mr. Valentine was head of the Clara Laughlin Travel Service, named after the indefatigable Midwestern maiden lady whose series of guidebooks, their titles beginning with the words, "So You're Going to—" (Paris, London, Germany, etc.), had become almost standard equipment for American tourists.

Eight days before he appeared on the ledge at the Gotham, John Warde had driven to a bridge at Hampton Bays, near Southampton, in his father's car, parked it, walked to the middle of the bridge, and stood there gazing down at the water. His manner and actions had aroused the suspicions of a bridge tender, who chased him off the bridge, took the license number of his car as he drove away, and informed the police. The police found John at his home, but as no actual suicide attempt had been made, no official action was taken beyond his being given a "talking to." His family was, of course, alarmed and told the Valentines. Thinking that a change of scene might help, the Valentines took John on a week-end trip to Chicago. John's twenty-two-year-old married sister, Katherine, of whom he was fond, accompanied them. In Chicago John swam in Lake Michigan, saw the Cubs, his favorite ball club, and attended a symphony concert in Grant Park Stadium. Although the Valentines and Katherine strove to make things as pleasant for him as they could, their efforts didn't seem to cheer him up much.

They returned to New York on Tuesday morning at about ten o'clock and went to the suite at the Gotham which the Valentines had been using as their city residence for about a year. Mrs. Valentine phoned Southampton and inquired about the children. Mr. Valentine departed for his office at the travel agency, which was situated a few blocks from the hotel, leaving John with the two women, who chatted about the heat and the things that each had to do that day. Katherine mentioned that she was going to phone a doctor and make an appointment for John to see him. "No!" John said. "All right, all right, keep your hair on," Katherine replied and changed the subject. John took off his coat, folded it carefully, and laid it over the back of an armchair; then he tucked the ends of his blue necktie inside his shirt. He was wearing neatly pressed gray flannel trousers, and his black shoes had a high shine on them. John really did look nice, Katherine reflected; he had always been fastidious about his appearance, poor darling. Several menus were slid under the door. The women examined them and commenced discussing what to have for lunch. Room service was rung, food orders were given.

There were no hard words, there was no quarrel. John merely said, "I'm going out the window," in a quiet voice and did so before Katherine or Mrs. Valentine could say or do anything about it. Katherine rushed to the phone and began screaming at the switchboard operator. Mrs. Valentine ran to the window, then turned and cried, "No, no, he's here, Katherine, here on the ledge. He's all right." Katherine went to the window and looked at her brother, then she looked down. The ledge on which he was standing is eighteen inches wide and 160 feet above the street. She looked at John again, started to speak to him, and fainted.

3.

THE MAN on the ledge was noticed almost immediately by pedestrians, who began forming in groups on the sidewalks and staring up at him. A policeman directing traffic at Fifth Avenue and Fifty-fifth Street left his post and hurried into the hotel. When he leaned out of the window of 1714 he shouted at John, "Hey, you, come in here! What are you doing out there, anyway?" John was backed away from the window, to the east of it, leaning against the architectural ornament. The balls of his feet were poised on the edge of the ledge, like those of a swimmer about to plunge into a pool. "Don't you come near me or I'll jump," he said to the policeman. There was a look in his eyes that made the policeman withdraw from the window at once and telephone Headquarters and the Fire Department. Soon the hook-and-ladder trucks, the rescue squad, the ambulance, and sixty men under an inspector arrived.

The Police and Fire Departments have many techniques for seizing a person threatening suicide, most of them based on his being contacted before he sees his rescuers; but the position John had taken made this impossible. He was standing too far out on the ledge to be touched, much less seized, from the window of 1714; and the window of 1716, directly to the east, was still farther away. Lieutenant William Klotzbach, a lariat and rope expert from the Emergency Division, went to the window directly above John on the eighteenth floor, but another protruding ledge there made the lassoing of him out of the question. The cornice of the hotel roof hung out so far that lowering a bosun's chair from it four floors could not have been accomplished without John's seeing the chair long before it got to him. He was too high to be reached by the fire ladders; the canvas life-net, with the red circle painted in its center, which the fireman had spread on the sidewalk ready to snatch up, would not hold a body falling more than six or seven stories. Had there been a building of approximately equal height opposite the Gotham, perhaps some kind of rescue contrivance might have been rigged from it. But there was only the Fifth Avenue Presbyterian Church with its comparatively low roof.

There was just one course for the police to follow, and that was to wait John out. At least once and probably twice before within the past year this boy had tried to end his life; now he could snap the thread of it at will by merely shifting his balance an inch or two. Also, it seemed clear that a policeman in uniform meant "keeper" to him, an enemy come to take him to some institution; and he instantly recognized as police several men in plainclothes who attempted to coax him in. John would have to be persuaded to save himself—by someone who already had his trust or could win it, or by his own thinking, or by his weariness.

Again and again Katherine and Mrs. Valentine went to the window to plead with him. Here is one conversation that took place:

"John, it's Katherine talking to you, it's your sister who loves you. Come in, darling. We all love you, John, you definitely know that. Come in and have a drink, John, darling. You have so much to live for, so many good times ahead of you. Oh, please, please, please, John, come on in. Johnny!"

"I want to be left alone," John replied quietly and politely but decidedly. "I've got to work things out for myself. I've got problems to think about."

"Oh, John, darling, everybody's got problems. You can work yours out somewhere else. We've always been so close, Johnny, haven't we? Just like brother and sister, I mean just like a couple of brothers, haven't we? You're the best brother in the world."

"No, I'm not. You think I haven't got character."

"Oh, darling, darling, I never said you didn't have character. You have character. You've got more character than I ever thought of having. Johnny, please, please, please, come back to us."

"I want to be left alone here awhile."

Katherine was overcome with weeping, and Mrs. Valentine took her place.

"Come on in, John. Forget all about everything that's happened. Please be nice and come in."

"Where's my sister? Where's Katherine?"

"Katherine's asking for you, John. Come in, dear, please do. Come along in and have a nice lunch and forget everything."

"She wants to send me away. Back to that asylum."

"No, she doesn't, John, I swear she doesn't. Nobody in the world wants to do you any harm. I promise that nothing will happen to you, if you'll just come in."

"I've got to think things out for myself."

Once he said, "I can't get over that fence." Mrs. Valentine thought that by "fence" he meant the architectural ornament which separated them.

"If you're frightened about crossing that fence, John, we'll get someone to help you. I'll have him here in no time."

"No, thank you," he said. "I'd like to be left alone for a while, please."

Summoned from his office, Mr. Valentine went to the window.

"Hello, there, John. Say, I've got a proposition to make to you. We have a nice lunch here. Come on in and help us eat it, and then you and I'll go to the ball game. The Cubs are playing here today, those Cubs of yours."

"Who are they playing?"

"The Dodgers."

"I wouldn't care to see the Dodgers," John said.

The police phoned John's father at Southampton, but Mr. Warde was on his vacation, touring Vermont in his car. Mrs. Warde didn't know what part of Vermont he might be in or near. She herself was confined to her bed with an illness and couldn't come to New York. The police asked her if she had any ideas on how her son might be induced to come in off the ledge, but she had none. The Vermont state police were asked to find Mr. Warde and have him get in touch with the Gotham at once. John asked for a glass of water, but refused to allow it to be handed to him, insisting that it be left on the ledge and nobody should be near either window while he drank it. When he stooped to pick up the filled tumbler, women screamed in the crowds below, and people who had started into the hotel entered on the run.

4.

BEFORE REPORTING to his superiors on the seventeenth floor, Patrolman Glasco stopped in the lobby to borrow a coat from the huskiest bellboy on duty; when he appeared at the window of 1714 he was wearing it unbuttoned because it would not quite button across the stomach and was somewhat tight under the arms. He had, of course, previously removed his cap, shield, pistol with holster, and cartridge belt. Glasco decided not to sit on the sill during his first appearance lest John should be suspicious of his police trousers, which didn't match the bellboy's coat, and he was also worried about the blue chambray shirt he had on;

under summer regulations the uniformed force had laid blouses aside. Would this boy recognize a police shirt? Glasco hoped not.

"Hello, John," he said easily.

"Who are you?" The suspicion in John's eyes bored into him. Glasco crossed himself mentally.

"I'm a new bellhop here at the Gotham, John. Matter of fact, I just got the job this morning. Listen, John, I don't want to butt in on what's strictly your own business, but I'd like to explain you my angle on this situation. John, I got a wife and three kids. Before the hotel took me on this morning, we'd all been on relief since I can't hardly remember when we wasn't. You ever been on relief, John?"

There was no answer, but the suspicion had gone out of John's eyes and his face had softened.

"Well, it's really tough, John, and I wouldn't kid you. Oh, I suppose if a man was single, it wouldn't be so bad, and the relief people mean well and do the best they can; but when you got a wife and three kids, boy, I'm telling you. Well, John, I'm just giving you my angle on this situation. Okay, you're out there on that ledge, and it's strictly your own business, but suppose something bad should happen to you? You know what it'd do? It'd besmirch the hotel, that's what it'd do. John, a hotel gets besmirched, its business gets lousy. Business gets lousy, the hotel starts laying off people. And who do they lay off first? The ones they took on last. Who did they take on last? Yours truly they took on last. So if anything should happen to you out there, John, it's back on relief for me and the wife and the three kids. John, I can't tell you how much I need this job, how much five people need it."

"Gosh, I wouldn't want you to have to go back on relief," John said. "Could I please have another drink of water?"

"You sure could," Glasco said, picking up the empty tumbler on the ledge and withdrawing into the room. He put the tumbler down and ripped off the bellboy's coat. "He's thirsty," he told the lieutenant from the Emergency Division. "Rope me up. This time I'll lay my prat on the sill and get as close to him as I can. When he takes the glass, I'll grab him by the wrist and then you can reel me in."

The lieutenant tied the slip noose securely around Glasco's right ankle. The rope ran under the bed and out the door into the hall, where eight men from the Emergency Division were holding on to it. They were all large men: the Emergency Division invariably wins the tug-of-war at the annual Police Athletic League games.

"If he falls or jumps after you get hold of him, keep hanging on," the lieutenant said. "You won't drop more than five feet."

Glasco gave him a cop's look, then filled the tumbler from a pitcher of ice water and went to the window. This time he sat on the sill. John backed away against the architectural ornament until there were several feet between himself and Glasco. His insteps were again resting on the edge of the ledge. He was as taut as a cat arching its back.

"Easy, now, take it easy," Glasco said, keeping his eyes on John's and thrusting the tumbler toward him. "Here it is, and it's good and cold, too."

But instead of taking it, John inched farther away. His eyes were once more filled with suspicion.

"No, I won't drink it unless you have a drink of it first."

Glasco grinned. "Why, John, you don't think I'd slip you a Mickey, do you?" He drank several mouthfuls from the tumbler. There was a long silence. "See, John, it's just plain water like you asked for. Here." He thrust the glass toward John, but not very far, hoping that in reaching for it John would come close enough to be seized. John stood his ground.

"Give it to me with your left hand," he said.

There was nothing for Glasco to do but to obey. John stayed glued against the architectural ornament, reached his right arm forward, and carefully seized the rim of the tumbler by squeezing his index and middle fingers together. Glasco noticed that his nails had been bitten to the quick. While he drank, his eyes never left Glasco. When he finished, he stooped and slid the tumbler along the ledge back to him. There were screams from below. John stood erect on the edge of the ledge. Slowly, slowly his body rocked forward on the balls of his feet and he stared down at the crowd. There was even more screaming. Glasco had a sick feeling in the pit of his stomach, and bit his lip to keep from shouting.

"Look at those morons," John said. Then slowly he rocked back on the balls of his feet. Glasco began breathing again.

"Like some more water, John?"

"No, thank you, not now."

"Care for a smoke?" Glasco shook an opened pack of cigarettes until one cigarette stuck up above the others.

"Why, yes, thank you, I would. Will you hold them in your left hand, please?"

Again not permitting Glasco to get close enough to grab him, he extracted the upstanding cigarette from the pack, lit it from a book of matches he had in his pocket, and smoked hungrily. Then he looked at the cigarette. "I see you're a Lucky smoker. I smoke Philip Morrises. I've got some in my coat pocket in the room. No reason I should be smoking your cigarettes."

"Think nothing of it."

A silence.

"Why should you be kind to me? You never set eyes on me before."

"It's like I already told you, John, we're both tied up in this thing together. The way I got it figured, as long as you're in trouble out there, so are my wife and kids. Besides, well, maybe this'll sound fresh from a bellboy, but you look regular to me, you look like the type of man I'd like to have for a friend. Do you think we could be friends, John?"

John swallowed. "Of course we could," he said. Glasco leaned far out of the window and stretched his right arm forward to shake hands. John's eyes focused back to cunning. With the tip of his right little finger he touched the palm of Glasco's hand for the fraction of a second and then immediately withdrew the finger from reach. Glasco laughed.

"You don't trust me much, do you, John? Well, listen, John, I trust you, and that not only goes for me but the wife and kids, too. We're trusting you not to let anything bad happen to you or to us."

There was another silence. The suspicion swirled out of John's eyes.

"I can't get over that fence," he said slowly. "I've got a momentous decision to make. This thing has got to be thought out."

"Sure, I appreciate that, John. Maybe I can help you."

"Thanks, but I have to work it out alone."

Glasco felt the rope around his ankle being jerked.

"Well, whatever you work out, John, I want you to promise me not to let anything bad happen to you."

"I'll be working it out."

"That's fine, John. I'll be back in ten minutes. Just don't forget that we're all in there rooting for you."

5.

IN FRONT of the hotel, Fifty-fifth Street had now been cleared of everyone except members of the Police and Fire Departments and the press. Newsreel cameramen were setting up their tripods; photographers from the daily papers and the wire services were lying on their backs on the sidewalk by the church, aiming up at John with their "Big Berthas"— cameras with lenses having a focal length of twenty-eight inches or greater, the kind used to cover mass-attended sporting events. The Fifth Avenue Presbyterian Church had curtly refused the use of its steeples for picture purposes; many photographers were working from rooftops and the upper windows of high office buildings, some as much as three hundred feet away. At 711 Fifth Avenue, half a block to the northeast of the hotel, the Television Section of the National Broadcasting Company was televising John. In the same building, Dave Driscoll, of the Special Features Section of the Mutual Broadcasting System, began putting John—or rather a breathless description of his plight—on the air. Hawkers circulated among the crowds in the streets and peddled cheap opera glasses so that John's fellow citizens might see him better. Passengers craned and goggled at John from the busses that crawled along Fifth Avenue. As though the crucial game of a World Series were being played, people all over Greater New York gathered about parked taxicabs equipped with radios. Switchboards at the West Forty-seventh and East Fifty-first Street precinct station houses were flooded with calls from persons with advice to give.

At ringside, so to speak, on the northeast corner of Fifth Avenue and Fifty-fifth Street, a cluster of John's co-mortals discussed his dilemma.

"It's a guy tryna settle a family scrap" . . . "Yeh, his wife trettena leavum" . . . "I hoid she did leavum awreddy" . . . "Fellow told me it's a broker attempting to get money out of his relatives" . . . "That's what I was told, except that he's an auditor wanted for absconding" . . . "Five'll gitcha eight he don't jump" . . . "Oh, it's probably just some advertising stunt, a publicity gag for the hotel" . . . "Lemme have those glasses a sec, Louise" . . . *"Geez, willya look-atum settin' down!"*

With nobody to talk to, John had seated himself on the ledge and was dangling one foot over the edge.

"Hold Fern a little higher, Daddy. See the funny man sitting way up there, dear? Oh, you aren't even looking at the right building. Look. Where Mamma's pointing. There" . . . "My God, Louise, the way he's got his head turned now, he's a dead ringer for Tyrone Power. Take the glasses quick" . . . "Five'll gitcha ten he don't jump" . . .

6.

GLASCO'S ANKLE had been tugged for a conference with his superiors. Present also was Dr. Jacques C. Presner, the house physician at the near-by Hotel Dorset, who had been summoned by the Gotham because its own house physician happened to be out of town that day. Dr. Presner was a French-Canadian by birth and a graduate of McGill University, a small, dark, neat man with tortoise-shell spectacles. He was not a psychiatrist, but every hotel physician has opportunities for observing the human mind and the strange things it sometimes does in some hotel guests.

"That kid out there is plenty smart, very foxy," Glasco told the conference. "The way things are now, you can't possibly get near enough to him to grab a belt or a sleeve or a trouser cuff, not speaking about an arm or a leg or a hand. I tried a couple of fast ones on him, but he saw through them in a flash. He does go, though, for that business about me being a bellhop with a wife and three kids. It has him worried. I got confidence I can talk him in, all right, only it'll take some time."

"Maybe if we could get one of those things they use in groceries to take cans and stuff down off the high shelves," a voice said. "Snap that on his ankle and, bing, you got him."

"Or how about you catch hold of him with a pair of ice tongs?" another suggested. "You whip them into something like a leg or somewheres, and right away his mind gets off whatever's bothering him upstairs and goes right down to where the pain is. Be a cinch to sew him up later, wouldn't it, Doc?"

But before Dr. Presner could answer, a third voice spoke up. "Neither of those things make any sense. If Glasco went out there carrying ice tongs or a grocery grabber, that kid might take off. You're forgetting that all he's got to do is give the least little twitch and he's away. No, sir, this thing is strictly a kid-glove proposition. It can't be licked by anything but patience. You got to tire him out. Glasco, get as much of that drinking water in him as you can; pretty soon he should be having to go to the bathroom and maybe he'll be wanting to come in. Keep right on being nice to him like you been doing. Get him talking about himself. You started out fine making friends with him, so stay with it. Will you take a look at him now, Doc?"

Glasco slipped the noose off his leg and went out into the hall. It was becoming crowded. He could hear the clatter of a typewriter, telephones ringing, and somebody saying, "Gimme the city desk." Across the way loud, excited German male voices boomed from behind a door slightly open. Glasco knew a little German and could catch a word or two.

"Absolut phantastisch!" . . . *"Ja, aber vollkommen meschugge!"* . . . *"Ganz ausgeschlossen!"*

His eight anchor men from the Emergency Division were leaning against the walls.

"How goes it, Charlie?"

"Well, it's slow, but I think we'll make it okay. What's with his sister?"

"Lying down in there. She ain't in too good shape."

"Listen, Charlie, all I ask is you get him in by four. I got a very important date then or thereabouts."

"You think I'm dawdling? I got a date myself to eat some liver and bacon."

"Say, Charlie, does that kid out there go for dames?"

"How should I know? We haven't got around to that yet. Why?"

"Oh, nothing. I was just thinking."

Glasco smoked a couple of cigarettes and chatted until a sergeant stuck his head out of 1714 and hailed him. He went inside at once and shut the door. Dr. Presner had just come back from the window.

"He's asking for you," he told Glasco. " 'Where's that bellboy, where's that bellboy?' was the last thing he said to me. We had a nice talk. I tried to impress on him that everybody in here is his friend. He wasn't hostile at all, but courteous throughout. I think he'd like to come in, on the one hand, but on the other he's afraid of the humiliation and possible punishment he'd have to face if he did come in after causing all this hullabaloo. It strikes me, though, that he's also getting quite a kick out of causing it, of being for once the monarch of all he surveys, you might say. I get a feeling of power drive there. Did he teeter on the edge and look down below while you were talking to him?"

"My God, yes," Glasco said, "and it scared the hell out of me."

"He has remarkable control of his equilibrium. And here's another thing. I've read quite a lot about the subconscious mind, but this is the first time I've ever had a definite sense of watching it in operation. You see it whenever you put something up to him and he starts thinking it over. It's in the way his face and hands and his limbs behave when the thinking is going on. You can almost hear one part of his mind tell him, 'You're a brave boy, John, you're wonderful. All these people admire you for standing New York on its ear. That man who just talked to you is your admirer and friend.' And while this is going on, there's what might be called a bodily nod. His head's nodding slightly and the rest of his body seems to be telling you, 'Yes, I know you're there. Give me time. What you just said is getting my most favorable consideration.' Then the bodily nod will stop while the other part of his mind seems to say, 'Watch out! Don't do anything rash. There may be danger ahead. Don't trust this man.' This part of his mind will finally dominate, and suddenly he'll shake his head and say out loud, 'Nope, I can't do it. Sorry.' I'd say his will power is by no means weak at this time, and he has control over his faculties."

"Any ideas on what we can do, Doc?"

"I think that our plan of attack ought to be to influence his mental attitude in the right direction. Glasco here is absolutely our best bet. Let him talk with him as long as he can, and whenever he gets tired, I'll spell him."

Glasco went back to the window.

"You're late," John said, looking at his wrist watch. "You said you'd be back in ten minutes, and it's more than fifteen. Nearly sixteen."

They talked for almost an hour and a half. They discussed picnics and which was better, a day picnic or a night picnic. John thought that night picnics were more colorful and romantic, but Glasco pointed out that by day the bugs weren't so bad, poison ivy was easier to dodge, children did not tread or sit on food as frequently, and added attractions like fat men's races and ball games between the marrieds and the singles could be held. This led naturally to a discussion of baseball. John declared that he didn't think the Brooklyn club would finish in the first division, and again he refused an invitation to attend the Cubs-Dodgers game. From there the talk turned to what sports John liked to indulge in himself. The first two mentioned were ping-pong, which Glasco had seen but never played, and badminton, which he had never heard of and at first confused with backgammon. Swimming, however, was John's favorite sport. He loved to take a long swim and then lie on the beach covered with sun-tan oil.

"Gee, that must be a great life, John. It shows in that streamlined build of yours. Do you take exercises regular besides?"

"Oh, sure, and I work with dumbbells, too. Listen, when I come in there, I'll take you out to my house and show you the swellest pair of dumbbells you ever saw."

Glasco stared at him and his heart pounded. He strove to keep the elation out of his voice.

"Well, let's get going then," he said casually.

"What do you mean?"

"Let's go see those dumbbells of yours. Matter of fact, for a long time now I've been wanting to get rid of some of this lard I'm carrying, and probably working with dumbbells is exactly what I need. If I like yours, I'll get me a pair of them and you can coach me what to do to develop a decent build. Come on, John, you got me all hopped up. Let's grab a train before that commuters' rush starts."

Until then, Glasco had not seen what Dr. Presner called "the bodily nod," but now he saw it.

"Not for a while yet," John said at last.

"When, then?"

"I'll let you know."

But Glasco was not discouraged. He was convinced that the jam had begun finally to break in the right direction. During this long conversation, John had drunk quite a few glasses of water, each of which Glasco had been forced to drink from first and then to deliver with his left hand. In the end it was Glasco and not John who went to the bathroom. Dr. Presner replaced him at the window.

As the afternoon wore on, the crowds below swelled, and Chief Inspector Alexander C. Anderson, now at the hotel supervising the case, kept sending for more police until he had three hundred on hand. Deputy Mayor Henry H. Curran arrived to see if he could be of assistance, as did Supreme Court Justice John E. McGeehan. Among other arrivals at the Gotham that afternoon were Miss Evelyn MacDonnell, "the Angel of the Bowery," from the Beacon Relief Mission; an individual dressed in white who described himself simply as "an army man" and offered to rescue John by jujitsu; a woman who insisted on kneeling in the lobby and praying because she was a faith healer with scientifically worked-out slogans; and a Miss Diane Gregal, who had prevented the suicide of Maurice Wast, broker, aged sixty-five, the previous December by coaxing him in off a ledge at the Pennsylvania Hotel. Miss Gregal informed the press that an unidentified male voice had summoned her by telephone. So many volunteers and persons claiming to possess special skills were swarming into the hotel that the police set up a check-point at the entrance, with the Gotham's register available, and admitted only bona-fide guests and those who could prove that they had legitimate business inside. Meanwhile the Gotham's flawlessly dressed manager had been striding through the building, doing his best to co-operate, and wringing his hands.

Dr. Presner's wife and his sister, who was in town on a visit from Montreal, were strolling down Fifth Avenue when they were stopped by the throngs at Fifty-fifth Street. They stared in the direction everybody else was staring. The doctor's sister screamed slightly. "Isn't that Jacques up there hanging out of that window?" she said. "Yes," said Mrs. Presner. As the neighboring *aficionados* could give them no coherent explanation for the unusual situation of their husband and brother, the two women struggled to the hotel, but were refused permission to enter. A little later, in the home of a friend who had invited them to tea, everything was made clear by the radio blow-by-blow account of the event, which millions were now listening to all over the Western Hemisphere.

Sitting on the sill of 1714, Dr. Presner could hear booming through the hotel's open windows the voices of announcers describing John's actions, and his own, as they took place. He reported this, and the police made the thoughtless guests close their windows or shut off their sets. Countless suburban mothers, who had been drinking in the broadcasts all afternoon, phoned sons and daughters working in the midtown section to be sure to stop on their way home for a look at the spectacle on Fifty-fifth Street. (When quitting time came, many firms with offices affording good views of the Gotham's façade were unable to get their employees to leave.) That night in his news broadcast, Gabriel Heatter outdid himself. Altogether it was a great day for those principles of electrical phenomena first given to the world by that eminent physicist, Heinrich Rudolph Hertz.

One person who tuned in late was Mrs. Charles V. Glasco. She had been totally occupied all day with housework at her home out in Queens. Around a quarter to six her telephone rang. It was Augie Schmidt, the neighborhood butcher and a friend of the family.

"Well, Maggie, with your old man out on that ledge, I guess you'll be keeping that liver and bacon on the back of the stove this evening."

"Oh, dear," Mrs. Glasco said resignedly, "what is it with him now?"

"You didn't hear yet? Ho, ho, ho! Turn your radio on."

7.

SINCE BREAKFAST John had been subsisting solely on Lucky Strikes and water. Toward the end of the afternoon he asked for coffee and was given a cup of it, black. Having submitted it to the Glasco test for noxious drugs, he ordered cream and sugar. "More sugar," he demanded, handing the coffee back to Glasco after tasting it. The strategy of filling John up with liquids had so far worked only on Glasco. Nor did John appear at all wearied after standing in one spot for hours under conditions of tension which had long since affected the spectators on the streets below. Relieved at intervals by Dr. Presner, Glasco had conversed with John the whole afternoon on the friendliest possible terms, and by six o'clock he had extracted numerous half-promises from him that he would come inside. But as the daylight began to go, a change seemed to come over John.

For the first time he refused to give Glasco even a half-promise.

"No," he said abruptly.

"No? Oh, now look, fella, what kind of talk is that? This is your pal the bellhop here, the guy with the wife and kids that'll go back on relief if you don't co-operate. You already told me a dozen times you'd take me out to your house and show me those dumbbells of yours, don't you remember? Don't you, John?"

No answer.

"Did I do or say anything to make you sore? John, if I did I'm sorry and I apologize. Is there anything you want, John? Anything I can do for you? Just name it and you can have it."

There was a silence, and then John said, "I want to talk to my sister."

"John, your sister's in bed with a terrible sick headache. She's taken this thing very hard and she's in bad shape. We better not bother her right now, John."

"I want to talk to Katherine," John said. Glasco could not dissuade him from his wish.

The police had set up a field telephone system to speed communication between their key elements stationed in various parts of the hotel, and to relieve the Gotham's swamped switchboard. One line of the network extended across Fifty-fifth Street to a sergeant standing on the steps of the church. His job was to keep his superiors inside the hotel informed of John's movements. A small cordon had to be thrown about this sergeant to protect him from zealots who squirmed through the police lines and pressed advice upon him. There was, of course, an installation in room 1714, and also one in 1716. Glasco brought a telephone to the window, rang Katherine in the next room, got her, and then started to pass the telephone to John. John shook his head. Glasco switched the instrument from his right to his left hand and gave it to him. John talked in such a low voice that Glasco could not hear what he said, but from the way John was frowning when he lowered the telephone from his face, he inferred that the conversation hadn't been satisfactory to either participant. It had not been. In room 1716 Katherine put the telephone down and wept hysterically. Mrs. Valentine, who had been looking after her, picked it up. She spoke very gently.

"The children need you, darling. We all need you, so why don't you come in? We'll play ping-pong, we'll go swimming together. Come on, darling, take one little step here, one little step there, show them you can do it. We want you, Johnny, we need you. . . . Oh, Johnny, what do you mean, you can't come in? If you'll just come in, there'll be nothing."

Out on the ledge Glasco heard John say, "I'd be ashamed now, with all those people down there." He lowered the telephone from his face. Glasco pushed the phone cradle along the ledge. When John put the phone on it, perhaps he would be able to seize him. But once more John was too cunning. He tossed the phone to Glasco. "You do it," he said. Glasco put the phone on its cradle, withdrew from the window, and found Dr. Presner.

"Something's happened to him, Doc. You better take a look."

Glasco opened the door to the corridor. The crush reminded him of the lobby of Madison Square Garden on the night of a big fight. He caught the eye of the anchor man who had had the very important date at four o'clock and was glared at with mock rage. Another anchor man was in deep conversation with a blond young woman. Above the babble in the hall he could hear snatches from the Germans still talking the case over. *"Es ist ja unerhört!"* . . . *"Absolut phantastisch!"* Glasco shut the door and went to a bed, sat down, and held his head in his hands. His head ached. His eyes smarted. From the shifting and stretching he had been doing all afternoon on the sill, his sacro-iliac pained him. Dr. Presner appeared from behind the window curtains.

"He'll come in if he gets a document signed by the Police Commissioner promising that nothing will happen to him."

Glasco wearily rose from the bed.

Dr. Presner went into a huddle with Deputy Mayor Curran, the

Chief Inspector, other high brass from the Police and Fire Departments, and three more doctors—all psychiatrists—who had arrived. Two of them were from Bellevue Hospital, and the third, a Chicagoan, was a guest in the hotel. Glasco was about to part the curtains to mount the sill again when he was waylaid by the anchor man and the blond young woman from the hallway. The anchor man spoke in an undertone.

"Listen, Charlie, I wish you'd give this friend of mine here a chance at that kid out there. She worked with us before and knows her stuff. She's okay."

"Well—" Glasco said, shooting a doubtful glance toward the huddle.

"Aw, come awn, Charlie! What can you lose?"

"Well, all right, but—"

The blond young woman knifed between the curtains and got up on the sill. Glasco and the anchor man strained their ears.

"Hello. Remember me?"

"No. Who are you? Where are you from?"

"Baltimore. Remember?"

"No."

"Look, aren't you lonesome out there?"

A silence.

"I'm lonesome. Why don't you come in here?"

Another silence. Then John said, "I want to be loved in the right way."

"Break it up," Glasco said, parting the curtains.

8.

AT ONE POINT Glasco was given a tumbler of water containing one-half a milligram of benzedrine for John. The doctors thought it might "heighten his mood." Although one New York newspaper the next day mentioned "hypnotic tablets," and a weekly magazine later spoke of "coffee liberally doped," this half-milligram of benzedrine, scarcely enough to brighten the outlook of a be-bop drummer, was actually all the pharmaceutic stimulant that John received. He did not receive even that much, scientifically speaking, for, as usual whenever liquid was offered him, he made Glasco drink part of it first. When an attempt was made to repeat the dosage, a cloudiness in the water, caused by an imperfectly dissolved tablet, so roused John's suspicions that he made Glasco drink it all. The benzedrine-laced water failed to "heighten the mood" of either drinker.

Representing the Police Department, Captain William O'Brien, of the West Forty-seventh Street station, went to the window and told John that the document of immunity he had demanded from the Police Commissioner was being prepared.

"But you don't really need it," Captain O'Brien said. "You can go to your friends in Scarsdale, or anywhere you want, without hindrance, if you'll only come in. You believe me, don't you? Don't I look honest to you?"

"No, you don't," John said.

The Reverend James McCarthy, summoned from St. Patrick's Cathedral near by, went to the window and did the best he could, but soon realized that he was not making progress.

"By the way, are you a Catholic?"

"No. I'm an Episcopalian," John said in a detached tone.

The police again called the Warde home in Southampton. Mr. Warde was still somewhere in Vermont and had not been heard from. Mrs. Warde consented to appeal to John over the telephone. When John heard who was calling, however, he refused to take the telephone from Glasco.

The sun went down at seven twenty-three that day, but long before then, searchlights set up by the police were playing against the Gotham's façade, and the photographers were shooting their flash bulbs. The crowds grew steadily after dark, and traffic in the entire vicinity became even more clogged than during the day. The heaviest concentrations of spectators were on Fifty-fifth Street west of the hotel clear to Sixth Avenue, and along Fifth Avenue on the northeast corners of Fifty-fifth, Fifty-sixth, Fifty-seventh, and Fifty-eighth Streets. On Sixth Avenue between Fifty-sixth and Fifty-seventh, spectators milled and jostled for positions on a patch of sidewalk about eight feet square;

somebody had discovered that from it, through a space between two buildings, John's tiny figure could be seen, picked out by the search-lights. An angry, sweating policeman tried to keep this patch of side-walk clear, but as soon as he cleared it the spectators would swarm back. "Go on home and look after your own children," he kept shouting at the women, but they merely laughed at him. With so many thousands staring into the air, it was a productive evening for pickpockets.

Dr. Presner and the three psychiatrists took turns at the window. Once Dr. Presner heard a woman call from a near-by roof, "Don't do it, John. We all love you. Go on back in like a good boy now."

Glasco went to the window again. He had the key to the room in his hand.

"John, I'd like to make a deal with you. You been out there eight, nine, ten hours now and you're all dirty and tired and you must feel awful. Look at your nails; you've bitten them down to the elbow almost. Well, John, this room's been cleared, and here's the key: I'm leaving it right here on this ledge. For the next twenty minutes the room'll be absolutely yours alone. If you want to, you can come in and have a good wash and get that dirt off and feel better. Then, if you want to, you can go back on out there."

"I'll think it over," John said, and it was obvious that he was inter-ested. His voice and manner had not been so friendly since he had offered to show Glasco his dumbbells. He looked at his wrist watch and then looked at Glasco without suspicion.

"All right, John, you think it over. If you get cleaned up, I believe you'll find you can think clearer. Here's the key on the sill. I'll open the curtains so you can see for yourself the room's empty. Be back in twenty minutes."

John nodded and looked at his wrist watch again. Glasco withdrew from the window, fixed the curtains, and hurried to the door leading to the hall.

"Okay, Johnny, take it away," he said, raising his voice. He went into the hall and slammed the door.

In the room, concealed behind a bureau, was the fastest man in the Emergency Division at snapping on a pair of handcuffs. There was another Emergency Division man in the bathroom.

"Twenty-minute break, fellas," Glasco called to the anchor men, who at once moved off to make phone calls. Glasco stood with his ear against the door of 1714, listening for any sound from within, keeping his hand on the knob. There were still many people wandering up and down the hall, but he paid no attention to them. His mind was inside the room.

"I want to talk to that boy," he heard a voice say. Glasco turned from the door and saw a gaunt man with blazing eyes. He wore a high stiff collar of a cut that had gone out of style years before. The man identified himself as a Protestant clergyman. "I can save that boy," he said. "He doesn't understand the fear of God, that's all. I will explain it to him and save him."

"Sorry, sir," Glasco said, "but I have orders from the Chief Inspector not to let anybody in the room just now. Maybe if you'd call back in half an hour and see the Chief Inspector personally."

The clergyman turned away impatiently and moved down the hall toward the Fifth Avenue end of the building. Glasco put his ear to the door again and glanced at his watch. Five minutes had passed.

Inside 1714 a short while later, the handcuff expert, peeking through a slit below the bureau mirror, was surprised to see a gaunt man wearing an old-fashioned stiff collar enter from 1716 by a connecting door, which the police had had unlocked, and close it carefully behind him. No sooner had he closed it than John's figure appeared outside the window, doubled over, his face down by his knees, his eyes staring into the room. John saw the gaunt man immediately. His head swung up and his body disappeared from view. It had all happened in a split second.

"Sweet jumping Christ!" Glasco heard the handcuff expert say in fury. He shoved the door open and rushed into the room. Both Emergency Division men were coming out of their hiding places. "Go look at him quick," the handcuff expert said. Glasco ran to the window. John was on the ledge, back in his old niche, holding on to the architectural ornament. Glasco exhaled with relief, but the look on John's face worried him.

"I'm awful sorry, John. That party got in by mistake. He sneaked into the next room on me and came in here through the side door. So many people in that next room, they didn't notice him. I swear it won't happen again. Will you give it another try, please?"

John didn't answer. Glasco knew that he would never give it another try.

The clergyman was removed from the room, and Dr. Presner went to the window. Glasco was sitting on the bed holding his head in his hands when he became aware that the Chief Inspector was standing in front of him. He rose to his feet.

"You've done a good job, Glasco, but we'll all have to keep punching at this thing a while longer. We've sent to the Coast Guard for a cargo net that we'll anchor one edge of along the windows directly below these; then we'll jerk the other edge up quick to the floor above this one and pin him against the side of the building. At the same time we'll lower a couple of bosun's chairs from the eighteenth, too. But it'll take a while to get the net here and get it set up. So as soon as the Doc comes in, I want you to take over for another hour."

Dr. Presner came in from the window; Glasco tore open a fresh pack of Philip Morris cigarettes.

"He just told me he knows everyone's interested in his welfare," the doctor said, "and he's asking for that bellboy again."

Glasco mounted the sill, drew the curtains around him, and began to talk. He started all over, from the beginning. He talked about his bellboy's job and the hotels he had worked in and his hope of staying off relief. He talked about his wife and children. He talked about picnics and baseball and ping-pong and badminton, about swimming and lying on the beach in the sun getting tanned and the satisfaction there must be in achieving a fine build through dumbbell exercise. He passed John cigarettes with his left hand automatically now, without having to be told. John smoked and listened, never answering the questions Glasco kept shooting at him. He dropped each butt on the ledge and carefully extinguished it with his heel, as he had done since Glasco had given him his first cigarette. When Glasco had gone over everything he could think of he paused for breath, and John said, "I wish you could convince me that life's worth living."

9.

THE CARGO NET, forty by twenty-five feet, was raised by ropes lowered from eighteenth-floor windows to the east and west of where John was standing. It rose slowly in steady jerks, passing the ledges on the eighth and twelfth floors, but just as it reached the sixteenth, some of the ropes it was being raised by fouled, and the net sagged against the hotel like a monster empty reticule. Firemen on the ground tried to spread it by ropes attached to its lower end, but could not. Riggers with pikes, who had been stationed at sixteenth-floor windows to keep a belly in the net when it was in position, began using their pikes in an effort to extend it.

"I'm ashamed to be doing this before all those people," John said. "They're anticipating something."

"We'll frustrate their intentions, Johnny," Glasco said.

"I've made up my mind."

"That's the way to talk. We'll frustrate the hell out of them."

Instead of crushing his cigarette under his heel, John threw it down at the street.

A hand holding a telephone thrust at Glasco through the curtains and a voice said, "It's for him."

"Got a call for you, John."

John took the telephone.

"Hello . . . Yes . . . Who is this? . . . Oh? Well, if you're my girl friend, what's our favorite poem?"

It was evident to Glasco that the lady was clueless. He suspected the Emergency Division man who had sponsored Miss Gregal. Just as John passed the telephone back, Glasco felt a tug on his ankle rope.

"I'll be right back, John. Just keep swinging, fella."

A coatless young man was standing with the Chief Inspector.

"He's been a friend of John's since they were kids together," the Chief Inspector explained. "Go ahead, son. Have a breather, Glasco."

The young man went to the window and leaned out. Glasco sat on the bed and rubbed his left leg, which had gone to sleep.

"How's it with that net?"

"Should be all set in a few minutes, Charlie. You think he can see it?"

"No, but I think he'll see those bosun's chairs when they come down from above."

"Well, they'll have that net ready in a few shakes, and then there'll be nothing to worry about."

"Gosh, I sure hope so," Glasco said, rubbing his leg. "It's been quite a day. I got all those stubs on my summonses to make out yet before I can go home."

Suddenly there was a tremendous roar from the crowd below.

"There he goes!"

Glasco thought of "They're off!" which the railbirds roar at the start of every horse race, and then he burst into tears.

10.

As JOHN'S BODY passed the sixteenth floor a policeman, who had been stationed there to seize the strands of the net when it was raised before his window, made a lunge for him and barely missed. A magnesium flare was set off by the newsreel cameramen. John fell feet first as far as the eighth floor, where he grazed the ledge, then he whirled end-over-end until he struck the hotel marquee, almost hit a Homicide Squad lieutenant coming from under it, and landed partly on the sidewalk and partly in the gutter. A priest sprang forward to administer the last rites, but John was beyond all rites.

When John leaped, the crowds burst through the police lines and rushed toward the marquee. It took most of the Chief Inspector's detail of three hundred men to stop them. Scores of women fainted. John's body was swiftly put into an ambulance and taken to the West Forty-seventh Street station. A quarter of an hour after John's death, the new moon appeared in the sky, and, in its light, souvenir hunters scrambled for bits of the broken marquee glass.

The next day the nation's newspapers broke out with a rash of some of the worst editorials in the history of American journalism. The most offensive of these seemed to fall into three categories: those which compared John to the European dictators teetering on the brink of war; those which compared Patrolman Glasco to Neville Chamberlain trying to make Adolf Hitler see reason; and those which deplored mob hysteria. Nearly all the newspapers which viewed mob hysteria with alarm simultaneously ran harrowing pictures of John's broken body lying on the sidewalk.

Three days after his death, John was buried in Evergreen Cemetery, Brooklyn. The funeral services, which had been scheduled to take place at 2 P.M. in a Brooklyn funeral home, were advanced four hours by the family in order to avoid curious throngs.

At closing time that Tuesday afternoon, while John was on the ledge trying to decide what to do, the manager of a Fifth Avenue department store estimated that his indecisiveness had cost the merchants of the district at least $100,000. But by the end of the week the motion-picture industry was reporting that the newsreels showing John's final decision had already added $1,000,000 to the regular grosses of the theaters which exhibited them in Greater New York. Perhaps it can be argued that in the end John William Warde more than paid his debt to metropolitan society.

The Night
the Martians Came

BY CHARLES JACKSON

Charles Jackson was working as a script writer for the Columbia Broadcasting System at the time Orson Welles staged his "invasion from Mars" on the radio. In the following article he analyzes the extraordinary panic which was caused by that incident, and draws some interesting parallels with actual news events of the time. Mr. Jackson was one of the most successful authors of radio plays of the 1930's, and continued to work on his radio serial *Sweet River* during the time he was writing *The Lost Weekend* (1944), the novel about an alcoholic which was highly successful as a book and as a motion picture. Mr. Jackson is also the author of *The Fall of Valor* (1946) and *The Outer Edges* (1948). He lives in Orford, New Hampshire, with his wife and two daughters.

✵ 1.

AT MOMENTS OF crisis or disaster people are fond of telling where they were at the time, how they happened to hear the news, or what they were doing when they heard it, as if their personal reaction were more important than the event itself. Thus, on Monday morning, October 31, 1938, while everybody in the radio business collected in excited knots to discuss the panic the country had been thrown into on the previous evening by the medium they worked in, my own story went something like this:

My wife and I had returned from dinner in Greenwich Village. I went into the bedroom, lay down on my bed, and dialed WABC to see how the Orson Welles show was going. I was interested in the show for several reasons. I worked for the Columbia Broadcasting System and I had been in on the first audition. The Mercury Theater of the

Air was one of the most expensive sustainers in radio. An hour-long program, it had been on the air for over three and a half months, and there was still no sponsor in sight. Nor was there likely to be, for the show occupied one of the toughest spots of the week, eight to nine on Sunday night, bucking the fantastically popular Charlie McCarthy at the same hour. Sponsors showed little interest in the Welles program, for the talk in radio was that it had no listening audience whatever.

As usual, Orson was presenting a dramatization of a book. The opening announcement said: "The Columbia Broadcasting System and its affiliated stations present Orson Welles and the Mercury Theater of the Air in *The War of the Worlds,* by H. G. Wells."

But strangely, no dramatic program seemed to ensue. A prosaic weather report was given instead. Then an announcer remarked that the program would be continued from a New York hotel, with dance tunes. For a few moments, one heard the music of a swing band. Then came a sudden break-in with a "flash" which declared dramatically that a professor had just noted from his observatory a series of gas explosions on the planet Mars. The clever Welles—not H. G. (indeed, the dramatization had little connection with H. G.'s original at any point) —was up to one of his tricks.

Simulated news bulletins followed in rapid succession, interspersed with "remotes": on-the-spot broadcasts of actual "scenes." These reported brilliantly, with the extraordinary technique which radio had long since perfected for news events, the landing of a meteor near Princeton, New Jersey, killing fifteen hundred persons—and then the discovery that it was no meteor at all but a metal cylinder containing Martian creatures armed with death rays, come to open hostilities against the inhabitants of the earth.

I could not but admire Orson for the marvelous reality he was able to bring to such a fantastic story, but after a few moments, it seemed to me, he succeeded too well; the very grotesqueness of the broadcast soon caused me to lose interest—it outraged all my sense of belief— and by eight-fifteen or so, I switched off the dial and took a nap.

Arriving at the office the next morning, I was dumfounded—and somewhat ashamed for my fellow Americans—to discover that a national panic had been generated by the broadcast. But I needn't have been so damn smug. I happened to know beforehand, after all, just what program had been scheduled on CBS between eight and nine on Sunday evening; moreover, from working in the studios myself, I was familiar with the radio techniques which purported to reproduce actual events, and thus I was less likely to be taken in than the average listener.

Orson Welles had made a monkey of somebody: the non-existent sponsor, Charlie McCarthy, CBS, the radio industry itself, or the vast gullible United States public—no one was quite sure which. But a certain frightening fact was clear beyond doubt: to the radio listeners of the United States, their nerves already strained by the war jitters which had gripped the world for six months, nothing coming over the air could be too fantastic; *any*thing might happen. It was the epitome of what W. H. Auden called our "age of anxiety," but concentrated in the hours of a single evening.

2.

SUNDAY NIGHT'S WAVE of mass hysteria took strange forms. Throughout New York City, families fled their apartments in panic, some to near-by parks, many to seek verification of the horrendous report, hundreds of others, in a state of terror, to find out how they could follow the broadcast's advice and flee from the city.

In Newark, New Jersey, in a single block, more than twenty families rushed out of their homes with wet handkerchiefs and towels over their heads and faces, to flee from what they believed to be a gas raid.

In San Francisco, the general impression of listeners was that an overwhelming force had invaded the United States from the sky; New York was in the process of being destroyed, and the frightful Martians were even now moving westward. "My God," roared one man into a phone, "where can I volunteer my services? We've got to stop this awful thing!"

In Caldwell, New Jersey, a terror-stricken parishioner rushed into the First Baptist Church during the evening service and shouted that a meteor had fallen, showering death and destruction, and that North Jersey was threatened with annihilation. The Reverend Thomas Thomas attempted to quiet his congregation by leading them in prayer for deliverance from the catastrophe.

A man in Pittsburgh returned home in the midst of the broadcast and found his wife in the bathroom, a bottle of poison in her hand, screaming, "I'd rather die this way than like that!" Another man, in Mt. Vernon, New York, called police to tell them that his brother, a hopeless invalid, had been listening to the broadcast and when he heard the report, he got into an automobile and "disappeared."

In Harlem, extreme panic was created. Thirty men and women rushed into the West 123rd Street Police Station and twelve into the West 135th Street Station saying they had their household goods packed and were ready to quit Harlem if the police would tell them where to go to be evacuated. One man insisted he had heard "the President's voice" over the radio, advising all citizens to leave the city. One could hardly blame him, for at a dramatic point in the broadcast the President's voice was exactly imitated by a Mercury Theater actor telling the listeners to do just that.

Nor was credulity confined to the susceptible citizenry alone. Men of science were not immune. Dr. Arthur F. Buddington, chairman of the department of geology, and Dr. Harry Hess, professor of geology, Princeton University, received the first alarming reports in a form indicating that a meteor had fallen near Dutch Neck, some five miles away. They armed themselves with "the necessary equipment" and set out to find the specimen. What they found was a group of excited natives, searching, like themselves, for the meteor.

Later, a detailed study of the entire panic and its effects was made by the Princeton Radio Project, operating on a grant of the Rockefeller Foundation to Princeton University. Some of the comments recorded by interviewers for the Project were as follows:

A New Jersey housewife: "I knew it was something terrible and I was frightened. But I didn't know just what it was. I couldn't make myself believe it was the end of the world. I've always heard that when the world would come to an end, it would come so fast nobody would know—so why should God get in touch with this announcer? When they told us what road to take and get up over the hills and the children began to cry, the family decided to go out. We took blankets and my granddaughter wanted to take the cat and the canary. We were outside the garage when the neighbor's boy came back and told us it was only a play."

A high-school girl in Pennsylvania: ". . . I was really hysterical. My two girl friends and I were crying and holding each other and everything seemed so unimportant in the face of death. We felt it was terrible we should die so young. . . ."

A Negro housewife in Newark: "We listened, getting more and more excited. We all felt the world was coming to an end. Then we heard, 'Get gas masks!' That was the part that got me. I thought I was going crazy. It's a wonder my heart didn't fail me because I'm nervous anyway. I felt if the gas was on, I wanted to be together with my husband and nephew so we could all die together. So I ran out of the house. I guess I didn't know what I was doing. I stood on the corner waiting for a bus and I thought every car that came along was a bus and I ran out to get it. I kept saying over and over again to everybody I met: 'New Jersey is destroyed by the Germans—it's on the radio!' I was all excited and I knew that Hitler didn't appreciate President Roosevelt's telegram a couple of weeks ago. While the United States thought everything was settled, they came down unexpected. The Germans are so smart they were in something like a balloon, and when the balloon landed—that's when they announced the explosion—the Germans landed. . . ."

A man in a Midwest town: "That Halloween boo had our family on its knees before the program was half over. God knows but we prayed to him last Sunday. It was a lesson in more than one thing to us. My mother went out and looked for Mars. Dad was hard to convince, and skeptical, but even he got to believing it. Brother Joe, as usual, got more excited than anyone. Brother George wasn't home. Aunt Grace, a good Catholic, began to pray with Uncle Henry. Lillie got sick to her stomach. I don't know what I did exactly, but I know I prayed harder and more earnest than ever before. Just as soon as we were convinced that this thing was real, how petty all things on earth seemed, and how soon we put our trust in God!"

An unskilled laborer in Massachusetts spent his savings trying to escape. When he heard, later, of the Princeton investigation, he wrote: "I thought the best thing to do was to go away, so I took $3.25 out of my savings and bought a ticket. After I had gone sixty miles I heard it was a play. Now I don't have any money left for the shoes I was saving up for. Would you please have someone send me pair of black shoes, size 9-B."

3.

ORSON WELLES, in behalf of the Mercury Theater of the Air, is deeply regretful to learn that the H. G. Wells fantasy, *War of the Worlds*, which was designed as entertainment, has caused some apprehension among Columbia's network listeners. Far from expecting the radio audience to take the program as fact rather than as a fictional presentation, we feared that the classic H. G. Wells story, which has served as inspiration for so many moving pictures, radio serials, and even comic strips, might appear too old-fashioned for modern consumption. We can only suppose that the special nature of radio, which is often heard in fragments, or in parts disconnected from the whole, has led to this misunderstanding.

This statement, signed by Welles, appeared in papers the day after the broadcast. Whether or not the "classic H. G. Wells story" had served as inspiration for *quite* that many pictures, serials, and comics, it is true that the Mercury Theater group did not expect the radio audience to take the fantastic dramatization seriously.

After the program had been on the air half an hour, Orson Welles, at the microphone, was nudged by his fellow actors Ray Collins and Paul Stewart. He glanced toward the studio control room and, to his astonishment, saw it filling up with police. True, the show went on, as all shows must—everywhere, under any conditions—but not without a few interruptions.

During the broadcast, CBS made four announcements to the full network to the effect that It Was Only a Play: one at the beginning, one before and one after the "station break," and one at the end of the program. But before the hour was over, the panic had grown to such proportions that the network was obliged to make similar announcements during the rest of the evening, up to midnight, when this final announcement was made:

For those listeners who tuned in to Orson Welles' Mercury Theater of the Air broadcast from 8 to 9 P.M. E.S.T. tonight and did not realize that the program was merely a modernized adaptation of H. G. Wells' famous novel *War of the Worlds,* we are repeating the fact which was made clear four times on the program, that, while the names of some American cities were used, as in all novels of dramatization, the entire story and all of its incidents were fictitious.

Besides this, sixty per cent of all stations carrying the program interrupted the broadcast to make local announcements when it became apparent that a dangerous misunderstanding was abroad. But the damage had been done, for the most terrifying part of the broadcast came before the station broadcast. Susceptible listeners who failed to hear the first announcement did not stay for the others; they beat it into the night.

After the broadcast, Orson Welles and company had to go from the CBS studio at 485 Madison Avenue to the Mercury Theater on West Fortieth Street. At Times Square, they saw thousands of people standing in the street reading the startling news over the New York *Times* moving electric sign. Orson and his colleagues got out of the cab and took a look too, and panic seized them as well—panic of a different kind. Joseph Cotten told Welles that he was finished, washed up, a dead pigeon; show business would have no more of him from then on. Welles doubted it meant an end to his career; he argued that the American sense of humor would relish the hoax. And since Orson is still going strong, he seems to have been right.

In an interview with Ed Sullivan some years later, Welles was asked what, in his opinion, had made the broadcast so convincing. He replied, "It was the legitimate way in which we did it, I think. The background of the entire broadcast was legit radio. There was a second-rate band playing popular tunes apparently from a night club. Suddenly we broke in with a news flash of the Martian invasion near Princeton, New Jersey. Then we went back to the band and it went on playing popular tunes. Then a second news flash. Then the clincher: an actor imitating a State Department official's tones urged the country to stay calm. That did it!"

"Did you know," Sullivan asked, "that the broadcast would alarm the country?"

Orson: "My agent turned off his radio, because he thought it was such a silly show."

4.

THE PANIC became such a tremendous news story that psychologists were called upon to "analyze" it. Dr. Raymond H. Paynter, professor of psychology at Long Island University, was inclined to blame the public delusion, at least partly, on lack of imagination. "These people had been excited by the thought of war," he said, "and their imaginations, instead of carrying them into the fantastic at first, really held them back from the realization that the broadcast was only a dramatization. . . . The War Department couldn't have devised a cheaper or broader experiment. The panic can't help but reveal to the Department the extent to which emotion can be lifted by false terrifying reports. People have been conditioned to the idea of catastrophe. The war scare has done it. They naturally are quick to misconstrue anything in the nature of a threat. It shows how near the surface are the basic terrifying emotions."

The panic becomes more understandable, I think, when we recall that just one month before the broadcast, on September 30, the Big Four of Western Europe—Chamberlain, Daladier, Hitler, and Mussolini— had agreed at Munich to the terms which sold Czechoslovakia down the river and led to the beginning of World War II one year later.

Munich ended, temporarily, a month of war scares, a month in which the world became radio-conscious as never before. In December of 1936, the abdication of Edward VIII had kept listeners all over the world glued to their seats by the radio. In March, 1938, the Nazi *anschluss* with Austria did it again, with people everywhere on the *qui vive* in the hope that war might be averted. But neither the abdication crisis nor the *anschluss* was as sustained in intensity or duration as the Czechoslovakian crisis.

In September, 1938, there could no longer be any doubt that Nazi Germany was preparing for war with a seriousness of intent which had been completely lacking in the democracies. During the month before the Orson Welles panic—on every single day of that month, in fact—radio programs the world over (but particularly in the United States where the news coverage was more complete and the censorship *nil*) were constantly being interrupted by flash announcements threatening disaster to our shaky peace. Beginning with September 12 and continuing through October 1, some of the alarms and excursions that assailed us daily, often even hourly, over the air, are listed here. Radio stations stayed on the air all night, the names of news commentators became household words, horrific black headlines in our daily papers competed with radio flashes all day long—and Orson Welles was innocently preparing his spectacular broadcast, the perfect timing of which could not have been predicted by even so expert a showman as he:

Sept. 12, 1938	At Nuremberg, Adolph Hitler declares that the right of self-determination must be given to the Sudeten Germans.
Sept. 13	An outbreak of rioting leads the Czechoslovak Government to impose martial law in several Sudeten areas; the Henleinists serve an ultimatum on the Government giving it six hours in which to cancel its decrees.
Sept. 14	Prague ignores Henleinist ultimatum and sends more troops into the Sudeten area.
Sept. 15	In a dramatic move to avert war, Prime Minister Chamberlain flies to Berchtesgaden to see Hitler.
Sept. 16	Chamberlain returns to London to report on the German dictator's demands.
Sept. 17	The Prague Government puts all of Czechoslovakia under martial law.
Sept. 18	Premier Daladier and Foreign Minister Bonnet of France fly to London to consult with British Government.
Sept. 19	Britain and France accept Hitler's demands for a quick surrender to Germany of all predominantly German areas of Czechoslovakia.

Sept. 20   Beneš announces that the Anglo-French plan ·to partition
                Czechoslovakia is unacceptable.

Sept. 21   Under pressure from London and Paris, Prague agrees to
                cede Sudeten German areas to Germany.

Sept. 22   Chamberlain flies to Bad Godesberg for a second meeting
                with Hitler; General Jan Syrovy becomes Premier of
                Czechoslovakia.

Sept. 23   Hitler increases his demands on Czechoslovakia, threaten-
                ing invasion; Beneš orders general mobilization of the
                Czechoslovak Army; Paris prepares for partial mobilization.

Sept. 24   Chamberlain flies back to London; Mussolini assures Hitler
                of support; Britain and France speed their defenses.

Sept. 25   Daladier and Bonnet fly to London again; the Czechoslovak
                Government rejects the new German demands.

Sept. 26   As fear of war grows, President Roosevelt appeals to Hitler
                to negotiate; an "authoritative" statement is issued in Lon-
                don declaring that Britain and Russia will support France
                in the defense of Czechoslovakia.

Sept. 27   In a radio broadcast, Chamberlain calls Hitler's Godesberg
                demands "unreasonable" and makes a final plea to the Ger-
                man dictator; President Roosevelt sends a second appeal to
                Hitler; the British fleet is partially mobilized.

Sept. 28   With Europe on verge of war, Hitler calls a four-power con-
                ference in Munich.

Sept. 29   Chamberlain, Daladier, and Mussolini meet Hitler.

Sept. 30   The four powers reach an agreement in Munich allowing
                Germany to occupy the Sudeten areas progressively over a
                ten-day period beginning October first; Czechoslovakia,
                feeling that she has been betrayed, capitulates.

War had been averted; there was "peace in our time"—and on October 1 the Nazis crossed the border of Czechoslovakia. Thirty days
later, in this period of the war of nerves, Orson Welles produced his

Martian invasion, and millions of jittery Americans were instantly convinced that the war had come to them.

5.

OF COURSE, reactions in the public press were many and varied.

Quick to take advantage of the American panic was the Nazi party
newspaper, the *Völkischer Beobachter,* which characteristically blamed
the whole thing on the Jews for the war scare caused in the United
States; while the Italian Fascist sheet, *Resto del Carlino* of Bologna,
reported (one can imagine with almost as much glee as exaggeration)
that many deaths were caused in the United States by heart attacks,
suicides, and panics resulting from the broadcast. This paper called the
American public (rightly enough, God knows) "incredible," adding
that the mythical Martians "put a third-grade democracy into tragic
confusion." It wound up: "The Americans live under fear of invasion; and upon its announcements, no matter how ridiculous they may
be, people start firing guns, drinking poison, throwing themselves from
windows, and dashing madly to insane asylums."

Soberer reflections came from New York editorial writers. The
Times paused in its appraisal of more solemn affairs and wrote sternly:

> Radio ought to act promptly to prevent a repetition of the wave of panic
> in which it inundated the nation Sunday night. . . . Thousands, from one
> end of the country to the other, were frightened out of their senses, starting
> an incipient flight of hysterical refugees from the designated area, taxing the
> police and hospitals, confusing traffic, and choking the usual means of com-
> munication. . . . Common sense might have warned the projectors of the
> broadcast that our people are just recovering from a psychosis brought on by
> fear of war. But the trouble goes much deeper than that. It is inherent in the
> method of radio broadcasting as maintained at present in this country. It can
> only be cured by a deeply searching self-regulation in which every element of
> the radio industry should join. Radio is new, but it has adult responsibilities.
> It has not mastered itself or the material it uses. . . .

In more tolerant and judicious vein, the New York *World-Telegram*
said editorially:

It is strange and disturbing that thousands of Americans, secure in their homes on a quiet Sunday evening, could be scared out of their wits by a radio dramatization. . . . Unlike Hamlet, young Mr. Welles did not plan deliberately to demoralize his audience. And no guilty consciences, but nerves made jittery by actual though almost incredible threats of war and disaster, had prepared a good many radio listeners to believe the completely incredible "news" that Martian hordes were here. Of course it should never happen again. But we don't agree with those who are arguing that the Sunday night broadcast showed a need for strict government censorship of radio programs. On the contrary, we think it is evidence of how dangerous political control of radio might become. If so many people could be misled unintentionally, when the purpose was merely to entertain, what could designing politicians not do through control of broadcasting stations? The dictators in Europe use radio to make their people believe falsehoods. We want nothing like that here. Better have American radio remain free to make occasional blunders than start on a course that might, in time, deprive it of freedom to broadcast uncensored truth.

Nevertheless, radio executives everywhere were in the anxious seat, none more so than certain nervous officials on the eighteenth and nineteenth floors at 485 Madison Avenue. CBS feared an investigation by the Federal Communications Commission, and penalties. But on December 5, the Associated Press reported that the FCC had decided to take no action. The Commission said that it believed steps already taken by CBS were sufficient to protect the public interest. "While it is regrettable that the broadcast alarmed a substantial number of people," the FCC said, "there appeared to be no likelihood of a repetition of the incident and no occasion for action by the Commission."

Nevertheless, a chastened industry had learned its lesson. The "steps already taken by CBS" were summarized in a statement by William (Bill) Lewis, vice-president in charge of CBS programs, who expressed regret for the incident and said that the techniques employed in the Welles broadcast would not be used henceforth. "In order that this may not happen again, the Program Department hereafter will not use the technique of simulated news broadcasts within a dramatization when the circumstances of the broadcast could cause immediate alarm to numbers of listeners."

Still and all, like the fellow says—and in view of that fateful anxious month—the statement which seems to have made the most common sense was Heywood Broun's very human reaction in the *World-Telegram*:

I'm still scared. I didn't hear the broadcast, and I doubt that I would have called up the police to complain merely because I heard that men from a strange machine were knocking the daylights out of Princeton. . . . But I live in terror that almost any time now a metal cylinder will come to earth, and out of it will step fearsome creatures carrying death-ray guns.

Perhaps, to the inhabitants of Hiroshima or Nagasaki, that would be almost a relief.

Wendell Willkie: A Study in Courage

BY ROSCOE DRUMMOND

Roscoe Drummond has spent his whole newspaper career with *The Christian Science Monitor,* serving it as reporter, assistant city editor, chief editorial writer, executive editor, and, since 1940, chief of its Washington news bureau. He reported the Willkie campaign of 1940 and remained in close personal touch with Willkie up to within a few days of the latter's death. His intimate account of Willkie's relations with President Roosevelt, and of his own final interview with Willkie in the hospital where he died, are valuable contributions to the history of our times. Mr. Drummond was—and is—a frank admirer of Willkie, and in the following article he seeks to evaluate as well as describe him.

✵ 1.

AMERICANS, I believe, will never forget Wendell Willkie. We will never forget how this Wilson Democrat who voted for Franklin Roosevelt in 1932, this "barefoot Wall Street lawyer"—as Harold Ickes sneered in the 1940 campaign—seized the Republican Presidential nomination by popular demand; we will not forget the prodigious crusade he conducted against the New Deal's Third Term, how the country became familiar with his disheveled suits, necktie askew, hair flying in the breeze or falling down over his forehead, his voice getting hoarser and hoarser, as he impatiently used to elide "Presen-Unide-States." We will not forget his repeated and still pertinent appeal that "only the productive can be strong and only the strong can be free."

It happened that I was present, with other correspondents, in his suite in the Benjamin Franklin Hotel when he was nominated in Philadelphia in 1940, and I was the last correspondent to talk with him in

1944, spending an hour and a half with him discussing the Roosevelt-Dewey campaign in his hospital room just seven days before his death. There were numerous newspapermen who had an intimate and mutually trusted relationship with him, and I think we came to know his motivations and his purposes, his hopes and his disappointments.

At a time when Wendell Willkie still had a fair chance and a large hope of becoming the Republican Presidential nominee for the second time, in 1944, he told me, as he no doubt told some others, "If I could write my own epitaph, and if I had to choose between saying, 'Here lies an unimportant President' or, 'Here lies one who contributed to saving freedom at a moment of great peril,' I would prefer the latter."

Willkie would never have made an unimportant President. But he might well have secured the nomination on terms which would have made him the prisoner of his compromises. Instead, he deliberately chose the prospect of political defeat in order to improve America's prospect of winning the war and building the peace.

Willkie would today be an asterisk leading to a footnote in a history book if he had simply been another Republican Presidential candidate defeated by Franklin Roosevelt. But his defeat was only the beginning of Wendell Willkie's claim to a place in our history.

Willkie's brief public career spanned one of the three most critical periods of American history, equal in danger and equal in opportunity to the Revolution and the founding of the Republic, and to the War Between the States and the preservation of the Union. Hitler was not always wrong; he was right when he said that he was gambling for control of the world for a thousand years to come. If freedom had been wiped from the face of the globe by Axis victory, it might well have taken a thousand years of pain and pestilence and suffering and sacrifice to have won it back.

No American leader saw more clearly than Wendell Willkie the nature of the Axis threat to the freedom of free men everywhere in the world. The total impact of his leadership was directed toward deflecting that threat, toward defeating that threat, toward forging the Allied coalition which would ultimately win the war into an Allied coalition determined to secure a just and workable peace.

During his campaign for the Presidency in 1940, he spurned the most alluring advice on how he could win if he would only shut up about the war. He wouldn't.

During his campaign for renomination from 1940 to April, 1944, he spurned the most astute political counsel on how he could influence Republicans and not damage his conscience too much if he would only come out for a "soft" war and quit harping on what America had to do to win the peace. He wouldn't.

Instead, at a time when every isolationist, pacifist, America First, hate-Roosevelt, head-in-the-sand pressure group was waiting to clutch his coattail if he would give them the slightest encouragement, and his own party leaders were wringing their hands at his missed "opportunities," what did he do? He ridiculed, resisted, and rejected all such actions.

No wonder the Republican organization leaders were displeased, dismayed, and alarmed. They didn't quite know what they had on their hands and, whatever it was, they were anxious to get rid of it as soon as possible. From some firsthand knowledge of what brought him to the top of the G.O.P. in 1940 and what thrust him to the bottom in 1944, my own judgment of Mr. Willkie's difficulties with the Republican party can be put this way:

The Republicans reluctantly accepted Wendell Willkie in 1940 because they did not know him.

The Republicans eagerly rejected Wendell Willkie four years later because they did know him, and he had not proved an adequately conservative and tractable political leader.

In the four years between, Willkie became the most influential American never to hold national office.

He made a larger contribution to the security, the welfare, the progress, and the vision of the nation than many elected Presidents.

Though he was unable greatly to shape the course of the Republican party, he was able greatly to help shape the course of history.

2.

WENDELL WILLKIE was as American as the two-pants suit and the general store. With his three brothers and two sisters, he lived as a youngster in a ramshackle, three-story house, painted in two shades of green and with maples shading the yard, which still stands in Elwood, Indiana. In high school and college he distinguished himself as a debater of slightly radical tinge. At sixteen he helped his father, Herman F. Willkie, prepare a case for union labor in opposition to a picketing injunction. In later years he was fond of repeating the old maxim: "Any man who is not something of a Socialist before he is forty has no heart; any man who is still a Socialist after he is forty has no head."

Elwood's composite recollection of young Willkie is something of a mixture of Peck's bad boy, a juvenile Norman Thomas, and a misplaced Oxford don. He used to amuse himself by playing Hamlet from memory, wearing his mother's old petticoat for a cape. With one of his husky brothers, he once took on the whole police force of Bloomington, Indiana, with his bare fists. He fried eggs, made steel, milked cows, and taught history with such vivid reality that his students remember his descriptions to this day—all this to work his way through college.

Willkie's racial strains stemmed from the Germany of democratic revolution and took deep root in the soil of Indiana. He grew up in a family environment of intellectual curiosity and individual self-reliance. He never really left the America of the Midwest, for he took Indiana with him, its manners and its mood, when he went to New York to make a living in the law and business. His views were never bounded by the limited horizons of business, and while he believed profoundly in a dynamic private enterprise, his concern was not primarily for business or businessmen but for a productive economy capable of sustaining a social security for the whole people. He inherited this social view, he expanded this social view for himself, and he never departed from this social view while he was practicing law in New York, while he was conducting the affairs of the billion-dollar utility Commonwealth and Southern, or while he was conducting a liberal crusade within and, more often than not, against both the Republican party and the Democratic party, then commonly tagged the political home of liberals.

Willkie's was a notably favored background and environment for the life and tasks ahead of him. His four grandparents were political refugees who emigrated from Germany when that country's democratic revolutionaries of 1848 were being suppressed. His parents, Herman Francis and Henrietta Trisch Willkie, brought up their six children on a fare of unlimited discussion and limited resources. His father and mother practiced law together and Wendell—or Lewis, as he was then called—had the advantage of having to work his way through college at Indiana University. These were the favors with which Willkie started his life. He discovered *Das Kapital* as an undergraduate and persuaded the college to add a study of Socialism to its curriculum because he wanted to know more about it. He spent most of his extracurricular time with the University debating team and his early political attachments were toward the ideas of the elder Bob La Follette and Woodrow Wilson's New Freedom. Young Willkie lost his first law case to his father, but after he had established himself in Akron, Ohio, won so many of his cases that he was invited by Bernard Capen Cobb, president of Commonwealth and Southern, to accept a partnership in its law firm in New York. Four years later, at forty-one, he succeeded Mr. Cobb in the presidency of Commonwealth and Southern.

Willkie was entirely aware that utilities had a bad record and that reasonable government regulation was both necessary and desirable. He carried out many reforms in the management and financing of Commonwealth and Southern, and in the middle of the depression he succeeded in reducing his company's residential rates and increasing the use of electric power to farms and private homes. That was what the government was trying to do, too.

The government's offer to buy the Tennessee Electric Power Company for $55,000,000 Mr. Willkie considered too low, and, confident of the fairness of his position, he boldly proposed arbitration by the Federal Securities and Exchange Commission. The government refused arbitration, but finally increased its offer to $78,600,000; the sale at this figure enabled Willkie to pay off outstanding bonds and preferred stock at par value and realize about $6,000,000 for holders of the common stock.

3.

As a frequent witness at Congressional and administrative agency committee hearings during this period, later as Presidential candidate, and finally as public advocate, Wendell Willkie gained a wide acquaintanceship among the Washington press corps.

Many Washington correspondents knew him well. He liked newspapermen and it was his habit to talk with us frankly on almost any provocation, to disclose his real opinions of men and affairs without the caution and reserve which mark so many public men.

Thinking out loud was his pastime; exchanging ideas was his passion. He loved to listen—admittedly somewhat less than he loved to talk. He was, however, a reasonably good listener whenever there was something worth listening to, but his open disdain of what he often described as the "pedestrian thinking" of most professional politicians sometimes won him unnecessary ill will and political difficulty. He acquired his ideas through thought processes, not through social osmosis. He was brought up on ideas, could look a new one in the face without blanching, regarded ideas as the tools of social, economic, and political progress.

Willkie always seemed to me a more forceful, a more persuasive, a more impressive personality in give-and-take conversation than he did over the radio. His informality, his spontaneity were more convincing when you sat opposite him in his office and when he was holding a five-hour "bull session" with correspondents in Washington than from the platform. He never cultivated the ornaments of the "great executive" —neither the commanding look nor the efficient affability. He got on better with his critics than his adulators and he enjoyed the company of newspapermen who argued back better than those whose duty it was to take down what he said and rush to the telephone.

He was his own closest adviser. He was independent, occasionally stubborn. He was something of a revivalist even in private conversation. His mind was stimulated in his contact with people, and his thought processes seemed more inspirational than logical. Not that he was illogical; he just didn't tick things off under Roman numerals I, II, and III. The impression of one of his writing friends is that he used to snipe at a subject from all sides; then, finally grabbing hold, he would roll it up in a ball and throw it at you.

Willkie was no more humble than he was simple. There was no self-doubt in his make-up. He was neither modest nor immodest; it just never occurred to him that he could be anything other than successful.

He was an engaging, disarming, compelling, fascinating, stirring personality. I choose these adjectives carefully. He had few of the little graces, though in his personal relations he could show an extraordinary and imaginative sensitivity. He was a warmhearted, unwavering, loyal friend and expected the same loyalty in return.

As a political leader he did not know how to play it safe.

It seems to me that Mr. Willkie's great and incalculable influence for good upon the course of the nation stemmed in large degree from this fact. He had no ability to express cautious, discreet, expedient opinions on issues that seemed to him important. However, he was not consciously a "fearless" man. He was either something more than that or something different from that. I mean that he was a political leader of such intellectual honesty that he never seriously considered whether he was being courageous or fearless. Because he was free of political fear, he never needed to strive to be fearless.

Wendell Willkie was publicly and privately the same man; he was himself.

American democracy nurtured and made possible Wendell Willkie. It defeated him at the polls for reasons which will be later discussed, but it responded to him more warmly after he was defeated than at the peak of his Presidential campaign.

Willkie did not tarnish upon intimate association, and when he was suddenly stricken at a time when many were waiting his lead, it was evident that he had become the conscience and the symbol of the best hopes of much of mankind.

4.

THE EMERGENCE of Wendell Willkie in 1940, the nature of the Presidential campaign he conducted, and his greatness in political defeat were decisive factors in enabling America to win the war.

There were four main contributions which Mr. Willkie made toward winning the war and in total they constituted, I believe, an indispensable factor on the side of victory. They were these:

1. He defied and weakened the isolationist forces of the Republican party.

2. Immediately after the hard-fought election of 1940, during which emotions were high and partisanship was deep, he gave an expression of American democracy at its purest and its best by summoning the "loyal opposition" to strengthen, rather than to weaken, the administration.

3. He carried weight with the people outside the confines of his own party and he exerted a compulsion upon the government to take bolder and stronger measures of defense than it was taking.

4. His leadership was felt beyond the boundaries of America and helped to give heart and faith to the heroic struggles of all people who were fighting the enemies of freedom.

At a time when Britain alone was holding the outer rim of freedom against the Axis, the Old Guard G.O.P. leadership was fiercely resisting every effort of the administration to aid the cause Britain was upholding. No Republican could have won the election of 1940, but any Republican leadership other than Willkie's would have confirmed the party in a position of implacable isolationism. If Willkie's dynamic influence and will to co-operate had not prevailed, aid to Britain would have been feeble and failing and those democratic remnants who were still standing out against Hitler would have seen themselves abandoned. America then would have been without strong Allies and without time in which to prepare first for defense and later for offensive action. Even the limited measures which the administration was advancing would probably not have passed the Congress without Willkie's active help.

After the 1940 election it would have been in the political tradition for the defeated Presidential nominee to have continued to harass the national administration; it would have been to Willkie's immediate political advantage. He could have retired into aloofness and silence; and many of his political colleagues advised him that that was the smart thing to do. He could have technically kept his own record straight by saying a few polite and proper words and leaving it to the man who defeated him to carry the ball. He did none of these things. Against all political counsel, he issued a clear call to his followers to bury partisan differences, to adjourn domestic disputes, and to give their whole support to the President in mobilizing the strength of the free world against the Axis.

On November 11, 1940, Mr. Willkie called the "loyal opposition" into being—"a vigorous, public-spirited loyal opposition which would not oppose for the sake of opposition."

Soon thereafter, in a series of speeches, Mr. Willkie went to the furthest lengths in summoning the nation to unite as one people behind the elected government because of the peril of war.

If you will think back to the bitter, uncertain, controversial, divisive months from 1939 through 1941, while the Nazi armies were conquering all of Europe, you will recapture some sense of the political dangers and difficulties which faced the President in his efforts to win the nation's support for a dynamic defense—a defense which would keep the Axis as far as possible from American shores and which would strengthen the arm of every country resisting Hitler.

There was the personally popular and persuasive Lindbergh who was advising the world that Nazi Germany was unbeatable, that Russia was militarily helpless, that America couldn't be attacked.

There were the "America First" organizations in many parts of the country constantly repeating and repeating that "This isn't our war; it's of no concern to the United States."

There was the instinctive, deep-seated peace-loving tradition of the American people on which Hitler relied to keep the United States on the sidelines until the rest of the world had fallen to the Axis.

These forces, which were saying in effect, "Leave us alone; everything will be all right" were never in a majority. But they were powerful, articulate, cleverly led. If they had increased their strength, if they had retained their strength, if they had not had their influence decisively wrested from them, these forces would have constituted a barrier to effect aid to Britain, to every venturesome act of American defense against the encircling Axis. I suggest that without the Willkie-created climate of national unity, the government would have been perilously delayed and enfeebled and Britain might easily have gone down.

In August, 1940, when the Presidential campaign was just about to get under way, Willkie was told by a representative of the White House that the President would like to arrange the exchange of fifty American destroyers for Western Hemisphere bases, but that the President did not think this could be done unless Mr. Willkie would agree not to make a political issue of it. It would have been "smart" politics for him to attack it. It couldn't have hurt him politically; it probably would have helped him politically. But Willkie believed that aid to Britain was America's best defense and he chose to serve his beliefs rather than enhance his political prospects.

When he was preparing his acceptance speech, he was urged by the Old Guard politicians to come out against Selective Service. They contended that the pacifist instincts of the American people could be so effectively played upon if he would take sharp issue with the administration over the draft that he could not fail to be elected. Weight must be given to this political appraisal because, even as the war clouds grew blacker, the demobilization of the nation's draft army in the fall of 1941 was averted by only one lone vote in the House of Representatives. But Mr. Willkie believed that the draft was essential to the defense of America, and he chose to serve his beliefs.

Wendell Willkie's concrete advocacy of an all-out war effort began early in 1940 before his nomination at Philadelphia; he never let up. At nearly every turn he either advocated obvious measures more forcibly than was already being done or advocated more forcible measures than were elsewhere being urged. The record shows that:

He was constantly preparing and pressing public opinion to accept unstinting aid to Britain as essential to America's own defense.

By his flying trip to the storm shelters of London, he dramatized what it meant to the United States to keep beleaguered Britain afloat.

After he had braved the bombs to find out for himself, he hurried home to appear before the Senate Foreign Relations Committee. It was his firsthand testimony which gave the Lend-Lease Act its most formidable support and which put behind it the kind of national unity which enabled the President to implement it to the full.

He early advocated the end of the helpless, hopeless concept of cash and carry—the concept that America would sell its arms to any nation that could come and carry them away. And when Lend-Lease removed the cash from the carry, he was first to urge that American merchantmen be armed and escorted by the fleet to deliver the tools of war to the outstretched hands of the Allies.

He advocated total repeal of the outmoded neutrality law which the administration was attacking in such piecemeal manner that it never succeeded in getting rid of it until it was wiped out by the Japanese on December 7.

I remember how dismayed many of us were when at one of President Roosevelt's press conferences during the early stages of our prewar efforts toward preparedness, the President sought to assure the country that nobody was "going to be discombobulated." Obviously the President was gravely concerned lest too vigorous action play into the hands of the isolationist, this-isn't-our-war opposition.

But Mr. Willkie did not coddle this opposition. He told the people from the beginning that the nation's whole economy and everybody's lives would have to be "discombobulated" if America was to gear for war, arm the Allies, and be prepared to defend its freedom. He believed that the American people did not need to be cushioned from the impact of the war but only shown what vast dedication was needed—that they would respond. He advocated total conversion to war individually, industrially, financially.

Willkie did not hesitate to brand the obstructionists of the Republican party as sabotaging the nation's will and he put principle above partisanship when he declared in August of 1941:

"We can have only one administration and only one foreign policy at any one time. And when through our elected representatives we have determined that policy, every American citizen should help to make it effective. Legitimate debate is wise—and our duty—but attempts to stultify action and disunite our people by mere political harangue are in effect sabotaging their will."

I submit—and I believe the historians will ultimately concur—that the leadership of Wendell Willkie was a decisive event in our war for "the preservation of America and freedom."

5.

HE DID MORE than play a huge role in winning the war. From its beginning he was concerned with the shape of the peace. He lost no opportunity to tell the American people that there could be no durable peace after World War II, as there was none after World War I, unless the United States played a full-bodied role in the world and did not attempt to secede from it. During the early days of the war, while high officials of the government, including the President, were saying, in effect, that it was too early to begin creating the machinery of the peace, Mr. Willkie was saying that now is the time, now is the time.

He said, "We must not listen to those who say, 'Win the war now,' and leave postwar solutions to our leaders and our experts."

He said, "It is idle to talk about creating after the war is over a machinery for preventing economic warfare and promoting peace between nations, unless the parts of that machinery have been assembled under the unifying effort and common purpose of seeking to defeat the enemy."

He said, "What we need is not the hope of a grand council after the war. What we need is a council today of the United Nations—not a paper council but an actual working council. A common council in which all plan together, not a council of a few, who direct and merely aid others as they think wise. . . . Let us resolve that the United Nations shall be more than a symbol, that it shall be a working reality today, in order that the things for which we fight may have a chance to be realized tomorrow."

At a time when most of the Republican leaders were hoping against hope that he would somehow find his way into political oblivion, Willkie mounted a four-engine Consolidated bomber on August 26, 1942, and forty-nine days later had traveled thirty-one thousand miles around the globe, visited a dozen countries, and had intimate conversations with the world's leaders—and hundreds of other "men and women, important and anonymous, whose heroism and sacrifices give meaning and life to their beliefs."

The flight of the *Gulliver* and its distinguished passenger made significant and controversial news. At every turn, Willkie was exhorting the Allied fighters to an ever greater united war effort. But more important, the trip lent fire and focus to Willkie's concept of the future peace. His forty-nine-day, thirty-one thousand miles around the world gave him an impression "not of distance from other peoples, but of closeness to them"—the indelible impression of "a world become small and interdependent"; in short: One World.

The account which Willkie wrote of his travels was a compelling piece of narrative literature. He had seen One World. He wrote *One World*. He perceived that One World was a fact, not an intellectual argument—a fact which must be the cornerstone of the only successful peace which could make us secure against a third World War.

To the acute distress of his political critics, *One World* instantly became one of the all-time best sellers. In an amazingly brief time more than two million copies were sold in the United States. It was translated into almost every language in the world, sometimes into several dialects. And in Nazi-conquered countries it was printed for freedom-loving people by underground movements, at the risk of death. Apart from the war itself, nothing could have contributed more to holding aloft the goal of One Freedom, One Peace.

These words about One World from *One World* deserve to be recalled:

At the end of the last war, not a single plane had flown across the Atlantic. Today that ocean is a mere ribbon, with airplanes making regular scheduled flights. The Pacific is only a slightly wider ribbon in the ocean of the air, and Europe and Asia are at our doorstep.

America must choose one of three courses after this war: narrow nationalism, which inevitably means the ultimate loss of our own liberty; international imperialism, which means the sacrifice of some other nation's liberty; or the creation of a world in which there shall be an equality of opportunity for every race and every nation. I am convinced the American people will choose, by overwhelming majority, the last of these courses. To make this choice effective, we must win not only the war but also the peace, and we must start winning it now.

To win this peace three things seem to me necessary—first, we must plan now for peace on a world basis; second, the world must be free, politically and economically, for nations and for men, that peace may exist in it; third, America must play an active, constructive part in freeing it and keeping its peace.

When I say that peace must be planned on a world basis, I mean quite literally that it must embrace the earth. Continents and oceans are plainly only parts of a whole, seen, as I have seen them, from the air. England and America are parts, Russia and China, Egypt, Syria and Turkey, Iraq and Iran are also parts. And it is inescapable that there can be no peace for any part of the world unless the foundations of peace are made secure throughout all parts of the world.

It is easy and it is accurate to say that the haggard and harried peace which has thus far emerged is a far cry from the One World of Wendell Willkie's conception; that the United Nations is feeble; that national sovereignty has been "hoarded," not "used" as he urged; that Indo-China or Indonesia hardly seems to be enjoying "equality of opportunity"; that Eastern Europe is free neither politically nor economically; that America's clutching for military bases in the Arctic and in the Far Pacific looks more altruistic and peaceful to Americans than to others.

True, but Willkie never said achieving one peace and one freedom would be easy. He did say—and today who will deny him—that until the world's leaders conform their policies to the fact of One World, there will be no just and durable peace.

In *One World,* you will remember, Willkie wrote: "It is inescapable that there can be no peace for any part of the world unless the foundations of peace are made secure throughout all parts of the world."

At the opening meeting of the Security Council's Atomic Energy Commission, Bernard Baruch, the American representative, said that any prospect of atomic control must rest upon the basis of a sound foreign policy and that in this new age, such a foreign policy for all the United Nations must be: "That anything that happens, no matter where or how, which menaces the peace of the world, or the economic stability, concerns each and all of us."

There is no reason to believe that Mr. Willkie would have taken any tolerant, condoning attitude toward Russia's imposition of police state regimes in Eastern Europe. He was one of the first to condemn Moscow for what it was doing to Poland before the full extent of the Polish conquest was evident. But denial of the One World concept by the Russian expansionists makes it no less valid than its denial by American isolationists. Ultimately peace can be had only on the terms in which Wendell Willkie conceived it.

6.

THE FAME and the name and something of the galvanic personality of Wendell Willkie had, by the spring of 1940, become known to millions of newspaper and magazine readers and radio listeners, primarily through his own writing and speaking, and partly through his Commonwealth and Southern-T.V.A. tussle with the government.

Two months before the Philadelphia convention he was hardly being more than mentioned as a "dark horse" candidate—very "dark horse," so dark he was scarcely visible to the political eye. He himself did not begin to exert any effort to obtain the nomination until about six weeks before the opening of the convention, and at no time, even when the balloting began, did he have any orthodox organization working for him, or more than a few delegates pledged to him. He had no official manager.

Willkie won the Republican Presidential nomination on June 28, 1940, for three reasons:

The convention was not satisfied with its two leading candidates. It instinctively felt that the then District Attorney of New York County, Thomas E. Dewey, would not be counted by the country as ready for the White House and that Senator Robert A. Taft of Ohio would not make a vote-getting appeal.

The convention knew little about Willkie as a politician, but it had plenty of evidence that he was the public's favorite; that he was the most appealing figure who had come along to carry the Republican banner since Teddy Roosevelt. It responded to the battering waves of popular demand. Willkie was no more "put over" on the Philadelphia convention than Babe Ruth was "put over" on the New York Yankees. It was obvious to the party leaders that Willkie could hit and it was assumed he could be managed without too much difficulty.

The conservative leadership of the Republican party which wrote its platform and could have successfully resisted his nomination accepted Willkie because they assumed that as a businessman in the White House he could be counted on to perform conservative acts. They thought that Willkie's "liberal lapses" were not dangerous and wouldn't last if he were elected. They believed that on his business record—a record they had never closely read—Willkie would be only a phraseological liberal and a practicing conservative.

How wrong they were! How deeply they regretted their decision. What a relief when Willkie wasn't elected. How energetically they went to work to see that it shouldn't happen again.

Long before his nomination, Willkie had conclusively aligned himself with social and economic progressivism. He was saying again and again that "the system of 1929 could not be permitted to stand"; that democracy in a modern industrial society "needed more social controls"; that an "extension of federal authority" was proper and inevitable in view of the "national character of the great American corporations and of many businesses and financial operations."

The attitudes which Willkie took, the policies he advocated, stemmed logically from his background and from the publicly stated positions he had previously taken. They were consistent expressions, not violations, of his whole record as a student, as a lawyer, as a liberal businessman, as writer, speaker, and advocate.

The Republican Old Guard had no excuse for being misled about Wendell Willkie. The reason they were misled is that they either had not paid attention to what he said, or did not believe he meant it. Or some of both.

During the 1940 campaign itself—in the course of which the *Willkie Special* carried the candidate on an 18,759-mile canvass of the nation, covering 31 states in 51 days—Willkie literally picked up the

Republican party by its bootstraps and planted it on a new front line of social and economic policy.

He pledged his support to progressive social legislation, opposition to which in the past had come principally from the Republican party.

He defended labor legislation, opposition to which in the past had come principally from the Republican party.

He gave his unqualified backing to full-bodied internationalism in foreign policy, unstinting aid to Britain, Selective Service, and other bold measures of defense, to all which the majority of the Republican party was in opposition.

Willkie's positive and progressive stand on foreign and domestic issues was far more than passing allegiance to political catchwords, far more than convenient endorsement of political promises. He was ready to proclaim these purposes and to practice them and to help bring them about—whether the Republican party gained control of Congress or remained in the minority.

There was, of course, a gulf between Willkie and the Roosevelt administration. His central and repeated charge was that the New Deal had failed to rescue the nation from the 1930 depression—had failed because its excesses of capricious and class-conscious regulation were applying a deadening hand to the energies of private enterprise—and that incentives and freedoms were disappearing.

Willkie put it this way in his acceptance speech at Elwood:

I say that we must henceforth ask certain questions of every reform and of every law to regulate business or industry. We must ask: Has it encouraged our industries to produce? Has it created new opportunities for our youth? Will it increase our standard of living? Will it encourage us to open up a new and bigger world?

A reform that cannot meet these tests is not a truly liberal reform. It is an "I pass" reform. It does not tend to strengthen our system, but to weaken it. It exposes us to aggressors, whether economic or military. It encourages class distinctions and hatreds. And it will lead us inevitably, as I believe we are now headed, toward a form of government alien to ours, and a way of life contrary to the way that our parents taught us here in Elwood.

For the first time in our history, American industry has remained stationary for a decade. It offers no more jobs today than it did ten years ago—and there are six million more persons seeking jobs. As a nation of producers we have become stagnant. Much of our industrial machinery is obsolete. And the national standard of living has declined.

It is a statement of fact, and no longer a political accusation, that the New Deal has failed in its program of economic rehabilitation. And the victims of its failures are the very persons whose cause it professes to champion.

He submitted that after eight years of New Deal economic experimentation, the box score remained: One-third of the nation still in need; ten million still unemployed; the federal deficit still going up and up.

He submitted that there was no evidence whatsoever that New Deal "recovery" policies had raised the standard of living, had increased employment, had created opportunities for youth or for adults, had resulted in expansion of enterprise.

I traveled those 18,759 miles on the *Willkie Special* in the fall of 1940, was aboard that hectic campaign train for most of its fifty-one days of touring, and listened to most of the candidate's six to ten daily speeches, no two of which were ever alike. On the basis of the campaign record I would say that the main differences on domestic policy which Willkie drew between himself and the Roosevelt administration were these:

The New Deal brought needed social and economic reform legislation into being, but did not make a single significant contribution to economic recovery.

The New Deal sought to save private enterprise by subjecting it to the maximum of government control and ended by hamstringing it.

The New Deal sought to promote social reform by belaboring private enterprise and ended by endangering both social reform and private enterprise.

The New Deal sought to combine forms of collectivism with a degree of private capitalism and ended by imperiling private capitalism and impairing democracy.

Willkie held that private enterprise and democracy were indispensable to each other.

He wished to see private enterprise freed from a governmental atmosphere of hostility and released from a degree of federal control which, he believed, had domination rather than regulation as its objective.

He contended that only by releasing private enterprise and restoring its proper incentives could we achieve a productive economy which would sustain the social securities he favored.

He held that liberal reforms could only be saved and expanded by enabling private enterprise to function.

It is, of course, clearer in retrospect than it was at the time that Wendell Willkie was perpetually, in 1940 and ever afterward, campaigning against *both major parties*!

He was opposing the New Deal more for what it had failed to do than for what it had done—its failure to bring economic recovery to the nation. He was opposing the New Deal because it was "power hungry," because it had no answer for an economic ill other than to spend more money, because it promoted class conflict and disunity for political purposes.

And he was, in effect, opposing the Republican party for having fought during the previous eight years the principle and substance of virtually every social reform to which he gave his support during the 1940 campaign. He was, in effect, opposing the Republican party for having led the country down the lonely road of isolationism during the 1920's and for pursuing a head-in-the-sand, do-as-little-as-possible attitude on defense in face of the Axis conquests.

In his deep disagreements with the New Deal, yes, but also in his unyielding advocacy of liberal reform within the framework of the free enterprise system, Willkie meant what he said, meant it all the way, meant it all the time.

This is why the Republican Old Guard stand-patters, who controlled the party machinery, were horrified before Willkie was halfway through the campaign, why they deserted him before the election, why they began at once to arrange that they should never be troubled with him again.

This is why it can be accurately said that the Republican leaders permitted the nomination of Wendell Willkie in 1940 before they came to know him and arranged to reject him in 1944 because they came to know him.

The fact is that from November 11, 1940, when he delivered his post-election "loyal opposition" broadcast, to April 5, 1944, when he withdrew from the race for renomination, after his overwhelming Wisconsin defeat, Wendell Willkie conducted an open, vigorous, and unrelenting campaign for the reform—for the liberalization on domestic and foreign policies—of the Republican party.

It was just too much for the great majority of Republican leaders to have their 1940 Presidential nominee characterize the past record of their party as one of "narrow nationalism and economic Toryism."

It was just too much for most of the Republican members of Congress to listen to Willkie warn that the voters would "separate the gold from the dross" if the Republican party didn't press "for more efficient ways of winning the war" instead of engaging in "blind opposition" and "fence sitting."

Willkie was saying that the Republican party could not win a victory with the nation in 1944 "until it first won a victory within itself."

He was saying that the Republican party, because it had "become corrupted by vested interests in its own ranks and by reactionary forces" and had forgotten "its own great liberal traditions," had seen the country lose confidence in it and "never quite regain it."

Willkie didn't change his tune in the fateful Wisconsin primary of 1944. He had undertaken the task of reforming the Republican party and getting it to like him at the same time, the task of simultaneously thumping the G.O.P. elephant on the rear and patting its head. He may have made some converts to his purposes in Wisconsin, but he made no friends, and Wisconsin Republicans showed decisively that they, like the party leaders, didn't want Willkie.

Wisconsin Republicans may or may not have decided, like the rest of the country, that isolationism would no longer work, but they didn't want to nominate a candidate who had so emphatically told them so. The party simply wouldn't take its disciplinarian even if it did take some of his discipline.

Willkie was out of the race and the Republican leaders were still so afraid of his vast influence with the country that they gave him no opportunity to appear before the platform committee or to attend the 1944 convention in any official capacity. Republican Chairman Harrison E. Spangler sent him a ticket which indicated that he could enter the convention hall in Chicago if he sat at a sufficiently safe distance so as not to interrupt the harmony of the proceedings.

Even Governor Thomas E. Dewey was a more liberal and independent dose of medicine than they wanted. But he looked a lot more palatable than Willkie, and they swallowed him quickly.

Some have said that Franklin Roosevelt was the reason Wendell Willkie didn't win in 1940 and dismiss the question as a matter of political personalities. Others have said that Willkie was too inexperienced politically to conduct an effective campaign or to handle his own party, and dismiss the matter as political tactics. I think neither of these explanations is adequate. I suggest these conclusions:

That in 1940 Wendell Willkie won a Presidential nomination from a surprised and unregenerate Republican party and ended by disclosing to the country—even persuading the country—that the policies and purposes he was advocating were not the policies and purposes of the party which, in the event of his election, would control Congress. The country refused the risk.

That from 1940 to 1944 Wendell Willkie set out to reform the Republican party *from within* in order to win a Presidential renomination—and found that while his party might swallow some of his reforms it wouldn't reward the reformer.

Indeed, though writing as one who wished to see him President of the United States, I believe that it would not be inaccurate to say that Willkie "deserved" to lose in 1940; that is, he asked for and insured his losing by exhibiting to the voters the tremendous gap between the voting record of the majority of the Republican members of Congress and the progressive social and economic measures and international foreign policy he offered.

That is why this political appraisal seems to me inescapable: the country defeated Wendell Willkie in 1940 because of his party, and in spite of what he stood for—and in 1944, when he might have been elected, his party rejected Wendell Willkie because of what he stood for.

7.

AFTER THE 1944 Republican and Democratic conventions Willkie wrote two articles for *Collier's* concerning the "evasive mockeries put over at Chicago," dealing in particular with foreign policy and racial minorities. He referred to the "vast disappointment of millions of thoughtful men and women in these platforms—a disappointment which I shared."

These two articles were an indictment of both platforms for inadequacy, evasion, and cowardice. He was again bitingly and bluntly campaigning against both major parties and both major candidates in a last attempt to hold them up to public responsibility. He died suddenly early Sunday morning, October 8, without disclosing what choice he would ultimately have made between the parties and between the nominees.

Immediately after his death both sides in rather unseemly fashion began claiming him for their own. Dewey's campaign managers were out with instant statements that Willkie had made it apparent that he intended to support the Governor. And Democratic spokesmen were equally insistent that his silence during the campaign assured his ultimate backing of President Roosevelt.

I can state with definite knowledge and evidence that both claims were untrue. I discussed the trend of Governor Dewey's campaign several times with Mr. Willkie following the Republican convention and on the basis of these talks I wrote a dispatch for *The Christian Science Monitor* outlining the large reservations which he held concerning Mr. Dewey. Since Mr. Willkie did not wish to declare his position on the record at that time, he cited this dispatch to numerous correspondents, who came to query him, as an accurate exposition of his views.

The pertinent paragraphs from this dispatch are as follows:

Those who are fully acquainted with Mr. Willkie's present views also know that acts more than speeches by Mr. Dewey will influence his course the most. For example, a matter which concerns Mr. Willkie as much as any of the "wrong-headedness" of the platform is the Governor's deliberate inclusion in his top campaign cabinet of the man whom the party rejected as

National Chairman eighteen months ago because he stood for extreme isolationism and the extreme isolationist associations which the G.O.P. appeared to be trying to escape. That man was Werner Schroeder, National Committeeman from Illinois, who holds office as a willing spokesman for the Chicago *Tribune*.

Mr. Willkie does not expect Governor Dewey to go around making political enemies for the fun of it, but he does question whether the American people will be persuaded that a presidential nominee who embraces the most extreme isolationist symbol in his inner council can be trusted to carry out collaborationist foreign policies which these isolationists bitterly oppose. . .

It also is apparent that Mr. Willkie is not going to allow himself to be dragooned into support of the ticket and platform by threats of punishment for party irregularity. As he views it, politics is more than an athletic match. To him, the question isn't whether he is a "good sport" or a "bad sport"; it is whether he can conscientiously put party unity ahead of deeply held convictions and ahead of a course of national and international action he considers vital to the welfare of the United States.

This is why Mr. Willkie is not rushing to back the Dewey-Bricker ticket. He is in no hurry to declare himself. He intends to wait and see—to wait to see whether Mr. Dewey and Mr. Bricker come reasonably close to meeting the conditions he feels essential to justify his support.

There are those who foresee that Mr. Willkie's support and his demonstrated influence with the independent voter could be decisive in the election this year, and certainly many Republican organization leaders are showing unusual anxiety to bring into line a man whom they profess to believe is a "has-been."

Few informed persons expect Mr. Willkie to support President Roosevelt. He has gone too far in his denunciation of the New Deal's mistakes and blind spots to do that. Rather, the choice is between supporting Mr. Dewey and "taking a walk"—and it would be probable that Mr. Willkie would do a good deal of talking while taking that walk. That is, he would expound the issues of the campaign to the country in a series of speeches without advising his followers how they should vote.

The questions which will be logically asked are: Did Governor Dewey's first weeks of campaigning resolve the foregoing doubts which were foremost in Mr. Willkie's mind? Had Mr. Willkie decided under any circumstances to support the Republican nominee against a Roosevelt fourth term?

The answer to both questions is unqualifiedly no. His reservations about Governor Dewey had not been withdrawn. He had not determined to support him despite his reservations.

I can say of my own knowledge that as late as a week before his death he had not made up his mind which candidate he would back because on Saturday morning, September 30, I canvassed the whole political situation with him in a long private conversation at the Lenox Hill Hospital. He had telephoned me at my hotel to come to see him and conspiratorily told me how to get to his room by a side elevator so I wouldn't run into objecting nurses.

He was looking rested, robust, and buoyant. He was eager to talk of everything and his energy filled the little hospital room to overflowing. All the New York Sunday newspapers were strewn on the floor where he had tossed them after reading and a dozen of the latest books were piled helter-skelter on a little table by his elbow. The sum of our conversation was that he had seen nothing thus far in Mr. Dewey's commitments to justify his calling on those who thought as he did to vote for him, and he had certainly not reconciled himself to back the President he had tried to defeat four years earlier. It was a hard decision for Mr. Willkie, because he was not one to "take a walk," to declare a "plague on both your houses."

My confidence that these statements faithfully depict Mr. Willkie's attitude does not rest alone on the recollections of my last interview. On the Monday morning following that interview I received a letter from him, the first paragraph of which reads as follows:

"I enjoyed our talk this morning very much. Frankly, I cannot answer your ultimate question [i.e., whom would he support?] yet because I have not finally decided."

Wendell Willkie died not of a broken heart, as some like to suggest, but after an abundant, zestful, rewarding life—a career lived in accord with his conscience and devoted to promoting the highest principles and purposes he could conceive. I never could detect that he was either bitter or depressed. He was too intellectually resourceful, too morally confident ever to feel he had come to the end of the road. There was no end to Wendell Willkie's road. He died, I believe, not looking backward, but looking ahead.

8.

THOUGH, in all my conversations with him, he rarely—and only in passing—discussed President Roosevelt, I would say that Wendell Willkie of Elwood, Indiana, had no liking for Franklin Delano Roosevelt of Hyde Park, New York. There was no real affinity between them. But this I never felt was due to any sense of political rivalry toward Roosevelt. It was evident in many small ways—though never made evident in large ways—that Willkie entertained no personal cordiality toward the man he tried his best to remove from American political life, and whom later he did his best to help in winning the war and building the peace. It would be my sense that Willkie's towering political objectivity after 1940 and his incalculable services to the government in dissolving what would have been a perilous partisan controversy over the war were performed more despite President Roosevelt than because of him.

When Willkie met Roosevelt for the first time—during his protracted Commonwealth and Southern-T.V.A. negotiations—he telegraphed to his wife, a strong anti-New Dealer: "CHARM EXAGGERATED STOP I DIDN'T TELL HIM WHAT YOU THINK OF HIM."

The personal relations between the two men were not fundamentally important and deserve to be explored only to the extent that they affect the politically inspired and baseless charge that Willkie had some kind of understanding or alliance or allegiance with Roosevelt, and that this accounted for some kind of charted course of action between them.

The opposite is nearer the truth. It would be more accurate to say that not even his antipathetic personal feeling toward Roosevelt could influence Willkie to oppose the President when he felt Roosevelt was pursuing a useful course, not to hamper the President when the great issues of the war and the peace required a national unity above partisanship.

There was never any political or personal agreement between the two on any subject at any time for any purpose; there was no under-standing, no alliance, no allegiance.

Before he became a Presidential candidate, Willkie conferred with the President perhaps a dozen times, usually on Commonwealth and Southern-T.V.A. matters, never on political matters. They did not meet during the 1940 campaign, and between 1940 and 1944 I find that they had six brief exchanges wherein the President was either giving Willkie a letter to Churchill or to Stalin or to Chiang Kai-shek, or Willkie was giving the President a candid and not too well-received earful on his trip around the world.

In answer to a series of questions contributed to *Look* magazine, April 7, 1942, dealing with the report that he and the President "had fallen out" because of the failure of the administration to find a place for him in the war effort, Willkie wrote:

"To say that two men have 'fallen out,' implies that there was once some sort of agreement or understanding between them. I don't have and never have had any personal relationship with President Roose-velt. . . . There has never been any understanding between us that I should do or say certain things or that he should do or say certain things."

In the fall of 1941 the Australian government invited Willkie to visit Australia. They needed the tonic he had already given to Britain. Two days before Pearl Harbor the President wrote Willkie a gracious letter indicating that he would count it an asset to Australian-American relations and to the Allied cause if he would accept the invitation and make the trip in any capacity he chose. The letter arrived after Pearl Harbor, and Mr. Willkie replied as follows:

My dear Mr. President:

I congratulate you very much on your Tuesday night talk.

I have your letter of December 5, which I appreciate. I am unable presently to appraise the potentialities or the wisdom of going to Australia since the Japanese attack. Perhaps it would now constitute a nuisance. I will think about it further.

I am coming to Washington on Monday, and, if your schedule presents a free moment, would you have one of your secretaries let me know before that date if it would be convenient to you for me to call on you in accordance with the suggestion in your letter. Please disregard this if you are at all pressed for time.

In case I do not see you Monday, there is something I would like to say to you. Of late a few people, friends of yours, have suggested to me various ways in which they thought you might make use of me in our national emergency. Since they have talked to me about this, I am afraid they may also have troubled you. You have incredibly anxious and burdensome days ahead and it should be plain to anyone that you can function with least strain and most effectiveness if you are free to choose your helpers and advisers for whom you must bear the responsibility, without any consideration other than your conception of the public welfare.

What I am trying to say—honestly, but awkwardly I am afraid, because it is not easy—is this: If any such well-meant suggestions about me are brought to you, I beg you to disregard them. There is on your shoulders the heaviest responsibility any man can carry and I would not add to it in the slightest way. Even to volunteer a willingness to serve seems to me now only an imposition on your attention. Every American is willing to serve.

In all sincerity, I am
Respectfully yours, . . .

Willkie made it clear to the White House that he preferred not to be associated with the administration because he thought he could be more useful outside; he did not want his right to comment on its policies and conduct curtailed. When in the course of a conversation he was having with the British Prime Minister at the White House early in 1942, Churchill asked him if he was going to join the government, Willkie put to him this question: "Would you have joined the Chamberlain Government when you did if you had thereby felt under the obligation to refrain from expressing your views?" Willkie later remarked that it was "inappropriate" for him to quote the Prime Minister's reply.

It was evident to many of us in Washington that the periodic and tenuous personal relations between Willkie and Roosevelt, never really cordial except on the surface, became increasingly strained with the fall of 1942. I would cite the following as the main reasons:

There was the fact that the President appeared to take no pains to correct a false impression, which derived from one of his press conferences, that he had said news stories about Willkie statements abroad were "not worth reading." The President was actually referring to the controversy growing out of these statements as not worth noting. But Willkie certainly felt the President was so unconcerned about correcting the impression as to indicate his approval of it.

There was the seventy-five-minute conference which the two had at the White House on the afternoon of Willkie's return from his *One World* trip, and it added to the strain. There were few gentle words spoken during this interview. Mr. Willkie was deadly serious and set out to tell the President what he considered the truth—how the nation's economy was not adequately mobilized for total war, how the reservoir of the world's good will toward America was beginning to leak in a dozen different places because the administration was promising big and delivering little, how it was imperative that the United States and Britain speed up their plans to open the second front in Europe—the latter view now shown by former Secretary of War Henry L. Stimson's memoirs to have been favored by General Marshall, who wanted the second front in 1942, but who was overruled by President Roosevelt in favor of the North African campaign.

There was the time when, at his first press conference after the North African invasion, President Roosevelt talked of how he had to sit smilingly and take it on the chin while ignorant outsiders were clamoring for a second front when a second front had already been determined upon. Correspondents knew that he was not excluding Willkie from this category of ignorant outsiders.

Even when Steve Early, the President's wise press secretary, leaned over to his chief to suggest that perhaps the word "ignorant" might cause a wrong impression, Roosevelt did not ask that his remark be struck from the printable record of the press conference.

There was the President's 1942 New York *Herald Tribune* Forum speech in which he renewed his "ignorant outsider" theme and referred pointedly to "criticism from those who, as we know in our hearts, are actuated by political motives."

Finally, there was the White House pressure brought to bear on

Willkie to drop from his *Herald Tribune* Forum speech all critical references regarding the North African arrangements with Admiral Jean Darlan.

The President caused Secretary of War Henry L. Stimson to telephone to Willkie demanding that he delete these references on the ground that such criticism would endanger the lives of American soldiers. Though skeptical of the argument, it was one Mr. Willkie could not well defy, so he agreed to omit the criticism. But when the President himself twelve hours later released a carefully prepared explanation of the Darlan deal in which he said that the government opposes "Frenchmen who support Hitler and the Axis," and that he "approved" the feeling which had produced wide suspicion of the arrangement with Admiral Darlan, Willkie was convinced that the White House was using disingenuous and high-handed means to suppress criticism until the President had full opportunity to set the stage his own way.

Actually, all the Presidential talk about "ignorant outsiders" seemed wide of the mark, for the significant fact remains that even without full military information, thoughtful laymen like Willkie had reached the conclusion that an Anglo-American second-front operation against Germany was imperative and possible at exactly the same time the military leaders had concluded it was imperative and possible.

There was never any substantial exchange of correspondence between Willkie and Roosevelt, and, as with their brief interviews, nothing in their letters to give the faintest color to the idea that there was an "understanding" between them. There wasn't. There were not more than a half-dozen letters which each wrote to the other and they usually bore upon some service which Willkie had performed or was going to perform in the cause of the war or the peace.

Only one letter ever gave even any appearance of political implications. On July 13, 1944, President Roosevelt wrote the following:

Dear Wendell:

I will not be able to sign this because I am dictating it just as I leave on a trip to the Westward.

What I want to tell you is that I want to see you when I come back, but not on anything in relationship to the present campaign. I want to

talk with you about the future, even the somewhat distant future, and in
regard to the foreign-relations problems of the immediate future.

When you see in the papers that I am back, will you get in touch
with General Watson? We can arrange a meeting either here in Wash-
ington, or, if you prefer, at Hyde Park—wholly off the record or other-
wise, just as you think best.

Always sincerely yours,
FRANKLIN D. ROOSEVELT

As I happened to be in his law office on Broad Street shortly after
Willkie received this letter, he showed it to me, and we discussed—
which means that mostly I listened—whether he should accept. It was
evident that he had already decided not to see Roosevelt at that time,
and after going through the appearance of weighing with me the arguments, pro and con, he drew from his desk drawer a tentative draft
reply and read it to me. I later learned that he never sent his answer to
the President. He never told me why, but I think the reason can be
safely deduced. First, courtesy required no prompt reply because Mr.
Roosevelt would be away quite a while. Secondly, this "personal" letter
from the President, proposing a confidential meeting, leaked—Willkie
believed from the White House to one or two newspaper columnists
who usually spoke for the administration. Anyway, Willkie let the matter go, and the following unmailed letter was found in his files:

My dear Mr. President:

I have your gracious note of the thirteenth. The subjects concerning
which you suggest we have a talk on your return from the West are, as
you know, subjects in which I am intensely interested. I am fearful,
however, that any talk between us before the campaign is over might
well be the subject of misinterpretation and misunderstanding. And I
do not believe, however much you and I might wish or plan otherwise,
that we could possibly have such a talk without the fact becoming
known.

Therefore, if it is agreeable with you, I would prefer postponement
of any such talk until after the November election.

I hope you will understand that I make this suggestion solely be-
cause you in a great way, and I in a small one, have the trust and con-

fidence of people who might see in the most innocent meeting between us at this time some betrayal of the principles which each of us respectively holds so deeply.

Believe me, with great respect,

Sincerely yours, . . .

And so, the two letters were each unsigned. Possibly Willkie's belief that the Roosevelt proposal for a pre-election conference with Willkie was officially "leaked" to friendly Washington correspondents should not have given the impression that the President, knowing that Willkie had great reservations concerning Governor Dewey, hoped to gain a political benefit from the projected meeting. But Wendell Willkie was not playing ball with Roosevelt personally at the end of his political career any more than at the beginning.

9.

WHAT, then, was the contribution of Wendell Willkie to the America of the fateful forties? I suggest that at the very minimum it was not less than this:

That Willkie, by persuading many that the Republican party could be made a liberal organ of government, set into motion a stirring of political forces from which it is possible that America may later get not the much-discussed and useless third party but, in effect, a realignment within both the major national parties.

That Willkie was indispensable in paving the way for the public acceptance of nearly every bold measure which the Roosevelt administration took to sustain the nations that were fighting the Axis while America frantically prepared.

That Willkie, by the character of his 1940 campaign and by his attitude of "loyal opposition" after the verdict was in, created a climate in which national unity could develop and without which the great decisions of defense before Pearl Harbor—from Lend-Lease to the renewal of Selective Service in 1941—would have been irreparably delayed and diluted.

That Wendell Willkie made a decisive, indispensable contribution to winning the war—a contribution without which the war could have been lost—by rescuing the nation from a bitter, bickering, devitalizing partisan division when every fiber of the country's resources was needed to oppose the oncoming attack from without and disunion from within.

That Wendell Willkie, more than most leaders of the Allied world, successfully summoned his own and other nations to the essential concept of the world which, if mankind is to get a just and humane and lasting peace, must follow this total war: The concept of *One World*. By precept and practice he added a new phrase to the minds and hopes of the Allied peoples and gave new power to the concept that the only guarantee against another total war is total freedom, one and indivisible.

Pearl Harbor Sunday: The End of an Era

BY JONATHAN DANIELS

Jonathan Daniels became well acquainted with the inside of the White House as administrative assistant and press secretary for President Roosevelt from 1943 to 1945, and, for a brief interval after that, for President Truman. Before that he was a Washington correspondent, a writer for *Fortune*, editor of the Raleigh *News and Observer*, and assistant director of the Office of Civilian Defense. He has a particularly fine flair for reporting and interpreting American moods and places. He has written *A Southerner Discovers the South* (1938), *A Southerner Discovers New England* (1940), *Tarheels: A Portrait of North Carolina* (1941), and *Frontier on the Potomac* (1946), a sensitive and historically valuable account of Washington in wartime.

✵ 1.

Even a blind pig can find some acorns if he roots under an oak.

All of history is spilled milk. If you don't study what caused the spilling, you won't be able to prevent it in the future.

—*Comments on the Pearl Harbor Investigation by Senator Homer Ferguson of Michigan.*

AND IN TERMS of the pig and the dairy maid, with perhaps a little more emphasis on politics than on history, the Congressional Committee investigating the surprise attack had by March, 1946, when it ended its hearing, accumulated nine and a half million words of testimony, reports, and exhibits. A good deal was left out still. Many of the witnesses who knew most about the event were dead. Also Pearl Harbor was clearly less the single violence of a morning in the Pacific than the punctuation mark at the end of an American period which had been twenty-three years and twenty-six days long, from armistice to attack. Politicians did not need to root to find politics. Obviously Pearl Harbor was a political event in the highest politics of mankind. Perhaps in all history no event had ever served so well to show both the difficulties and the durability of democracy, and the ease with which those contemptuous of democracy can move to both violence and folly. Pearl Harbor spilled not only milk but blood. It set a blaze which not only began the defeat of the tyrannies; it also threw back a light to illumine the whole period it ended. Lightning had hit the oak, but it had not restored the sight of the blind.

Indeed, the strangest disclosure as the testimony piled up to tedium was that the chief interest in the investigation was taken by those who longest and most loudly doubted the menace to America which struck at Pearl Harbor that morning as the planes came in from the southwest over Diamond Head. Newspapers which had been completely wrong about the spread of war to America gave the widest headlines to mistakes made when it came—and there were mistakes. Politicians who had been most insistent on isolation were more shocked than any others that America could have been surprised. Franklin Roosevelt, they were sure, incited the attack or was stupidly surprised by it or both or either. The one thing they insisted upon, sometimes blatantly and often slyly, was that the victor had been the villain.

Senator Ferguson, who seemed the most determined investigator of the Past's mistakes and almost the seeker of home crime in foreign attack, is not only a better man than many of those from whom he drew the limited amount of applause he secured. Also, he was not in the Congresses which debated the danger of war. Of course, he is right about the necessity for studying spilled milk or dumped bombs. The whole procession to Pearl Harbor, indeed, is a process which could be repeated again. Sometimes it seems already moving in inescapable repetition. And basically it is the problem of leadership and decision in democratic government at home and in the tough politics of the world. The years between the great wars did not just end at Pearl Harbor. Pearl Harbor was the almost inescapable conclusion of those years.

2.

CERTAINLY THE DAY "will live in infamy." But already somehow the morning of the day itself has become a casualty along with the men and the ships and the planes. The time before the bombs fell has been reconstructed in the logic of the fact that the bombs did fall. The illogical but essentially American morning is gone. It is forgotten that the mood even of that morning was almost completely free from fear. And that mood is as important as the documents. The sinister timing of the Japs brought the planes with the symbol of the sun on their wings over Diamond Head while sailors and soldiers still slept, and the same timing meant that the news in America would cut the day into halves. The afternoon was war, but the morning lies in the years between wars. Perhaps the morning was as important as the afternoon. The news of death came at 1:50 P.M. Eastern Standard Time. But the whole portrait of a period about to be destroyed lay between cockcrow and catastrophe.

It was a beautiful morning in America. Along the Atlantic seaboard the sunshine was warm for December; the winds only began to whip gray clouds about the sun in the afternoon. It was Ham Fish's birthday and Senator Gerald P. Nye was confidently on his way to address an isolationist mass meeting in Pittsburgh. To loud applause in New York, Myron Taylor, the President's personal representative at the Vatican, praised the peace efforts of the Pope and the President at the annual communion breakfast of the Notre Dame Club of New York. But at the Riverside Church, Dr. Harry Emerson Fosdick saw a sickness in democracy.

"The world splits up," he said, "dictatorships naturally emphasizing loyalty but not liberty, democracy naturally emphasizing liberty but not loyalty. Somehow we must get these two indispensable qualities together."

They were not together at twelve o'clock when his congregation poured out into the sun. And not everybody had been to church even to contemplate the fission. In New York and Raleigh, North Carolina, and Washington, D.C., many people slept late in the American celebration of Sunday morning. Some who on December 6 had enjoyed a gay

American Saturday night slept later still. And some others like Donald Nelson, who was to have responsibility for American industrial production for war, got up early out of habit rather than apprehension and gave long, lazy reading to the Sunday papers.

There were the big headlines which afterward were warnings in the record. But there were also big advertisements of new automobiles. The Matson Line was advertising vacation cruises to Hawaii. The upsweep hair-do was receiving early attention. Traffic accidents in the country were already up sixteen per cent above "the lamentable record" of 1940. John L. Lewis was about to win a decision in his contention that miners in the captive coal mines of the steel companies must join his United Mine Workers of America. A New York gambling house had been raided in which "prosperous businessmen" were robbed of many thousands of dollars with dice which had only twos, fours, and sixes on them. An editor wondered how such businessmen got "prosperous" or stayed so. Department stores advertised white shirts at two dollars (regular two-fifty and three-dollar values—and plenty of them). The Tecla Pearl people were preparing an annual bargain sale at which five-thousand-dollar necklaces might be snapped up for twenty-five hundred. Americans were urged to say, "Merry Christmas with fragrant whimsies by Coty." People were reading *The Keys to the Kingdom*, by A. J. Cronin, and—in a sort of undeciphered code of coincidence—*The Sun Is My Undoing*, by Marguerite Steen, and *Reveille in Washington*, by Margaret Leach.

Like a lot of Americans that morning, Donald Nelson was in no great hurry. He dressed slowly to go to a Sunday luncheon at the "Headwater" farm of old Harold Ickes and his pretty young red-headed wife at Olney, Maryland. He drove out in the sun to find good company and good talk. Behind the fat columns of the Ickes' country house, surrounded by the fat Ickes pigs and cattle and the hundreds of cackling Ickes hens, Ickes and Nelson, and Supreme Court Justice Hugo Black and Senator Tom Connally, chairman of the Senate Foreign Relations Committee, talked about the Japs with whom old Secretary of State Cordell Hull was still talking in special conversations that had begun twenty days before. And the representatives of the Court and the Cabinet and the Congress agreed (Nelson remembers) that there would be no war with Japan—not, at least, in the foreseeable future. While they talked there were other noises already in the Pacific, but at Olney they could only hear the Ickes hens.

It was very quiet at the White House that morning. In the middle of Washington it was still an unguarded mansion with no sign of soldiers about it. Mrs. Charles Hamlin, of Albany, an old Hudson Valley friend of the Roosevelts, woke up in the Lincoln bed. Across the north lawn she could see the warm sun casting the shadow of the portico toward the fountain. She got up quietly, as a familiar and considerate guest. Across the long dark corridor the doors to the President's bedroom and to his oval study were shut. She went off alone across La Fayette Square to old St. John's Church, whose bells ring into the White House on such quiet mornings. She found her old seat in the church. She met "the Conrad girls and Susie Stone from Milton." A gentleman named Russell Sard, of Albany, walked back with her to the portico of the White House through unguarded gates. And there she met a long line of people coming upstairs from the East Entrance for luncheon.

There were thirty people for lunch and they lined up alphabetically in the Blue Parlor. The President did not join them, but that seemed natural enough to those guests familiar with his habits. There were no guests who would have attracted him from his Sunday rest and seclusion. It was, indeed, a casual sort of company, some Roosevelt relatives and friends, a couple of New Dealers, some minor government officials, some Army Medical Corps people, some of the sort of people who for one reason or another (and there were always many reasons) had to be invited to the White House.

"It looks," said one guest who had been there often before, "as if Mrs. Roosevelt's secretary has been cleaning up around the edges of the list."

They went into the dining room at about one-thirty. Mrs. Roosevelt told them good-by at about two forty-five, though one guest stayed a little later to talk to her, at her request, about a matter about which she was concerned. Beyond the big entrance hall the sun was still very bright outside, but there was already a little sharpness in the wind. And about the same time the party at the Ickes farm broke up too. Nelson, driving along slowly on the road back to Washington, turned

on his radio to hear the regular Sunday afternoon concert of the New
York Philharmonic Orchestra. It began at 3:03:15 P.M. in Carnegie
Hall and on the Maryland highway. A voice suddenly came in with
"more news about Pearl Harbor." Even earlier one of the White House
luncheon guests had gotten across La Fayette Square to the Cosmos
Club to find a body of its gray-headed habitués clustered about a radio
eagerly hoping for amplification of the news which the President had
announced at 2:25 P.M., from his oval study—while the luncheon party
was still in progress and in ignorance in the dining room below.

3.

IN THE SERIOUS BUSINESS of history the day began perhaps when
Cordell Hull came at ten-fifteen into the empty, echoing halls of the
old baroque State Department. Hull had got to be seventy years old
that fall on the very day on which Hitler in an order of the day to the
German forces in Russia announced the beginning of the last great decisive battle of the year. The day before that Charles A. Lindbergh in
Fort Wayne had suggested that a warmongering administration might
not permit Congressional elections in 1942. The procession to war was
a march to tyranny. Since November 17, Hull had been talking, with
increasing fears and suspicions, to a special Japanese "peace" envoy.
He was awaiting that Sunday morning an answer to proposals which
the United States had made to Japan on November 26.

A little later in the morning Secretary of War Henry L. Stimson and
Secretary of the Navy Frank Knox came to the State Department to
discuss the situation with Hull. They had been kept informed of the
situation. Stimson went home afterward to the old estate of Woodley,
where Francis Scott Key had stayed long before. Knox drove down to
the Navy Department. Hull remained in conference with his Far Eastern experts. And at one-ten there was a call from the beautiful Japanese
Embassy (one of the architects of which had been a Delano) asking
for an appointment with the Secretary to deliver the answer to the
American proposals. (Already then at 12:32 P.M., Washington time,
7:02 A.M. Hawaii time, a U. S. Army private listening on a radio plane
detector in Hawaii had reported a large flight of planes to the north,

but the assumption had been made that they were American.) The Japs asked for an appointment at two o'clock, but the hour set was one forty-five. They arrived, nevertheless, at two-five, and were kept waiting for fifteen minutes in the Secretary's anteroom, which looked like a parlor in a conservative undertaking establishment. Those were the fifteen minutes in which an American period came to an end.

Other people also had gone to work in Washington that day. Watch No. 3 (about thirty-five men and a watch officer) was on duty at Radio Central in the Navy Department handling the usual flow of Sunday traffic on Radio Washington, the Navy's biggest communication station. The clocks above them turned in precision and at about 1848 G.C.T. (1:48 P.M. E.S.T.) the traffic chief of the watch, Chief Radioman Frank A. Ackerson, U.S.N., was summoned to the Washington-Honolulu circuit by the operator, E. E. Harris, Radioman First Class, U.S.N., in response to an alert to stand by for an urgent message by the Honolulu operator. At 1850 (1:50 P.M. E.S.T.) Harris gave the Honolulu operator his receipt for the following message:

NPM 1516
Z ØF2 183Ø ØF3 ØF4 Ø2FØ O

From: CINCPAC
ACTION: CINCLANT CINCAF OPNAV

AIR RAID ON PEARL HARBOR THIS IS NOT DRILL

The message moved from Harris to Ackerson to the communication watch officer, Lieutenant William L. Tagg, U.S.N., to Rear Admiral Richmond K. Turner, of the War Plans Division, to Admiral Harold R. Stark, Chief of Naval Operations. They took it to Secretary Knox. Soon after the event good reporters recorded the conversation which took place when Knox got through to the President. Roosevelt, who had looked worn the night before, at a large White House dinner, was lunching from a tray in his study with Harry Hopkins. His incredulous "No," in response to Knox's report, has been set down. There is also the record of his immediate commands about acts and safeguards to be taken. The sinuses from which he had been suffering were forgotten.

The room became a conning tower. He began the process of direction by a call to Cordell Hull.

Some confusion has slipped into the first historical efforts to fix the exact timing of that first afternoon of war. It has been reported that when the President received the news, the brass hands of the ship's clock on his desk stood at 1:47 P.M. What happened, however, is precisely timed by the receipt of the message by Radio Washington at 1:50 P.M. and the flash of the news, which he personally dictated, at 2:25 P.M. The Japanese diplomats must have been coming into the State Department while Roosevelt talked to Hull, who afterward let them sweat before he saw them. The news had been flashed to the country before they left Hull's office, running before news cameramen down the dim marble halls. In the interim, old man Hull, whose dignity is not damaged, nor the expression of his indignations dulled, by a lisp ("Jesus Quist"), had given the first American characterization to the sneak infamy of such liars in governmental power as the old man had not before believed could exist on this planet. The morning was gone; the afternoon was of a different time in a wholly altered world.

The President's phone summoned staff and Cabinet. The radio broke the beginnings of a lazy afternoon. Crowds began to gather about the Japanese Embassy, where a little gray spiral of burning diplomatic papers rose above the neoclassic building and men and women in the street stood as ominously quiet (as one woman witness remembers) "as a lynch mob I once saw in Valdosta, Georgia." Two Japs drove up in a taxicab and scurried across the pavement and the brief lawn to the chancellery. The only actual violence reported was that some anonymous idiots chopped down one of the capital's Japanese cherry trees. In general, there was an amazing mass calm which was all Fiorello LaGuardia, as chief of Civilian Defense, could have wanted while he cried in New York for "Calm! Calm! Calm!" after a flight in a sirening police car to a radio station to announce that "We are not out of the danger zone by any means." Before sunset people looked not only at the White House and the Japanese Embassy, but fearfully, if a little apologetically, at the sky. There was a steady and spontaneous mobilization in the War, Navy, and State Departments, and the War Production Board, of men who poured in, called only by the news.

The calmest place in town and the most exciting was the White House. Hull came from across the street. Stimson and General Marshall arrived together. Knox led his admirals. Other Cabinet members arrived. Vice-President Henry Wallace in New York phoned that he was coming by the next plane. Among them all the Commander in Chief wore a turtle-neck sweater. Not since the first days of his arrival in the White House, when the national economy had seemed to be collapsing, had he seemed so clearly the genius of leadership in crisis. Swiftly and easily plans were made for the meeting of the Cabinet and the Congressional leaders. An address to the Congress had to be prepared. The report to the nation itself began to shape up. It was not, however, a time of great leadership merely. Before the day was over, among plain people and politicians, Republicans and Democrats, the emphasis on loyalty had swung neatly into place beside the emphasis on liberty in the defense of democracy.

Quickly guards appeared at the gate of the White House and new security restrictions were placed around other government buildings. Also in the White House, and without fuss, housekeeping under Mrs. Roosevelt met the occasion. There had been two trays at lunch, but many others were needed, as the day proceeded, by people called to work that could not be interrupted. And despite Pearl Harbor a supper party already invited for the evening was held as usual. The guests saw the officials and the admirals waiting and moving in the halls. One guest came in a state of excitement and passed on to others his confidence that bombs would be falling above them soon. His remained a private panic. But another guest was Edward R. Murrow, who had covered the spread of the war in Europe since 1937 for the Columbia Broadcasting System. He was a good witness for history.

"There was," he said later, "ample opportunity to observe at close range the bearing and expression of Mr. Stimson, Colonel Knox, and Secretary Hull. If they were not surprised by the news from Pearl Harbor, then that group of elderly men were putting on a performance which would excite the admiration of any experienced actor."

Late in the evening, as the admirals and generals, Congressmen and

Cabinet officers began to disappear, sometime after midnight, the President sent for Murrow to come up to his study.

"I have seen," Murrow reported, "certain statesmen in times of crisis. Never have I seen one so calm and steady. He was completely relaxed."

They talked and as Murrow was leaving, the President asked him, "Did this surprise you?"

"Yes, Mr. President."

Roosevelt shook his head. "Maybe you think it didn't surprise us!"

4.

SOMETIMES SINCE, as politics and history have been put together, that statement has been made to seem the part of a debate as to whether Roosevelt was actually surprised or should have been. Actually the only question revolves around the understanding—or sometimes the deliberate misunderstanding—of the meaning of surprise. In February, 1946, after both Roosevelt and Harry Hopkins were dead, much was made of the testimony of a young naval officer who on the night before the attack went to the same oval study in which Roosevelt received the news of Pearl Harbor. This naval officer, Lester R. Schultz, was then a lieutenant and an assistant naval aide at the White House. He came with a locked brief case to bring the President a paper—the intercepted and decoded first thirteen parts of the Japanese reply to Hull's final proposals which the Japanese believed would be taken to Hull only after the Japanese attack on Pearl Harbor was begun. There was no hint of the attack itself in the violence of the Japanese rejection of the proposals. But the President read them, handed them to Hopkins, waited until he had read, then spoke.

"This means war."

As a junior officer to be trusted but not consulted, young Schultz stood listening, surprised at the President's conviction. Senior officers who had seen the decoded message had reached no such conclusion. The President and Hopkins discussed the deployment of Japanese forces. Indo-China, about which the President had written in his final peace appeal to the Emperor, was particularly mentioned. There was no mention of Pearl Harbor. There was no mention of time.

Then Hopkins said, "It's too bad we can't strike first and prevent a surprise."

The young officer quoted later the answer of the President.

"No, we can't do that. We are a democracy of peaceful people. We have a good record. We must stand on it."

5.

THE VIOLENT ALTERATION of America which began the next day was a long process which was almost the story of the period. And the man to whom the message of attack came in his oval study at the White House while he relaxed a little from long strain was himself the figure of the period. There are portraits of the man still vivid in the memories of the soldiers and sailors and politicians who came that afternoon and evening to the study which had become a sort of conning tower, certainly a G.H.Q. of America at war. They check with the memories of his leadership as he entered the White House in the midst of domestic disaster in 1933. Obviously his extraordinary vigor, on those occasions, his energy, calmness, his complete control over men, policies, and details were parts of the greatness of the man. But those characteristics were not merely individual; they represented also the possibilities of leadership in democracy in those periods of pressure and danger in which not only leadership but democracy works. But unfortunately destiny is often determined in the doldrums. And the problems of leadership in democracy lie in those hours when the dramatic is missing. It is important to remember that Roosevelt was not always followed by all the people or even a majority of them. That is essential to understanding of the man and the period and the quality of his leadership at the end of it.

There are other pictures that need to be remembered. Roosevelt was a young man who came back to America from Europe on the *George Washington* with Woodrow Wilson at the time of Wilson's first confidence in the vision of his League. Roosevelt was a young man as Vice-Presidential candidate who made the hopeless fight for that League in 1920 when not only Harding but America preferred "normalcy" to even the noblest notions about peace. Perhaps too much has been made by his friends as well as his enemies, by the sentimentalists, the money raisers, and the politicians, of his crippling illness. It was probably because he was the man who was stricken that he was the man who triumphed over it. But it is not remembered often enough that his image of the Happy Warrior was not merely a simile for Al Smith but a clean ideal in a country in which Ku Kluxery was only a little less hateful than the general smug and unimaginative materialism which surrounded it. Later also his idealism, like his sickness, was sentimentalized. Nobody knew better than he the almost comic impotence of many of the ineffectuals of earnestness in home reforms as well as in the realm of world peace. In the service of both he was a practical politician who in New York and America outsmarted those who thought they were its first professionals. Nobody in his time was so qualified to meet the toughest politicians of the world, whose purposes were still political even though they employed bombs instead of ballots.

Much has been written about his sense of timing, but sometimes the history of the period almost seemed to have timed his own arrivals and departures. Even his sickness coincided with the vulgar vacuum of the first American postwar years. The recognition of his competence grew in a country ready for creativeness beyond collapse. But the amazing coincidence in time is only rarely remembered. America, under its new President, was too desperately self-concerned beyond the inauguration of March 4, 1933, to make much note of the fact that before the following midnight the German Reichstag had passed the Enabling Act, putting absolute power into the hands of Chancellor Adolf Hitler.

Obviously the same forces of world failure had brought the two men to power. It should be equally obvious now that theirs was the basic antagonism of the period. One student of history has suggested that the fundamental difference between the men was that Hitler regarded the economic disaster which had brought him to leadership as a crime while Roosevelt recognized it as the product of stupidity. Certainly the essential differences in the tools the two men used were clearly and immediately apparent. And the intent showed in the tools: Roosevelt believed he could make security for Americans; Hitler believed he could take it for Germans. Roosevelt built schools and bridges, highways. Hitler built an army. There is no sense now in denying the fact that Hitler won to the extent that he forced the ultimate alteration of the American direction to hard conformity with his own. In aftermath certainly some saw Roosevelt as the dreamer and Hitler as the realist. It must seem an odd notion today in the rubble of Berlin. The important fact, however, is that there was no alteration, or interruption, of the democracy which, under Roosevelt's leadership, America set out to perfect and defend.

6.

ONLY THE SIMPLE will miss the fact that the struggle of Roosevelt and Hitler was one of the great political struggles in the history of mankind and that only a great politician could have won it. The notion that dictators need not bother with politics must include the belief that Hitler built up his vast propaganda machine beside his military forces without purpose. Its effectiveness was demonstrated by the fact that he took the Rhineland, Austria, a whole part of Czechoslovakia before war seemed a necessity or an inevitability. His fate—or the world's—was that he met Roosevelt, who understood even better than Hitler did the calculated risks which must be taken in the politics of the world.

Roosevelt's task was infinitely more difficult than Hitler's. His purposes did not include war. The belligerency of Hitler pulled him from his own plans, which were not merely his own but America's. It is significant that he made his famous quarantine speech about the dictators in 1937 at the dedication of such a public-works project as a bridge, not a battleship. Also, though such an isolationist as Charles Lindbergh charged two months before Pearl Harbor that there might not be another election, Roosevelt worked without interruption within the framework of democracy. (At no point in the war was there such a suspension of civil rights—for instance, the right of habeas corpus, when Lincoln found it necessary to set aside during the Civil War.) His enemies have charged (1) that he was late in recognizing and preparing for the danger and (2) that he was a man who plotted from the beginning the involvement of the American nation in war against a peaceful people's will. Perhaps no one will ever know at what point Roosevelt accepted the inevitability of American involvement. It is certain that he took his position against aggression in Europe and the East early, that he held it inflexibly, and that, by a variety of brilliantly conceived devices, each increasingly hostile in effect and purpose, he increased the pressure of American power upon the Axis, which was engaged in the destruction of the philosophy of government to which he devoted his life and to which the American people had entrusted their destiny.

His problem was essentially simple and altogether difficult. He was the leader of a democracy which had to be led every step of the way against angry resistance to aid of the allies and preparation for possible war. Beyond Dunkirk haste was of the essence, but as late as August, 1941, the extension of Selective Service requested by the President was secured by only a one-vote margin in the House of Representatives. In the Pacific, however, the problem was not haste but delay. On September 27, 1940, the same Saburo Kurusu who waited as the "peace envoy" in Hull's anteroom on December 7, 1941, had signed the pact which took Japan into the Axis. Yet it was a year and three months later before the Japanese struck. The problem of the President, seeking more time for both England and our own armed forces in preparing their defenses, was "to baby along" the Japs. The "babying" paid off. What was not visible to Jap aviators in the Pacific was that in December, 1941, we produced over 900 tanks; in December, 1939, we had produced none. In 1939, we had turned out a few more than 2,100 military planes. In 1941, we produced 19,500. Our active Army had increased from 174,000 enlisted men on July 1, 1939, to more than a million and a half by December 7, 1941. The important fact was that war plants were already built, shipyards were already producing the ships. The mechanism of victory was in being.

But Jap troops in Indo-China were already pointed toward Singapore. German troops fought less than fifty miles from Moscow. There were no Allied troops fighting on the Continent of Europe except in beleagured Russia. The British fought desperately in Lybia. Denmark and Norway, Holland and Belgium, Poland, France, Czechoslovakia,

Austria, Greece, and other countries had disappeared as nations while American opinion was torn in angry division.

It was at least a little strange that the people who accused Roosevelt of headlong dictatorship in warmongering then afterward were sure that he moved too slowly and too blindly. There was a mass of warning before Pearl Harbor. As a matter of fact, warning had been clear for many months before Pearl Harbor. The increasing menace had been understood and accepted. Of course, even Senators can now read to precise clarity—to the place and the hour—the warnings we possessed. Then Senators, along with admirals, generals, diplomats, politicians, even those among them who possessed the best information, were surprised. And Roosevelt was among them.

7.

OF COURSE, he was surprised. But he had deliberately taken the chance of surprise as he had won the strategy of successful militant delay. The blow was heavier than he had hoped it would necessarily be. Some men upon whom he and the nation depended were inadequate to that faith. But the risks paid off; even the loss was worth the price in terms of times secured in which the power of victory had already been built, and built against all the forces of division in America which continued to the last day. It was a day of tragedy but a day also in which America not only put loyalty and liberty together but put them together under a leadership which in the processes of democracy had already prepared the victory in the violent politics of the world.

It is the fashion to emphasize the uniqueness of heroes. Men have talked of Roosevelt since he died not merely in hostility but a sort of homesickness for the guidance he gave in the problems of peace as well as those of war. It is not a strange nostalgia in history. But Roosevelt, for all his individual strength and skill, was not a man alone. As clearly as any figure in our past, he was the product of his times. There were weaknesses in those times. But they grew out of a smug complacency through vigorously and sharply debated reforms to a readiness for greatness. That greatness in man and nation together was clear when Roosevelt came to the Presidency in domestic crisis. It was clear when the planes came to Diamond Head. There was American greatness in the sleepy morning as well as in the surprised afternoon. Perhaps a democracy and its leadership must wait—though not in idleness—for surprise. And surprise today increasingly leaves less and less time for debate. An inevitable threat to the processes of democracy lies in the new speed of danger. But Roosevelt and America in the years between the wars preserved democracy and safety together. Perhaps Pearl Harbor was the price. It does not now seem too much to have paid. But certainly it deserves the study of the succeeding period. Spilled milk has now turned into the fission of the atom. In the metaphor of the blind pig under the oak, the acorns to be sought cannot merely be mistakes of the past. Blind pigs may be satisfied with acorns. Some men may find nourishment in other men's old mistakes. But men without prophetic vision, a people who could be surprised again, need creative contemplation of the times when, only twice in a generation, a people and a President touched greatness together with loyalty and liberty side by side—and each time in disaster. They did not solve the democratic dilemma of long debate and swift danger. They survived it without the loss of either liberty or security, but only under great leadership as devoted to the democratic process at home as to the defense of democracy in the world.

"We are a democracy of peaceful people," Roosevelt said that evening when the Jap carriers were already moving to release their planes. "We have a good record. We must stand on it."

The next morning and all that made it needs remembering.

But the job of democracy in the future began in the afternoon. It involves the survival of not only democracy but of ourselves.